COMMON CORE MATHEMATICS

A Story of Units

Grade 5, Module 6: Problem Solving with the Coordinate Plane

COMMON CORE™ consider the source

JB JOSSEY-BASS™

A Wiley Brand

Cover design by Chris Clary

Published by Jossey-Bass
A Wiley Brand
One Montgomery Street, Suite 1200, San Francisco, CA 94104-4594—www.josseybass.com

ISBN: 978-1-118-81129-0

Printed in the United States of America
FIRST EDITION
PB Printing   10 9 8 7 6 5 4 3 2

WELCOME

Dear Teacher,

Thank you for your interest in Common Core's curriculum in mathematics. Common Core is a non-profit organization based in Washington, DC dedicated to helping K-12 public schoolteachers use the power of high-quality content to improve instruction.[1] We are led by a board of master teachers, scholars, and current and former school, district, and state education leaders. Common Core has responded to the Common Core State Standards' (CCSS) call for "content-rich curriculum"[2] by creating new, CCSS-based curriculum materials in mathematics, English Language Arts, history, and (soon) the arts. All of our materials are written by teachers who are among the nation's foremost experts on the new standards.

In 2012 Common Core won three contracts from the New York State Education Department to create a PreKindergarten–12th grade mathematics curriculum for the teachers of that state, and to conduct associated professional development. The book you hold contains a portion of that work. In order to respond to demand in New York and elsewhere, modules of the curriculum will continue to be published, on a rolling basis, as they are completed. This curriculum is based on New York's version of the CCSS (the CCLS, or Common Core Learning Standards). Common Core will be releasing an enhanced version of the curriculum this summer on our website, commoncore.org. That version also will be published by Jossey-Bass, a Wiley brand.

Common Core's curriculum materials are not merely aligned to the new standards, they take the CCSS as their very foundation. Our work in math takes its shape from the expectations embedded in the new standards—including the instructional shifts and mathematical progressions, and the new expectations for student fluency, deep conceptual understanding, and application to real-life context. Similarly, our ELA and history curricula are deeply informed by the CCSS's new emphasis on close reading, increased use of informational text, and evidence-based writing.

Our curriculum is distinguished not only by its adherence to the CCSS. The math curriculum is based on a theory of teaching math that is proven to work. That theory posits that mathematical knowledge is most coherently and

---

1. Despite the coincidence of name, Common Core and the Common Core State Standards are not affiliated. Common Core was established in 2007, prior to the start of the Common Core State Standards Initiative, which was led by the National Governors Association and the Council for Chief State School Officers.

2. *Common Core State Standards for English Language Arts & Literacy in History/Social Studies, Science, and Technical Subjects* (Washington, DC: Common Core State Standards Initiative), 6.

effectively conveyed when it is taught in a sequence that follows the "story" of mathematics itself. This is why we call the elementary portion of this curriculum "A Story of Units," to be followed by "A Story of Ratios" in middle school, and "A Story of Functions" in high school. Mathematical concepts flow logically, from one to the next, in this curriculum. The sequencing has been joined with methods of instruction that have been proven to work, in this nation and abroad. These methods drive student understanding beyond process, to deep mastery of mathematical concepts. The goal of the curriculum is to produce students who are not merely literate, but fluent, in mathematics.

It is important to note that, as extensive as these curriculum materials are, they are not meant to be prescriptive. Rather, they are intended to provide a basis for teachers to hone their own craft through study, collaboration, training, and the application of their own expertise as professionals. At Common Core we believe deeply in the ability of teachers and in their central and irreplaceable role in shaping the classroom experience. We strive only to support and facilitate their important work.

The teachers and scholars who wrote these materials are listed beginning on the next page. Their deep knowledge of mathematics, of the CCSS, and of what works in classrooms defined this work in every respect. I would like to thank Louisiana State University professor of mathematics Scott Baldridge for the intellectual leadership he provides to this project. Teacher, trainer, and writer Robin Ramos is the most inspired math educator I've ever encountered. It is Robin and Scott's aspirations for what mathematics education in America *should* look like that is spelled out in these pages.

Finally, this work owes a debt to project director Nell McAnelly that is so deep I'm confident it never can be repaid. Nell, who leads LSU's Gordon A. Cain Center for STEM Literacy, oversees all aspects of our work for NYSED. She has spent days, nights, weekends, and many cancelled vacations toiling in her efforts to make it possible for this talented group of teacher-writers to produce their best work against impossible deadlines. I'm confident that in the years to come Scott, Robin, and Nell will be among those who will deserve to be credited with putting math instruction in our nation back on track.

Thank you for taking an interest in our work. Please join us at www.commoncore.org.

Lynne Munson
President and Executive Director
Common Core
Washington, DC
October 25, 2013

Common Core's K-5 Math Staff

Scott Baldridge, Lead Mathematician and Writer
Robin Ramos, Lead Writer, PreKindergarten-5
Jill Diniz, Lead Writer, 6-12
Ben McCarty, Mathematician

Nell McAnelly, Project Director
Tiah Alphonso, Associate Director
Jennifer Loftin, Associate Director
Catriona Anderson, Curriculum Manager,
    PreKindergarten-5

Sherri Adler, PreKindergarten
Debbie Andorka-Aceves, PreKindergarten

Kate McGill Austin, Kindergarten
Nancy Diorio, Kindergarten
Lacy Endo-Peery, Kindergarten
Melanie Gutierrez, Kindergarten
Nuhad Jamal, Kindergarten
Cecilia Rudzitis, Kindergarten
Shelly Snow, Kindergarten

Beth Barnes, First Grade
Lily Cavanaugh, First Grade
Ana Estela, First Grade
Kelley Isinger, First Grade
Kelly Spinks, First Grade
Marianne Strayton, First Grade
Hae Jung Yang, First Grade

Wendy Keehfus-Jones, Second Grade
Susan Midlarsky, Second Grade
Jenny Petrosino, Second Grade
Colleen Sheeron, Second Grade
Nancy Sommer, Second Grade
Lisa Watts-Lawton, Second Grade
MaryJo Wieland, Second Grade
Jessa Woods, Second Grade

Eric Angel, Third Grade
Greg Gorman, Third Grade
Susan Lee, Third Grade
Cristina Metcalf, Third Grade
Ann Rose Santoro, Third Grade
Kevin Tougher, Third Grade
Victoria Peacock, Third Grade
Saffron VanGalder, Third Grade

Katrina Abdussalaam, Fourth Grade
Kelly Alsup, Fourth Grade
Patti Dieck, Fourth Grade
Mary Jones, Fourth Grade
Soojin Lu, Fourth Grade
Tricia Salerno, Fourth Grade
Gail Smith, Fourth Grade
Eric Welch, Fourth Grade
Sam Wertheim, Fourth Grade
Erin Wheeler, Fourth Grade

Leslie Arceneaux, Fifth Grade
Adam Baker, Fifth Grade
Janice Fan, Fifth Grade
Peggy Golden, Fifth Grade
Halle Kananak, Fifth Grade
Shauntina Kerrison, Fifth Grade
Pat Mohr, Fifth Grade
Chris Sarlo, Fifth Grade

Additional Writers

Bill Davidson, Fluency Specialist
Robin Hecht, UDL Specialist
Simon Pfeil, Mathematician

Document Management Team

Tam Le, Document Manager
Jennifer Merchan, Copy Editor

Mathematics Curriculum

Table of Contents

GRADE 5 • MODULE 6

Problem Solving with the Coordinate Plane

NOTE: Student sheets should be printed at 100% scale to preserve the intended size of figures for accurate measurements. Adjust your copier or printer settings to *actual size* and set page scaling to *none*.

Grade 5 • Module 6

Problem Solving with the Coordinate Plane

OVERVIEW

In this 40-day module, students develop a coordinate system for the first quadrant of the coordinate plane and use it to solve problems. Students use the familiar number line as an introduction to the idea of a coordinate and construct two perpendicular number lines to create a coordinate system on the plane. They see that just as points on the line can be located by their distance from 0, the plane's coordinate system can be used to locate and plot points using two coordinates. They then use the coordinate system to explore relationships between points, ordered pairs, patterns, lines and, more abstractly, the rules that generate them. This study culminates in an exploration of the coordinate plane in real world applications.

In Topic A, students come to realize that *any* line, regardless of orientation, can be made into a number line by first locating zero, choosing a unit length, and partitioning the length-unit into fractional lengths as desired. They are introduced to the concept of a coordinate as describing the distance of a point on the line from zero. As students construct these number lines in various orientations on a plane, they explore ways to describe the position of points *not* located on the lines. This discussion leads to the discovery that a second number line, perpendicular to the first, creates an efficient, precise way to describe the location of these points. Thus, points can be located using coordinate pairs, (a, b), by starting at the origin, travelling a distance of a units along the x-axis, and b units along a line parallel to the y-axis. Students describe given points using coordinate pairs as well as use given coordinate pairs to plot points (**5.G.1**). The topic concludes with an investigation of patterns in coordinate pairs along lines parallel to the axes, which leads to the discovery that these lines consist of the set of points whose distance from the x- or y-axis is constant.

Students move in to plotting points and using them to draw lines in the plane in Topic B (**5.G.1**). They investigate patterns relating the x- and y-coordinates of the points on the line and reason about the patterns in the ordered pairs, laying important groundwork for Grade 6 proportional reasoning. Topic B continues as students use given rules (e.g., multiply by 2, then add 3) to generate coordinate pairs, plot points, and investigate relationships. Patterns in the resultant coordinate pairs are analyzed, leading students to discover that such rules produce collinear sets of points. Students next generate two number patterns from two given rules, plot the points, and analyze the relationships within the sequences of the ordered pairs (**5.OA.3**). Patterns continue to be the focus as students analyze the effect on the steepness of the line when the second coordinate is produced through an addition rule as opposed to a multiplication rule (**5.OA.2, 5.OA.3**). Students also create rules to generate number patterns, plot the points, connect those points with lines, and look for intersections.

Topic C finds students drawing figures in the coordinate plane by plotting points to create parallel, perpendicular, and intersecting lines. They reason about what points are needed to produce such lines and angles, and then investigate the resultant points and their relationships. Students also reason about the relationships among coordinate pairs that are symmetric about a line (**5.G.1**).

Problem solving in the coordinate plane is the focus of Topic D. Students draw symmetric figures using both angle size and distance from a given line of symmetry (**5.G.2**). Line graphs are also used to explore patterns and make predictions based on those patterns (**5.G.2, 5.OA.3**). To round out the topic, students use coordinate planes to solve real world problems.

Topic E provides an opportunity for students to encounter complex, multi-step problems requiring the application of concepts and skills mastered throughout the Grade 5 curriculum. They use all four operations with both whole numbers and fractions in varied contexts. The problems in Topic E are designed to be non-routine, requiring students to persevere in order to solve them. While wrestling with complexity is an important part of Topic E, the true strength of this topic is derived from the time allocated for students to construct arguments and critique the reasoning of their classmates. After students have been given adequate time to ponder and solve the problems, two lessons are devoted to sharing approaches and solutions. Students will partner to justify their conclusions, communicate them to others, and respond to the arguments of their peers.

In this final topic of Module 6, and in fact, *A Story of Units*, students spend time producing a compendium of their learning. They not only reach back to recall learning from the very beginning of Grade 5, but they also expand their thinking by exploring such concepts as the Fibonacci sequence. Students solidify the year's learning by creating and playing games, exploring patterns as they reflect back on their elementary years. All materials for the games and activities are then housed for summer use in boxes created in the final two lessons of the year.

Distribution of Instructional Minutes

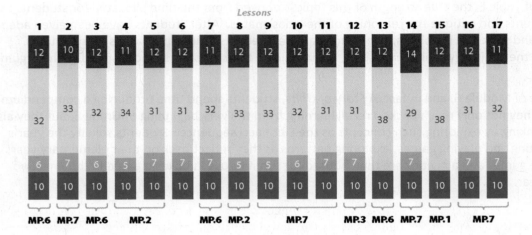

This diagram represents a suggested distribution of instructional minutes based on the emphasis of particular lesson components in different lessons throughout the module.

■ Fluency Practice
□ Concept Development
▪ Application Problems
■ Student Debrief

Lessons

Lesson	1	2	3	4	5	6	7	8	9	10	11	12	13	14	15	16	17
Fluency	12	10	12	11	12	12	11	12	12	12	12	12	12	14	12	12	11
Concept	32	33	32	34	31	31	32	33	33	32	31	31	38	29	38	31	32
Application	6	7	6	5	7	7	7	5	5	6	7	7		7		7	7
Debrief	10	10	10	10	10	10	10	10	10	10	10	10	10	10	10	10	10

MP.6 MP.7 MP.6   MP.2   MP.6 MP.2   MP.7   MP.3 MP.6 MP.7 MP.1   MP.7

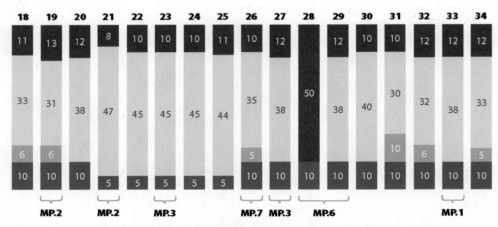

Lesson	18	19	20	21	22	23	24	25	26	27	28	29	30	31	32	33	34
Fluency	11	13	12	8	10	10	10	11	10	12		12	10	10	12	12	12
Concept	33	31	38	47	45	45	45	44	35	38	50	38	40	30	32	38	33
Application	6	6							5					10	6		5
Debrief	10	10	10	5	5	5	5	5	10	10	10	10	10	10	10	10	10

MP.2   MP.2   MP.3   MP.7 MP.3 MP.6   MP.1

MP = Mathematical Practice

Focus Grade Level Standards

Write and interpret numerical expressions.

5.OA.2 Write simple expressions that record calculations with numbers, and interpret numerical expressions without evaluating them. *For example, express the calculation "add 8 and 7, then multiply by 2" as 2 × (8 + 7). Recognize that 3 × (18932 + 921) is three times as large as 18932 + 921, without having to calculate the indicated sum or product.*

Analyze patterns and relationships.

5.OA.3 Generate two numerical patterns using two given rules. Identify apparent relationships between corresponding terms. Form ordered pairs consisting of corresponding terms from the two patterns, and graph the ordered pairs on a coordinate plane. *For example, given the rule "Add 3" and the starting number 0, and given the rule "Add 6" and the starting number 0, generate terms in the resulting sequences, and observe that the terms in one sequence are twice the corresponding terms in the other sequence. Explain informally why this is so.*

Graph points on the coordinate plane to solve real-world and mathematical problems.

5.G.1 Use a pair of perpendicular number lines, called axes, to define a coordinate system, with the intersection of the lines (the origin) arranged to coincide with the 0 on each line and a given point in the plane located by using an ordered pair of numbers, called its coordinates. Understand that the first number indicates how far to travel from the origin in the direction of one axis, and the second number indicates how far to travel in the direction of the second axis, with the convention that the names of the two axes and the coordinates correspond (e.g., x-axis and x-coordinate, y-axis and y-coordinate).

5.G.2 Represent real world and mathematical problems by graphing points in the first quadrant of the coordinate plane, and interpret coordinate values of points in the context of the situation.

Foundational Standards

4.OA.1 Interpret a multiplication equation as a comparison, e.g., interpret 35 = 5 × 7 as a statement that 35 is 5 times as many as 7 and 7 times as many as 5. Represent verbal statements of multiplicative comparisons as multiplication equations.

4.OA.5 Generate a number or shape pattern that follows a given rule. Identify apparent features of the pattern that were not explicit in the rule itself. *For example, given the rule "Add 3" and the starting number 1, generate terms in the resulting sequence and observe that the terms appear to alternate between odd and even numbers. Explain informally why the numbers will continue to alternate in this way.*

4.MD.5 Recognize angles as geometric shapes that are formed wherever two rays share a common endpoint, and understand concepts of angle measurement:

    a.   An angle is measured with reference to a circle with its center at the common endpoint of the rays, by considering the fraction of the circular arc between the points where the two

rays intersect the circle. An angle that turns through 1/360 of a circle is called a "one-degree angle," and can be used to measure angles.

    b.   An angle that turns through *n* one-degree angles is said to have an angle measure of *n* degrees.

4.MD.6   Measure angles in whole-number degrees using a protractor. Sketch angles of specified measure.

4.MD.7   Recognize angle measure as additive. When an angle is decomposed into non-overlapping parts, the angle measure of the whole is the sum of the angle measures of the parts. Solve addition and subtraction problems to find unknown angles on a diagram in real world and mathematical problems, e.g., by using an equation with a symbol for the unknown angle measure.

4.G.1   Draw points, lines, line segments, rays, angles (right, acute, obtuse), and perpendicular and parallel lines. Identify these in two-dimensional figures.

5.NF.2   Solve word problems involving addition and subtraction of fractions referring to the same whole, including cases of unlike denominators, e.g., by using visual fraction models or equations to represent the problem. Use benchmark fractions and number sense of fractions to estimate mentally and assess the reasonableness of answers. *For example, recognize an incorrect result 2/5 + 1/2 = 3/7, by observing that 3/7 < 1/2.*

5.NF.3   Interpret a fraction as division of the numerator by the denominator ($a/b = a \div b$). Solve word problems involving division of whole numbers leading to answers in the form of fractions or mixed numbers, e.g., by using visual fraction models or equations to represent the problem. *For example, interpret 3/4 as the result of dividing 3 by 4, noting that 3/4 multiplied by 4 equals 3, and that when 3 wholes are shared equally among 4 people each person has a share of size 3/4. If 9 people want to share a 50-pound sack of rice equally by weight, how many pounds of rice should each person get? Between what two whole numbers does your answer lie?*

5.NF.6   Solve real world problems involving multiplication of fractions and mixed numbers, e.g., by using visual fraction models or equations to represent the problem.

5.NF.7c   Apply and extend previous understandings of division to divide unit fractions by whole numbers and whole numbers by unit fractions.

    c.   Solve real world problems involving division of a unit fractions by non-zero whole numbers and division of whole numbers by unit fractions, e.g., by using visual fraction models and equations to represent the problem. *For example, how much chocolate will each person get if 3 people share 1/2 lb of chocolate equally? How many 1/3-cup servings are in 2 cups of raisins?*

5.MD.1   Convert among different-sized standard measurement units within a given measurement system (e.g., convert 5 cm to 0.05 m), and use these conversions in solving multi-step, real world problems.

5.MD.5   Relate volume to the operations of multiplication and addition and solve real world and mathematical problems involving volume.

	Module 6:	Problem Solving with the Coordinate Plane
	Date:	1/31/14

            vi

Focus Standards for Mathematical Practice

MP.1   **Make sense of problems and persevere in solving them.** Students make sense of problems as they use tape diagrams and other models, persevering to solve complex, multi-step word problems. Students check their work and monitor their own progress, assessing their approach and its validity within the given context and altering their method when necessary.

MP.2   **Reason abstractly and quantitatively.** Students reason abstractly and quantitatively as they interpret the steepness and orientation of a line given by the points of a number pattern. Students attend to the meaning of the values in an ordered pair and reason about how they can be manipulated in order to create parallel, perpendicular, or intersecting lines.

MP.3   **Construct viable arguments and critique the reasoning of others.** As students construct a coordinate system on a plane, they generate explanations about the best place to create a second line of coordinates. They analyze lines and the coordinate pairs that comprise them, then draw conclusions and construct arguments about their positioning on the coordinate plane. Students also critique the reasoning of others and construct viable arguments as they analyze classmates' solutions to lengthy, multi-step word problems.

MP.6   **Attend to precision.** Mathematically proficient students try to communicate precisely to others. They endeavor to use clear definitions in discussion with others and in their own reasoning. These students state the meaning of the symbols they choose, including using the equal sign, consistently and appropriately. They are careful about specifying units of measure, and labeling axes to clarify the correspondence with quantities in a problem. The students calculate accurately and efficiently, expressing numerical answers with a degree of precision appropriate for the problem context. In the elementary grades, students give carefully formulated explanations to each other. By the time they reach high school, they have learned to examine claims and make explicit use of definitions.

MP.7   **Look for and make use of structure.** Students identify and create patterns in coordinate pairs and make predictions about their effect on the lines that connect them. Students also recognize patterns in sets of coordinate pairs and use those patterns to explain why a line is parallel or perpendicular to an axis. They use operational rules to generate coordinate pairs and, conversely, generalize observed patterns within coordinate pairs as rules.

Overview of Module Topics and Lesson Objectives

Standards		Topics and Objectives	Days
5.G.1	A	**Coordinate Systems**	6
		Lesson 1: Construct a coordinate system on a line.	
		Lesson 2: Construct a coordinate system on a plane.	
		Lessons 3–4: Name points using coordinate pairs, and use the coordinate pairs to plot points.	
		Lessons 5–6: Investigate patterns in vertical and horizontal lines, and interpret points on the plane as distances from the axes.	
5.OA.2 **5.OA.3** **5.G.1**	B	**Patterns in the Coordinate Plane and Graphing Number Patterns from Rules**	6
		Lesson 7: Plot points, use them to draw lines in the plane, and describe patterns within the coordinate pairs.	
		Lesson 8: Generate a number pattern from a given rule, and plot the points.	
		Lesson 9: Generate two number patterns from given rules, plot the points, and analyze the patterns.	
		Lesson 10: Compare the lines and patterns generated by addition rules and multiplication rules.	
		Lesson 11: Analyze number patterns created from mixed operations.	
		Lesson 12: Create a rule to generate a number pattern, and plot the points.	
		Mid-Module Assessment: Topics A–B (assessment 1 day, return 1 day, remediation or further applications 1 day)	3
5.G.1 **5.G.2**	C	**Drawing Figures in the Coordinate Plane**	5
		Lesson 13: Construct parallel line segments on a rectangular grid.	
		Lesson 14: Construct parallel line segments, and analyze relationships of the coordinate pairs.	
		Lesson 15: Construct perpendicular line segments on a rectangular grid.	
		Lesson 16: Construct perpendicular line segments, and analyze relationships of the coordinate pairs.	
		Lesson 17: Draw symmetric figures using distance and angle measure from the line of symmetry.	

Standards		Topics and Objectives	Days
5.OA.3 **5.G.2**	D	**Problem Solving in the Coordinate Plane** Lesson 18: Draw symmetric figures on the coordinate plane. Lesson 19: Plot data on line graphs and analyze trends. Lesson 20: Use coordinate systems to solve real world problems.	3
		End-of-Module Assessment: Topics A–D (assessment 1 day, return 1 day, remediation or further applications 1 day)	3
5.NF.2 **5.NF.3** **5.NF.6** **5.NF.7c** **5.MD.1** **5.MD.5** **5.G.2**	E	**Multi-Step Word Problems** Lessons 21–25: Make sense of complex, multi-step problems and persevere in solving them. Share and critique peer solutions.	5
	F	**The Years in Review: A Reflection on *A Story of Units*** Lessons 26–27: Solidify writing and interpreting numerical expressions. Lesson 28: Solidify fluency with Grade 5 skills. Lessons 29–30: Solidify the vocabulary of geometry. Lesson 31: Explore the Fibonacci sequence. Lesson 32: Explore patterns in saving money. Lessons 33–34: Design and construct boxes to house materials for summer use.	9
Total Number of Instructional Days			**40**

Terminology

New or Recently Introduced Terms

- Axis (fixed reference line for the measurement of coordinates)
- Coordinate (number that identifies a point on a plane)
- Coordinate pair (two numbers that are used to identify a point on a plane; written (x, y) where x represents a distance from 0 on the x-axis and y represents a distance from 0 on the y-axis)
- Coordinate plane (plane spanned by the x-axis and y-axis in which the coordinates of a point are distances from the two perpendicular axes)
- Ordered pair (two quantities written in a given fixed order, usually written as (x, y))
- Origin (fixed point from which coordinates are measured; the point at which the x-axis and y-axis

intersect, labeled (0, 0) on the coordinate plane)
- Quadrant (any of the four equal areas created by dividing a plane by an x-axis and y-axis)

Familiar Terms and Symbols[1]

- Angle (union of two different rays sharing a common vertex)
- Angle measure (number of degrees in an angle)
- Degree (unit used to measure angles)
- Horizontal (parallel to the x-axis)
- Line (two-dimensional object that has no endpoints and continues on forever in a plane)
- Parallel (two lines in a plane that do not intersect)
- Perpendicular (two lines are *perpendicular* if they intersect, and any of the angles formed between the lines are 90-degree angles)
- Point (zero-dimensional figure that satisfies the location of an ordered pair)
- Rule (procedure or operation(s) that affects the value of an ordered pair)
- Vertical (parallel to the y-axis)

Suggested Tools and Representations

- Ruler
- Protractor
- Set square
- Tape diagrams

Scaffolds[2]

The scaffolds integrated into *A Story of Units* give alternatives for how students access information as well as express and demonstrate their learning. Strategically placed margin notes are provided within each lesson elaborating on the use of specific scaffolds at applicable times. They address many needs presented by English language learners, students with disabilities, students performing above grade level, and students performing below grade level. Many of the suggestions are organized by Universal Design for Learning (UDL) principles and are applicable to more than one population. To read more about the approach to differentiated instruction in *A Story of Units,* please refer to "How to Implement *A Story of Units.*"

---

[1] These are terms and symbols students have seen previously.
[2] Students with disabilities may require Braille, large print, audio, or special digital files. Please visit the website, www.p12.nysed.gov/specialed/aim, for specific information on how to obtain student materials that satisfy the National Instructional Materials Accessibility Standard (NIMAS) format.

Assessment Summary

Type	Administered	Format	Standards Addressed
Mid-Module Assessment Task	After Topic B	Constructed response with rubric	5.OA.2 5.OA.3 5.G.1
End-of-Module Assessment Task	After Topic D	Constructed response with rubric	5.OA.2 5.OA.3 5.G.1 5.G.2

Topic A

Coordinate Systems

5.G.1

Focus Standard:	5.G.1	Use a pair of perpendicular number lines, called axes, to define a coordinate system, with the intersection of the lines (the origin) arranged to coincide with the 0 on each line and a given point in the plan located by using an ordered pair of numbers, called its coordinates. Understand that the first number indicates how far to travel from the origin in the direction of one axis, and the second number indicates how far to travel in the direction of the second axis, with the convention that the names of the two axes and the coordinates correspond (e.g., x-axis and x-coordinate, y-axis and y-coordinate).
Instructional Days:	6	
Coherence -Links from:	G3–M5	Fractions as Numbers on the Number Line
-Links to:	G6–M1	Ratios and Unit Rates
	G6–M3	Rational Numbers

In Topic A, students revisit a Grade 3 activity in which lined paper is used to subdivide a length into n equal parts. In Grade 5, this activity is extended as students explore that *any* line, regardless of orientation, can be made into a number line by first locating zero, choosing a unit length, and partitioning the length-unit into fractional lengths. Students are introduced to the concept of a coordinate as describing the distance of a point on the line from zero.

As they construct these number lines in various orientations on a plane, students explore ways to describe the position of points *not* located on the lines. This discussion leads to the discovery that a second number line, perpendicular to the first, creates an efficient, precise way to describe the location of these points. Thus, points can be located using coordinate pairs, (a, b), by travelling a distance of a units from the origin along the x-axis, and b units along a line parallel to the y-axis.

Students describe given points using coordinate pairs, and then use given coordinate pairs to plot points (**5.G.1**). The topic concludes with an investigation of the patterns in coordinate pairs along vertical or horizontal lines, which leads to the discovery that these lines consist of the set of points whose distance from the x- or y-axis is constant.

A Teaching Sequence Towards Mastery of Coordinate Systems

Objective 1: Construct a coordinate system on a line.
(Lesson 1)

Objective 2: Construct a coordinate system on a plane.
(Lesson 2)

Objective 3: Name points using coordinate pairs, and use the coordinate pairs to plot points.
(Lessons 3–4)

Objective 4: Investigate patterns in vertical and horizontal lines, and interpret points on the plane as distances from the axes.
(Lessons 5–6)

Lesson 1

Objective: Construct a coordinate system on a line.

Suggested Lesson Structure

- Fluency Practice (12 minutes)
- Application Problem (6 minutes)
- Concept Development (32 minutes)
- Student Debrief (10 minutes)

Total Time (60 minutes)

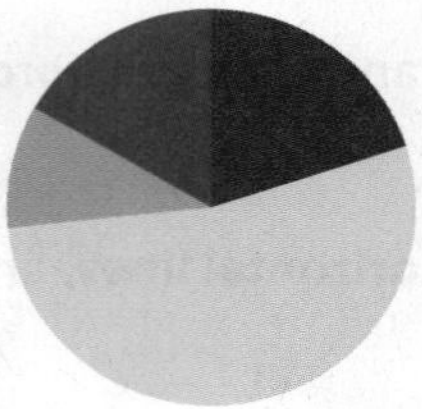

Fluency Practice (12 minutes)

- Count by Equivalent Fractions **4.NF.1** (6 minutes)
- Find the Missing Number on a Number Line **5.G.1** (4 minutes)
- Physiometry **4.G.2** (2 minutes)

NOTES ON MULTIPLE MEANS OF REPRESENTATION:

The Count by Equivalent Fractions fluency activity supports language acquisition for English language learners as it offers valuable practice speaking fraction names, such as *fourths.* Model and assist students' enunciation of the ending digraph /th/. Couple the counting with prepared visuals to increase comprehension.

Count by Equivalent Fractions (6 minutes)

Materials: (S) Personal white boards

Note: This fluency activity prepares students for G5–M6–Lesson 1.

T: Count by 1 half to 10 halves. Start at zero halves. (Write as students count.)

$\frac{0}{2}$	$\frac{1}{2}$	$\frac{2}{2}$	$\frac{3}{2}$	$\frac{4}{2}$	$\frac{5}{2}$	$\frac{6}{2}$	$\frac{7}{2}$	$\frac{8}{2}$	$\frac{9}{2}$	$\frac{10}{2}$
0,	$\frac{1}{2}$	1	$\frac{3}{2}$	2	$\frac{5}{2}$	3	$\frac{7}{2}$	4	$\frac{9}{2}$	5

S: $\frac{0}{2}, \frac{1}{2}, \frac{2}{2}, \frac{3}{2}, \frac{4}{2}, \frac{5}{2}, \frac{6}{2}, \frac{7}{2}, \frac{8}{2}, \frac{9}{2}, \frac{10}{2}$.

T: 2 halves is the same as 1 of what unit?

S: 1 one.

T: (Beneath $\frac{2}{2}$, write 1.) 2 ones is the same as how many halves?

S: 4 halves.

T: (Beneath $\frac{4}{2}$, write 2.) 3 ones is the same as how many halves?

Repeat the process through $\frac{10}{2}$ or 5.

T: (Beneath $\frac{10}{2}$, write 5.) Let's count to 10 halves again, but this time when you come to a fraction that is equal to a whole number, say the whole number.

S: $0, \frac{1}{2}, 1, \frac{2}{2}, 2, \frac{5}{2}, 3, \frac{7}{2}, 4, \frac{9}{2}, 5.$

Repeat the process, counting by fourths to $\frac{10}{4}$.

Find the Missing Number on a Number Line (4 minutes)

Materials: (S) Personal white boards

Note: This fluency activity prepares students for G5–M6–Lesson 1.

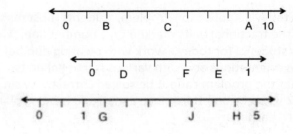

T: (Project a number line partitioned into 10 unit intervals. Label 0 and 10 as the endpoints. Point to the A.) What's the value of A?

S: 9.

T: (Point to B.) What's the value of B?

S: 2.

T: Write the value of C.

S: (Write 5.)

Continue the process for the other number lines.

Physiometry (2 minutes)

Note: This fluency activity prepares students for G5–M6–Lesson 2.

T: (Stretch one arm up, directly toward the ceiling. Stretch the other arm out, directly toward a wall and parallel to the floor.) What type of angle do you think I am making?

S: Right angle.

T: What is the relationship of the lines formed by my arms?

S: Perpendicular.

T: (Point to a wall on the side of the room.) Point to the walls that run perpendicular to the wall I'm pointing to.

S: (Point to the front and back walls.)

T: (Point to the back wall.)

S: (Point to the side walls.)

Continue the exercise, pointing to remaining walls and asking students to respond.

T: (Point to the back wall.) Point to the wall that runs parallel to the wall I'm pointing to.

Lesson 1:   Construct a coordinate system on a line.
Date: 1/31/14

6.A.4

S: (Point to the front wall.)

Continue the exercise, pointing to remaining walls and asking students to respond.

Application Problem (6 minutes)

A landscaper is planting some marigolds in a row. The row is 2 yards long. The flowers must be spaced $\frac{1}{3}$ yard apart so that they will have proper room to grow. The landscaper plants the first flower at 0. Place points on the number line to show where the landscaper should place the other plants. How many marigolds will fit on this row?

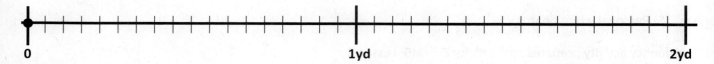

Note: In today's Application Problem, students must make sense of the fractional units marked on a number line. This prepares students for today's work with creating number lines in various orientations and with various fractional units. Be aware that the problem cannot be solved correctly by simply dividing 2 yards by one-third since a marigold is being planted at the zero hash mark.

7 marigolds will fit.

Concept Development (32 minutes)

Materials: (T) Teacher created number lines in various orientations and scales (see Problem 3 in the Concept Development) (S) Straightedge or ruler, 2 pieces of unlined paper, 1 piece of lined paper, 2 1" × 4¼" tag board strips

NOTES ON MULTIPLE MEANS OF ENGAGEMENT:

The use of parallel lines to create equidistant intervals is outlined in G3–M5–Lesson 30. Please see that lesson for more detail.

Problem 1: Create a number line by choosing a unit length, an origin, and a direction of increase.

T: (Distribute tag board strips, unlined paper, lined paper, and straightedges.) Tell me all you know about number lines. (Record what students say.)

S: Number lines start with zero. → They count from zero. → Numbers increase from left to right as far as you want. Really, they don't ever stop; we just stop writing down the numbers. → We can count by ones, twos, or even by fractions. → When you draw a number line, you have to be sure that the tick marks are the same distance apart.

T: The things you've said are true. We can think of 0 as the starting point for a number line, even when we don't actually show it. They do count by anything, and the distance between the marks must be the same. (Display the collection of lines at the right or a similar collection.) These are all number lines, too. What do you notice that is different? Turn and talk.

Lesson 1:   Construct a coordinate system on a line.
Date: 1/31/14

6.A.5

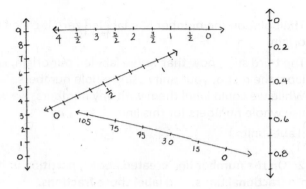

S: Some go up and down, not side-to-side. → Some vertical lines have zero at the top, and the numbers increase from the top to the bottom. → Some are at an angle. → Some increase from right to left.

T: Use your straightedge to draw a long line on your plain paper. You may draw your line at any angle.

S: (Draw lines.)

T: Let's draw an arrow on both ends to show that the line goes on forever in both directions.

S: (Draw arrows on the lines.)

T: We can turn the line that we've drawn into a number line. (If possible, list three steps on the board, as shown below.) First, choose a unit length. Use the tag board to pick a unit length. Cut one of your tag board strips so that it is at least 1 inch long. How can we be sure our cut is straight?

S: Fold it so that the edges meet and cut on the fold. (Cut tag board strip.)

T: Compare your unit length to your partner's. Are they the same or different?

S: (Compare unit lengths. There should be a variety.)

T: Use this unit length to mark off equal distances on our lines with hash marks. Start at either end, and mark as many equal units as you can. (Demonstrate, if necessary.)

T: Now that our number lines show equal units, read our second step.

 MP.6

S: (Read.) Choose a direction of increase of the numbers and label zero.

T: Label a hash mark as zero on one end of your line so that your numbers increase in the direction you chose. Show your partner what you did. (Allow students time to work and discuss with a partner.)

> 1. Choose a unit length by cutting a piece of tag board.
> 2. Choose a direction of increase of the numbers, and label zero.
> 3. Label the units starting with the origin.

COMMON CORE™   Lesson 1:   Construct a coordinate system on a line.
Date: 1/31/14

6.A.6

T: The point on the number line labeled zero is called the **origin.**

T: The third step, now that we've labeled our origin, is to label the rest of your units using whole numbers. While we could label them with any numbers, we will use whole numbers for this line.

S: (Label units.)

Problem 2: On the number line created above, partition unit lengths into fractional units, and label those fractions.

T: Now that we've marked the whole units on our number lines, let's partition these wholes into fractional units. We can use lined paper to mark off *any* fractional unit *precisely* without the use of a ruler. Place your lined paper on your desk so that the red margin is horizontal.

S: (Place paper so that red margin is horizontal.)

T: Angle your tag board unit so that the left top corner touches one line, and the right top corner touches another line. Mark the intersection of your unit with the lines on the paper.

S: (Mark intersection.)

T: What fractional unit did you mark? How do you know?

S: I marked thirds. I see 3 equal parts. → I marked fourths. I made my paper touch a line, and then I counted 4 lines over and marked where they touched. This made 4 equal parts.

T: Use the vertical lines to mark a different fractional unit on the other long edge of your tag board. Then, flip your unit over and mark two more fractional units on those edges as well.

S: (Mark additional units.)

T: Why does this method work?

S: Because the lines on the paper are parallel and the same distance apart, it doesn't matter how you lay your paper strip across them; the distance between each mark is still the same. → Because the lines are equal distances, we can choose how many marks we want and angle the paper across that many lines. → If we want halves, we touch a line and count two spaces to figure out the line to touch with the other end of the unit. If we want thirds, we touch a line and count three spaces to figure out the line to touch with the other corner.

T: Now choose one of the fractional units you've marked on your tag board, and use it to partition your number line. Label the fractional units.

S: (Label the units.)

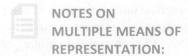

NOTES ON MULTIPLE MEANS OF REPRESENTATION:

Students with fine motor deficits may find number line creation difficult. Allow students to partner such that one draws the lines and partitions, and the other labels the tick marks.

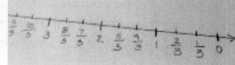

T: Try to find someone in our class whose number line is exactly the same as yours. What do you
      notice?

S: I couldn't find anybody's that was exactly like mine. Some counted in the same direction, but the
      units were different size. → Number lines can increase in any direction. → Units can be whatever
      size you choose, and the line can be at any angle. → We can choose to show any fraction of our unit
      on the number line.

Problem 3: Identify the coordinate of a given shape placed on a number line.

T: (Display Number Line 1.) Here is a number line that I created. I want to describe the location of one
      of the shapes on this number line without pointing to it. What can I say? Turn and talk.

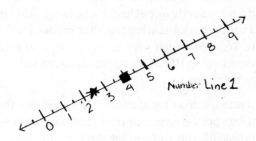

S: You could tell how far it is from another shape. → You
      could tell how far the shape was from one end of the
      line. → You could tell how far it is from zero.

T: Because every number line has an origin, we can
      use it as a reference point to tell the location of
      other points on and off the line. We can describe
      the location of a shape on this line by telling its
      coordinate. (Write *coordinate* on the board.) Say
      coordinate.

S: (Repeat *coordinate*.)

T: The coordinate tells the distance from zero to the shape. On Number Line 1, the square's coordinate
      is 4. (Point.) That's another way to say that the distance from zero to the shape is 4 units. (Show the
      distance by running a finger along the line from 0 to 4.) What is the star's coordinate?

S: $2\frac{1}{2}$.

T: Remind your partner what the coordinate tells.

S: (Share with partner.)

T: (Display Number Lines 2 and 3.) A point has been plotted on each of these number lines. What is
      the coordinate of point A on Number Line 2? The coordinate of point B on Number Line 3? Tell
      your partner.

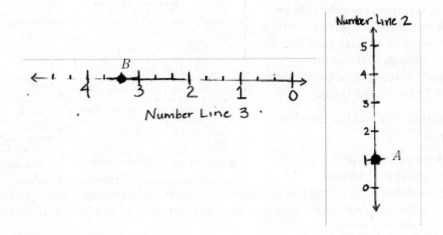

S: Point A is 1 unit from the origin. → The coordinate of point B is $3\frac{1}{3}$.

T: Plot 2 points on your number line and label them C and D. Have your partner give the coordinate of the points.

S: (Plot and label points; partner gives coordinates.)

Problem Set (10 minutes)

Students should do their personal best to complete the Problem Set within the allotted 10 minutes. Some problems do not specify a method for solving. This is an intentional reduction of scaffolding that invokes MP.5, Use Appropriate Tools Strategically. Students should solve these problems using the RDW approach used for Application Problems.

For some classes, it may be appropriate to modify the assignment by specifying which problems students should work on first. With this option, let the careful sequencing of the Problem Set guide your selections so that problems continue to be scaffolded. Balance word problems with other problem types to ensure a range of practice. Assign incomplete problems for homework or at another time during the day

Student Debrief (10 minutes)

Lesson Objective: Construct a coordinate system on a line.

The Student Debrief is intended to invite reflection and active processing of the total lesson experience.

Invite students to review their solutions for the Problem Set. They should check work by comparing answers with a partner before going over answers as a class. Look for misconceptions or misunderstandings that can be addressed in the Debrief. Guide students in a conversation to debrief the Problem Set and process the lesson.

You may choose to use any combination of the questions below to lead the discussion.

- Share your answer for Problem 4 with a partner. (Discuss with students that the cultural convention for single number lines is that the numbers increase from left to right, but in reality it doesn't matter. This will help prepare students to encounter concepts of absolute value in later

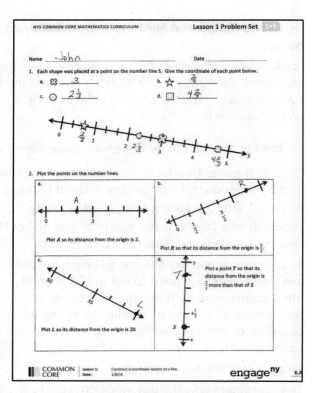

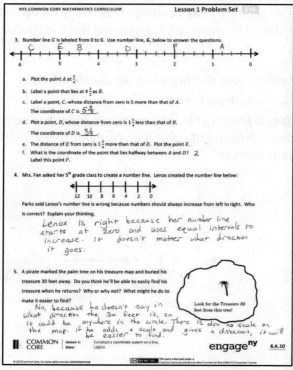

Lesson 1:   Construct a coordinate system on a line.
Date: 1/31/14

6.A.9

grades.)

- What advice did you have for the pirate in Problem 5? Share and explain your thinking to a partner.

- What did you learn about the number line that you did not know before?

- G5–Module 6 is rich in new vocabulary. A word wall for this new vocabulary (e.g., *origin, coordinate, plot*) may be a helpful scaffold for all students. The word wall might even take on the appearance of a coordinate plane in future lessons with words plotted at different coordinates each day. Students could be asked to explain the word plotted at (2, 4), for example.

Exit Ticket (3 minutes)

After the Student Debrief, instruct students to complete the Exit Ticket. A review of their work will help you assess the students' understanding of the concepts that were presented in the lesson today and plan more effectively for future lessons. You may read the questions aloud to the students.

| Lesson 1: | Construct a coordinate system on a line. |
| Date: | 1/31/14 |

6.A.10

Name _____ Date _____

1. Each shape was placed at a point on the number line S. Give the coordinate of each point below.

    a. ✖ _____   b. ★ _____

    c. ● _____   d. ■ _____

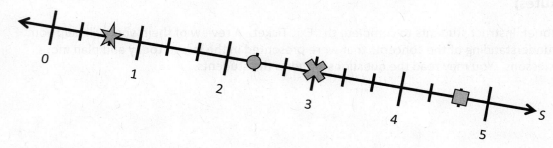

2. Plot the points on the number lines.

    a.

    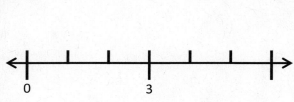

    Plot A so its distance from the origin is 2.

    b.

    Plot R so that its distance from the origin is $\frac{5}{2}$.

    c.

    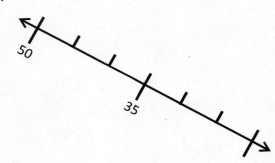

    Plot L so its distance from the origin is 20

    d.

    Plot a point T so that its distance from the origin is $\frac{2}{3}$ more than that of S

COMMON CORE™

Lesson 1:   Construct a coordinate system on a line.
Date: 1/31/14

6.A.11

3. Number line G is labeled from 0 to 6. Use number line G below, to answer the questions.

G

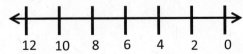

6   5   4   3   2   1   0

a. Plot point A at $\frac{3}{4}$.

b. Label a point that lies at $4\frac{1}{2}$ as B.

c. Label a point, C, whose distance from zero is 5 more than that of A.

The coordinate of C is _____.

d. Plot a point, D, whose distance from zero is $1\frac{1}{4}$ less than that of B.

The coordinate of D is _____.

e. The distance of E from zero is $1\frac{3}{4}$ more than that of D. Plot point E.

f. What is the coordinate of the point that lies halfway between A and D?
Label this point F.

4. Mrs. Fan asked her fifth-grade class to create a number line. Lenox created the number line below:

12   10   8   6   4   2   0

Parks said Lenox's number line is wrong because numbers should always increase from left to right. Who

is correct? Explain your thinking.

5. A pirate marked the palm tree on his treasure map and buried his

treasure 30 feet away. Do you think he'll be able to easily find his

treasure when he returns? Why or why not? What might he do to

make it easier to find?

Look for the treasure 30
feet from this tree!

Lesson 1:   Construct a coordinate system on a line.
Date: 1/31/14

6.A.12

Name _____ Date _____

1. Use number line ℓ to answer the questions.

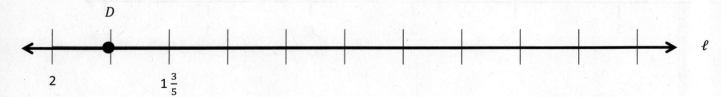

D

2        $1\frac{3}{5}$

a. Plot point C so its distance from the origin is 1.

b. Plot point E $\frac{4}{5}$ closer to the origin than C. What is its coordinate? _____

c. Plot a point at the midpoint of C and E. Label it H.

Name _____   Date _____

1. Answer the following questions using number line Q, below.

    a. What is the coordinate, or the distance from the origin, of the 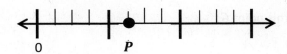 ? _____

    b. What is the coordinate of ⚡ ? _____

    c. What is the coordinate of ♥ ? _____

    d. What is the coordinate at the midpoint of ⚡ and ♥ ? _____

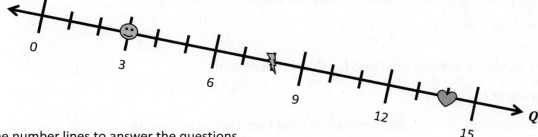

2. Use the number lines to answer the questions.

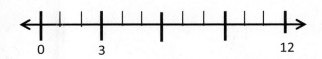

    Plot T so its distance from the origin is 10.

Plot M so its distance is $\frac{11}{4}$ from the origin.

What is the distance from P to M?

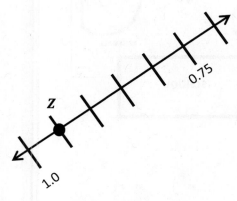

    Plot a point that is 0.15 closer to the origin than Z.

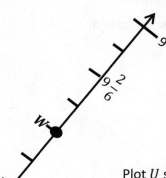

Plot U so that its distance from the origin is $\frac{3}{6}$ closer than that of W.

3. Number line K shows 12 units. Use number line K, below, to answer the questions.

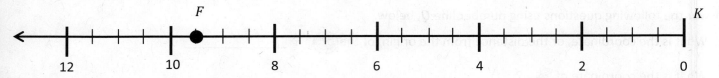

a. Plot a point at 1. Label it A.

b. Label a point that lies at $3\frac{1}{2}$ as B.

c. Label a point, C, whose distance from zero is 8 units farther than that of B.

   The coordinate of C is _____.

d. Plot a point, D, whose distance from zero is $\frac{6}{2}$ closer to zero than B.

   The coordinate of D is _____.

e. What is the coordinate of the point that lies $\frac{17}{2}$ farther from the origin than D?

   Label this point E.

f. What is the coordinate of the point that lies halfway between F and D?

   Label this point G.

4. Mr. Baker's fifth-grade class buried a time capsule in the field behind the school. They drew a map and marked the location of the capsule with an X so his class can dig it up in ten years. What could Mr. Baker have done to make the capsule easier to find?

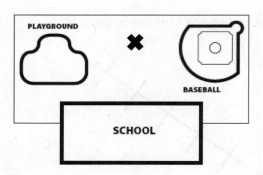

COMMON CORE   Lesson 1: Construct a coordinate system on a line.
              Date: 1/31/14   6.A.15

© 2014 Common Core, Inc. All rights reserved. commoncore.org

Lesson 2

Objective: Construct a coordinate system on a plane.

Suggested Lesson Structure

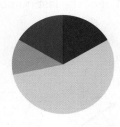

■ Fluency Practice   (10 minutes)
■ Application Problem   (7 minutes)
■ Concept Development   (33 minutes)
■ Student Debrief   (10 minutes)
   Total Time   **(60 minutes)**

Fluency Practice (10 minutes)

- Count by Equivalent Fractions **4.NF.1**   (6 minutes)
- Find the Missing Number on a Number Line **5.G.1**   (4 minutes)

Count by Equivalent Fractions (6 minutes)

Note: This fluency activity reviews G5–M6–Lesson 1 and prepares students for today's lesson.

  T: Count from 0 to 10 by ones.

$\frac{0}{4}$	$\frac{1}{4}$	$\frac{2}{4}$	$\frac{3}{4}$	$\frac{4}{4}$	$\frac{5}{4}$	$\frac{6}{4}$	$\frac{7}{4}$	$\frac{8}{4}$	$\frac{9}{4}$	$\frac{10}{4}$
0	$\frac{1}{4}$	$\frac{2}{4}$	$\frac{3}{4}$	1	$\frac{5}{4}$	$\frac{6}{4}$	$\frac{7}{4}$	2	$\frac{9}{4}$	$\frac{10}{4}$

  S: 0, 1, 2, 3, 4, 5, 6, 7, 8, 9, 10.

  T: Count by 1 fourth to 10 fourths. Start at zero fourths. (Write as students count.)

  S: $\frac{0}{4}, \frac{1}{4}, \frac{2}{4}, \frac{3}{4}, \frac{4}{4}, \frac{5}{4}, \frac{6}{4}, \frac{7}{4}, \frac{8}{4}, \frac{9}{4}, \frac{10}{4}.$

  T: 4 fourths is the same as 1 of what unit?

  S: 1 one.

  T: (Beneath $\frac{4}{4}$, write 1.) 2 ones is the same as how many fourths?

  S: 8 fourths.

  T: (Beneath $\frac{8}{4}$, write 2.) Let's count to 10 fourths again, but this time say the whole numbers when you come to a whole number. Start at 0.

  S: 0, $\frac{1}{4}, \frac{2}{4}, \frac{3}{4}$, 1, $\frac{5}{4}, \frac{6}{4}, \frac{7}{4}$, 2, $\frac{9}{4}, \frac{10}{4}.$

Lesson 2:	Construct a coordinate system on a plane.
Date:	1/31/14

6.A.16

Repeat the process, counting by thirds to 10 thirds.

Find the Missing Number on a Number Line (4 minutes)

Materials: (S) Personal white boards

Note: This fluency activity reviews G5–M6–Lesson 1. For the last number line, challenge students by having them write simplified fractions.

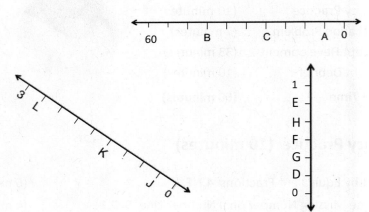

- T: (Project a number line partitioned into 10 intervals. Label 60 and 0 as the endpoints. Point at A.) What is the value of A?
- S: 6
- T: What's the value of B?
- S: 42.
- T: Write the value of C.
- S: (Write 24.)

Continue the process for the other number lines.

Application Problem (7 minutes)

The picture shows an intersection in Stony Brook Village.

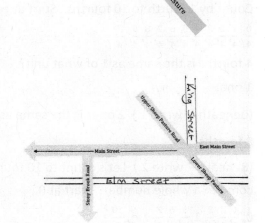

a. The town wants to construct two new roads, Elm Street and King Street. Elm Street will intersect Lower Sheep Pasture Road, run parallel to Main Street, and be perpendicular to Stony Brook Road. Sketch Elm Street.

b. King Street will be perpendicular to Main Street and begin at the intersection of Upper Sheep Pasture Road and East Main Street. Sketch King Street.

Note: The Application Problem prepares students for today's discussions regarding parallel and perpendicular lines. To expedite the sketches, you might suggest to students that they abbreviate the street names as SBR, MS, and USPR.

Lesson 2:   Construct a coordinate system on a plane.
Date: 1/31/14

6.A.17

Concept Development (33 minutes)

Materials: (S) Set square, equal unit strip created during G5–M6–Lesson 1, unlined paper, coordinate plane
template (multiple sheets per student)

Note: In this lesson, the axes are drawn with arrows that show the increasing direction of the numbers only.
Students should be reminded that although the arrows are not visible on both ends of the axes, they still
represent lines that continue in both directions infinitely.

**Problem 1: Construct a second number line, perpendicular to the x-axis, to give the coordinates of points
that do not fall directly on the x- or y-axis.**

T: Turn your paper on its side.

S: (Turn the paper to a landscape
orientation.)

T: (Post or read the step-by-step directions
pictured to the right.)

S: (Draw the number line.)

T: (Draw number line on board.) Our unit for
this number line is ones. Label this line as
x. (Model for students.)

S: (Label the line.)

Directions for Drawing the Number Line.

1.   Draw a horizontal number line using your
straightedge along the bottom of the paper.

2.   Label the origin on the left at the first hash mark.

3.   Draw 20 more equally spaced hash marks using one
of your fractional units from yesterday's strip.

4.   Mark every other hash mark with the whole numbers
from 1 to 10.

T: (Point to 2.) What is the coordinate for the point at this location on x?

S: 2.

T: (Point to 6.) What is the coordinate for this point?

S: 6.

T: What does this point's coordinate tell us?

S: It tells us the point is 6 units from zero. → The distance from zero to that point is 6.

T: Remember that our unit is 1 whole. What is the coordinate of the point that is $\frac{1}{2}$ unit farther from
zero than 3? When you've found it, put your finger on the point, and show your partner.

S: (Point to $3\frac{1}{2}$.) That hash mark is halfway between 3 and 4, so we can call it $3\frac{1}{2}$. → The point's
coordinate is $3\frac{1}{2}$.

T: (Point to $1\frac{1}{2}$.) What is the coordinate for this point?

S: $1\frac{1}{2}$.

T: Plot a point at $1\frac{1}{2}$ and name it A.

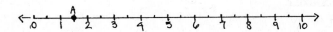

S: (Plot A.)

T: We have a great strategy for describing the locations of points, such as point A, that fall directly *on* a
number line.

T: How can we describe the location of a point that does not lie directly on line x? (Point to a location approximately 2 units above 1 on the x-axis.) Turn and talk.

S: We could just say go about an inch above 1 on x. → We could measure how far up we need to go above the 1 with a ruler.

T: I hear you saying that if we could somehow measure the distance above x, we could describe the point's location. True! Let's construct a second number line perpendicular to x to do just that.

T: (Draw a line intersecting x at the origin at a right angle)

T: Construct this second number line. Place your set square on x, and draw a perpendicular line that goes through the origin like mine does. (Model on board.)

S: (Draw a perpendicular line.)

T: Let's mark the same unit length on this number line as on x. Use your unit strip to do so. Draw 20 more hash marks using the same fractional units as on line x. Label the whole numbers just like before.

S: (Draw hash marks and label.)

T: Now we have two perpendicular number lines that intersect at the origin. This arrangement allows us to describe the location of any point that falls in this plane. (Point.)

T: We call the horizontal number line the **x-axis.** Let's label it by writing *x-axis* down by the arrow on the right. (Demonstrate.)

S: (Label the horizontal line.)

T: The vertical number line is called the **y-axis**. Label the y-axis up by the arrow toward the top. (Demonstrate.)

S: (Label the vertical line.)

T: Let's look again at the location of the point that stumped us earlier. (Plot a point at (1, 2) and label it B.) How can having both number lines help us describe the location of point B? Turn and talk.

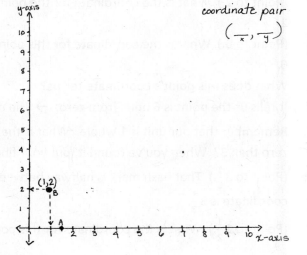

S: It's about an inch up and to the right of the origin at about a 60 degree angle. → We could say it is above the 1 on the x-axis and to the right of 2 on the y-axis.

T: When describing the location of point, we want to be precise. I'm going to draw a dotted-perpendicular line from B to both the x- and y-axes. (Model on board.)

T: At what coordinate does the line I drew intersect the x-axis?

S: At 1.

T: Yes, it intersects the x-axis at a distance of 1 from the origin. (Move a finger to the right 1 unit on the x-axis.) We say that this point has an x-coordinate of 1. At what coordinate on the y-axis does the dotted-line intersect?

Lesson 2: Construct a coordinate system on a plane.
Date: 1/31/14

6.A.19

S: 2.

T: It intersects the y-axis at a distance of 2 from the origin. (Move a finger up from the x-coordinate 2 units.) Point B has a y-coordinate of 2.

T: We can describe the location of this point by giving directions. Starting at the origin, move 1 unit to the right along the x-axis. Then, move 2 units up, parallel to the y-axis. These two numbers, taken together, are called a **coordinate pair**. (Write *coordinate pair* on the board.) Repeat this term.

S: Coordinate pair.

T: Why does this term make sense? Turn and talk.

S: Pair means two. We need two coordinates to tell where the point is. → It just says what it is. We have two coordinates. Coordinate pair means two coordinates!

T: We have a convention when we write coordinate pairs. We always write the x-coordinate first (write a blank with an x under it), followed by a comma, and then the y-coordinate second (write a blank with a y under it). We show that these two distances describe the same point by putting parentheses around the pair. (Place parentheses around the blanks.)

T: Let's write the coordinate pair for this point. Remind me, what was the x-coordinate of the point?

S: 1.

T: (Fill in the first blank on the board with a 1.)

T: What was the y-coordinate?

S: 2.

T: (Fill in the second blank on the board with a 2.)

T: The coordinate pair for this point is (1, 2). Put your finger on the origin. (Model.)

S: (Point to the origin.)

T: Our x-coordinate is 1, so travel 1 unit on the x-axis. (Model.)

S: (Drag finger.)

T: Our y-coordinate is 2, so now we travel 2 units up, parallel to the y-axis. (Model.)

S: (Drag finger.)

T: Say the coordinate pair that names the location of your finger.

S: (1, 2).

T: What do these coordinates tell us? Turn and talk.

S: They tell us the location of our finger. → We have to go over 1 unit and go up from there 2 units. → The first one means that we started at the origin and traveled 1 unit along the x-axis; then, we traveled up 2 units parallel to the y-axis. → We travel along the x-axis 1 unit. Then, we travel parallel to the y-axis 2 units up to find the point.

T: Write the coordinate pair on your boards.

S: (Write and show.)

T: (Write (4, 8) on the board.) Start at the origin. Which coordinate tells us how far to travel on the x-axis?

S: The first one. → 4.

T: Now we'll travel parallel to the *y*-axis. What distance do we travel parallel to the *y*-axis?

S: Eight units.

T: Plot the point.

Repeat the process with (5, 3), (7, 7), and (9, 0).

Problem 2: Name the coordinate pairs of shapes on the coordinate plane.

T: (Display the coordinate plane and give a coordinate plane template to each student.) This coordinate plane is printed on grid paper. Label the *x*- and *y*-axes. Also, notice that the axes on this plane only show the direction that the numbers increase. Leaving off the arrows on the other end of the line just helps the plane be a bit neater, but remember that the axes continue in both directions forever.

S: (Label the axes.)

T: Label the point where the axes intersect as zero. Remind me what we call this point.

S: The origin.

T: Starting at the origin, on every other blue grid line, draw 10 hash marks on both axes. Label them using whole numbers up to 10. (Model on board.) Our unit for these axes will be ones.

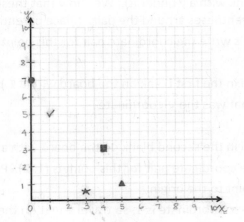

MP.7 S: (Label the hash marks.)

T: (Draw a square at (4, 3) on the plane.) How can we name the location of this square? Turn and talk.

S: It's 3 up and 4 over. → It's over 4 and up 3. → It's above the 4 on the *x*-axis and across from 3 on the *y*-axis. → It's 4 units above the *x*-axis and 3 units to the right of the *y*-axis. → It's at (4, 3).

T: Use the grid lines to help you. What is the *x*-coordinate of the square?

S: 4.

T: (Write (4, ____) on the board.) Tell a neighbor how you know.

S: I just counted over from the *y*-axis, and there were 8 spaces; since we labeled every other grid line, that makes 4 for an *x*-coordinate. → I can see that the little blue line that comes down from the square intersects the *x*-axis at 4.

T: What is the *y*-coordinate of the square?

S: 3.

T: (Write (4, 3) on board.) Tell a neighbor how you know.

S: (Share answer with neighbor.)

NOTES ON
MULTIPLE MEANS OF
ENGAGEMENT:

Some students can lose motivation because they do not recognize the progress they are making. Teachers can explicitly help students recognize their accomplishments by constructing systems that help students see their progress. A chart that monitors progress is one way students can visibly see and track accomplishments.

Lesson 2:   Construct a coordinate system on a plane.
Date: 1/31/14

T: Say the coordinate pair for the square.

S: Four, three.

T: Draw a square on your coordinate plane at (4, 3). Compare your work with your partner's.

Follow a similar sequence with the suggested shapes and locations.

Triangle: (5, 1)   Check Mark: (1, 5)

Circle: (0, 7)   Star: $(3, \frac{1}{2})$

Note: Be sure to watch for students who may reverse the coordinates when graphing—especially the locations of the triangle and check mark.

Problem Set (10 minutes)

Students should do their personal best to complete the Problem Set within the allotted 10 minutes. For some classes, it may be appropriate to modify the assignment by specifying which problems they work on first. Some problems do not specify a method for solving. Students solve these problems using the RDW approach used for Application Problems.

Student Debrief (10 minutes)

Lesson Objective: Construct a coordinate system on a plane.

The Student Debrief is intended to invite reflection and active processing of the total lesson experience.

Invite students to review their solutions for the Problem Set. They should check work by comparing answers with a partner before going over answers as a class. Look for misconceptions or misunderstandings that can be addressed in the Debrief. Guide students in a conversation to debrief the Problem Set and process the lesson.

You may choose to use any combination of the questions below to lead the discussion.

- Share your thinking about Problem 4. What did we learn today that could help the pirate locate his treasure more easily?

- When answering questions about the coordinate plane

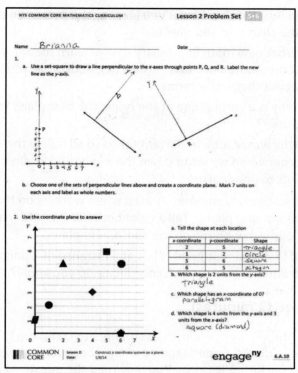

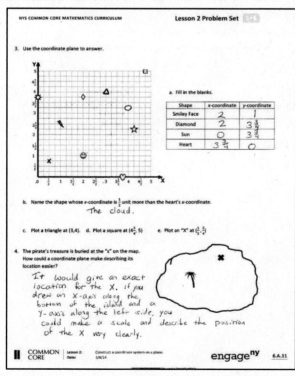

COMMON CORE

Lesson 2:   Construct a coordinate system on a plane.
Date: 1/31/14

6.A.22

in Problem 3, how did you identify the y-coordinate of the Diamond and the Sun?

- What new math vocabulary did we learn today? (***Coordinate pair, axis***.) Tell a neighbor what you know about these new terms.

- Why is a vertical line at the origin the best place for the y-axis?

- Why would it be important for us to all follow the same order when we write down the x- and y-coordinates? Talk to your partner.

- Grid paper is sometimes used when working on the coordinate plane. Tell a neighbor how this grid paper is helpful in working on the coordinate plane.

- If I tell you that point A lies at a distance of 3 units from the x-axis, which coordinate do you know?

NOTES ON MULTIPLE MEANS OF ENGAGEMENT:

Offering learners choices can develop self-determination, instill pride, and increase the level in which they feel connected to their learning. One way to offer choice is to let students decide the sequence of some components of their learning. Menus from which students may choose tasks are one way to offer such academic choice.

Exit Ticket (3 minutes)

After the Student Debrief, instruct students to complete the Exit Ticket. A review of their work will help you assess the students' understanding of the concepts that were presented in the lesson today and plan more effectively for future lessons. You may read the questions aloud to the students.

Lesson 2:   Construct a coordinate system on a plane.
Date: 1/31/14

6.A.23

Name _____　　Date _____

1.

   a.　Use a set square to draw a line perpendicular to the x-axes through points P, Q, and R. Label the new line as the y-axis.

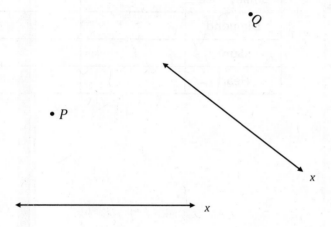
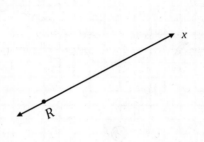

   b.　Choose one of the sets of perpendicular lines above and create a coordinate plane. Mark 7 units on each axis and label as whole numbers.

2.　Use the coordinate plane to answer.

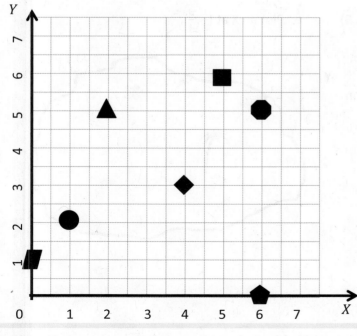

   a. Tell the shape at each location.

x-coordinate	y-coordinate	Shape
2	5	
1	2	
5	6	
6	5	

   b. Which shape is 2 units from the y-axis?

   c. Which shape has an x-coordinate of 0?

   d. Which shape is 4 units from the y-axis and 3 units from the x-axis?

3. Use the coordinate plane to answer.

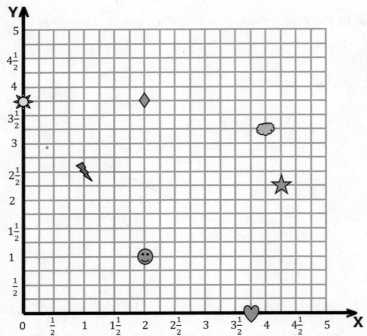

a. Fill in the blanks.

Shape	x-coordinate	y-coordinate
Smiley Face		
Diamond		
Sun		
Heart		

b. Name the shape whose x-coordinate is $\frac{1}{2}$ unit more than the heart's x-coordinate.

c. Plot a triangle at (3, 4).   d. Plot a square at $(4\frac{3}{4}, 5)$.   e. Plot an X at $(\frac{1}{2}, \frac{3}{4})$.

4. The pirate's treasure is buried at the X on the map. How could a coordinate plane make describing its location easier?

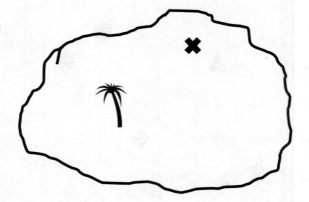

Name _____   Date _____

1. Name the coordinates of the shapes below.

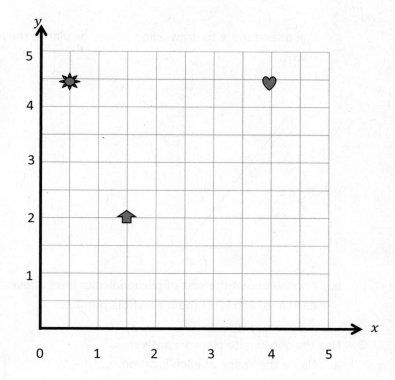

Shape	x-coordinate	y-coordinate
Sun		
Arrow		
Heart		

2. Plot a square at $(3, 3\frac{1}{2})$.

3. Plot a triangle at $(4\frac{1}{2}, 1)$.

Name _____   Date _____

1.
    a.   Use a set-square to draw a line perpendicular to the x-axis through point P. Label the new line as the y-axis.

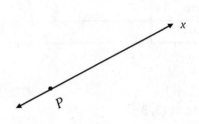

    b.   Choose one of the sets of perpendicular lines above and create a coordinate plane. Mark 5 units on each axis, and label them as whole numbers.

2.   Use the coordinate plane to answer.
    a.   Name the shape at each location.

x-coordinate	y-coordinate	Shape
2	4	
5	4	
1	5	
5	1	

    b.   Which shape is 2 units from the x-axis?

    c.   Which shape has the same x- and y-coordinate?

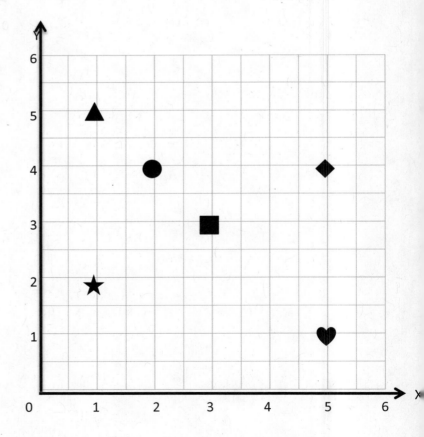

3. Use the coordinate plane to answer.

a. Name the coordinates of each shape.

Shape	x-coordinate	y-coordinate
Moon		
Sun		
Heart		
Cloud		
Smiley Face		

b. Which 2 shapes have the same *y*-coordinate?

c. Plot an X at (2, 3).

d. Plot a square at $(3, 2\frac{1}{2})$.

e. Plot a triangle at $(6, 3\frac{1}{2})$.

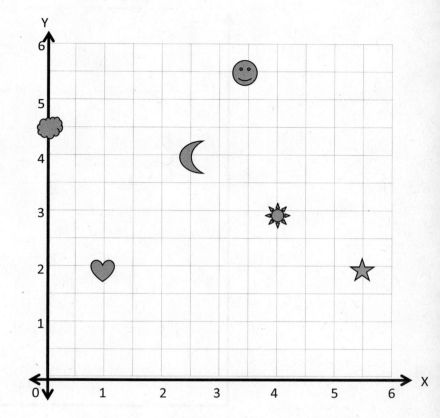

4. Mr. Palmer plans to bury a time capsule 10 yards behind the school. What else should he do to make naming the location of the time capsule more accurate?

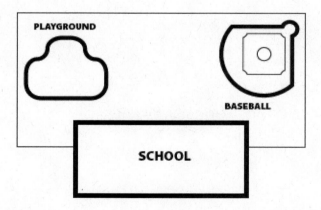

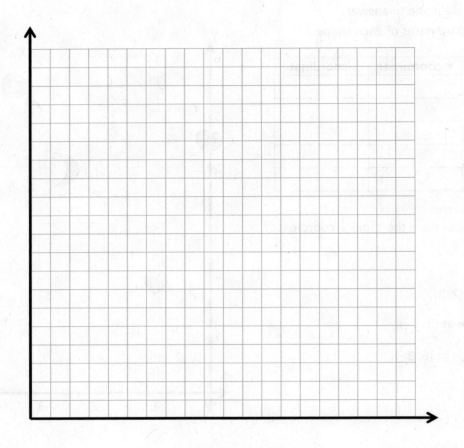

Lesson 2:   Construct a coordinate system on a plane.
Date: 1/31/14

6.A.29

© 2014 Common Core, Inc. All rights reserved. **commoncore.org**

Lesson 3

Objective: Name points using coordinate pairs, and use the coordinate pairs to plot points.

Suggested Lesson Structure

■ Fluency Practice   (12 minutes)
■ Application Problem   (6 minutes)
■ Concept Development   (32 minutes)
■ Student Debrief   (10 minutes)

  Total Time   **(60 minutes)**

Fluency Practice (12 minutes)

▪ Name the Parts of the Coordinate Grid **5.G.1**   (1 minutes)
▪ Find the Missing Number on a Number Line **5.G.1**   (5 minutes)
▪ Name Coordinates on a Coordinate Grid **5.G.1**   (6 minutes)

Name the Parts on the Coordinate Grid (1 minute)

Materials: Coordinate plane template from G5–M6–Lesson 2.

Note: This fluency activity reviews G5–M6–Lesson 2.

    T: (Project the coordinate plane template. Point at the horizontal axis.) Name the axis.

    S: x-axis.

    T: (Point at the vertical axis.) Name the axis.

    S: y-axis.

    T: The x-axis and y-axis intersect at what angle measure?

    S: 90 degrees.

    T: Lines that intersect at right angles are called?

    S: Perpendicular lines.

    T: (Point at the origin.) Name the coordinate.

    S: Zero, zero.

    T: What else can we call this point?

    S: Origin.

	Lesson 3:	Name points using coordinate pairs, and use the coordinate pairs to plot points.	
	Date:	1/31/14	

6.A.30

Find the Missing Number on a Number Line (5 minutes)

Materials: (S) Personal white boards

Note: This fluency activity reviews G5–M6–Lesson 1.

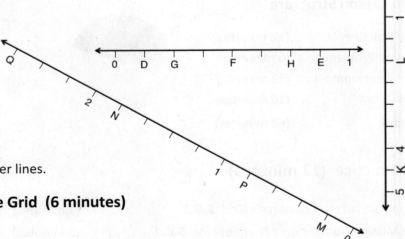

T: (Project a number line partitioned into 10 intervals. Label 0 and 50 as the endpoints. Point to *A*.) What is the value of *A*?

S: 10.

T: What's the value of B?

S: 45.

T: Write the value of C.

S: (Write 30.)

Continue the process for the other number lines.

Name Coordinates on a Coordinate Grid (6 minutes)

Materials: (S) Personal white boards

Note: This fluency activity reviews G5–M6–Lesson 2.

T: (Project coordinate planes shown below.) Write the coordinate pair for A.

S: (Write (1, 1).)

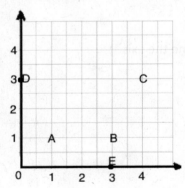
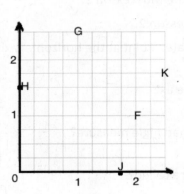

Continue the process for letters B–E.

T: (Project a coordinate grid.) Write the coordinate pair for F.

S: (Write (2, 1).)

Continue the process for the remaining letters.

Lesson 3:   Name points using coordinate pairs, and use the coordinate pairs to plot points.

Date: 1/31/14

6.A.31

Application Problem (6 minutes)

The captain of a ship has a chart to help him navigate through the islands. He must follow points that show the deepest part of the channel. List the coordinates the captain needs to follow in the order he will encounter them.

1. (_____, _____)   2. (_____, _____)

3.   4.

5.   6.

Note: Today's Application Problem not only asks students to identify the coordinates of points, but also provides them with an example of how a basic coordinate plane is used in the real world.

1. $(5, 1\frac{1}{2})$ 2. $(3\frac{1}{2}, 3)$
3. $(2, 4\frac{1}{2})$ 4. $(4, 6)$
5. $(5\frac{1}{2}, 7\frac{1}{2})$ 6. $(7\frac{1}{2}, 9)$

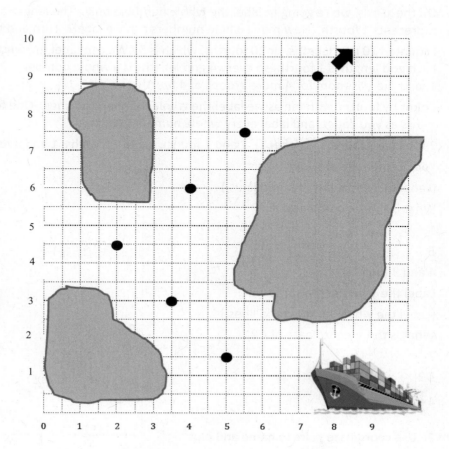

Concept Development (32 minutes)

Materials: (S) Ruler, coordinate plane template

Problem 1: Construct a coordinate plane.

T: (Distribute 1 copy of the coordinate plane template to each student.) Use your ruler to draw an x-axis so that it goes through points A and B, and label it x-axis. (Model on the board.)

MP.6

S: (Draw and label the axis.)

T: Use your ruler to draw the y-axis so that it goes through points C and D, and label it y-axis.

S: (Draw and label the axis.)

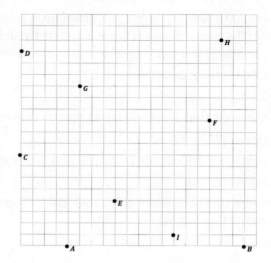

MP.6

T: Label 0 at the origin.

S: (Label the origin.)

T: On the x-axis, we're going to label the whole numbers only. The length of one square on the grid represents 1 fourth. How many whole numbers can we label? Turn and talk.

S: I counted 20 grid lengths, or 20 fourths, which is 5. We can label the whole numbers 0 through 5. → Each grid length is 1 fourth, so every 4 grid lengths is a whole number. → Point A is at 4 fourths, or 1, and there is room for 4 more groups of 4 fourths.

T: Count by fourths with me as we label the whole number grid lines. One fourth…. (Move along the x-axis as you count, and label every whole number grid line.)

S: 2 fourths, 3 fourths, 1 (label 1), 1 and 1 fourth, 1 and 2 fourths, 1 and 3 fourths, 2 (label 2).

T: You do the same on your x-axis.

S: (Label the whole number grid lines.)

T: What is the x-coordinate of A?

S: 1.

T: B?

S: 4 and 3 fourths.

T: Label the y-axis in the same way.

S: (Label the whole number grid lines.)

T: What is the y-coordinate of C?

S: 2.

T: D?

S: $4\frac{1}{4}$.

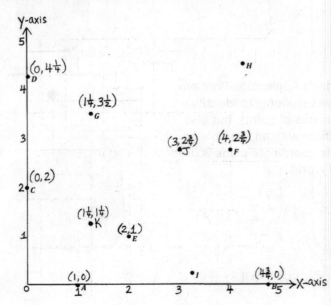

Problem 2: Use coordinate pairs to name and plot points.

T: Put your finger on E. How do we find the x-coordinate of E? Turn and talk.

S: I can just follow the grid line down from E to the x-axis, and it falls at a distance of 2 from the origin. So, the x-coordinate is 2. → E is directly above 2 on the x-axis, so its x-coordinate is 2. → Start at the origin, and move on x-axis to the x-coordinate of E.

T: What is the x-coordinate of E?

S: 2.

T: Show me that x-coordinate as part of a coordinate pair.

S: (Show (2, ___).)

T: Find the y-coordinate of E. (Pause.) Show me the coordinate pair for E.

S: (Show (2, 1).)

T: Write that coordinate pair above point E on your plane. Work with a partner to name the coordinate pair for F.

Lesson 3: Name points using coordinate pairs, and use the coordinate pairs to plot points.

Date: 1/31/14

6.A.33

S: (Share and show F, $(4, 2\frac{3}{4})$.)

Repeat for points G, B, and C, respectively $(1\frac{1}{4}, 3\frac{1}{2})$, $(4\frac{3}{4}, 0)$, $(0, 2)$.

T: Name the point located at $(1, 0)$.

S: A.

T: Name the point located at $(0, 4\frac{1}{4})$.

S: D.

T: I want to name the point whose distance from the y-axis is $4\frac{1}{4}$. How is this question different from the other questions I've asked you about points in this plane? Turn and talk.

S: You are asking us about the distance from the whole line, not the distance from the origin on x. →
    We are looking at the distance away from the y-axis, rather than going a distance down the x-axis.

T: Work with a neighbor to name the point whose distance from the y-axis is $4\frac{1}{4}$.

S: H.

T: Which point lies at a distance of $\frac{1}{4}$ from the x-axis?

S: I.

T: Plot a point J at $(3, 2\frac{3}{4})$. Have a neighbor check your work.

S: (Work and share.)

T: Turn and tell a partner how to find the distance between J and F.

S: Since they both have a y-coordinate of $2\frac{3}{4}$, I can just count the number of 1 fourth lengths on the x-axis from J to F. → It's just like finding the distance between 3 and 4 on a ruler. It's just 1 unit away.

T: What is the distance between J and F? (Gesture between the points.)

S: One unit.

T: Yes. Now, plot a point K so that the x- and y-coordinates are both $1\frac{1}{4}$, then find the distance between K and G.

S: (Work.)

T: Say the distance between K and G.

S: $2\frac{1}{4}$ units.

**NOTES ON
MULTIPLE MEANS OF
REPRESENTATION:**

G5–Module 6, "Problem Solving with the Coordinate Plane," has many new vocabulary words. Here are a few strategies to help students make these new words their own:

- Have students tap and whisper a new word three times.

- Allow students to explore online vocabulary builders such as, Word2Word, an online collection of dictionaries of multiple languages.

- Have students continue to add to their collection of math words on 3" × 5" cards held together by a metal ring.

- Have students continue building their illustrated glossary.

(The last two options assume students have been using these tools all year, which may not be the case.)

COMMON CORE™ | Lesson 3: | Name points using coordinate pairs, and use the coordinate pairs to plot points.
Date: | 1/31/14

6.A.34

Problem Set (10 minutes)

Students should do their personal best to complete the Problem Set within the allotted 10 minutes. For some classes, it may be appropriate to modify the assignment by specifying which problems they work on first. Some problems do not specify a method for solving. Students solve these problems using the RDW approach used for Application Problems.

Student Debrief (10 minutes)

Lesson Objective: Name points using coordinate pairs and use the coordinate pairs to plot points.

The Student Debrief is intended to invite reflection and active processing of the total lesson experience.

Invite students to review their solutions for the Problem Set. They should check work by comparing answers with a partner before going over answers as a class. Look for misconceptions or misunderstandings that can be addressed in the Debrief. Guide students in a conversation to debrief the Problem Set and process the lesson.

You may choose to use any combination of the questions below to lead the discussion.

- Explain your thought process as you decided how to label the whole numbers along the x- and y-axes.
- Share your answer to Problem 2(j) with your neighbor.
- Explain how locating a point at (1, 4) is different from locating a point at (4, 1).
- In the Application Problem, the captain of the ship used coordinate pairs. Why was it important for him know the difference between $(5, 1\frac{1}{2})$ and $(1\frac{1}{2}, 5)$?
- Problem 1(m) asks you to compare lengths. What strategies did you use to answer this question?
- Again thinking about Problem 1(m), will a square's diagonal be longer or shorter than the sum of two side lengths? Is one side of a triangle longer or shorter than the sum of the other two sides? How do you know?

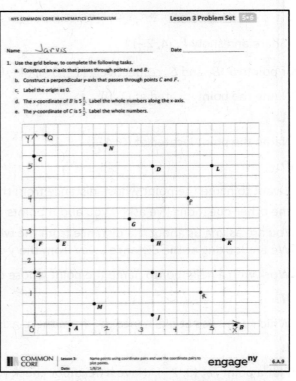

COMMON CORE™

Lesson 3:   Name points using coordinate pairs, and use the coordinate pairs to plot points.
Date: 1/31/14

6.A.35

Exit Ticket (3 minutes)

After the Student Debrief, instruct students to complete the Exit Ticket. A review of their work will help you assess the students' understanding of the concepts that were presented in the lesson today and plan more effectively for future lessons. You may read the questions aloud to the students.

COMMON CORE

Lesson 3: Name points using coordinate pairs, and use the coordinate pairs to plot points.
Date: 1/31/14

6.A.36

Name _____   Date _____

1. Use the grid below, to complete the following tasks.

    a. Construct an x-axis that passes through points A and B.

    b. Construct a perpendicular y-axis that passes through points C and F.

    c. Label the origin as 0.

    d. The x-coordinate of B is $5\frac{2}{3}$. Label the whole numbers along the x-axis.

    e. The y-coordinate of C is $5\frac{1}{3}$. Label the whole numbers.

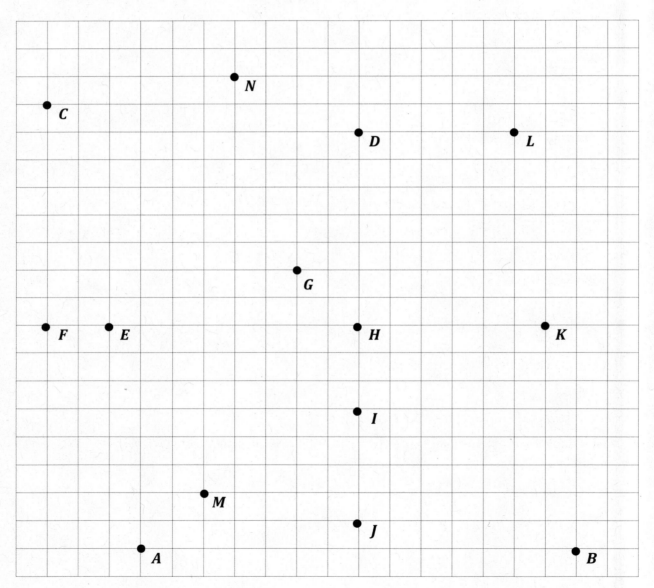

Lesson 3:	Name points using coordinate pairs, and use the coordinate pairs to plot points.
Date:	1/31/14

6.A.37

2. For all of the following problems, consider the points A through N on the previous page.

   a. Identify all of the points that have an x-coordinate of $3\frac{1}{3}$.

   b. Identify all of the points that have a y-coordinate of $2\frac{2}{3}$.

   c. Which point is $3\frac{1}{3}$ units above the x-axis **and** $2\frac{2}{3}$ units to the right of the y-axis? Name the point and give its coordinate pair.

   d. Which point is located $5\frac{1}{3}$ units from the y-axis?

   e. Which point is located $1\frac{2}{3}$ units along the x-axis?

   f. Give the coordinate pair for each of the following points.

   K: _____ I: _____ B: _____ C: _____

   g. Name the points located at the following coordinates.

   $(1\frac{2}{3}, \frac{2}{3})$ _____ $(0, 2\frac{2}{3})$ _____ $(1, 0)$ _____ $(2, 5\frac{2}{3})$ _____

   h. Which point has an equal x- and y-coordinate? _____

   i. Give the coordinates for the intersection of the two axes. _____ Another name for this point on the plane is the _____.

   j. Plot the following points.

   P: $(4\frac{1}{3}, 4)$ Q: $(\frac{1}{3}, 6)$ R: $(4\frac{2}{3}, 1)$ S: $(0, 1\frac{2}{3})$

   k. What is distance between E and H, or EH?

   l. What is the length HD?

   m. Would the length ED be greater or less than $EH + HD$?

   n. Jack was absent when the teacher explained how to describe the location of a point on the coordinate plane. Explain it to him using point J.

COMMON CORE™

Lesson 3:   Name points using coordinate pairs, and use the coordinate pairs to plot points.

Date: 1/31/14

6.A.38

Name _____   Date _____

1. Use a ruler on the grid below to construct the axes for a coordinate plane. The x-axis should intersect points L and M. Construct the y-axis so that it contains points K and L. Label each axis.

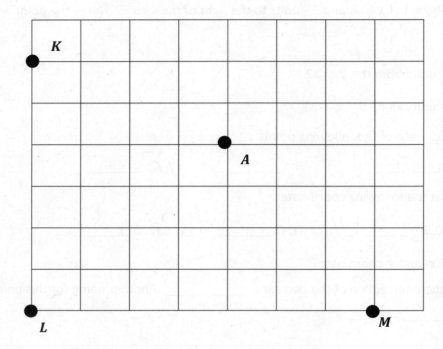

a. Place a hash mark on each grid line on the x- and y-axis.

b. Label each hash mark so that A is located at (1, 1).

c. Plot the following points:

Point	x-coordinate	y-coordinate
B	$\frac{1}{4}$	0
C	$1\frac{1}{4}$	$\frac{3}{4}$

Lesson 3: Name points using coordinate pairs, and use the coordinate pairs to plot points.

Date: 1/31/14

6.A.39

Name _____   Date _____

1. Use the grid below to complete the following tasks.

    a. Construct a y-axis that passes through points Y and Z.

    b. Construct a perpendicular x-axis that passes through points Z and X.

    c. Label the origin as 0.

    d. The y-coordinate of W is $2\frac{3}{5}$. Label the whole numbers along the y-axis.

    e. The x-coordinate of V is $2\frac{2}{5}$. Label the whole numbers.

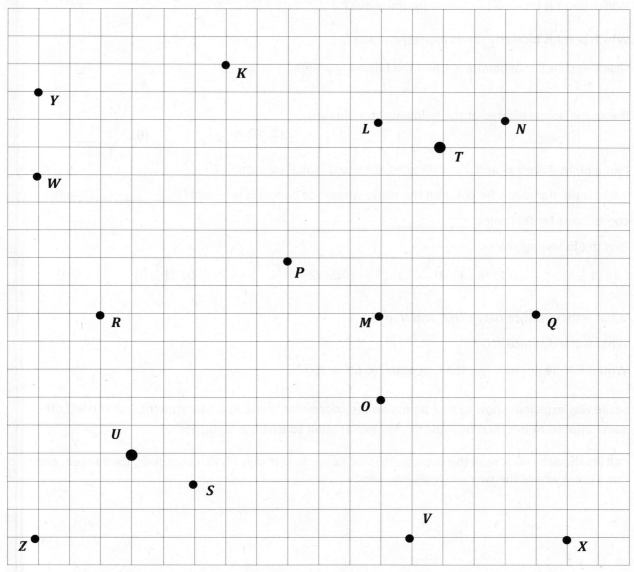

Lesson 3:   Name points using coordinate pairs, and use the coordinate pairs to
            plot points.
Date: 1/31/14

6.A.40

2. For all of the following problems, consider the points K through X on the previous page.

    a. Identify all of the points that have a y-coordinate of $1\frac{3}{5}$.

    b. Identify all of the points that have an x-coordinate of $2\frac{1}{5}$.

    c. Which point is $1\frac{3}{5}$ units above the x-axis *and* $3\frac{1}{5}$ units to the right of the y-axis? Name the point and give its coordinate pair.

    d. Which point is located $1\frac{1}{5}$ units from the y-axis?

    e. Which point is located $\frac{2}{5}$ units along the x-axis?

    f. Give the coordinate pair for each of the following points.

        T: _____ U: _____ S: _____ K: _____

    g. Name the points located at the following coordinates.

        $(\frac{2}{5}, \frac{3}{5})$ ____ $(3\frac{2}{5}, 0)$ ____ $(2\frac{1}{5}, 3)$ ____ $(0, 2\frac{3}{5})$ ____

    h. Plot a point whose x- and y-coordinates are equal. Label your point E.

    i. What is the name for the point on the plane where the two axes intersect? _____ Give the coordinates for this point. _____

    j. Plot the following points.

        A: $(1\frac{1}{5}, 1)$ B: $(\frac{1}{5}, 3)$ C: $(2\frac{4}{5}, 2\frac{2}{5})$ D: $(1\frac{1}{5}, 0)$

    k. What is the distance between L and N, or LN?

    l. What is the distance MQ?

    m. Would RM be greater, less than, or equal to $LN + MQ$?

    n. Leslie was explaining how to plot points on the coordinate plane to a new student, but she left off some important information. Correct her explanation so that it is complete.

        "All you have to do is read the coordinates; for example, if it says (4, 7), count four, then seven, and put a point where the two grid lines intersect."

COMMON CORE™

Lesson 3:   Name points using coordinate pairs, and use the coordinate pairs to
              plot points.
Date: 1/31/14

6.A.41

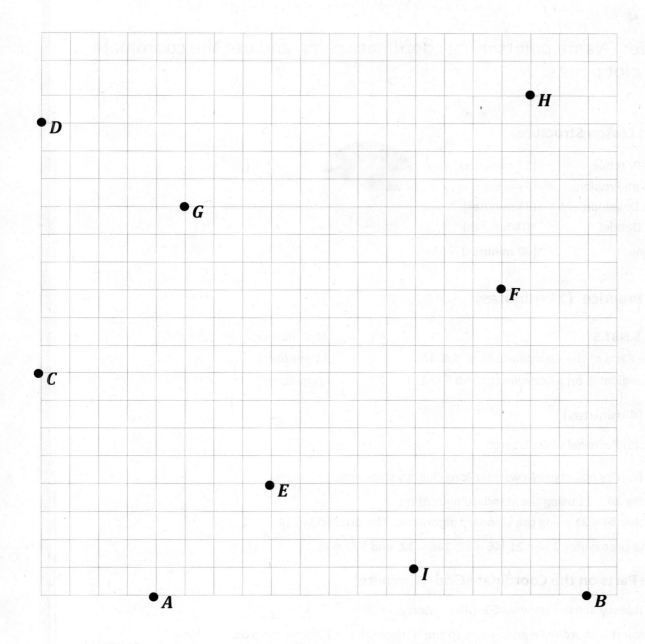

Lesson 3:	Name points using coordinate pairs, and use the coordinate pairs to plot points.
Date:	1/31/14

6.A.42

Lesson 4

Objective: Name points using coordinate pairs, and use the coordinate pairs to plot points.

Suggested Lesson Structure

■ Fluency Practice   (11 minutes)
■ Application Problem   (5 minutes)
■ Concept Development   (34 minutes)
■ Student Debrief   (10 minutes)

   Total Time   **(60 minutes)**

Fluency Practice (11 minutes)

- Multiply **5.NBT.5**   (4 minutes)
- Name the Parts of the Coordinate Grid **5.G.1**   (1 minutes)
- Name Coordinates on a Coordinate Grid **5.G.1**   (6 minutes)

Multiply (4 minutes)

Materials: (S) Personal white boards

Note: This fluency activity reviews year-long fluency standards.

    T: Solve 34 × 21 using the standard algorithm.
    S: (Solve 34 × 21 using the standard algorithm. The product is 714.)

Continue the process for 234 × 21, 46 × 32, 146 × 32, and 537 × 35.

Name the Parts on the Coordinate Grid (1 minute)

Note: This fluency activity reviews G5–M6–Lesson 2.

    T: (Project a coordinate grid. Point to the horizontal axis.) Name the axis.
    S: x-axis.
    T: (Point at the vertical axis.) Name the axis.
    S: y-axis.
    T: The x-axis and y-axis intersect at a 90° angle. What kinds of line intersect at this angle?
    S: Perpendicular.
    T: (Point to the origin.) Name the coordinate.

COMMON CORE™   Lesson 4:   Name points using coordinate pairs, and use the coordinate pairs to plot points.   6.A.43
                    Date: 1/31/14

S: Zero, zero.

T: What's the term for the coordinate zero, zero?

S: Origin.

Name Coordinates on a Coordinate Grid (6 minutes)

Materials: (S) Personal white boards

Note: This fluency activity reviews G5–M6–Lesson 2.

T: (Project coordinate grid.)
      Write the coordinate pair for A.

S: (Write (2, 1).)

Continue the process for letters B–E.

T: (Project coordinate grid.)
      Write the coordinate pair for F.

S: (Write (2, 1).)

Continue the process for the remaining letters.

Application Problem (5 minutes)

Violet and Magnolia are shopping for boxes to organize the materials for their design company. Magnolia wants to get small boxes, which measure 16 in × 10 in × 7 in. Violet wants to get large boxes, which measure 32 in × 20 in × 14 in. How many small boxes will equal the volume of four large boxes?

Note: Today's Application Problem reviews the volume work done in G5–Module 5.

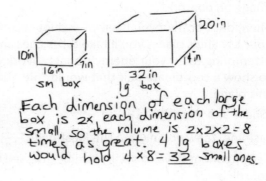

Each dimension of each large box is 2x each dimension of the small, so the volume is 2×2×2=8 times as great. 4 lg boxes would hold 4 × 8 = 32 small ones.

Concept Development (34 minutes)

Materials: (S) *Battleship* Rules, Problem Set with Enemy Ships and My Ships grids (1 per student/per game), red pencil or crayon (1 per student), black pencil or crayon (1 per student), folder (1 per pair of students)

Note: Today, students will be playing a version of the board game, *Battleship*. Depending on the level of experience your students have with this game, the following suggested discussion might be modified.

NOTES ON
MULTIPLE MEANS OF
ENGAGEMENT:

One possible extension of today's Concept Development would be to have students write a handbook for winning at *Battleship*. To write such a guide, students must articulate strategic thinking, which gives them an opportunity to use critical thinking and communication skills.

Lesson 4:   Name points using coordinate pairs, and use the coordinate pairs to
              plot points.

Date: 1/31/14

6.A.44

T: Raise your hand if you've heard of, or have ever played, *Battleship*.

T: (Distribute a copy of the Problem Set to each student.) Take four minutes to read and talk about *Battleship* Rules with a partner.

S: (Read and share.)

T: Find your My Ships coordinate plane and hold it up.

S: (Hold up paper.)

T: Once we get started, one of the first things you'll do with your opponent is label the axes using halves, thirds, fourths, or fifths. (Display image on board.) This is an example of a coordinate plane that has already been prepared for play. What fractional unit is designated by the grid lengths? Turn and talk.

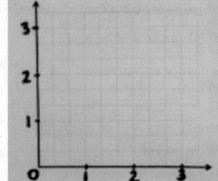

S: Thirds!

T: The next step is the fun part. You get to secretly select locations for your fleet on the coordinate plane. How many ships does each player get?

S: 5.

T: Exactly, and some ships are small, such as the patrol boat, while others are large, such as the aircraft carrier. Let's look at an example of how a fleet might be set up on the coordinate plane. (Display image on board.)

T: Then, once both of you have your ships secretly placed on your My Ships plane, you'll take turns guessing attack shots, attempting to hit your enemy's boats. Work with a neighbor to show a coordinate pair that would "hit" the submarine on this plane.

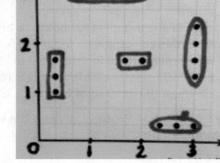

S: (Share and show.)

T: Jasmine, I saw you named the location $(2\frac{2}{3}, \frac{1}{3})$. What would her opponent have to say if Jasmine guessed these coordinates?

S: Hit!

T: That's right! Then, Jasmine would record those coordinates on her paper, and mark a red check on her Enemy Ships plane. What would the opponent have to do?

S: Mark a red check on the hit coordinate of the submarine.

T: You got it! Then, it's Jasmine's opponent's turn to make an attack shot. When does the game end? How do you win?

S: The game ends when one person sinks all of the opponent's ships!

T: Or, when time is up, the winner is the player who has sunk the most ships. Let's play!

Game Play (20 minutes)

MP.2 Students should select or be assigned an opponent and begin play. Early finishers may choose to play a rematch or be assigned another opponent. Please note that a new copy of the Problem Set is needed for each game. However, the grid sheets can be inserted into page protectors for multiple uses.

Student Debrief (10 minutes)

Lesson Objective: Name points using coordinate pairs, and use the coordinate pairs to plot points.

Note: Today's Debrief may take place at the end of the math session, or may prove more purposeful after about 10 minutes of play. Students could count ships to declare a winner and then engage in a short discussion about their game strategy before beginning a second game with a new opponent.

You may choose to use any combination of the questions below to lead the discussion.

- What was your strategy in choosing where to set up your fleet? Did it work? What would you do differently next time? (These strategies can be recorded and displayed for future use.)
- How did you decide where to make your attack shots?
- When you did hit an opponent's ship, how did you plan your next shot?
- What did your opponent do that seemed to work well for him or her?
- What could be done to the coordinate plane to make the game easier or more challenging?
- How did today's game strengthen your understanding of the coordinate plane?
- Do you think coordinate pairs are actually used in war? Why or why not?

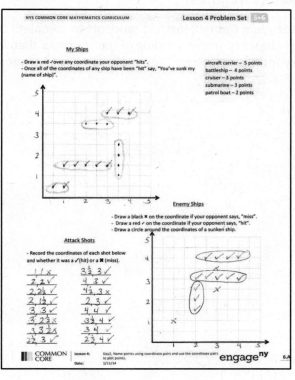

NOTES ON MULTIPLE MEANS OF ACTION AND EXPRESSION:

One goal of playing *Battleship* is to use strategic thinking, rather than using trial and error, or simply guessing. Teachers can help students develop strategic planning and thinking by employing these suggestions:

- Require students to play with a partner. Partners can collaborate on strategy while playing.
- Encourage each student to verbalize why a move is made before it is made. These think-alouds may not result in a competitive game, but it can help students learn to play in a more strategic way.

Lesson 4: Name points using coordinate pairs, and use the coordinate pairs to plot points.
Date: 1/31/14

6.A.46

Exit Ticket (3 minutes)

After the Student Debrief, instruct students to complete the Exit Ticket. A review of their work will help you assess the students' understanding of the concepts that were presented in the lesson today and plan more effectively for future lessons. You may read the questions aloud to the students.

Lesson 4:   Name points using coordinate pairs, and use the coordinate pairs to
            plot points.
Date: 1/31/14

6.A.47

Battleship Rules

Goal: To sink all of your opponent's ships by correctly guessing their coordinates.

Materials

- Each player gets 1 grid sheet(per game)
- Red crayon/marker for hits
- Black crayon/marker for misses
- Folder to place between players

Ships

- Each player must mark 5 ships on the grid.
  - Aircraft Carrier – Plot 5 points
  - Battleship – Plot 4 points
  - Cruiser – Plot 3 points
  - Submarine – Plot 3 points
  - Patrol Boat – Plot 2 points

Setup

- With your opponent, choose a unit length and fractional unit for the coordinate plane.
- Label chosen units on both grid sheets.
- Secretly select locations for each of the 5 ships on your My Ships grid.
  - All ships must be placed horizontally or vertically on the coordinate plane.
  - Ships can touch each other, but may not occupy the same coordinate.

Play

- Players take turns firing one shot to attack enemy ships.
- On your turn, call out the coordinates of your attacking shot. Record the coordinates of each attack shot.
- Your opponent checks his My Ships grid. If that coordinate is unoccupied, he says, "Miss." If you named a coordinate occupied by a ship, he says, "Hit."
- Mark each attempted shot on your Enemy Ships grid. Mark a black ✖ on the coordinate if your opponent says, "Miss." Mark a red ✓ on the coordinate if your opponent says, "Hit."
- On your opponent's turn, if he hits one of your ships, mark a red ✓on that coordinate of your My Ships grid. When one of your ships has every coordinate marked with a ✓, say, "You've sunk my [name of ship]."

Victory

- The first player to sink all (or the most) opposing ships wins.

6.A.48

My Ships

- Draw a red ✓ over any coordinate your opponent hits.
- Once all of the coordinates of any ship have been hit, say, "You've sunk my [name of ship]."

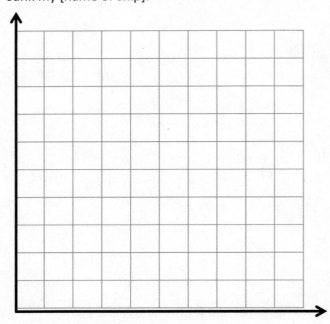

aircraft carrier – 5 points
battleship – 4 points
cruiser – 3 points
submarine – 3 points
patrol boat – 2 points

Enemy Ships

- Draw a black ✖ on the coordinate if your opponent says, "Miss."
- Draw a red ✓ on the coordinate if your opponent says, "Hit."
- Draw a circle around the coordinates of a sunken ship.

Attack Shots

- Record the coordinates of each shot below and whether it was a ✓ (hit) or a ✖ (miss).

_____ _____

_____ _____

_____ _____

_____ _____

_____ _____

_____ _____

_____ _____

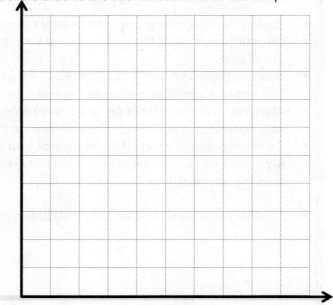

COMMON CORE™

Lesson 4:   Name points using coordinate pairs, and use the coordinate pairs to plot points.

Date: 1/31/14

6.A.49

Name _____ Date _____

Fatima and Rihana are playing *Battleship*. They labeled their axes using just whole numbers.

a. Fatima's first guess is (2, 2). Rihana says, "Hit!" Give the coordinates of four points that Fatima might guess next.

b. Rihana says, "Hit!" for the points directly above and below (2, 2). What are the coordinates that Fatima guessed?

Lesson 4:	Name points using coordinate pairs, and use the coordinate pairs to plot points.	
Date:	1/31/14	6.A.50

Name _____   Date _____

Your homework is to play at least one game of *Battleship* with a friend or family member. You can use the directions from class to teach your opponent. You and your opponent should record your guesses, hits, and misses on the sheet as you did in class.

When you have finished your game, answer these questions.

1. When you guess a point that is a hit, how do you decide which points to guess next?

2. How could you change the coordinate plane to make the game easier or more challenging?

3. Which strategies worked best for you when playing this game?

Lesson 4:	Name points using coordinate pairs, and use the coordinate pairs to plot points.	6.A.51
Date:	1/31/14	

Lesson 5

Objective: Investigate patterns in vertical and horizontal lines, and interpret points on the plane as distances from the axes.

Suggested Lesson Structure

■ Application Problem   (7 minutes)
■ Fluency Practice   (12 minutes)
■ Concept Development   (31 minutes)
■ Student Debrief   (10 minutes)

   Total Time   **(60 minutes)**

Application Problem (7 minutes)

A company has developed a new game. Cartons are needed to ship 40 games at a time. Each game is 2 inches high by 7 inches wide by 14 inches long.

How would you recommend packing the board games in the carton? What are the dimensions of a carton that could ship 40 board games with no extra room in the box?

Note: Today's Application Problem reviews the volume work done in G5–Module 5. It precedes the fluency work so that the decimal practice in today's Fluency Practice flows directly into the Concept Development where it is applied.

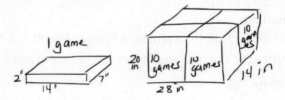

Fluency Practice (12 minutes)

- Multiply **5.NBT.5**   (4 minutes)
- Count by Decimals **5.NBT.1**   (4 minutes)
- Decimals on Number Lines **5.G.1**   (4 minutes)

Multiply (4 minutes)

Materials: (S) Personal white boards

Note: This fluency activity reviews year-long fluency standards.

   T: (Write 4 tens 5 ones × 3 tens 1 one = __ × __.) Write the multiplication expression in standard form.

Lesson 5:   Investigate patterns in vertical and horizontal lines, and interpret points on the plane as distances from the axes.

Date: 1/31/14

6.A.52

S: (Write 45 × 31.)

T: Solve 45 × 31 using the standard algorithm or the area model.

S: (Solve 45 × 31. The product is 1,395.)

Continue the process for 345 × 31, 47 × 23, 247 × 23, and 753 × 35.

Count by Decimals (4 minutes)

Materials: (S) Personal white boards

Note: This fluency activity prepares students for G5–M6–Lesson 6.

T: Count with me by ones to ten, starting at zero.

S: 0, 1, 2, 3, 4, 5, 6, 7, 8, 9, 10.

T: Count by tenths to 10 tenths, starting at zero.

S: 0 tenths, 1 tenth, 2 tenths, 3 tenths, 4 tenths, 5 tenths, 6 tenths, 7 tenths, 8 tenths, 9 tenths, 10 tenths.

T: (Write 10 tenths = 1 ___.) Write the number sentence.

S: (Write 10 tenths = 1 one.)

T: Starting at zero, count by tenths again. This time, when you come to a whole number, say the whole number.

S: 0 tenths, 1 tenth, 2 tenths, 3 tenths, 4 tenths, 5 tenths, 6 tenths, 7 tenths, 8 tenths, 9 tenths, 1.

T: Write the fraction equivalent to zero point one.

S: (Write $\frac{}{10}$.)

T: Count from 0 tenths to 1 again. When I raise my hand, stop.

S: 0 tenths, 1 tenth, 2 tenths, 3 tenths.

T: (Raise hand.) Write 3 tenths as a decimal.

S: (Write 0.3.)

Continue the process counting up to 1 one and down from 1 one to zero, stopping students at various points to write numbers in decimal form.

Decimals on Number Lines (4 minutes)

Materials: (S) Personal white boards

Note: This fluency activity reviews G5–M6–Lesson 1.

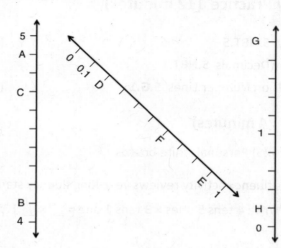

T: (Project a number line partitioned into 10 intervals. Label 4 and 5 as the endpoints. Point to A.) What is the value of A as a decimal?

S: 4.9.

Lesson 5:   Investigate patterns in vertical and horizontal lines, and interpret points on the plane as distances from the axes.

Date: 1/31/14

6.A.53

T: What's the value of B?

S: 4.1.

T: Write the value of C.

S: (Write 4.7.)

Continue the process for the other number lines.

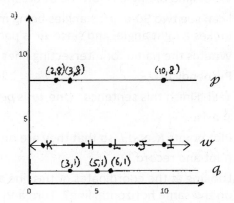

Concept Development (31 minutes)

Materials: (S) Straightedge, coordinate plane template

Problem 1: Identify the pattern in coordinate pairs that results in horizontal lines.

T: (Distribute a copy of the coordinate plane template to each student, and project a copy on the board.) On coordinate plane (a), plot a point H, that is 3 units from the x-axis and 4 units from the y-axis.

S: (Plot H.)

T: Say the coordinates of this point.

S: (4, 3). (Plot H on the board.)

T: Write the coordinates of H in the chart.

S: (Fill in the chart.)

T: Plot a second point, I, at (10, 3), and write its coordinates in the chart.

S: (Plot I, and fill in the chart.)

T: Plot a third point, J, at (8, 3), and put the coordinates in the chart.

S: (Plot J.)

T: What do you notice about these three points and their coordinates? Turn and talk.

S: They have different x-coordinates, but the y-coordinates are all threes. → All of the points are the same distance away from the x-axis.

T: Use a straightedge to draw a line that goes through H, I, and J. Label the line w.

S: (Construct line.)

T: What do you notice about line w?

S: It's a perfectly straight line. → It goes from left to right across the page. It's a horizontal line. → It's almost like another x-axis, except it's been shifted up.

**NOTES ON
MULTIPLE MEANS OF
ENGAGEMENT:**

Many of the math lessons in *A Story of Units,* although scaffolded, are meant to be challenging. Therefore, some students may need support in developing perseverance. There are several websites endorsed by the Universal Design for Learning Center dedicated to this end:

- *Coping Skills for Kids: Brain Works Project.* This website addresses the varying ways one can cope and learn to cope.

- *Lesson Planet: 386 Coping Skills Strategies Lesson Plans Reviewed by Teachers.* These lesson plans are rated by teachers and sorted by grade level.

Lesson 5:   Investigate patterns in vertical and horizontal lines, and interpret points on the plane as distances from the axes.

Date: 1/31/14

6.A.54

T: Does line *w* ever intersect with the *x*-axis?

S: No.

T: Tell a neighbor the term for lines that never intersect?

S: Parallel.

T: Right! Finish my sentence. Line *w* is *parallel* to the…?

S: *x*-axis.

T: Does line *w* ever intersect with the *y*-axis?

S: Yes.

T: Give the coordinates of the intersection.

S: (0, 3).

T: What kind of angle is formed at the intersection of line *w* and the *y*-axis? Turn and talk.

S: I can see two 90-degree angles being made when they intersect. → When the *x*- and *y*-axis meet, it makes a right angle, and since *w* is parallel to the *x*-axis, it must also make a right angle.

T: What is the name for intersecting lines that form right angles?

S: Perpendicular.

T: Yes! Finish this sentence. Line *w* is *perpendicular* to the…?

S: *y*-axis.

T: Plot points K and L so that they are on line *w*; then, record their coordinates in the chart.

S: (Plot and record.)

T: Looking at the coordinates of this line again, what can you conclude about the coordinates of points on the same horizontal line? Turn and talk.

S: The *y*-coordinate doesn't change for any points on the line. → No matter what the *x*-coordinate is, the *y*-coordinate stays the same.

T: Tell your neighbor the coordinates of two other points that would fall on line *w*, but whose *x*-coordinates are greater than 12. Would these points be visible on the part of the plane we see here? Why or why not?

MP.2 S: (Share.) You couldn't see them on this part. → We would have to extend both axes a little farther to see points with *x*-coordinates greater than 12.

T: Would the point with coordinates $(15\frac{1}{2}, 3)$ fall on line *w*? Tell a neighbor how you know.

S: Yes, it would, because it has 3 as a *y*-coordinate. → It doesn't matter what the *x*-coordinate is. If the *y*-coordinate is 3, then the point will be on line *w*.

T: Would the point with coordinates (3, 5) fall on line *w*? Tell your partner how you know.

S: (Share.)

T: Work with a neighbor to create a line that would also be parallel to the *x*-axis. If we wanted this line to be a greater distance from the *x*-axis than *w*, what will we need to think about?

S: We will have to pick a *y*-value that is greater than 3. → We can use the same *x*-values, but our *y*-values will have to be greater than *w*'s.

T: What about a line whose distance from the *x*-axis is less than *w*'s?

Lesson 5:   Investigate patterns in vertical and horizontal lines, and interpret points on the plane as distances from the axes.

Date: 1/31/14

6.A.55

S:　The *y-coordinate* for all our points will have to be less than 3. → We can use anything for x, but y will have to be between 0 and 3 for every point we plot.

T:　One partner should construct his line so that it is closer to the x-axis, while the other should draw her line so that it is farther than w from the x-axis. Partner 1 should label the line p, and Partner 2 should label the line q. Record the coordinates of three points that your line contains, and compare your work with your partner. (Circulate to check student work.)

S:　(Work and share.)

T:　Look at the two lines you created. What is their distance from the x-axis? Distance from w? Distance from each other?

S:　(Discuss. Answers will vary.)

Problem 2: Identify the pattern in coordinate pairs that results in vertical lines.

T:　Look at the coordinate pairs found in the chart next to coordinate plane (b). What do you notice about these coordinate pairs? Turn and talk.

S:　This time, the y-coordinate is always changing, but the x-coordinate stays the same. → x is always $2\frac{1}{2}$.

T:　Imagine that we have plotted the points found in this chart and connected them to make a line. Make a prediction about what that line would look like. Turn and talk.

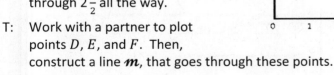

Point	x	y	(x, y)
D	$2\frac{1}{2}$	0	$(2\frac{1}{2}, 0)$
E	$2\frac{1}{2}$	2	$(2\frac{1}{2}, 2)$
F	$2\frac{1}{2}$	4	$(2\frac{1}{2}, 4)$

S:　Well, since the x-coordinate is always $2\frac{1}{2}$, I think the line will go straight up and down. → I think it will be a vertical line that goes through $2\frac{1}{2}$ all the way.

T:　Work with a partner to plot points D, E, and F. Then, construct a line m, that goes through these points.

S:　(Plot and draw.)

T:　Line m is parallel to which axis?

S:　The y-axis.

T:　Line m is perpendicular to which axis?

S:　The x-axis.

T:　What is the distance of point D from the y-axis? Point E? Point F? What do you notice about these points' distances from y? Turn and talk.

S:　The distance from y is the same number that we use for the x-coordinates. → The distances are all equal to each other and are the same as the x-coordinates.

Lesson 5:	Investigate patterns in vertical and horizontal lines, and interpret points on the plane as distances from the axes.	6.A.56
Date:	1/31/14	

T: Create another vertical line, **n**, that is also perpendicular to the x-axis, but whose distance is more or less than $2\frac{1}{2}$. Record the coordinates of three points that line **n** contains. Share your work with a neighbor when you're finished. Then, copy your partner's line onto your plane. (Circulate to check student work.)

S: (Work and share.)

T: What is the distance of every point on your line from the y-axis? What is the distance from your line to your partner's that you copied?

Problem Set (10 minutes)

Students should do their personal best to complete the Problem Set within the allotted 10 minutes. For some classes, it may be appropriate to modify the assignment by specifying which problems they work on first. Some problems do not specify a method for solving. Students solve these problems using the RDW approach used for Application Problems.

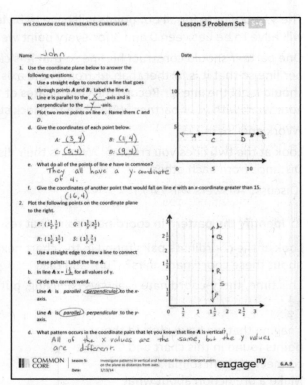

Student Debrief (10 minutes)

Lesson Objective: Investigate patterns in vertical and horizontal lines, and interpret points on the plane as distances from the axes.

The Student Debrief is intended to invite reflection and active processing of the total lesson experience.

Invite students to review their solutions for the Problem Set. They should check work by comparing answers with a partner before going over answers as a class. Look for misconceptions or misunderstandings that can be addressed in the Debrief. Guide students in a conversation to debrief the Problem Set and process the lesson.

You may choose to use any combination of the questions below to lead the discussion.

- In Problem 1, what's the relationship of line e to the x-axis and y-axis? Explain to a partner.

- Explain to a partner how you solved Problem 1(f).

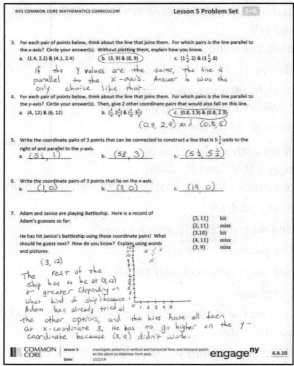

Lesson 5:   Investigate patterns in vertical and horizontal lines, and interpret
             points on the plane as distances from the axes.
Date: 1/31/14

6.A.57

- In Problem 2, what's the relationship of line h to the x-axis and y-axis? Explain to a partner.
- Share your answer to Problem 2(d) with a partner.
- In Problem 3, how did you know that the points were on a line that was not parallel to x? For the lines that were parallel to x, what was the distance of every point on those lines from the x-axis?
- In Problem 4, how did you know that the points were on a line that was not parallel to the y-axis?
- Share your idea for solving Problem 7 with a partner. What kinds of lines do you need to think about to be a winner at *Battleship*?

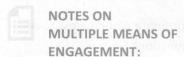

NOTES ON MULTIPLE MEANS OF ENGAGEMENT:

Some students, when asked to work cooperatively with a partner, may need more direction. It may be necessary to develop roles and guidelines for each person in the group. In addition, a collaboratively produced set of expectations or class norms for all group work should be part of the class culture for small group success.

Exit Ticket (3 minutes)

After the Student Debrief, instruct students to complete the Exit Ticket. A review of their work will help you assess the students' understanding of the concepts that were presented in the lesson today and plan more effectively for future lessons. You may read the questions aloud to the students.

Lesson 5:	Investigate patterns in vertical and horizontal lines, and interpret points on the plane as distances from the axes.
Date:	1/31/14

Name _____   Date _____

1. Use the coordinate plane below to answer the
   following questions.

   a. Use a straightedge to construct a line that goes
      through points A and B. Label the line e.

   b. Line e is parallel to the _____-axis and is
      perpendicular to the _____-axis.

   c. Plot two more points on line e. Name them C and
      D.

   d. Give the coordinates of each point below.

      A: _____ B: _____

      C: _____ D: _____

   e. What do all of the points of line e have in common?

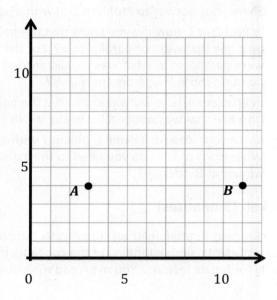

   f. Give the coordinates of another point that would fall on line e with an x-coordinate greater than 15.

2. Plot the following points on the coordinate plane
   to the right.

   P: $(1\frac{1}{2}, \frac{1}{2})$ Q: $(1\frac{1}{2}, 2\frac{1}{2})$

   R: $(1\frac{1}{2}, 1\frac{1}{4})$ S: $(1\frac{1}{2}, \frac{3}{4})$

   a. Use a straightedge to draw a line to connect
      these points. Label the line h.

   b. In line h, $x =$ ____ for all values of y.

   c. Circle the correct word.

      Line h is *parallel* *perpendicular* to the x-
      axis.

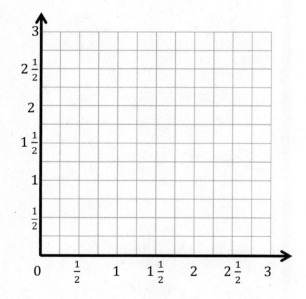

      Line h is *parallel* *perpendicular* to the y-
      axis.

   d. What pattern occurs in the coordinate pairs that let you know that line h is vertical?

COMMON CORE™ | **Lesson 5:**   Investigate patterns in vertical and horizontal lines, and interpret points on the plane as distances from the axes.   6.A.59

Date: 1/31/14

3. For each pair of points below, think about the line that joins them. For which pairs is the line parallel to the x-axis? Circle your answer(s). Without plotting them, explain how you know.

   a. (1.4, 2.2) and (4.1, 2.4)   b. (3, 9) and (8, 9)   c. ($1\frac{1}{4}$, 2) and ($1\frac{1}{4}$, 8)

4. For each pair of points below, think about the line that joins them. For which pairs is the line parallel to the y-axis? Circle your answer(s). Then, give 2 other coordinate pairs that would also fall on this line.

   a. (4, 12) and (6, 12)   b. ($\frac{3}{5}$, $2\frac{3}{5}$) and ($\frac{1}{5}$, $3\frac{1}{5}$)   c. (0.8, 1.9) and (0.8, 2.3)

5. Write the coordinate pairs of 3 points that can be connected to construct a line that is $5\frac{1}{2}$ units to the right of and parallel to the y-axis.

   a. _____   b. _____   c. _____

6. Write the coordinate pairs of 3 points that lie on the x-axis.

   a. _____   b. _____   c. _____

7. Adam and Janice are playing *Battleship*. Presented in the table is a record of Adam's guesses so far.

   He has hit Janice's battleship using these coordinate pairs. What should he guess next? How do you know? Explain, using words and pictures.

(3, 11)	hit
(2, 11)	miss
(3, 10)	hit
(4, 11)	miss
(3, 9)	miss

COMMON CORE™

Lesson 5:   Investigate patterns in vertical and horizontal lines, and interpret points on the plane as distances from the axes.

Date: 1/31/14

6.A.60

Name _____   Date _____

1. Use a straightedge to construct a line that goes
    through points A and B. Label the line ℓ.

2. Which axis is parallel to line ℓ?

    Which axis is perpendicular to line ℓ?

3. Plot two more points on line ℓ. Name them C and D.

4. Give the coordinates of each point below.

    A: _____ B: _____

    C: _____ D: _____

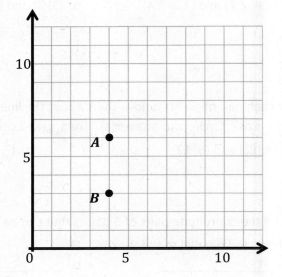

5. Give the coordinates of another point that falls on line ℓ with a y-coordinate greater than 20.

COMMON CORE™ | Lesson 5:   Investigate patterns in vertical and horizontal lines, and interpret
                              points on the plane as distances from the axes.
                 Date: 1/31/14

6.A.61

Name _____   Date _____

1. Use the coordinate plane to answer the questions.

   a. Use a straightedge to construct a line that goes through points A and B. Label the line g.

   b. Line g is parallel to the _____-axis and is perpendicular to the _____-axis.

   c. Draw two more points on line g. Name them C and D.

   d. Give the coordinates of each point below.

        A: _____ B: _____

        C: _____ D: _____

   e. What do all of the points on line g have in common?

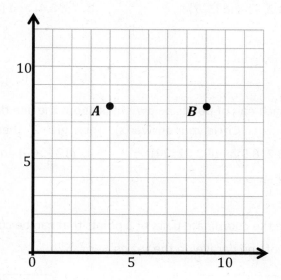

   f. Give the coordinates of another point that falls on line g with an x-coordinate greater than 25.

2. Plot the following points on the coordinate plane to the right.

   H: $(\frac{3}{4}, 3)$ I: $(\frac{3}{4}, 2\frac{1}{4})$

   J: $(\frac{3}{4}, \frac{1}{2})$ K: $(\frac{3}{4}, 1\frac{3}{4})$

   a. Use a straightedge to draw a line to connect these points. Label the line f.

   b. In line f, $x = $ _____ for all values of y.

   c. Circle the correct word:

   Line f is *parallel*   *perpendicular*   to the x-axis.

   Line f is *parallel*   *perpendicular*   to the y-axis.

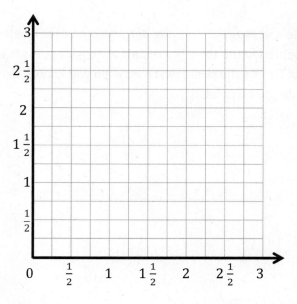

   d. What pattern occurs in the coordinate pairs that make line f vertical?

COMMON CORE™   **Lesson 5:**   Investigate patterns in vertical and horizontal lines, and interpret points on the plane as distances from the axes.   6.A.62

                        Date: 1/31/14

3. For each pair of points below, think about the line that joins them. For which pairs is the line parallel to the x-axis? Circle your answer(s). Without plotting them, explain how you know.

   a. (3.2, 7) and (5, 7)   b. (8, 8.4) and (8, 8.8)   c. ($6\frac{1}{2}$, 12) and (6.2, 11)

4. For each pair of points below, think about the line that joins them. For which pairs is the line parallel to the y-axis? Circle your answer(s). Then, give 2 other coordinate pairs that would also fall on this line.

   a. (3.2, 8.5) and (3.22, 24)   b. ($13\frac{1}{3}$, $4\frac{2}{3}$) and ($13\frac{1}{3}$, 7)   c. (2.9, 5.4) and (7.2, 5.4)

5. Write the coordinate pairs of 3 points that can be connected to construct a line that is $5\frac{1}{2}$ units to the right of and parallel to the y-axis.

   a. _____   b. _____   c. _____

6. Write the coordinate pairs of 3 points that lie on the y-axis.

   a. _____   b. _____   c. _____

7. Leslie and Peggy are playing *Battleship* on axes labeled in halves. Presented in the table is a record of Peggy's guesses so far. What should she guess next? How do you know? Explain using words and pictures.

(5, 5)	miss
(4, 5)	hit
($3\frac{1}{2}$, 5)	miss
($4\frac{1}{2}$, 5)	miss

COMMON CORE™

Lesson 5:   Investigate patterns in vertical and horizontal lines, and interpret
              points on the plane as distances from the axes.
Date: 1/31/14

6.A.63

Point	x	y	(x, y)
H			
I			
J			
K			
L			

a)

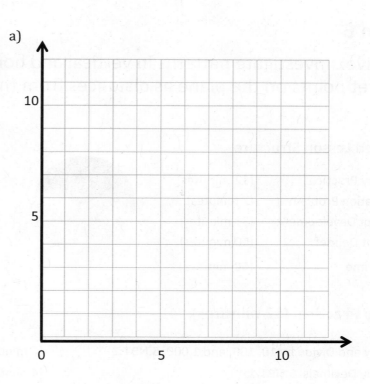

b)

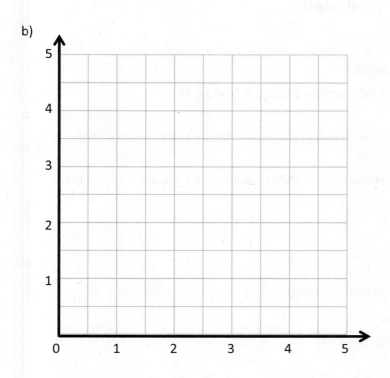

Point	x	y	(x, y)
D	$2\frac{1}{2}$	0	$(2\frac{1}{2}, 0)$
E	$2\frac{1}{2}$	2	$(2\frac{1}{2}, 2)$
F	$2\frac{1}{2}$	4	$(2\frac{1}{2}, 4)$

COMMON CORE | **Lesson 5:**   Investigate patterns in vertical and horizontal lines, and interpret
points on the plane as distances from the axes.   **6.A.64**

Date: 1/31/14

Lesson 6

Objective: Investigate patterns in vertical and horizontal lines, and interpret points on the plane as distances from the axes.

Suggested Lesson Structure

■ Fluency Practice   (12 minutes)
■ Application Problem   (7 minutes)
■ Concept Development   (31 minutes)
■ Student Debrief   (10 minutes)

   Total Time   **(60 minutes)**

Fluency Practice (12 minutes)

- Multiply and Divide by 10, 100, and 1,000 **5.NBT.2**   (4 minutes)
- Count by Decimals **5.NBT.1**   (4 minutes)
- Find the Missing Number on a Number Line **5.G.1**   (4 minutes)

Multiply and Divide by 10, 100, and 1,000 (4 minutes)

Materials: (T) Place value chart (S) Personal white boards

Note: This fluency activity reviews G5–Module 1 topics.

   T: (Project place value chart from millions to thousandths.) What is 0.003 × 10?
   S: 0.03

Repeat the process for this possible sequence: 0.005 × 100, 0.005 × 1000, 1.005 × 1,000, 1.035 × 100, 1.235 × 100, 1.235 × 10, 1.235 × 1,000.

Repeat the process for dividing by 10, 100 and 1,000 for this possible sequence: 2 ÷ 10, 2.1 ÷ 10, 2.1 ÷ 100, 21 ÷ 1,000, 547 ÷ 1,000.

Count by Decimals (4 minutes)

Materials: (S) Personal white boards

Note: This fluency activity prepares students for G5–M6–Lesson 6.

   T: Count by twos to twenty, starting at zero.
   S: 0, 2, 4, 6, 8, 10, 12, 14, 16, 18, 20.

Lesson 6:   Investigate patterns in vertical and horizontal lines, and
            interpret points on the plane as distances from the axes.   6.A.65
Date: 1/31/14

T: Count by 2 tenths to 20 tenths, starting at zero.

S: 0 tenths, 2 tenths, 4 tenths, 6 tenths, 8 tenths, 10 tenths, 12 tenths, 14 tenths, 16 tenths, 18 tenths, 20 tenths.

T: (Write 10 tenths = 1 ___.)   Write the number sentence.

S: (Write 10 tenths = 1 one.)

T: (Write 20 tenths = ___ ones.)

S: (Write 20 tenths = 2 ones.)

T: Starting at zero, count by 2 tenths again.   This time, when you come to a whole number, say the whole number.

S: 0 tenths, 2 tenths, 4 tenths, 6 tenths, 8 tenths, 1, 12 tenths, 14 tenths, 16 tenths, 18 tenths, 2.

T: (Write 0.2 = —.)

S: (Write $0.2 = \frac{2}{10}$.)

T: Count from zero tenths to 2 again.   When I raise my hand, stop.

S: 0 tenths, 2 tenths, 4 tenths, 6 tenths.

T: (Raise hand.)   Write 6 tenths as a decimal.

S: (Write 0.6.)

T: Continue.

S: 8 tenths, 1, 12 tenths, 14 tenths, 16 tenths.

Continue up to and down from 2 ones, stopping to have students write various numbers in decimal form.

Find the Missing Number on a Number Line   (4 minutes)

Materials: (S) Personal white boards

Note: This fluency activity reviews G5–M6–Lesson 1. For the last number line, challenge students by having them write simplified fractions.

T: (Project number line partitioned into 10 intervals. Label 0 and 1 as the endpoints. Point to A.)   What is the value of A?

S: 1 tenth.

T: What's the value of B?

S: 2 tenths.

T: Write the value of C.

S: (Write 0.8.)

Continue the process for the other number lines.

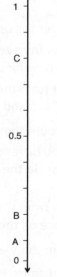
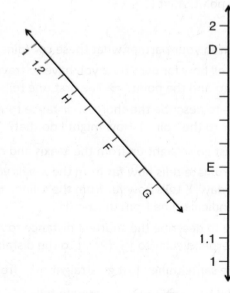

COMMON CORE™ | Lesson 6:   Investigate patterns in vertical and horizontal lines, and interpret points on the plane as distances from the axes.   **6.A.66**

Date: 1/31/14

Application Problem (7 minutes)

Adam built a toy box for his children's wooden blocks.

a. If the inside dimensions of the box are 18 inches by 12 inches by 6 inches, what is the maximum number of 2-inch wooden blocks that will fit in the toy box?

b. What if Adam had built the box 16 inches by 9 inches by 9 inches? What is the maximum number of 2-inch wooden blocks that would fit in this size box?

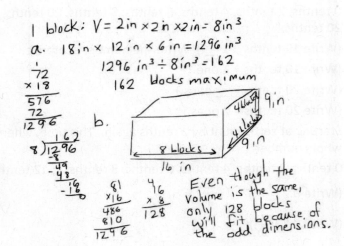

Note: Today's Application Problem reviews the volume work done in G5–Module 5. Part (b) extends the problem so that students must take into account the individual dimensions of the blocks.

Concept Development (31 minutes)

Materials: (S) Coordinate plane template, 1 red and 1 blue pencil or crayon, straightedge

Problem 1: Refer to locations as distances from the axes.

T: (Distribute one coordinate plane template to each student, and display an image of it on the board.) Plot a point, A, at $(2\frac{1}{2}, 1\frac{1}{4})$.

S: (Plot.)

T: Explain to your partner what these coordinates tell us.

S: They tell how far over on x you have to travel from zero, and then how far up parallel to y you have to go to find the point. → The first one tells how far over, and the second one tells how far up.

T: I'd like to describe the shortest distance to A from the x-axis. (Point to the perpendicular distance from x to the point.) How might I do that? Turn and talk.

S: You just go straight up from the x-axis and count the units. It's $1\frac{1}{4}$ straight up from the line. → The y-coordinate tells how far from the x-axis you have to go up. It's like the horizontal lines we did yesterday. Y tells how far from the x line. → Go the same distance as the y-coordinate in a perpendicular line from the x-axis.

T: I'd like to describe the shortest distance to A from the y-axis. How far is A from the y-axis along a line perpendicular to y? (Point to the distance on the plane.) Turn and talk.

S: It's the same thing. Just go straight over from the y-axis. It is $2\frac{1}{2}$ from y in a straight line that's parallel to x. → The x-coordinate tells the distance from y. It is $2\frac{1}{2}$ in a perpendicular line from y.

T: Let's record. What is the shortest distance to A from the x-axis?

Lesson 6:   Investigate patterns in vertical and horizontal lines, and interpret points on the plane as distances from the axes.
Date: 1/31/14

6.A.67

S: $1\frac{1}{4}$ units.

T: (Write on the board: *The shortest distance to A is $1\frac{1}{4}$ units from the x-axis.*)

T: What is the shortest distance to A from the y-axis?

S: $2\frac{1}{2}$ units.

T: (Write on the board: *The shortest distance to A from the y-axis is $2\frac{1}{2}$ units.*)

T: What do you notice about these distances from each of the axes? Turn and talk.

S: They are the same numbers as in the coordinates, but the order is switched. → The x-coordinate tells the shortest distance to the point from the y-axis, and the y-coordinate tells the shortest distance to the point from the x-axis.

Problem 2: Construct horizontal and vertical lines on the coordinate plane.

T: Construct a line, ℓ, so that it contains A and is perpendicular to the x-axis. (Draw line.)

S: (Draw line.)

T: Work with a neighbor to give the coordinates for another point on line ℓ that is $1\frac{1}{2}$ units farther from the x-axis than A. Label it B.

S: (Work and share.)

T: Name the coordinates of B.

S: $(2\frac{1}{2}, 2\frac{3}{4})$.

T: (Plot B on the board.) Give the coordinates for the point on ℓ that is halfway between A and B. How did you find it? Turn and talk.

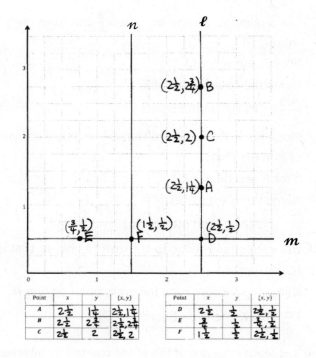

S: I used my fingers to go up 1 fourth from A and down 1 fourth from B until I found the middle. The middle was at $(2\frac{1}{2}, 2)$. → I counted up from A, and there were 6 fourths until I got to B. Half of 6 fourths is 3 fourths. So, the location of the point would have to have a y-coordinate that is $\frac{3}{4}$ more than A, which would be 2. → The length of AB is $1\frac{1}{2}$. I could find half of $1\frac{1}{2}$, which is $\frac{3}{4}$, and that would help me locate the point. → Since the point is on line ℓ, we know the x-coordinate is going to be $2\frac{1}{2}$. Halfway between the y-coordinates is 2. So, the location is $(2\frac{1}{2}, 2)$.

T: Name the coordinates of the point that is halfway between A and B.

S: $(2\frac{1}{2}, 2)$.

Point	x	y	(x, y)
A	$2\frac{1}{2}$	$1\frac{1}{4}$	$2\frac{1}{2}, 1\frac{1}{4}$
B	$2\frac{1}{2}$	$2\frac{3}{4}$	$2\frac{1}{2}, 2\frac{3}{4}$
C	$2\frac{1}{2}$	2	$2\frac{1}{2}, 2$

Point	x	y	(x, y)
D	$2\frac{1}{2}$	$\frac{1}{2}$	$2\frac{1}{2}, \frac{1}{2}$
E	$\frac{3}{4}$	$\frac{1}{2}$	$\frac{3}{4}, \frac{1}{2}$
F	$1\frac{1}{2}$	$\frac{1}{2}$	$2\frac{1}{2}, \frac{1}{2}$

Lesson 6: Investigate patterns in vertical and horizontal lines, and interpret points on the plane as distances from the axes.

Date: 1/31/14

6.A.68

T: Plot this point, name it C, and record its location in the chart.

S: (Plot and record.)

T: Now, work with a partner to draw a line, m, that is perpendicular to line ℓ and $\frac{1}{2}$ unit from the x-axis.

S: (Draw line.)

T: Plot a point, D, where lines ℓ and m intersect.

S: (Plot D.)

T: Record the coordinates of D in the chart.

S: (Record the coordinates.)

T: How far is D from the y-axis?

S: $2\frac{1}{2}$ units.

T: How far is D from the x-axis?

S: One half unit.

T: What are the coordinates of D.

S: $(2\frac{1}{2}, \frac{1}{2})$. (Plot D on the board.)

T: Plot a point, E, on line m, that is $\frac{3}{4}$ unit from the y-axis. Then, record the coordinates of E in the chart.

S: (Plot E and record.)

T: Name the coordinates of E.

S: $(\frac{3}{4}, \frac{1}{2})$. (Plot E on the board.)

T: Plot a point F, on line m, that is $\frac{3}{4}$ unit farther from the y-axis than E. Then, record the coordinates of F in the chart.

S: (Plot F and record.)

T: Name the coordinates of F.

S: $(1\frac{1}{2}, \frac{1}{2})$. (Plot F on the board.)

T: Use your straightedge to construct a line, n, that is parallel to line ℓ and contains point F.

S: (Construct n.)

T: Name the x-coordinate for every point on line n.

S: $1\frac{1}{2}$. (Draw line n on board.)

Problem 3: Identify regions of the plane created by intersecting lines.

T: I'm going to move my finger along the plane. Say, "Stop," when I get to a location that is $1\frac{1}{2}$ units from the y-axis. (Slowly drag finger horizontally across plane along any line perpendicular to the y-axis.)

Lesson 6:	Investigate patterns in vertical and horizontal lines, and interpret points on the plane as distances from the axes.
Date:	1/31/14

6.A.69

S: (Say, "Stop," when teacher's finger gets to x-coordinates of $1\frac{1}{2}$.)

T: (Run your finger vertically along line n.) Is every x-coordinate to the left of this line greater than or less than a distance of $1\frac{1}{2}$?

S: Less than $1\frac{1}{2}$.

T: And every x-coordinate to the right of this line is…?

S: Greater than $1\frac{1}{2}$.

T: Let's use our red pencil (or crayon) to shade the part of the plane that we can see that is more than $1\frac{1}{2}$ units from they y-axis. (Model on board.)

S: (Shade plane.)

T: Show your neighbor the portion of the plane that is less than $2\frac{1}{2}$ units from the y-axis.

S: (Indicate plane to the left of line ℓ.)

T: Shade this region of the plane using your blue pencil (or crayon).

S: (Shade plane.)

T: Work with a partner to name a point that would lie in the region that is double shaded.

S: (Work and share with partner.)

T: Show your neighbor the part of the plane that is double shaded and contains points which are farther from the x-axis than those on line m.

S: (Share with partner.)

T: On your boards, write the coordinates of a point that is in the double shaded part and is also closer to the x-axis than line m.

S: (Give an x-coordinate between $1\frac{1}{2}$ and $2\frac{1}{2}$ and a y-coordinate between 0 and $\frac{1}{2}$.)

Problem Set (10 minutes)

Students should do their personal best to complete the Problem Set within the allotted 10 minutes. For some classes, it may be appropriate to modify the assignment by specifying which problems they work on first. Some

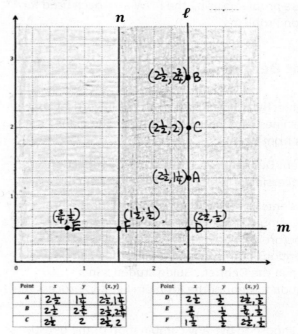

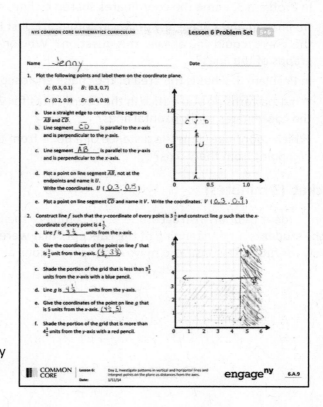

COMMON CORE™ | Lesson 6:   Investigate patterns in vertical and horizontal lines, and interpret points on the plane as distances from the axes.   **6.A.70**

Date: 1/31/14

problems do not specify a method for solving. Students solve these problems using the RDW approach used for Application Problems.

Student Debrief (10 minutes)

Lesson Objective: Investigate patterns in vertical and horizontal lines, and interpret points on the plane as distances from the axes.

The Student Debrief is intended to invite reflection and active processing of the total lesson experience.

Invite students to review their solutions for the Problem Set. They should check work by comparing answers with a partner before going over answers as a class. Look for misconceptions or misunderstandings that can be addressed in the Debrief. Guide students in a conversation to debrief the Problem Set and process the lesson.

You may choose to use any combination of the questions below to lead the discussion.

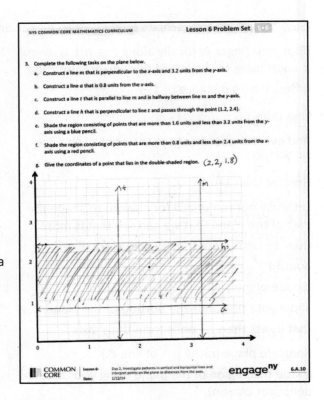

- In Problem 3, name the coordinates shared by lines t and h, m and h, m and a, t and a.
- Do lines m and t have any points in common? Just by looking at the distances of these lines from the y-axis, could you answer this question? Why or why not? How do you know by looking at the graphs of the lines?
- In Problem 3, what is the area of the shape enclosed by lines m, a, t, and h?
- What patterns do you notice in the coordinates for vertical lines? What patterns do you notice in the coordinates for horizontal lines?
- Which coordinate tells the distance of a point from the x-axis? Which coordinate tells the distance of a point from the y-axis?

Exit Ticket (3 minutes)

After the Student Debrief, instruct students to complete the Exit Ticket. A review of their work will help you assess the students' understanding of the concepts that were presented in the lesson today and plan more effectively for future lessons. You may read the questions aloud to the students.

Lesson 6: Investigate patterns in vertical and horizontal lines, and interpret points on the plane as distances from the axes.

Date: 1/31/14

6.A.71

Name _____   Date _____

1. Plot the following points, and label them on the coordinate plane.

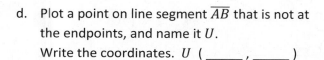

A: $(0.3, 0.1)$ B: $(0.3, 0.7)$

C: $(0.2, 0.9)$ D: $(0.4, 0.9)$

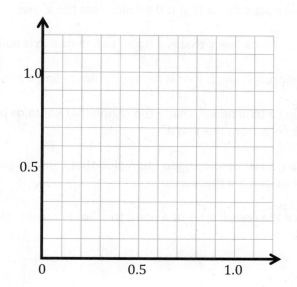

a. Use a straightedge to construct line segments $\overline{AB}$ and $\overline{CD}$.

b. Line segment _____ is parallel to the x-axis and is perpendicular to the y-axis.

c. Line segment _____ is parallel to the y-axis and is perpendicular to the x-axis.

d. Plot a point on line segment $\overline{AB}$ that is not at the endpoints, and name it U. Write the coordinates. U (_____ , _____)

e. Plot a point on line segment $\overline{CD}$ and name it V. Write the coordinates. V (_____ , _____)

2. Construct line f such that the y-coordinate of every point is $3\frac{1}{2}$, and construct line g such that the x-coordinate of every point is $4\frac{1}{2}$.

a. Line f is _____ units from the x-axis.

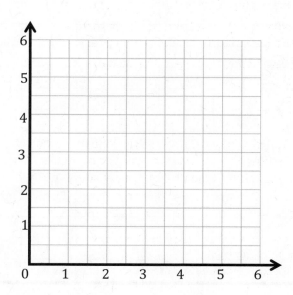

b. Give the coordinates of the point on line f that is $\frac{1}{2}$ unit from the y-axis. _____

c. With a blue pencil, shade the portion of the grid that is less than $3\frac{1}{2}$ units from the x-axis.

d. Line g is _____ units from the y-axis.

e. Give the coordinates of the point on line g that is 5 units from the x-axis. _____

f. With a red pencil, shade the portion of the grid that is more than $4\frac{1}{2}$ units from the y-axis.

COMMON CORE™   **Lesson 6:**   Investigate patterns in vertical and horizontal lines, and interpret points on the plane as distances from the axes.   **6.A.72**

Date: 1/31/14

3.   Complete the following tasks on the plane below.

   a.   Construct a line **m** that is perpendicular to the x-axis and 3.2 units from the y-axis.

   b.   Construct a line **a** that is 0.8 units from the x-axis.

   c.   Construct a line **t** that is parallel to line **m** and is halfway between line **m** and the y-axis.

   d.   Construct a line **h** that is perpendicular to line **t** and passes through the point (1.2, 2.4).

   e.   Using a blue pencil, shade the region that contains points that are more than 1.6 units and less than 3.2 units from the y-axis.

   f.   Using a red pencil, shade the region that contains points that are more than 0.8 units and less than 2.4 units from the x-axis.

   g.   Give the coordinates of a point that lies in the double-shaded region.

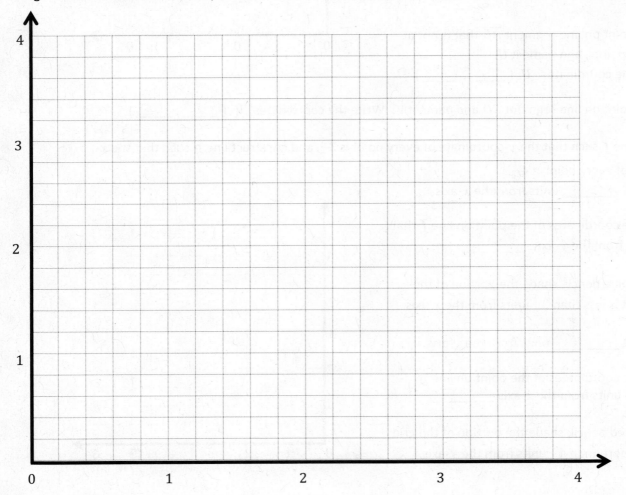

Lesson 6:	Investigate patterns in vertical and horizontal lines, and interpret points on the plane as distances from the axes.	6.A.73
Date:	1/31/14	

Name _____   Date _____

1. Plot the point H $(2\frac{1}{2}, 1\frac{1}{2})$.

2. Line ℓ passes through point H and is parallel to the y-axis. Construct line l.

3. Construct line m such that the y-coordinate of every point is $\frac{3}{4}$.

4. Line m is _____ units from the x-axis.

5. Give the coordinates of the point on line m that is $\frac{1}{2}$ unit from the y-axis.

6. With a blue pencil, shade the portion of the plane that is less than $\frac{3}{4}$ units from the x-axis.

7. With a red pencil, shade the portion of the plane that is less than $2\frac{1}{2}$ units from the y-axis.

8. Plot a point that lies in the double-shaded region. Give the coordinates of the point.

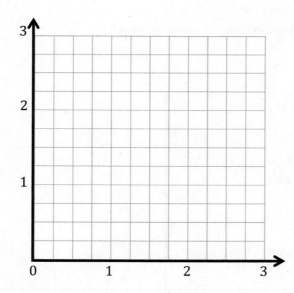

COMMON CORE™ | Lesson 6:   Investigate patterns in vertical and horizontal lines, and
                                      interpret points on the plane as distances from the axes.   6.A.74
                       | Date: 1/31/14

Name _____   Date _____

1. Plot and label the following points on the coordinate plane.

    C: (0.4, 0.4) A: (1.1, 0.4) S: (0.9, 0.5) T: (0.9, 1.1)

    a. Use a straightedge to construct line segments $\overline{CA}$ and $\overline{ST}$.
    b. Name the line segment that is perpendicular to the x-axis and parallel to the y-axis.
    c. Name the line segment that is parallel to the x-axis and perpendicular to the y-axis.
    d. Plot a point on $\overline{CA}$ and name it E. Plot a point on line segment $\overline{ST}$ and name it R.
    e. Write the coordinates of points E and R.

    E (____ , ____) R (____ , ____)

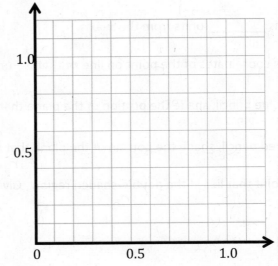

2. Construct line m such that the y-coordinate of every point is $1\frac{1}{2}$, and construct line n such that the x-coordinate of every point is $5\frac{1}{2}$.

    a. Line m is _____ units from the x-axis.

    b. Give the coordinates of the point on line m that is 2 units from the y-axis. _____

    c. With a blue pencil, shade the portion of the grid that is less than $1\frac{1}{2}$ units from the x-axis.

    d. Line n is _____ units from the y-axis.

    e. Give the coordinates of the point on line n that is $3\frac{1}{2}$ units from the x-axis. _____

    f. With a red pencil, shade the portion of the grid that is less than $5\frac{1}{2}$ units from the y-axis.

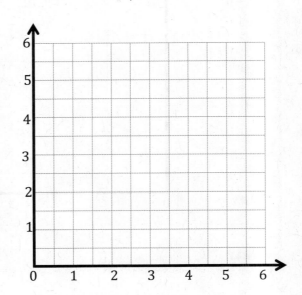

COMMON CORE™

Lesson 6:   Investigate patterns in vertical and horizontal lines, and interpret points on the plane as distances from the axes.

Date: 1/31/14

6.A.75

3. Construct and label lines e, r, s, o on the plane below.

   a. Line e is 3.75 units above the x-axis.

   b. Line r is 2.5 units from the y-axis.

   c. Line s is parallel to line e but 0.75 farther from the x-axis.

   d. Line o is to perpendicular to lines s and e and passes through the point $(3\frac{1}{4}, 3\frac{1}{4})$.

4. Complete the following tasks on the plane.

   a. Using a blue pencil, shade the region that contains points that are more than $2\frac{1}{2}$ units and less than $3\frac{1}{4}$ units from the y-axis.

   b. Using a red pencil, shade the region that contains points that are more than $3\frac{3}{4}$ units and less than $4\frac{1}{2}$ units from the x-axis.

   c. Plot a point that lies in the double shaded region, and label its coordinates.

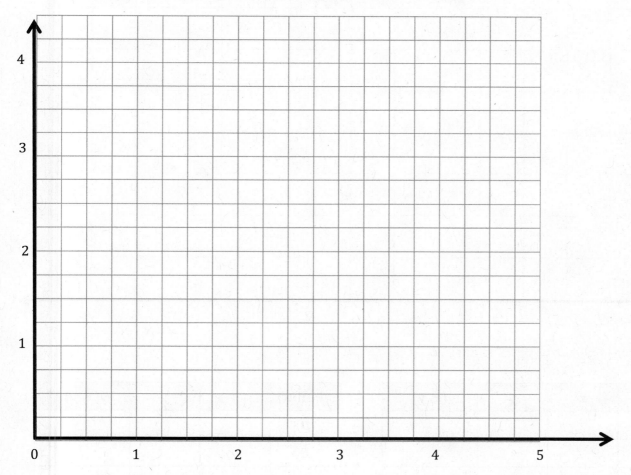

COMMON CORE | Lesson 6:   Investigate patterns in vertical and horizontal lines, and
                                 interpret points on the plane as distances from the axes.   **6.A.76**
                     Date: 1/31/14

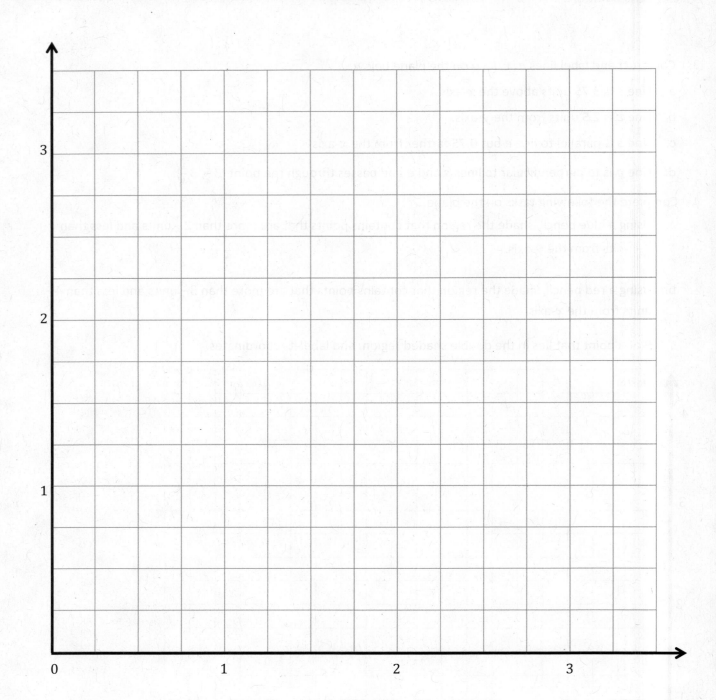

Point	x	y	(x, y)
A			
B			
C			

Point	x	y	(x, y)
D			
E			
F			

Lesson 6: Investigate patterns in vertical and horizontal lines, and interpret points on the plane as distances from the axes.

Date: 1/31/14

6.A.77

Topic B
Patterns in the Coordinate Plane and Graphing Number Patterns from Rules

5.OA.2, 5.OA.3, 5.G.1

Focus Standard:	5.OA.2	Write simple expressions that record calculations with numbers, and interpret numerical expressions without evaluating them. *For example, express the calculation "add 8 and 7, then multiply by 2" as 2 × (8 + 7). Recognize that 3 × (18932 + 921) is three times as large as 18932 + 921, without having to calculate the indicated sum or product.*
	5.OA.3	Generate two numerical patterns using two given rules. Identify apparent relationships between corresponding terms. Form ordered pairs consisting of corresponding terms from the two patterns, and graph the ordered pairs on a coordinate plane. *For example, given the rule "Add 3" and the starting number 0, and given the rule "Add 6" and the starting number 0, generate terms in the resulting sequences, and observe that the terms in one sequence are twice the corresponding terms in the other sequence. Explain informally why this is so.*
	5.G.1	Use a pair of perpendicular number lines, called axes, to define a coordinate system, with the intersection of the lines (the origin) arranged to coincide with the 0 on each line and a given point in the plan located by using an ordered pair of numbers, called its coordinates. Understand that the first number indicates how far to travel from the origin in the direction of one axis, and the second number indicates how far to travel in the direction of the second axis, with the convention that the names of the two axes and the coordinates correspond (e.g., x-axis and x-coordinate, y-axis and y-coordinate).
Instructional Days:	6	
Coherence -Links from:	G4–M4	Angle Measure and Plane Figures
	G4–M7	Exploring Measurement with Multiplication
-Links to:	G6–M1	Ratios and Unit Rates
	G6–M3	Rational Numbers
	G6–M4	Expressions and Equations

Topic B:	Patterns in the Coordinate Plane and Graphing Number Patterns from Rules
Date:	1/31/14

6.B.1

In Topic B, students plot points and use them to draw lines in the plane (**5.G.1**). Students begin by investigating patterns relating the x- and y-coordinates of the points on the line and reasoning about the patterns in the ordered pairs, which lays important groundwork for Grade 6 work with proportional reasoning. Topic B continues as students use given rules (e.g., multiply by 2, then add 3) to generate coordinate pairs, plot points, and investigate relationships. Patterns in the resultant coordinate pairs are analyzed to discover that such rules produce collinear sets of points, or lines. Students next generate two number patterns from two given rules, plot the points, and analyze the relationships within the sequences of the ordered pairs and the graphs (**5.OA.3**). Patterns continue to be the focus as students analyze the effect on the steepness of the line when the second coordinate is produced through an addition rule as opposed to a multiplication rule (**5.OA.3**). They also create rules to generate number patterns, plot the points, connect those points with lines, and look for intersections.

A Teaching Sequence Towards Mastery of Patterns in the Coordinate Plane and Graphing Number Patterns from Rules

Objective 1: Plot points, use them to draw lines in the plane, and describe patterns within the coordinate pairs.
(Lesson 7)

Objective 2: Generate a number pattern from a given rule, and plot the points.
(Lesson 8)

Objective 3: Generate two number patterns from given rules, plot the points, and analyze the patterns.
(Lesson 9)

Objective 4: Compare the lines and patterns generated by addition rules and multiplication rules.
(Lesson 10)

Objective 5: Analyze number patterns created from mixed operations.
(Lesson 11)

Objective 6: Create a rule to generate a number pattern, and plot the points.
(Lesson 12)

Lesson 7

Objective: Plot points, using them to draw lines in the plane, and describe patterns within the coordinate pairs.

Suggested Lesson Structure

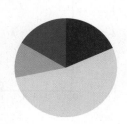

■ Fluency Practice   (11 minutes)
■ Application Problem   (7 minutes)
□ Concept Development   (32 minutes)
■ Student Debrief   (10 minutes)

Total Time   **(60 minutes)**

Fluency Practice (11 minutes)

▪ Multiply and Divide by 10, 100, and 1,000 **5.NBT.2**   (5 minutes)
▪ Name Coordinates **5.G.1**   (6 minutes)

Multiply and Divide Decimals by 10, 100, and 1,000 (5 minutes)

Materials: (T) Place value chart (S) Personal white boards

Note: This fluency activity reviews G5–Module 1 topics. The suggested place value chart allows students to see the symmetry of the decimal system around one.

    T: (Project place value chart from the one thousands place to the one thousandths place. Draw 4 disks in the tens column, 3 disks in the ones column, and 5 disks in the tenths column.) Say the value as a decimal.

    S: Forty-three and five tenths.

    T: Write the number on your personal boards. (Pause.) Multiply it by 10.

    S: (Write 43.5 on their place value charts, cross out each digit, and shift the number one place value to the left to show 435.)

    T: Show 43.5 divided by 10.

    S: (Write 43.5 on their place value charts, cross out each digit, and shift the number one place value to the right to show 4.35.)

Repeat the process and sequence for 43.5 × 100, 43.5 ÷ 100, 948 ÷ 1,000, and 0.529 × 1,000.

Lesson 7:   Plot points, using them to draw lines in the plane, and describe
                patterns within the coordinate pairs.

Date: 1/31/14

6.B.3

Name Coordinates (6 minutes)

Materials: (T) Coordinate grid template (S) Personal white boards

Note: This fluency activity reviews G5–M6–Lesson 6.

> T: (Project coordinate grid.) Write the coordinate positioned at A.
>
> S: (Write (5, 5).)

Continue the process for letters B–E.

> T: (Project coordinate grid.) Write the coordinate that is positioned at A.
>
> S: (Write (0.5, 1.0).)

Continue the process for the remaining letters.

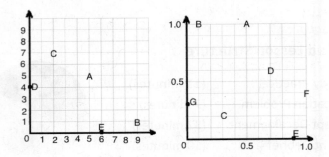

Application Problem (7 minutes)

An orchard charges $0.85 to ship a quarter kilogram of grapefruit. Each grapefruit weighs approximately 165 grams. How much will it cost to ship 40 grapefruits?

Note: This problem reviews fraction and decimal concepts from earlier in the year, in a multi-step, real world context.

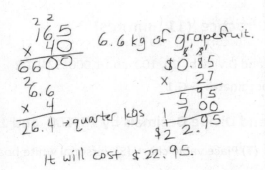

Concept Development (32 minutes)

Materials: (S) Coordinate plane template, straightedge

Problem 1: Describe patterns in coordinate pairs and name the rule.

> T: (Distribute 1 copy of coordinate plane template to each student. Display image of the chart, showing coordinate pairs A through D.) Work with a partner to plot points A through D on the first plane, and draw $\overleftrightarrow{AD}$.

Point	x	y	(x, y)
A	0	0	(0, 0)
B	1	1	(1, 1)
C	2	2	(2, 2)
D	3	3	(3, 3)

> S: (Draw the line.)
>
> T: Look at the coordinates of the points contained in $\overleftrightarrow{AD}$. What pattern do you notice about the x- and y-coordinates? Turn and talk.
>
> S: When x is 0, so is y. When x is 1, so is y, all the way up to 3. → The x-coordinate equals the y-coordinate.
>
> T: So, you're saying that the x-coordinate and the y-coordinate are always equal to one another. Will the point with coordinates (4, 4) also fall on $\overleftrightarrow{AD}$?
>
> S: Yes!

MP.6

Lesson 7:	Plot points, using them to draw lines in the plane, and describe patterns within the coordinate pairs.
Date:	1/31/14

6.B.4

MP.6

T: As long as the x- and y-coordinates are the same, the point will be on $\overleftrightarrow{AD}$. We can say that the relationship between these coordinates can be described by the rule x and y are equal. (Write on board: *Rule: x and y are equal.*) Or, we can also say the rule, y is equal to x. (Write, *Rule: y is equal to x.*)

T: Will $\overleftrightarrow{AD}$ contain the point with coordinates (10, 10)? Turn and talk.

S: I can't see it on this plane because the numbers stop at 5. However, if it kept going, we could see it. → Yes, as long as the x- and y-coordinates of the point are equal, the point will be on the line.

T: Show me a point on $\overleftrightarrow{AD}$ whose coordinates are mixed numbers.

S: (Show a coordinate pair where x and y are equal mixed numbers.)

T: Can $\overleftrightarrow{AD}$ contain a point where the x-coordinate is a mixed number and the y-coordinate is not? Turn and talk.

S: Don't they have to be the same? → x and y need to be equal. → If the x-coordinate is a mixed number, the y-coordinate will be the same mixed number, or it could be expressed in another equivalent form such as 3 halves and $1\frac{1}{2}$.

T: Give the coordinate pair of a point that would *not* fall on $\overleftrightarrow{AD}$.

S: (Show a coordinate pair where x and y are not equal.)

T: (Display image of chart, showing coordinate pairs for points G through J.) What pattern do you notice in these coordinate pairs? Turn and talk.

S: x and y aren't equal this time. The y is always more than the x-coordinate. → The x-coordinates are increasing by $\frac{1}{2}$ every time and so are the y-coordinates. → It goes from 0 to 3 and $\frac{1}{2}$ to $3\frac{1}{2}$, and 1 to 4. So, the y-coordinate is always 3 more than the x-coordinate.

T: Plot the points from the chart on the coordinate plane. Then, connect them in the order they were plotted.

S: (Plot and draw $\overleftrightarrow{GJ}$.)

T: What do you notice?

1.

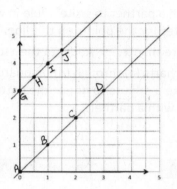

NOTES ON
MULTIPLE MEANS OF
ENGAGEMENT:

It may be difficult for some students to read the information displayed in the charts showing the coordinate pairs. The information in the charts can be managed in ways to help students:

- Shade alternate rows of information so that students can easily track information within the chart.

- Display the information one line at a time in order to help students see relevant information as needed.

Point	(x, y)
G	$(0, 3)$
H	$(\frac{1}{2}, 3\frac{1}{2})$
I	$(1, 4)$
J	$(1\frac{1}{2}, 4\frac{1}{2})$

Lesson 7:	Plot points, using them to draw lines in the plane, and describe patterns within the coordinate pairs.
Date:	1/31/14

6.B.5

S: They are all on the same line.

T: These points are collinear, so the relationship between each x and its corresponding y will be the same. Use this relationship to locate more points on this line. When x is 2, what is y? (Show (2, ?) on board.) Turn and talk.

S: y would be 5, because y is always 3 more than the x-coordinate for points on this line. → If I add 3 plus 2, then y is 5. → The coordinates would be (2, 5).

T: Work with a partner to write a rule in words that tells the relationship between the x- and y-coordinates for the points on this line. Be sure to include both x and y when you write the rule.

S: y is 3 more than x. → Add 3 to the x-coordinate to get y.

T: (Display charts (a) through (d) on board.) Each of these charts shows points on each of four different lines. Take a minute to notice the pattern within the coordinate pairs for each line. Share your thoughts with a partner.

a.

Point	(x, y)
L	$(0, 3)$
M	$(2, 3)$
N	$(4, 3)$

b.

Point	(x, y)
O	$(0, 0)$
P	$(1, 2)$
Q	$(2, 4)$

c.

Point	(x, y)
R	$(1, \frac{1}{2})$
S	$(2, 1\frac{1}{2})$
T	$(3, 2\frac{1}{2})$

d.

Point	(x, y)
U	$(1, 3)$
V	$(2, 6)$
W	$(3, 9)$

S: (Study and share.)

T: Which chart shows coordinate pairs for the rule y *is always 3*?

S: Chart (a).

T: (Write y *is always 3* beneath Chart (a).) Which chart shows every y-coordinate is less than every x-coordinate?

S: Chart (c).

T: How much less than x is each y-coordinate?

S: $\frac{1}{2}$ less.

T: Work with a partner to write a rule for finding points on the line shown in chart (c).

S: y is $\frac{1}{2}$ less than x. → Subtract $\frac{1}{2}$ from x to get y.

T: (Write y *is $\frac{1}{2}$ less than x* beneath chart (c).) Which chart shows coordinate pairs on a line that follows the rule, y *is x times 2*?

S: Chart (b). (Write students responses beneath chart (b).)

T: How else might we state this rule for this line? Turn and talk.

S: y is double x. → y is twice as much as x. → x is half of y.

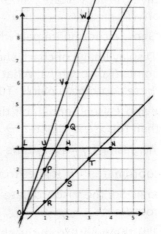

COMMON CORE™

Lesson 7: Plot points, using them to draw lines in the plane, and describe patterns within the coordinate pairs.

Date: 1/31/14

6.B.6

T: Write a rule for the coordinate pairs in chart (d).

S: y is x times 3. → y is 3 times more than x. → Triple x to get y. (Write student responses beneath chart (d).)

T: On the second plane, work with a neighbor to plot the three points from each chart, and the draw a line to connect the three points. (Circulate as students plot and construct lines.)

T: I'm going to show you some coordinate pairs. I'd like you to tell me which line the point would fall on. Be prepared to explain how you know. (Show coordinate pair (5, 10).)

S: x times 2. Because 5 times 2 is ten, and this follows the pattern in chart (b). → It's the same as the pattern in chart (b). If you double x, which is 5, you get 10, which is y. → The y-coordinate is twice as much as the x-coordinate in this pair. That's the same relationship as the other points on the line shown by chart (b).

T: (Show coordinate pair (5, $4\frac{1}{2}$).)

S: y is $\frac{1}{2}$ less than x.

T: Tell a neighbor how you know.

S: 5 minus $\frac{1}{2}$ is $4\frac{1}{2}$. → The y-coordinate is $\frac{1}{2}$ less than the x-coordinate.

T: (Show the coordinate pair ($\frac{1}{2}$, $1\frac{1}{2}$).)

S: x times 3.

T: Tell a neighbor how you know.

S: 3 times $\frac{1}{2}$ is 3 halves, which is $1\frac{1}{2}$. → The y-coordinate is 3 times as much as the x-coordinate.

T: (Show the coordinate pair, ($1\frac{1}{2}$, 3).)

S: x times 2. → y is always 3.

T: Some of you said the rule for the coordinate pair is, x times 2, and some of you said the rule is y is always 3. Which relationship is correct? How do you know? Turn and talk.

S: Both rules are correct because this point is on both lines. → The same point can be part of more than one line at a time.

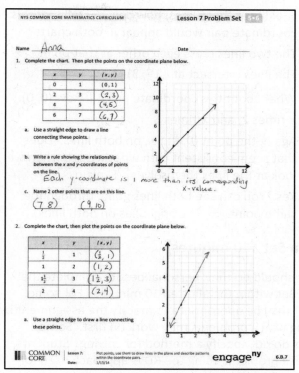

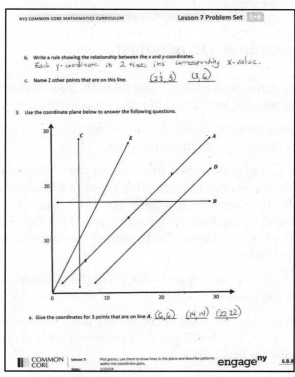

COMMON CORE™

6.B.7

T: Looking at these lines, how can you tell that this coordinate pair would appear in both charts?

S: The two lines cross each other at that point. → The lines intersect at ($1\frac{1}{2}$, 3).

T: What about this coordinate pair? (Show (0, 0).)

S: x times 2, and x times 3.

T: Again, the point (0, 0) lies on both lines. Does that seem consistent with what we see when we look at the lines themselves? Explain.

S: Yes. You can see both lines going through the same point. → The origin lies on both lines.

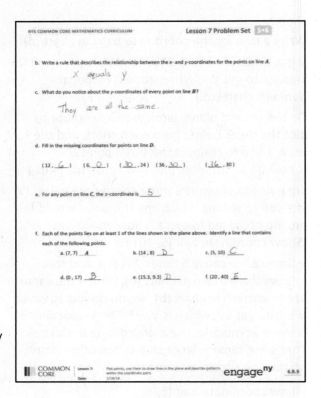

Problem Set (10 minutes)

Students should do their personal best to complete the Problem Set within the allotted 10 minutes. For some classes, it may be appropriate to modify the assignment by specifying which problems they work on first. Some problems do not specify a method for solving. Students solve these problems using the RDW approach used for Application Problems.

Student Debrief (10 minutes)

Lesson Objective: Plot points, using them to draw lines in the plane, and describe patterns within the coordinate pairs.

The Student Debrief is intended to invite reflection and active processing of the total lesson experience.

Invite students to review their solutions for the Problem Set. They should check work by comparing answers with a partner before going over answers as a class. Look for misconceptions or misunderstandings that can be addressed in the Debrief. Guide students in a conversation to debrief the Problem Set and process the lesson.

You may choose to use any combination of the questions below to lead the discussion.

- When you see a set of coordinate pairs, what is your strategy for identifying their pattern? What do you look for first? Then what?

NOTES ON
MULTIPLE MEANS OF
ENGAGEMENT:

One goal of the Student Debrief is to give all students time to articulate their thinking and make connections to prior knowledge. Whole group conversations may not always be the best way to give all students a chance to express themselves.

- Establish small groups with norms or protocols that give each member an opportunity to speak in turn.

- Ask students to talk to various classmates until they find a peer with a like viewpoint, opinion, or answer. This strategy requires students to express their ideas multiple times, perhaps improving as they go along.

- Pair students with peers with unlike opinions or answers. Require these pairs to talk to each other to find common understandings or errors in their ideas.

Lesson 7: Plot points, using them to draw lines in the plane, and describe patterns within the coordinate pairs.

Date: 1/31/14

6.B.8

- Compare your answers to Problems 1(c) and 2(c) with a neighbor. Are they the same or different? How many different sets of coordinate pairs are there for each rule?
- Look back at the coordinate pair (5, 10) in Problem 3 (f); how many lines shown on the plane contain this point? Compare and contrast the lines that contain this point.

Exit Ticket (3 minutes)

After the Student Debrief, instruct students to complete the Exit Ticket. A review of their work will help you assess the students' understanding of the concepts that were presented in the lesson today and plan more effectively for future lessons. You may read the questions aloud to the students.

| Lesson 7: | Plot points, using them to draw lines in the plane, and describe patterns within the coordinate pairs. |
| Date: | 1/31/14 |

6.B.9

Name _____   Date _____

1. Complete the chart. Then, plot the points on the coordinate plane below.

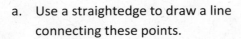

x	y	(x, y)
0	1	(0, 1)
2	3	
4	5	
6	7	

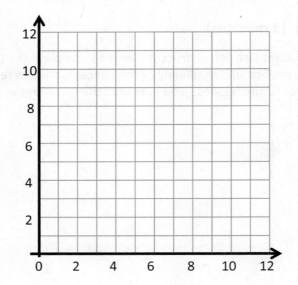

a. Use a straightedge to draw a line connecting these points.

b. Write a rule showing the relationship between the x- and y-coordinates of points on the line.

c. Name 2 other points that are on this line.

    _____   _____

2. Complete the chart. Then, plot the points on the coordinate plane below.

x	y	(x, y)
$\frac{1}{2}$	1	
1	2	
$1\frac{1}{2}$	3	
2	4	

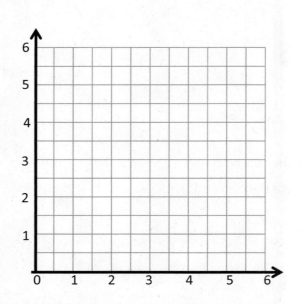

a. Use a straightedge to draw a line connecting these points.

COMMON CORE™

Lesson 7: Plot points, using them to draw lines in the plane, and describe patterns within the coordinate pairs.

Date: 1/31/14

6.B.10

b.   Write a rule showing the relationship between the x- and y-coordinates.

c.   Name 2 other points that are on this line.   _____   _____

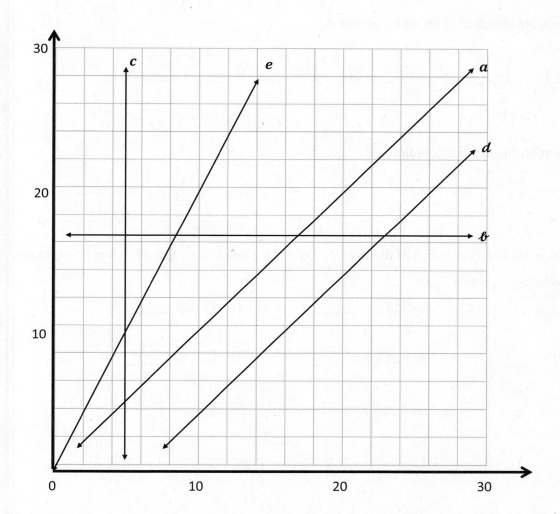

3.   Use the coordinate plane below to answer the following questions.

a. Give the coordinates for 3 points that are on line a. _____   _____   _____

b. Write a rule that describes the relationship between the x- and y-coordinates for the points on line a.

COMMON CORE™

Lesson 7:   Plot points, using them to draw lines in the plane, and describe
patterns within the coordinate pairs.

Date: 1/31/14

6.B.11

c. What do you notice about the y-coordinates of every point on line b?

d. Fill in the missing coordinates for points on line d.

(12, _____)   (6, _____)   (_____, 24)   (36 , _____)   (_____, 30)

e. For any point on line c, the x-coordinate is _____.

f. Each of the points lies on at least 1 of the lines shown in the plane above. Identify a line that contains each of the following points.

   a. (7, 7) __*a*__   b. (14 , 8) _____   c. (5, 10) _____

   d. (0 , 17) _____   e. (15.3, 9.3) _____   f. (20 , 40) _____

COMMON CORE™

Lesson 7:

Date:

Plot points, using them to draw lines in the plane, and describe patterns within the coordinate pairs.

1/31/14

6.B.12

Name _____   Date _____

Complete the chart. Then, plot the points on the coordinate plane.

x	y	(x , y)
0	4	
2	6	
3	7	
7	11	

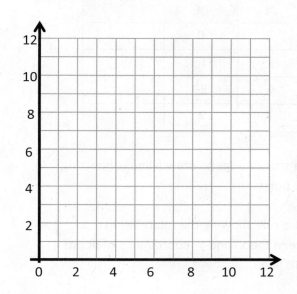

1.   Use a straightedge to draw a line connecting these points.

2.   Write a rule to show the relationship between the x- and y- coordinates for points on the line.

3.   Name two other points that are also on this line.

COMMON CORE™

Lesson 7:   Plot points, using them to draw lines in the plane, and describe patterns within the coordinate pairs.
Date: 1/31/14

6.B.13

Name _____   Date _____

1.   Complete the chart. Then, plot the points on the coordinate plane.

x	y	(x, y)
2	0	
$3\frac{1}{2}$	$1\frac{1}{2}$	
$4\frac{1}{2}$	$2\frac{1}{2}$	
6	4	

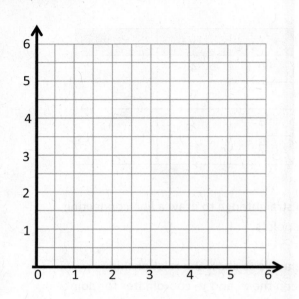

a.   Use a straightedge to draw a line connecting these points.

b.   Write a rule showing the relationship between the x- and y- coordinates of points on this line.

c.   Name two other points that are also on this line.   _____   _____

2.   Complete the chart. Then, plot the points on the coordinate plane.

x	y	(x, y)
0	0	
$\frac{1}{4}$	$\frac{3}{4}$	
$\frac{1}{2}$	$1\frac{1}{2}$	
1	3	

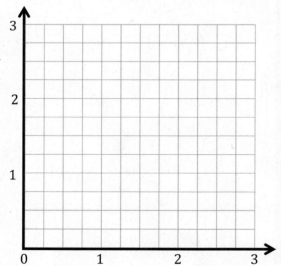

a.   Use a straightedge to draw a line connecting these points.

b.   Write a rule showing the relationship between the x- and y- coordinates for points on the line.

c.   Name two other points that are also on this line.

_____   _____

Lesson 7:   Plot points, using them to draw lines in the plane, and describe patterns within the coordinate pairs.

Date: 1/31/14

6.B.14

3. Use the coordinate plane to answer the following questions.

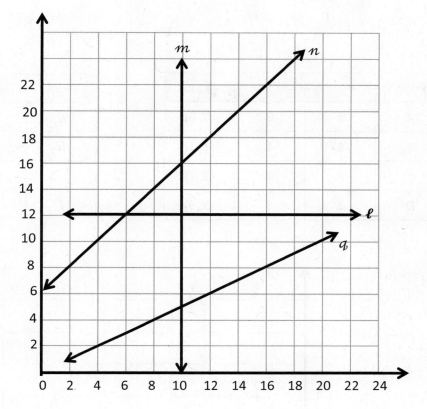

a. For any point on line *m*, the *x*-coordinate is _____.

b. Give the coordinates for 3 points that are on line *n*.

c. Write a rule that describes the relationship between the *x*- and *y*-coordinates on line *n*.

d. Give the coordinates for 3 points that are on line *q*.

e. Write a rule that describes the relationship between the *x*- and *y*-coordinates on line *q*.

f. For each point, identify a line on which each of these points lie.

(10,3.2) _____   (12.4, 18.4) _____   (6.45, 12) _____   (14, 7) _____

Name _____   Date _____

1.

a.

Point	x	y	(x, y)
A	0	0	(0, 0)
B	1	1	(1, 1)
C	2	2	(2, 2)
D	3	3	(3, 3)

b.

Point	x	y	(x, y)
G	0	3	(0, 3)
H	$\frac{1}{2}$	$3\frac{1}{2}$	($\frac{1}{2}$, $3\frac{1}{2}$)
I	1	4	(1, 4)
J	$1\frac{1}{2}$	$4\frac{1}{2}$	($1\frac{1}{2}$, $4\frac{1}{2}$)

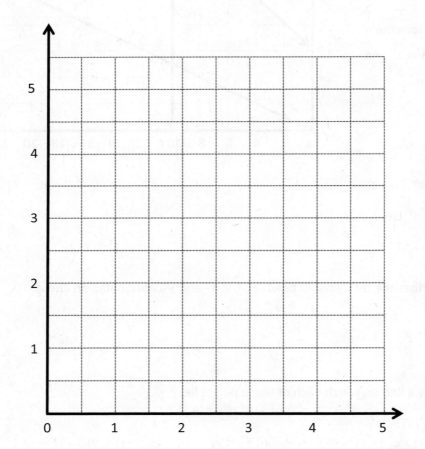

Lesson 7:   Plot points, using them to draw lines in the plane, and describe
patterns within the coordinate pairs.

Date: 1/31/14

6.B.16

2.

a.

Point	(x, y)
L	$(0, 3)$
M	$(2, 3)$
N	$(4, 3)$

b.

Point	(x, y)
O	$(0, 0)$
P	$(1, 2)$
Q	$(2, 4)$

c.

Point	(x, y)
R	$(1, \frac{1}{2})$
S	$(2, 1\frac{1}{2})$
T	$(2, 2\frac{1}{2})$

d.

Point	(x, y)
U	$(1, 3)$
V	$(2, 6)$
W	$(3, 9)$

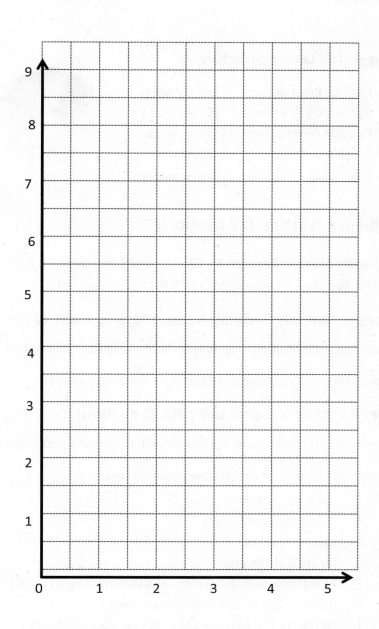

Lesson 8

Objective: Generate a number pattern from a given rule, and plot the points.

Suggested Lesson Structure

■ Fluency Practice   (12 minutes)
■ Application Problem   (5 minutes)
■ Concept Development   (33 minutes)
■ Student Debrief   (10 minutes)
  Total Time   **(60 minutes)**

Fluency Practice (12 minutes)

- Sprint: Multiply Decimals by 10, 100, and 1,000 **5.NBT.2**   (9 minutes)
- Plot Points on a Coordinate Grid **5.G.1**   (3 minutes)

Sprint: Multiply Decimals by 10, 100, and 1,000 (9 minutes)

Materials: (S) Multiply Decimals by 10, 100, and 1,000 Sprint

Note: This fluency activity reviews G5–Module 1 concepts.

Plot Points on a Coordinate Grid (3 minutes)

Materials: (S) Personal white boards with coordinate grid insert

Note: This fluency activity reviews G5–M6–Lesson 7.

    T: Label the x- and y-axes.
    S: (Label the axes.)
    T: Label the origin.
    S: (Write 0 at the origin.)
    T: Along both axes, label each interval, counting by ones to 5.
    S: (Label 1, 2, 3, 4, and 5 along each axes.)
    T: (Write (0, 1).) Plot the point on your coordinate grid.
    S: (Plot point at (0,1).)

Continue the process for the following possible sequence: (1, 2), (2, 3), and (3, 4).

T: Write 2 pairs of whole number coordinates on the line passing through the points you plotted.

S: (Possibly write (4, 5) and (5, 6).)

T: Erase your boards and label your axes and the origin.

S: (Label x-axis, y -axis, and origin.)

T: Label each interval along both axes, counting by halves to 4.

S: (Label $\frac{1}{2}$, 1, $1\frac{1}{2}$, 2, $2\frac{1}{2}$, 3, $3\frac{1}{2}$, and 4 along each axis.)

T: (Write $(1, \frac{1}{2})$.) Plot the point on your coordinate grid.

S: (Plot point at $(1, \frac{1}{2})$.)

Continue the process for (2, 1), (3, $1\frac{1}{2}$), and (4, 2).

T: Write another coordinate pair that is on the same line as the points you just plotted.

Application Problem (5 minutes)

The coordinate pairs listed locate points on two different lines. Write a rule that describes the relationship between the x- and y-coordinates for each line.

Line ℓ: $(3\frac{1}{2}, 7)$, $(1\frac{2}{3}, 3\frac{1}{3})$, (5, 10)

Line m: $(\frac{6}{3}, 1)$, $(3\frac{1}{2}, 1\frac{3}{4})$, $(13, 6\frac{1}{2})$

Line ℓ: y is 2 times X
Line m: y is ½ of X

Note: These problems review G5–M6–Lesson 7's objectives.

Concept Development (33 minutes)

Materials: (S) Personal white board, coordinate plane template, straightedge

Problem 1: Create coordinate pairs from rules.

   a. **y is equal to x**
   b. **y is 1 more than x**
   c. **y is 5 times x**
   d. **y is 1 more than 3 times x**
   e. **y is 1 less than 2 times x**

T: I will give you a rule that describes a relationship between the x- and y-coordinates for some points on a line. You will write a coordinate pair that has the same relationship and that follows the same rule on your board. (Write y *is equal to* x on the board.) Write and show a coordinate pair for y *is equal to x.*

S: (0, 0). → (2, 2). → (47, 47). → $(\frac{7}{8}, \frac{7}{8})$. → (0.21, 0.21).

T: This next rule describes a different relationship between the coordinates of a set of points. (Write *y is 1 more than x* on the board.)

T: How can you find the *y*-coordinate of a point on this line if you know the *x*-coordinate of the point is 0? Turn and talk.

S: The rule says that all the *y*'s are 1 more than all the *x*'s. So, if *x* is 0, then we have to add 1 to that to get *x*. → If *x* = 0, then *y* is 1. (0, 1) is the point's coordinate pair.

T: Write and show other coordinates for this rule.

S: (2, 3). → (3, 4). → $(10\frac{1}{2}, 11\frac{1}{2})$. → (0.1, 1.1).

T: (Write *y is 5 times x* on the board.)

T: What would be another way to state this rule? Turn and talk.

S: Multiply *x* by 5 to get *y*. → *x* times 5 is *y*.

T: Give the coordinate pair for this rule, if *x* is 1.

S: (Show (1, 5).)

T: Give the coordinate pair for this rule, if *x* is 0.

MP.2   S: (0, 0).

T: Give another coordinate pair for a point on this line.

S: (2, 10). → $(9\frac{1}{5}, 46)$. → (0.3, 1.5).

T: Explain to your partner how you thought about your coordinate pair.

S: I just multiplied *x* by 5. → I picked the number 2 to be my *x*, multiplied it by 5, and got 10 for *y*. My coordinate pair is (2, 10).

NOTES ON MULTIPLE MEANS OF REPRESENTATION:

Support English language learners and others as they articulate coordinate pairs based on rules such as *y is 1 more than x*. In addition to providing extra response time, you may want to rephrase questions in multiple ways, either simplifying or elaborating.

Students working below grade level may benefit from scaffolds such as sentence frames to find *y* using the rule *y is 5 times x*. You might present *x* = __ , so *y* = 5 times ___ = 5 × __.

Continue the sequence with (d) *y is 1 more than 3 times x* and (e) *y is 1 less than 2 times x.*

Problem 2: Create coordinate pairs from rules and plot the points.

Line *a:* *y* is 2 more than *x.*

Line *b:* *y* is 2 times *x.*

Line *c:* *y* is 1 more than *x* doubled.

NOTES ON MULTIPLE MEANS OF REPRESENTATION:

Simplify and clarify the phrase *range of values* for English language learners and others. While it may not be necessary to present the multiple meanings for each word, you may want to define the term as used here, or express your request in another manner, such as, "What are the greatest and smallest values on the *x* - and *y*-axes?"

T: (Hand out coordinate plane template to students. Display the coordinate plane on the board. Write *Line a*: *y is 2 more than x* on the board.) Say the rule for line *a.*

S: *y* is 2 more than *x.*

Lesson 8:   Generate a number pattern from a given rule, and plot the points.
Date: 1/31/14

6.B.20

T: Record the rule in the chart for line *a*.

S: (Record rule.)

T: What range of values do our axes show?

S: Both the *x*- and *y*-axis show even numbers from 0 to 14.

T: What will you need to think about as you pick your values for *x*? Talk to your partner, and then generate your coordinate pairs.

S: We have to make sure we don't pick *x*'s that are bigger than 14. → Since all our *y*'s will be 2 more than our *x*'s, we can't have an *x* that is bigger than 12 if we want to be able to put it on this part of the plane. → I'm going to pick whole number *x*'s so that adding 2 and putting the points on the gridlines will be easy.

S: (Create points and share with partner.)

T: Plot the 3 points on your grid paper.

S: (Plot points.)

T: Use a straightedge to draw line *a*. (Draw line *a*)

S: (Draw line *a*.)

Repeat a similar sequence for lines *b* and *c*.

T: Show your lines to your neighbor.

S: (Share.)

T: Raise your hand if your neighbor generated the exact same points as you.

S: (Most, if not all, should keep hands down.)

T: Raise your hand if your neighbor's lines were the same as yours.

S: (All should raise their hands.)

T: How is it possible that we all have the same lines on our plane, and, yet, we all plotted different points? Turn and talk.

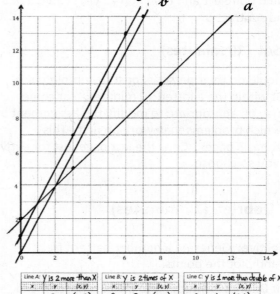

Line A: Y is 2 more than X			Line B: Y is 2 times of X			Line C: Y is 1 more than double of X		
x	y	(x, y)	x	y	(x, y)	x	y	(x, y)
0	2	(0,2)	0	0	(0,0)	0	1	(0,1)
3	5	(3,5)	4	8	(4,8)	3	7	(3,7)
8	10	(8,10)	7	14	(7,14)	6	13	(6,13)

S: The lines are all the same because we used the same rules to give the points. → There are a whole bunch of points on each line; we just picked a few of them to name. → We're doing the same operation to the *x*'s every time. So, no matter what numbers we put in, when we draw the line, they will have all the same lines drawn, which have all the same points.

T: Which lines appear to be parallel?

S: Lines *b* and *c*.

T: Do any of the lines intersect?

S: Yes. Line *a* intersects line *b*. → Line *a* intersects both lines *b* and *c*.

T: Line *a* intersects line *b*. What is the coordinate pair for the point at which these lines intersect?

S: (2, 4).

Lesson 8:   Generate a number pattern from a given rule, and plot the points.
Date: 1/31/14

6.B.21

T: Give the coordinate pair where a and c intersect.

S: (1, 3).

T: How can one coordinate pair follow more than one rule? Turn and talk.

S: In the point (2, 4), the y-coordinate is both 2 times greater than x, and it's 2 more than x, so it satisfies both rules. → With coordinates (1, 3), the y-coordinate is 2 more than x, so it's part of the rule y is 2 more than x; it's also 1 more than x doubled, so it's on that line, too! → There are lots of ways to get from 1 to 3. I can add two, or I could double 1 and then add 2. Or, I could add 5 and subtract 3.

Problem Set (10 minutes)

Students should do their personal best to complete the Problem Set within the allotted 10 minutes. For some classes, it may be appropriate to modify the assignment by specifying which problems they work on first. This Problem Set has 3 pages. Copy the last page just for early finishers if you so choose.

Student Debrief (10 minutes)

Lesson Objective: Generate a number pattern from a given rule, and plot the points.

The Student Debrief is intended to invite reflection and active processing of the total lesson experience.

Invite students to review their solutions for the Problem Set. They should check work by comparing answers with a partner before going over answers as a class. Look for misconceptions or misunderstandings that can be addressed in the Debrief. Guide students in a conversation to debrief the Problem Set and process the lesson.

You may choose to use any combination of the questions below to lead the discussion.

- How did you create the points for Problem 1? Explain to a partner.

- Share how you solved Problem 1(c) with a partner.

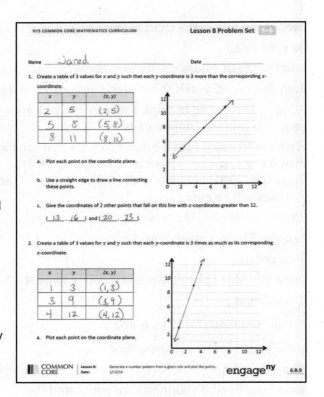

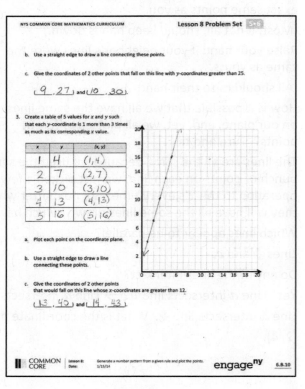

© 2014 Common Core, Inc. All rights reserved. commoncore.org

- How did you create the points for Problem 2? Explain to a partner.
- Share how you solved Problem 2(c) with a partner.
- How did you create the points for Problem 3? Explain to a partner.
- Share how you solved Problem 3(c) with a partner.
- Compare the three lines you drew for Problem 4. Do they look the same or different? Explain your thinking to a partner.
- (Note: Problem 4(d) should be viewed as a challenge and previews the work in G5–M6–Lesson 9.) In Problem 4(c), what did you notice about the two rules that created parallel lines? Share your solution to Problem 4(d) with a partner, and explain your thinking.

Exit Ticket (3 minutes)

After the Student Debrief, instruct students to complete the Exit Ticket. A review of their work will help you assess the students' understanding of the concepts that were presented in the lesson today and plan more effectively for future lessons. You may read the questions aloud to the students.

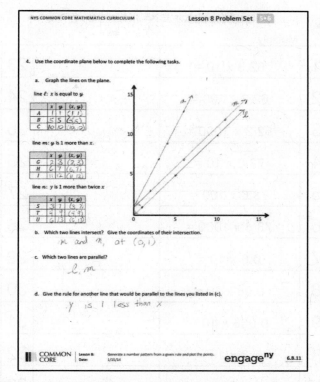

COMMON CORE™

Lesson 8: Generate a number pattern from a given rule, and plot the points.
Date: 1/31/14

6.B.23

© 2014 Common Core, Inc. All rights reserved. commoncore.org

A

Correct _____

Multiply.

1	62.3 x 10 =		23	4.1 x 1000 =	
2	62.3 x 100 =		24	7.6 x 1000 =	
3	62.3 x 1000 =		25	0.01 x 1000 =	
4	73.6 x 10 =		26	0.07 x 1000 =	
5	73.6 x 100 =		27	0.072 x 100 =	
6	73.6 x 1000 =		28	0.802 x 10 =	
7	0.6 x 10 =		29	0.019 x 1000 =	
8	0.06 x 10 =		30	7.412 x 1000 =	
9	0.006 x 10 =		31	6.8 x 100 =	
10	0.3 x 10 =		32	4.901 x 10 =	
11	0.3 x 100 =		33	16.07 x 100 =	
12	0.3 x 1000 =		34	9.19 x 10 =	
13	0.02 x 10 =		35	18.2 x 100 =	
14	0.02 x 100 =		36	14.7 x 1000 =	
15	0.02 x 1000 =		37	2.021 x 100 =	
16	0.008 x 10 =		38	172.1 x 10 =	
17	0.008 x 100 =		39	3.2 x 20 =	
18	0.008 x 1000 =		40	4.1 x 20 =	
19	0.32 x 10 =		41	3.2 x 30 =	
20	0.67 x 10 =		42	1.3 x 30 =	
21	0.91 x 100 =		43	3.12 x 40 =	
22	0.74 x 100 =		44	14.12 x 40 =	

COMMON CORE™

Lesson 8:   Generate a number pattern from a given rule, and plot the points.
Date: 1/31/14

6.B.24

B

Multiply.

Improvement _____   # Correct _____

#	Problem		#	Problem	
1	46.1 x 10 =		23	5.2 x 1000 =	
2	46.1 x 100 =		24	8.7 x 1000 =	
3	46.1 x 1000 =		25	0.01 x 1000 =	
4	89.2 x 10 =		26	0.08 x 1000 =	
5	89.2 x 100 =		27	0.083 x 10 =	
6	89.2 x 1000 =		28	0.903 x 10 =	
7	0.3 x 10 =		29	0.017 x 1000 =	
8	0.03 x 10 =		30	8.523 x 1000 =	
9	0.003 x 10 =		31	7.9 x 100 =	
10	0.9 x 10 =		32	5.802 x 10 =	
11	0.9 x 100 =		33	27.08 x 100 =	
12	0.9 x 1000 =		34	8.18 x 10 =	
13	0.04 x 10 =		35	29.3 x 100 =	
14	0.04 x 100 =		36	25.8 x 1000 =	
15	0.04 x 1000 =		37	3.032 x 100 =	
16	0.007 x 10 =		38	283.1 x 10 =	
17	0.007 x 100 =		39	2.1 x 20 =	
18	0.007 x 1000 =		40	3.3 x 20 =	
19	0.45 x 10 =		41	3.1 x 30 =	
20	0.78 x 10 =		42	1.2 x 30 =	
21	0.28 x 100 =		43	2.11 x 40 =	
22	0.19 x 100 =		44	13.11 x 40 =	

COMMON CORE

Lesson 8: Generate a number pattern from a given rule, and plot the points.
Date: 1/31/14

6.B.25

Name _____   Date _____

1. Create a table of 3 values for x and y such that each y-coordinate is 3 more than the corresponding x-coordinate.

x	y	(x, y)

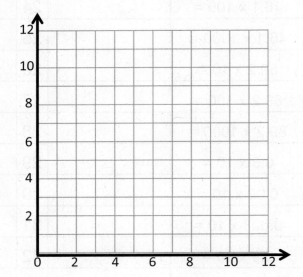

a. Plot each point on the coordinate plane.

b. Use a straightedge to draw a line connecting these points.

c. Give the coordinates of 2 other points that fall on this line with x-coordinates greater than 12.

(_____ , _____) and (_____ , _____).

2. Create a table of 3 values for x and y such that each y-coordinate is 3 times as much as its corresponding x-coordinate.

x	y	(x, y)

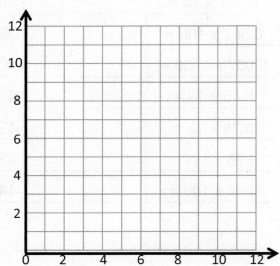

a. Plot each point on the coordinate plane.

b. Use a straightedge to draw a line connecting these points.

c. Give the coordinates of 2 other points that fall on this line with y-coordinates greater than 25.

(_____ , _____) and (_____ , _____).

3. Create a table of 5 values for x and y such that each y-coordinate is 1 more than 3 times as much as its corresponding x value.

x	y	(x, y)

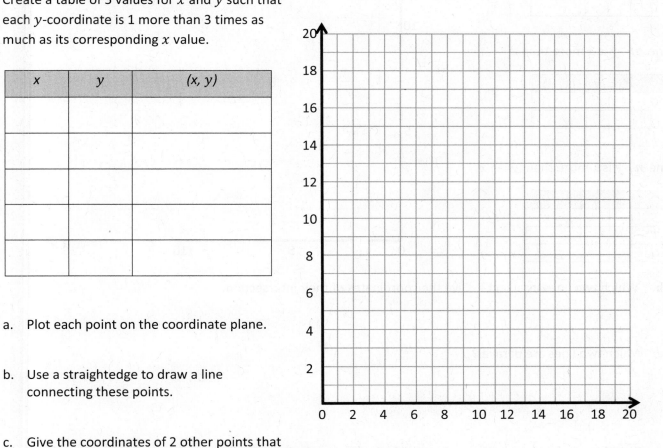

a. Plot each point on the coordinate plane.

b. Use a straightedge to draw a line connecting these points.

c. Give the coordinates of 2 other points that would fall on this line whose x-coordinates are greater than 12.

(_____ , _____) and (_____ , _____).

4. Use the coordinate plane below to complete the following tasks.

a. Graph the lines on the plane.

line ℓ: x is equal to y

	x	y	(x, y)
A			
B			
C			

line m: y is 1 more than x

	x	y	(x, y)
G			
H			
I			

line n: y is 1 more than twice x

	x	y	(x, y)
S			
T			
U			

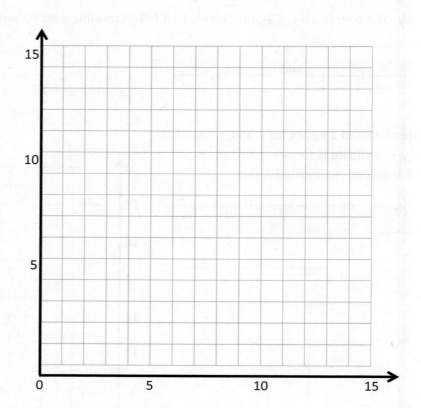

b. Which two lines intersect? Give the coordinates of their intersection.

c. Which two lines are parallel?

d. Give the rule for another line that would be parallel to the lines you listed in (c).

COMMON CORE™

Lesson 8: Generate a number pattern from a given rule, and plot the points.
Date: 1/31/14

6.B.28

Name _____   Date _____

1. Complete this table with values for x and y such that each y-coordinate is 5 more than 2 times as much

    as its corresponding x-coordinate.

x	y	(x, y)
0		
2		
3.5		

a. Plot each point on the coordinate plane.

b. Use a straightedge to draw a line connecting
    these points.

c. Name 2 other points that fall on this line with
    y-coordinates greater than 25.

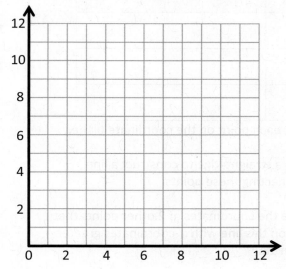

Name _____   Date _____

1. Complete this table such that each y-coordinate is 4 more than the corresponding x-coordinate.

x	y	(x, y)

a. Plot each point on the coordinate plane.

b. Use a straightedge to construct a line connecting these points.

c. Give the coordinates of 2 other points that fall on this line with x-coordinates greater than 18.

(_____ , _____) and (_____ , _____).

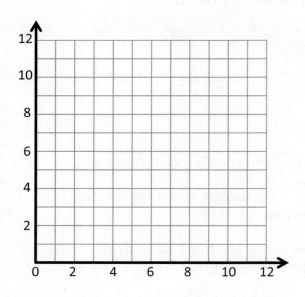

2. Complete this table such that each y-coordinate is 2 times as much as its corresponding x-coordinate.

x	y	(x, y)

a. Plot each point on the coordinate plane.

b. Use a straightedge to draw a line connecting these points.

c. Give the coordinates of 2 other points that fall on this line with y-coordinates greater than 25.

(_____ , _____) and (_____ , _____).

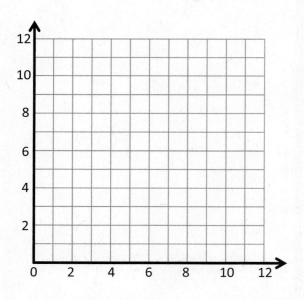

3. Use the coordinate plane below to complete the following tasks.
   a. Graph these lines on the plane.

   line ℓ: x is equal to y

	x	y	(x, y)
A			
B			
C			

   line **m**: y is 1 less than x

	x	y	(x, y)
G			
H			
I			

   line **n**: y is 1 less than twice x

	x	y	(x, y)
S			
T			
U			

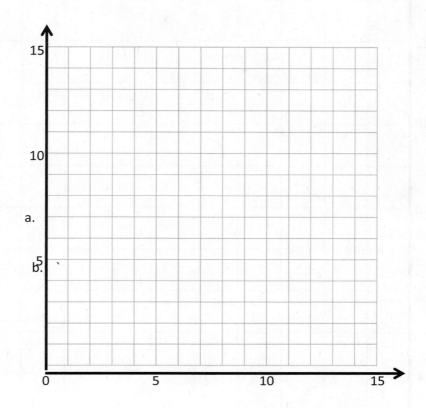

   b. Do any of these lines intersect? If yes, identify which ones, and give the coordinates of their intersection.

   c. Are any of these lines parallel? If yes, identify which ones.

   d. Give the rule for another line that would be parallel to the lines you listed in (c).

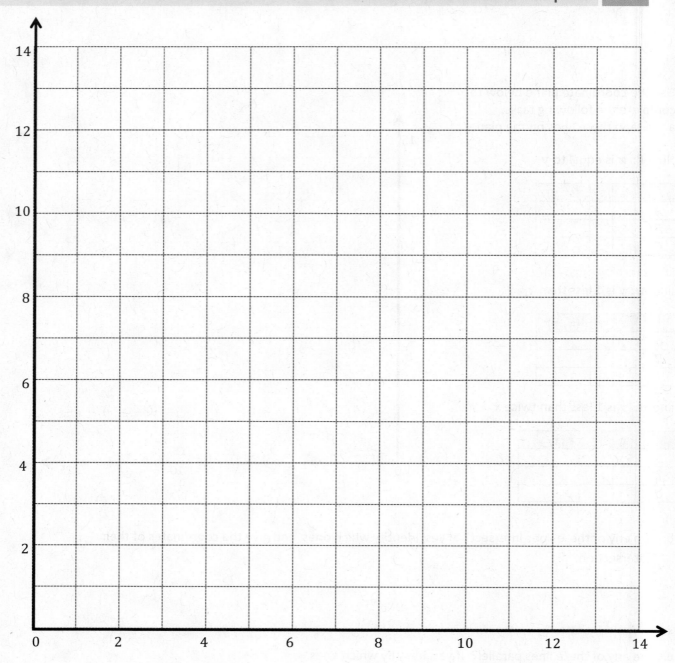

Line *a*:		
x	*y*	*(x, y)*

Line *b*:		
x	*y*	*(x, y)*

Line *c*:		
x	*y*	*(x, y)*

Lesson 9

Objective: Generate two number patterns from given rules, plot the points, and analyze the patterns.

Suggested Lesson Structure

■ Fluency Practice   (12 minutes)
■ Application Problem   (5 minutes)
■ Concept Development   (33 minutes)
■ Student Debrief   (10 minutes)
  Total Time   **(60 minutes)**

Fluency Practice (12 minutes)

■ Round to the Nearest One **5.NBT.4**   (4 minutes)
■ Add and Subtract Decimals **5.NBT.7**   (5 minutes)
■ Plot Points on a Coordinate Grid **5.G.1**   (3 minutes)

Round to the Nearest One (4 minutes)

Materials: (S) Personal white boards

Note: This fluency activity reviews G5–Module 1 concepts.

  T: (Write 4 ones 1 tenth.) Write 4 ones and 1 tenth as a decimal.
  S: (Write 4.1.)
  T: (Write 4.1 ≈ __.) Round 4 and 1 tenth to the nearest whole number.
  S: (Write 4.1 ≈ 4.)

Continue the process for 4.9, 14.9, 3.4, 23.4, 2.5, 32.5, 5.17, 8.76, and 17.51.

Add and Subtract Decimals (5 minutes)

Materials: (S) Personal white boards

Note: This fluency activity reviews G5–Module 1 concepts.

  T: (Write 5 + 1.) Say the answer.
  S: 6.
  T: 5 tenths + 1 tenth?

Lesson 9:   Generate two number patterns from given rules, plot the points, and
            analyze the patterns.
Date: 1/31/14   6.B.33

S: 6 tenths.

T: 5 hundredths + 1 hundredth?

S: 6 hundredths.

T: 5 thousandths + 1 thousandth?

S: 6 thousandths.

Continue the process with 5 – 1, 5 tenths – 1 tenth, 5 hundredths – 1 hundredth, and 5 thousandths – 1 thousandth.

T: (Write 4 + 1.) Write the number sentence.

S: (Write 4 + 1 = 5.)

T: (Write 4.8 + 1.) Write the number sentence.

S: (Write 4.8 + 1 = 5.8.)

Continue the process with 4.8 – 1, 4.83 + 1, 4.83 – 1, 0.6 + 0.2, 0.6 – 0.2, 0.63 + 0.2, 0.63 – 0.2, 0.638 + 0.2, 0.638 – 0.2, 1.746 + 0.02, 1.746 – 0.02, 3.456 + 0.003, and 3.456 – 0.003.

Plot Points on a Coordinate Grid (3 minutes)

Materials: (S) Personal white board with coordinate grid insert

Note: This fluency activity reviews G5–M6–Lesson 8.

T: Label the x- and y-axes.

S: (Label x- and y-axes.)

T: Label the origin.

S: (Write 0 at the origin.)

T: Along both axes, label every other grid line, counting by two's to 12.

S: (Label 2, 4, 6, 8, 10, and 12 along each axis.)

T: (Write (0, 2).) Plot the point on your coordinate grid.

S: (Plot point at (0, 2).)

Continue the process for the following possible sequence: (1, 4), (2, 6), (3, 8), and (4, 10).

T: Draw a line to connect these points.

S: (Draw line.)

T: Plot the points that fall on this line when x is 5 and when x is 6.

S: (Write (5, 12) and (6, 14).)

T: Erase your board. (Write (0, 0).) Plot the point on your coordinate grid.

S: (Plot point at the origin.)

Continue the process for (1, 1) and (2, 2).

T: Draw a line to connect these points.

T: Write 2 coordinate pairs for points that fall on this line whose x-coordinates are larger than 12.

S: (Write 2 coordinates with the same digit for x and y that is larger than 12.)

Lesson 9:   Generate two number patterns from given rules, plot the points, and
analyze the patterns.

Date: 1/31/14

6.B.34

Application Problem (5 minutes)

Maggie spent $46.20 to buy pencil sharpeners for her gift shop. If each pencil sharpener cost 60 cents, how many pencil sharpeners did she buy? Solve by using the standard algorithm.

Note: This Application Problem looks back to G5–Module 4 to review division of decimal numbers.

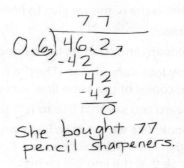

$$0.6\overline{)46.2}$$

```
        77
0.6)46.2
   -42
    42
   -42
     0
```

She bought 77 pencil sharpeners.

Concept Development (33 minutes)

Materials: (S) Coordinate plane template, straightedge

Problem 1: Graph two lines described by addition rules on the same coordinate plane, and compare/contrast them.

T: (Display chart for line ℓ on board. Distribute 1 coordinate plane template for each student.) Say the rule that describes line ℓ.

S: y is 2 more than x.

T: When x is 1, what is the y-coordinate if I apply the rule?

S: (Show (1 3).)

T: (Record on board.) Tell your partner how you generated this ordered pair.

S: The rule says, "y is 2 more than x," so if x is 1, y must be 3 because 3 is 2 more than 1. → I just added 2 to 1 and got 3 as the y-coordinate.

T: Complete the chart for the remaining values of x.

S: (Generate coordinate pairs.)

T: Plot each point on the plane, then use your straightedge to draw line ℓ.

S: (Plot and construct.)

T: Show your work to a neighbor and check to make sure line ℓ is drawn correctly.

S: (Share and check work. While students share, teacher constructs line ℓ on board.)

Repeat the sequence for m.

T: Look at lines ℓ and m. Do they intersect?

S: No.

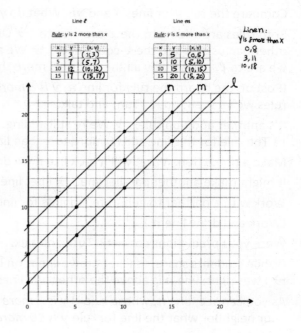

Line ℓ

Rule: y is 2 more than x

x	y	(x, y)
1	3	(1,3)
5	7	(5,7)
10	12	(10,12)
15	17	(15,17)

Line m

Rule: y is 5 more than x

x	y	(x, y)
0	5	(0,5)
5	10	(5,10)
10	15	(10,15)
15	20	(15, 20)

Line n:
y is 8 more than x
0,8
3, 11
10,18

NOTES ON MULTIPLE MEANS OF REPRESENTATION:

Use color to enhance learners' perception of the grid, pairs, and lines. You may want to present lines $l, m,$ and n in three different colors. It may be helpful to pick a consistent color for the numbers on the x- and y-axes and coordinate pairs. If students with visual impairments and others find plotting points challenging, you may want to magnify the grid, or use the Graphic Aid for Mathematics.

Lesson 9:	Generate two number patterns from given rules, plot the points, and analyze the patterns.	**6.B.35**
Date:	1/31/14	

T: What is the name we give to lines that do not intersect?

S: Parallel.

T: Compare and contrast lines ℓ and *m*. What do you notice about each line?

S: They look very similar. They're parallel, so they look like they go up at the same angle. → They look like copies of the same line, except line *m* is farther up than line ℓ.

T: I heard you say that line *m* is "farther up" than line ℓ. Farther up from what? Turn and talk.

S: It looks like we can take line ℓ and shift it up a bit to get the other one. → Each point is a little higher than the points on line ℓ. → The rule for line *m* is to add 5 to each x-coordinate; so, it makes sense that the line will be higher up than line ℓ, because line ℓ's rule is to only add 2. → All the y-coordinates on line *m* are 3 units above all the y-coordinates on line ℓ with the same x-coordinates.

T: Compare the rules for lines ℓ and *m*. What do you notice?

S: Both rules are adding to the x-coordinate. → One rule had us add 2 to the x-coordinate, and the other had us add 5 to the x-coordinate. → We are adding 3 more to the x-coordinates in *m* than we are to ℓ. That's why all the y's are 3 more than the y's on ℓ!

T: (Post on the board the rule for line *n*, *y is 8 more than x*.) Compare the rule for line *n* to the other rules we've seen today. Turn and talk.

S: It's another addition rule. → We're still adding, but this time we have to add 8 to the x-coordinate. → The rule for this line adds 6 more to x than line ℓ and 3 more to x than line *m*.

T: Make a prediction. What will it look like if we draw line *n* on this plane? Turn and talk.

S: It might make another parallel line. → I bet line *n* will be above the other two on the plane.

T: Work with a partner to generate 3 points for line *n*; then, draw it on the plane.

S: (Work and draw line *n*.)

T: Were your predictions correct? Turn and talk.

S: (While students share, teacher draws line *n* on board.) Yes, line *n* is parallel to the other two lines. → I was right; line *n* is above the other two lines.

T: As you can see, line *n*, whose rule is *y is 8 more than x* creates another parallel line. Tell and show your neighbor what the line for rule *y is 10 more than x* would look like.

S: (Share.)

T: The line for rule *y is 10 more than x* would again be parallel, and its y-coordinates would be greater than those for the same x-coordinates in the other lines. (Drag your finger across the plane to show the approximate location of this line.)

Problem 2: Graph 2 lines described by multiplication rules on the same coordinate plane, and compare and contrast them.

T: (Display chart for line *p* on board.) Say the rule for line *p*.

S: y is x times 2.

T: When x is 2, what is the y-coordinate if I apply the rule?

S: (Show (2, 4).)

T: (Record on board.) Tell your partner how you generated this ordered pair.

S: The rule says, "y is x times 2"; so, if x is 2, y must be 4, because 2 times 2 is 4. → I just multiplied 2

Lesson 9: Generate two number patterns from given rules, plot the points, and analyze the patterns.

Date: 1/31/14

6.B.36

times 2 and got 4 as the y-coordinate.

T: Great! Complete the chart for x-values of 0, 1, 3, and 4.

S: (Generate coordinate pairs.)

T: Plot each coordinate pair on the plane, then use your straightedge to draw line **p**.

S: (Plot and draw.)

T: Show your work to a neighbor, and check to make sure line **p** is drawn correctly.

S: (Share and check work. While students share, teacher draws line **p** on board.)

Follow a similar sequence for line **q**.

T: Compare and contrast the rules for lines **p** and **q**. Turn and talk.

S: They are both multiplication rules. → They're a little different cause **p** is multiplied by 2 and **q** is multiplied by 3.

T: Do lines **p** and **q** intersect?

S: Yes.

T: At what location do they intersect?

S: At (0, 0). → At the origin.

T: Compare lines **p** and **q** in terms of their steepness. What do you notice? Turn and talk.

S: They both seem to start at the origin, but then line **q** starts going up really quickly. It's steeper than line **p**. → Line **p** goes up more gradually than line **q**. Line **p** is less steep.

T: You noticed that line **q** is steeper than line **p**. Look again at the rules for these lines and at the coordinate pairs that you generated for each line. Can you explain why line **q** is steeper than line **p**? Turn and talk.

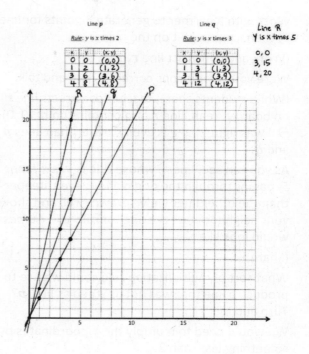

NOTES ON
MULTIPLE MEANS OF
REPRESENTATION:

Clarify math language for English language learners so that they may confidently explore and discuss lines on the coordinate plane. Define *steep* and *steepness*. Offer explanations in students' first language, if possible. Link the vocabulary to their experiences, such as walking a *steep* hill or paying a *steep* price.

S: We used all the same values for the x-coordinates, but we multiplied them by different numbers to get the y-coordinate. → I think line **q** is steeper because we tripled the x-coordinate, rather than doubling it as we did in line **p**. So, the y-coordinate gets higher faster when you triple it.

T: (Post the rule for line **r**, y is x times 5 on the board.) Compare the rule for line **r** to the rules for lines **p** and **q**. Turn and talk.

S: It's another multiplication rule. → We're still multiplying, but this time we have to quintuple the x-coordinate.

T: Make a prediction. What will it look like if we drew line **r** on this plane? Turn and talk.

S: I think it's going to start at the origin again. → I bet line **r** will be even steeper than the other two.

Lesson 9: Generate two number patterns from given rules, plot the points, and analyze the patterns.

Date: 1/31/14

6.B.37

T: Work with a partner to generate 3 points for line *r*; then, construct it on the plane.

S: (Work and construct line *r*.)

T: Were your predictions correct? Turn and talk.

S: (While students share, teacher constructs line *r* on board.) Yeah, line *r* also contains point (0, 0). → I was right; line *r* is even steeper than lines *p* and *q*.

MP.7

T: As you can see, line *r*, whose rule is *y is x times 5*, passes through the origin and is even steeper than the other lines we've drawn. Tell and show your neighbor what the line for rule *y is x times 6* would look like.

S: (Share.)

T: What sort of multiplication rule could we use to produce a line that was not as steep as line *p*? Turn and talk.

S: We would need to multiply the *x*-coordinates by something less than 2.

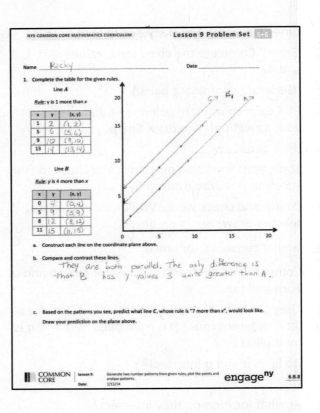

Problem Set (10 minutes)

Students should do their personal best to complete the Problem Set within the allotted 10 minutes. For some classes, it may be appropriate to modify the assignment by specifying which problems they work on first. Some problems do not specify a method for solving. Students solve these problems using the RDW approach used for Application Problems.

Student Debrief (10 minutes)

Lesson Objective: Generate two number patterns from given rules, plot the points, and analyze the patterns.

The Student Debrief is intended to invite reflection and active processing of the total lesson experience.

Invite students to review their solutions for the Problem Set. They should check work by comparing answers with a partner before going over answers as a class. Look for misconceptions or misunderstandings that can be addressed in the Debrief. Guide students in a conversation to debrief the Problem Set and process the lesson.

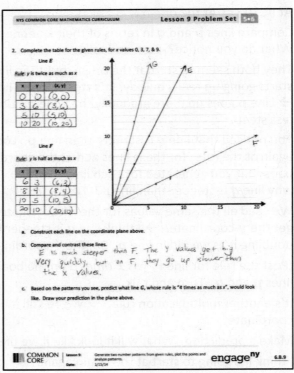

COMMON CORE

Lesson 9:
Date:

Generate two number patterns from given rules, plot the points, and analyze the patterns.
1/31/14

6.B.38

You may choose to use any combination of the questions below to lead the discussion.

- What pattern did you notice between lines *a* and *b*?
- If you could have chosen any values for x when generating points for line f, what would you have chosen? Why? What if the rule were, *y is one-third as much as x*?
- Explain to your partner how you made your predictions for Problems 1(c) and 2(c).
- Based on the patterns you saw in Problem 1, predict what the line for the rule, *y is 2 less than x* would look like. Use your finger to show your neighbor where you think the line would be.
- Compare the lines generated by addition and multiplication, for example $x + 2$ and $2x$. What effect does adding 2 to x have as compared to multiplying x by 2?

Exit Ticket (3 minutes)

After the Student Debrief, instruct students to complete the Exit Ticket. A review of their work will help you assess the students' understanding of the concepts that were presented in the lesson today and plan more effectively for future lessons. You may read the questions aloud to the students.

COMMON CORE™

Lesson 9: Generate two number patterns from given rules, plot the points, and analyze the patterns.
Date: 1/31/14

6.B.39

Name _____   Date _____

1. Complete the table for the given rules.

Line *a*

Rule: *y is 1 more than x*

x	y	(x, y)
1		
5		
9		
13		

Line *b*

Rule: *y is 4 more than x*

z	y	(x, y)
0		
5		
8		
11		

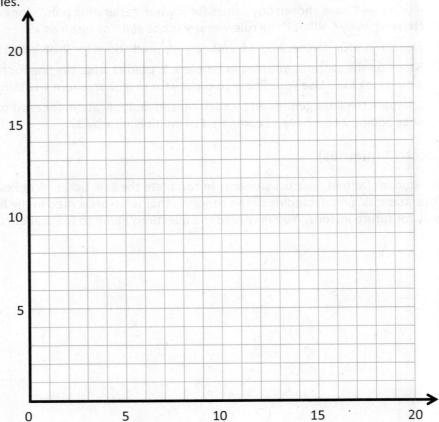

a. Construct each line on the coordinate plane above.

b. Compare and contrast these lines.

c. Based on the patterns you see, predict what line *c*, whose rule is *7 more than x*, would look like.

Draw your prediction on the plane above.

COMMON CORE   Lesson 9:   Generate two number patterns from given rules, plot the points, and analyze the patterns.   6.B.40

Date: 1/31/14

2.   Complete the table for the given rules for x values 0, 3, 7, and 9.

Line **e**

Rule: y is twice as much as x

x	y	(x, y)

Line **f**

Rule: y is half as much as x

x	y	(x, y)

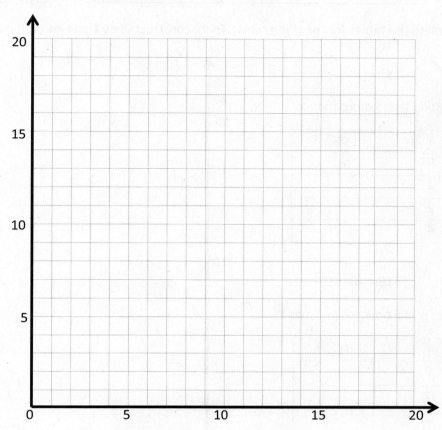

a.   Construct each line on the coordinate plane above.

b.   Compare and contrast these lines.

c.   Based on the patterns you see, predict what line **g,** whose rule is *4 times as much as x*, would look like. Draw your prediction in the plane above.

Name _____ Date _____

Complete the tables for the given rules. Then, construct lines ℓ and m on the coordinate plane.

Line ℓ

Rule: y is 5 more than x

x	y	(x, y)
0		
1		
2		
4		

Line m

Rule: y is 5 times as much as x

x	y	(x, y)
0		
1		
2		
4		

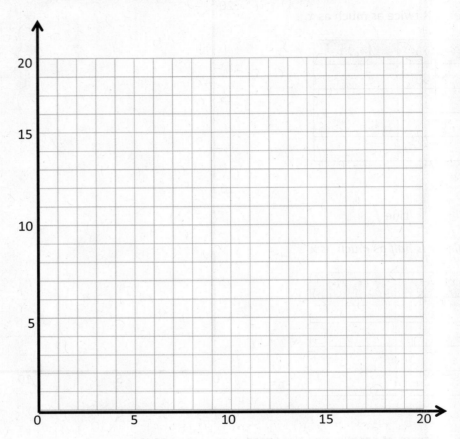

COMMON CORE™

Lesson 9: Generate two number patterns from given rules, plot the points, and analyze the patterns.

Date: 1/31/14

6.B.42

© 2014 Common Core, Inc. All rights reserved. commoncore.org

Name _____   Date _____

1. Complete the table for the given rules.

Line **a**

Rule: y is 1 less than x

x	y	(x, y)
1		
4		
9		
16		

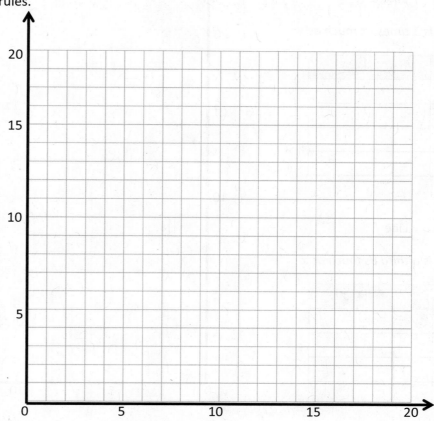

Line **b**

Rule: y is 5 less than x

x	y	(x, y)
5		
8		
14		
20		

a. Construct each line on the coordinate plane.

b. Compare and contrast these lines.

c. Based on the patterns you see, predict what line **c**, whose rule is *7 less than x*, would look like. Draw your prediction on the plane above.

COMMON CORE™

Lesson 9:   Generate two number patterns from given rules, plot the points, and
analyze the patterns.
Date: 1/31/14

6.B.43

2. Complete the table for the given rules for x values 0, 3, 4, and 6.

Line ***e***

Rule: *y is 3 times as much as x*

x	y	(x, y)

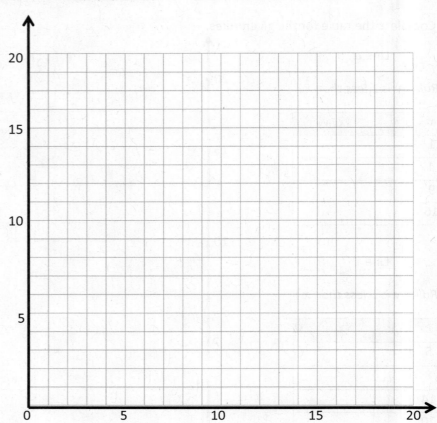

Line ***f***

Rule: *y is a third as much as x*

x	y	(x, y)

a. Construct each line on the coordinate plane.

b. Compare and contrast these lines.

c. Based on the patterns you see, predict what line ***g***, whose rule is *4 times as much as x*, and line ***h***, whose rule is one-fourth as much as x, would look like. Draw your prediction in the plane above.

COMMON CORE

Lesson 9:   Generate two number patterns from given rules, plot the points, and
              analyze the patterns.
Date: 1/31/14

6.B.44

Name _____   Date _____

Line *ℓ*

Rule: *y is 2 more than x*

x	y	(x, y)
1		
5		
10		
15		

Line *m*

Rule: *y is 5 more than x*

x	y	(x, y)
0		
5		
10		
15		

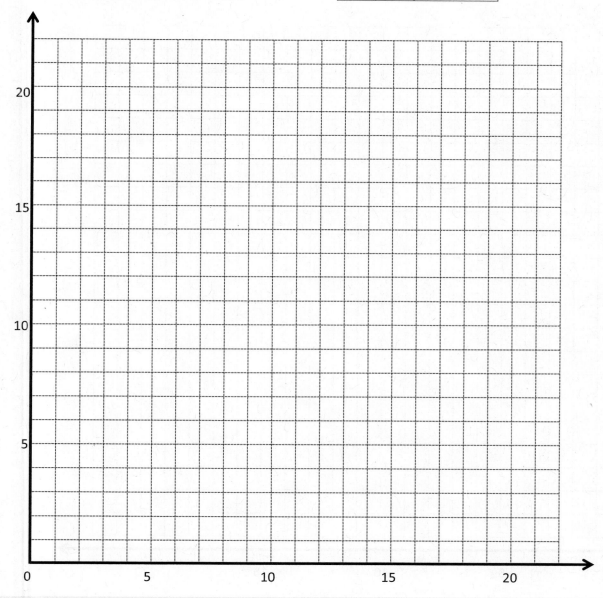

COMMON CORE™

Lesson 9: Generate two number patterns from given rules, plot the points, and analyze the patterns.

Date: 1/31/14

6.B.45

Line **p**

Rule: *y is x times 2*

x	y	(x, y)

Line **q**

Rule: *y is x times 3*

x	y	(x, y)

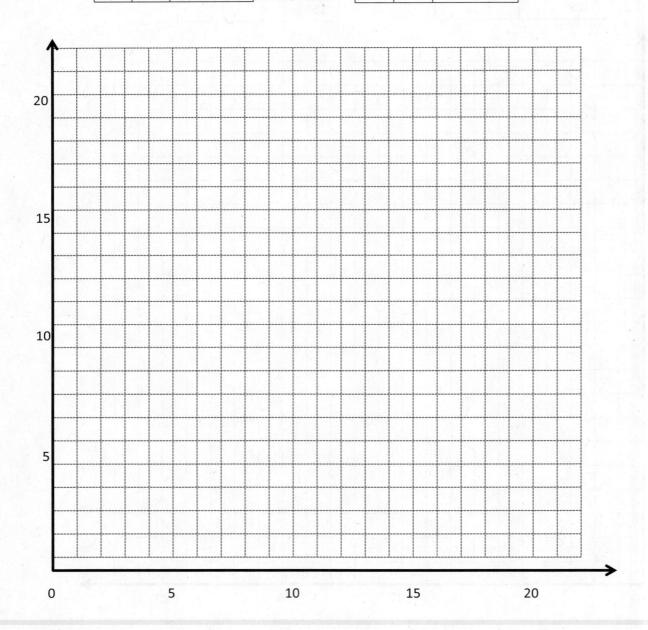

COMMON CORE™ | **Lesson 9:** Generate two number patterns from given rules, plot the points, and analyze the patterns.

Date: 1/31/14

6.B.46

Lesson 10

Objective: Compare the lines and patterns generated by addition rules and multiplication rules.

Suggested Lesson Structure

■ Fluency Practice   (12 minutes)
■ Application Problem   (6 minutes)
□ Concept Development   (32 minutes)
■ Student Debrief   (10 minutes)
   Total Time   **(60 minutes)**

Fluency Practice (12 minutes)

- Count by Equivalent Fractions **4.NF.1**   (4 minutes)
- Round to the Nearest One **5.NBT.4**   (4 minutes)
- Add and Subtract Decimals **5.NBT.7**   (4 minutes)

Count by Equivalent Fractions (4 minutes)

Note: This fluency activity prepares students for G5–M6–Lesson 11.

T: Count by ones to 9, starting at 0.
S: 0, 1, 2, 3, 4, 5, 6, 7, 8, 9.

$\frac{0}{3}$	$\frac{1}{3}$	$\frac{2}{3}$	$\frac{3}{3}$	$\frac{4}{3}$	$\frac{5}{3}$	$\frac{6}{3}$	$\frac{7}{3}$	$\frac{8}{3}$	$\frac{9}{3}$
$\frac{0}{3}$	$\frac{1}{3}$	$\frac{2}{3}$	1	$\frac{4}{3}$	$\frac{5}{3}$	2	$\frac{7}{3}$	$\frac{8}{3}$	3
$\frac{0}{3}$	$\frac{1}{3}$	$\frac{2}{3}$	1	$1\frac{1}{3}$	$1\frac{2}{3}$	2	$2\frac{1}{3}$	$2\frac{2}{3}$	3

T: Count by thirds from 0 thirds to 9 thirds. (Write as students count.)
S: $\frac{0}{3}, \frac{1}{3}, \frac{2}{3}, \frac{3}{3}, \frac{4}{3}, \frac{5}{3}, \frac{6}{3}, \frac{7}{3}, \frac{8}{3}, \frac{9}{3}.$
T: 1 is the same as how many thirds?
S: 3 thirds.
T: (Beneath $\frac{3}{3}$, write 1.) 2 is the same as how many thirds?
S: 6 thirds.

Lesson 10:   Compare with lines and patterns generated by addition rules and
              multiplication rules.
Date: 1/31/14

6.B.47

T: (Beneath $\frac{6}{3}$, write 2.)

Continue the process for 3.

T: Count by thirds again. This time, when you come to the whole number, say it. (Write as students count.)

S: $0, \frac{1}{3}, \frac{2}{3}, 1, \frac{4}{3}, \frac{5}{3}, 2, \frac{7}{3}, \frac{8}{3}, 3.$

T: (Point to $\frac{4}{3}$.) Say 4 thirds as a mixed number.

S: $1\frac{1}{3}$.

Continue the process for $\frac{5}{3}, \frac{7}{3}$, and $\frac{8}{3}$.

T: Count by thirds again. This time, convert to ones and mixed numbers. (Write as students count.)

S: $0, \frac{1}{3}, \frac{2}{3}, 1, 1\frac{1}{3}, 1\frac{2}{3}, 2, 2\frac{1}{3}, 2\frac{2}{3}, 3.$

T: Let's count by thirds again. This time, after saying 1, alternate between mixed numbers and improper fractions.

S: $\frac{0}{3}, \frac{1}{3}, \frac{2}{3}, 1, 1\frac{1}{3}, \frac{5}{3}, 2, 2\frac{1}{3}, \frac{8}{3}, 3.$

T: 3 is the same as how many thirds?

S: 9 thirds.

T: Let's count backwards alternating between fractions and mixed numbers. Start at $\frac{9}{3}$.

S: $\frac{9}{3}, 2\frac{2}{3}, \frac{7}{3}, 2, 1\frac{2}{3}, \frac{4}{3}, 1, \frac{2}{3}, \frac{1}{3}, \frac{0}{3}.$

NOTES ON MULTIPLE MEANS OF REPRESENTATION:

The Count by Equivalent Fractions fluency activity supports language acquisition for English language learners, as it offers valuable practice speaking fraction names, such as *thirds*. Couple the counting with prepared visuals to increase comprehension. Some learners may benefit from counting again and again until they gain fluency.

Round to the Nearest One (4 minutes)

Materials: (S) Personal white boards

Note: This fluency activity reviews G5–Module 1 concepts.

T: (Write 3 ones 2 tenths.) Write 3 ones and 2 tenths as a decimal.

S: (Write 3.2.)

T: (Write 3.2 ≈ __.) Round 3 and 2 tenths to the nearest whole number.

S: (Write 3.2 ≈ 3.)

Continue the process for 3.7, 13.7, 5.4, 25.4, 1.5, 21.5, 6.48, 3.62, and 36.52.

Add and Subtract Decimals (4 minutes)

Materials: (S) Personal white boards

Note: This fluency activity reviews G5–Module 1 concepts.

T: (Write 3.812 + 1.) Complete the number sentence.

Lesson 10:	Compare with lines and patterns generated by addition rules and multiplication rules.	
Date:	1/31/14	**6.B.48**

S: (Write 3.812 + 1 = 4.812.)

T: (Write 3.812 – 1.) Complete the number sentence.

S: (Write 3.812 – 1 = 2.812.)

Continue the process with 3.812 – 0.1, 3.812 + 0.1, 2.764 + 0.02, 2.764 – 0.02, 5.015 – 0.003, 5.015 + 0.003, and 8.426 – 0.006.

Application Problem (6 minutes)

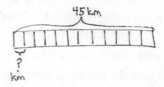

A 12-man relay team runs a 45 km race. Each member of the team runs an equal distance. How many kilometers does each team member run? One lap around the track is 0.75 km. How many laps does each team member run during the race?

Note: This Application Problem reviews several concepts explored earlier in the year, including division and measurement.

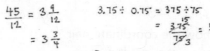

Concept Development (32 minutes)

Materials: (S) Personal white board, coordinate plane template, straightedge, set square or right angle template

Problem 1: Compare the lines and patterns generated by addition and subtraction rules.

T: (Distribute 1 coordinate plane template to each student. Display coordinate plane on board.) Say the rule for line p.

S: *y is the same as x.* → *x is equal to y.*

T: What point on this line has an *x*- coordinate of 3?

S: (Show (3, 3).)

T: Complete the chart for line ***p***.

S: (Complete chart.)

T: Can you find another way to name the rule for line ***p***? Turn and talk.

S: We could call it *y is equal to x.* → The rule could also be *y is x times 1.*

T: Plot each coordinate pair on the plane and then use your straight edge to construct line ***p***.

S: (As students work, construct line ***p*** on board.)

T: What do you notice about line ***p***, whose rule is *y is equal to x*? Turn and talk.

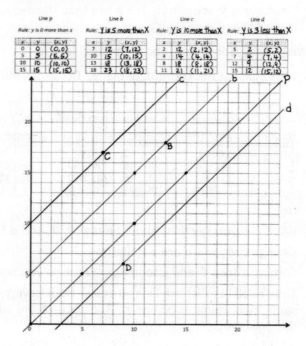

COMMON CORE™

Lesson 10:   Compare with lines and patterns generated by addition rules and multiplication rules.

Date: 1/31/14

6.B.49

S: It cuts the plane into 2 pieces. → It passes right through the origin.

T: On your plane, plot B at the following location. (Show B (13, 18) on board and plot B.)

S: (Plot B.)

T: On the coordinate plane, use your straight edge and set square to construct line *b* so that it's parallel to line *p* and contains point B. Check your work with a neighbor when you're finished.

S: (Work and check. Construct line *b* on board.)

T: Look at line *b*. (Point to location (10, 15) on board.) When x is 10, what is the y-coordinate?

S: 15.

T: Show the coordinate pair.

S: (Show (10, 15).)

T: Record the missing y-coordinates in the chart for line *b*. Share your work with a neighbor when you're finished.

S: (Record and share.)

T: What pattern do you notice in the coordinate pairs for line *b*? Turn and talk.

S: Every y-coordinate is 5 more than the x-coordinate. → If I add 5 to every x- value, I get the y-value.

MP.7 T: Work with a neighbor to identify the rule for line *b*. Show me the rule on your personal board.

S: (Show rule *y is 5 more than x*. → *x plus 5 is y*.)

T: Since every y-coordinate is 5 more than the x-coordinate, the rule for line *b* is, *y is 5 more than x*. Record the rule on your chart.

Repeat the process for lines *c*, and *d* as possible.

T: Look again at the coordinate plane. Do any of our lines intersect?

Line p		
Rule: y is 0 more than x		
x	y	(x, y)
0	0	(0,0)
5	5	(5,5)
10	10	(10,10)
15	15	(15,15)

Line b		
Rule: Y is 5 more than X		
x	y	(x, y)
7	12	(7,12)
10	15	(10,15)
13	18	(13,18)
18	23	(18,23)

Line c		
Rule: Y is 10 more than X		
x	y	(x, y)
2	12	(2,12)
4	14	(4,14)
8	18	(8,18)
11	21	(11,21)

Line d		
Rule: Y is 3 less than X		
x	y	(x, y)
5	2	(5,2)
7	4	(7,4)
12	9	(12,9)
15	12	(15,12)

S: No.

T: What can you say then about lines *p, c, b,* and *d*?

S: Lines *p, c, b,* and *d* are parallel lines.

T: Compare lines *b* and *c* to line *p*. What do you notice? Turn and talk.

S: They're all parallel. → Lines *c* and *b* both have y-coordinates that are greater than the ones for the same x-coordinates on line *p*. The y's on *b* are all 5 more, and the ones on *c* are all 10 more than the ones on *p*.

One way to help students with visual acuity differences to accurately locate points and give the correct coordinate pair is to provide a transparent, colored, cellophane sheet for aligning with the grid lines on the plane. Students can place the right corner of the sheet with the point. The edges of the sheet will then align with the x- and y-coordinates on the axes.

Lesson 10:	Compare with lines and patterns generated by addition rules and multiplication rules.
Date:	1/31/14

6.B.50

T: What do the rules for lines *c* and *b* have in common?

S: They're both addition rules. → They both require us to add to the *x*-coordinate, but line *c* is adding more to the *x*-coordinate.

T: What about line *d*? What operation is used in the rule for line *d*?

S: Subtraction.

T: And where does line *d* lie on the plane, in relation to the other lines? Turn and talk.

S: The points on this line will be closer to the *x*-axis than on the other lines. → The line will be drawn below the other lines on the plane.

Problem 2: Compare the lines and patterns generated by multiplication rules.

T: (Display a second coordinate plane on board.) What do you notice about line *p*? Turn and talk.

S: It's the same as line *p* on the other plane. → It's the line for rule *y is equal to x*.

T: This is the same line we drew on the other plane. It represents the rule, *y is equal to x*, or we can also think of it as *y is x times 1*. On your plane, plot point *G* at the following location. (Show *G* (3, 9) on board and plot point *G*.)

S: (Plot point *G*.)

T: Use your straight edge to draw line *g* so that it passes through the origin and contains point G. (Model on board.)

S: (Students construct line *g*.)

T: Look at line *g*. What point on the line has an *x*-coordinate of 1?

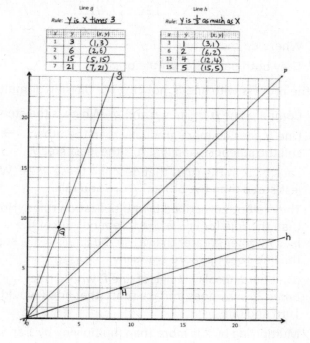

S: (1,3).

T: Record that in the chart for line g; then, work with a neighbor to fill in the rest of the missing *y*-coordinates.

S: (Record and share.)

T: What pattern do you see in the coordinate pairs for line *g*? Turn and talk.

S: The *y*-coordinate is always more than the *x*-coordinate. → If I multiply the *x*-values by 3, I get the *y*-coordinates. → I think the rule is *multiply x by 3*.

T: I hear that you noticed that the *y*-coordinate is always 3 times as much as the *x*-coordinate. Show me the rule for line *g*.

S: *y is 3 times as much as x.* → *y is x times 3.* → *Multiply x by 3.*

T: Record the rule on the chart for line *g*.

S: (Record.)

T: Compare line *g* to line *p*. Which is steeper? Turn and talk.

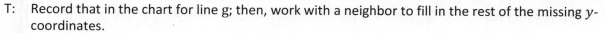

COMMON CORE   Lesson 10:   Compare with lines and patterns generated by addition rules and
                  multiplication rules.   6.B.51
                  Date: 1/31/14

S: Line **g** is steeper than line **p**.

T: Are lines **g** and **p** parallel?

S: No, they intersect.

Line g

Rule: Y is X times 3

x	y	(x, y)
1	3	(1,3)
2	6	(2,6)
5	15	(5,15)
7	21	(7,21)

Line h

Rule: Y is ⅓ as much as X

x	y	(x, y)
3	1	(3,1)
6	2	(6,2)
12	4	(12,4)
15	5	(15,5)

T: Where do they intersect?

S: They both pass through the origin.

Repeat the process with line **h**, noticing the division or multiplication by a fraction rule.

T: Compare line **h** to lines **p** and **g**. Which is the steepest? Turn and talk.

S: Line **h** goes up more gradually than the others. → Line **h** is less steep than the others. → Line **g** is still the steepest, and line **h** is the least steep.

T: Look back at the rules that describe these lines. Why do you think line **g** is the steepest and line **h** is less steep than the others? Turn and talk.

S: They're both described by multiplication rules. However, line **g's** rule multiplies by a larger number than the rule for line **h**. → It reminds me of the scaling work we did. The rule for line **g** multiplies by a number greater than 1, so the line is really steep; line **h** multiplies by a number less than 1, so the line goes up more gradually.

T: (On board, display image of line **i**, whose rule is, *y is x times 2*.) Line **i** represents the rule, *y is x times 2*. Why does it make sense that line **i** would be steeper than line **p**, but not as steep as line **g**? Turn and talk.

S: Multiplying by 2 is more than multiplying by 1 and less than multiplying by 3. → It's almost like measuring angles on a protractor. 60 degrees is in between 45 degrees and 80 degrees, so the line for multiplying by 2 should be in between the lines for multiplying by 1 and 3.

T: Show your neighbor where the line for rule, *y is x times 4* would be.

S: (Share with a neighbor.)

T: Would the line for rule, *y is x times $\frac{1}{10}$* be more steep or less steep than line **h**? Turn and talk.

S: It would be less steep because you're multiplying by a smaller number than $\frac{1}{3}$. → Line **h** would be steeper. The line for multiplying by $\frac{1}{10}$ would go through the origin and point (10, 1), which would be way less steep than line **h**.

T: That's right! The line for rule, *y is x times $\frac{1}{10}$* would be less steep than line **h**. (Drag your finger along plane showing its approximate location.)

COMMON CORE™

Lesson 10: Compare with lines and patterns generated by addition rules and multiplication rules.

Date: 1/31/14

6.B.52

Problem Set (10 minutes)

Students should do their personal best to complete the Problem Set within the allotted 10 minutes. For some classes, it may be appropriate to modify the assignment by specifying which problems they work on first. Some problems do not specify a method for solving. Students solve these problems using the RDW approach used for Application Problems.

Student Debrief (10 minutes)

Lesson Objective: Compare the lines and patterns generated by addition rules and multiplication rules.

The Student Debrief is intended to invite reflection and active processing of the total lesson experience.

Invite students to review their solutions for the Problem Set. They should check work by comparing answers with a partner before going over answers as a class. Look for misconceptions or misunderstandings that can be addressed in the Debrief. Guide students in a conversation to debrief the Problem Set and process the lesson.

You may choose to use any combination of the questions below to lead the discussion.

- In Problem 1, explain how you could create a rule that describes a line that is parallel to line *d* and whose points are even further from the *x*-axis.

- In Problem 2, explain how you could create a rule that describes a line that is less steep than line *w*.

- What point lies on any line that can be described by a multiplication rule?

- Explain to your partner how lines generated by addition and subtraction rules are different from those generated by multiplication rules.

Exit Ticket (3 minutes)

After the Student Debrief, instruct students to complete the Exit Ticket. A review of their work will help you assess the students' understanding of the concepts that were presented in the lesson today and plan more effectively for future lessons. You may read the questions aloud to the students.

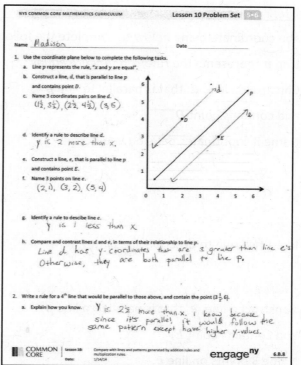

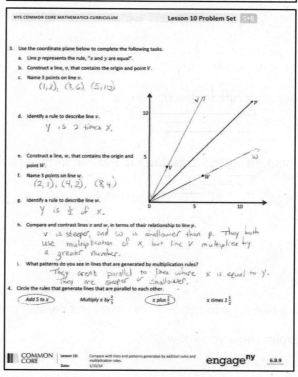

COMMON CORE

Lesson 10:   Compare with lines and patterns generated by addition rules and multiplication rules.
Date: 1/31/14

6.B.53

Name _____   Date _____

1. Use the coordinate plane below to complete the following tasks.

    a. Line **p** represents the rule, *x and y are equal*.

    b. Construct a line, **d**, that is parallel to line **p** and contains point D.

    c. Name 3 coordinates pairs on line **d**.

    d. Identify a rule to describe line **d**.

    e. Construct a line, **e**, that is parallel to line **p** and contains point E.

    f. Name 3 points on line **e**.

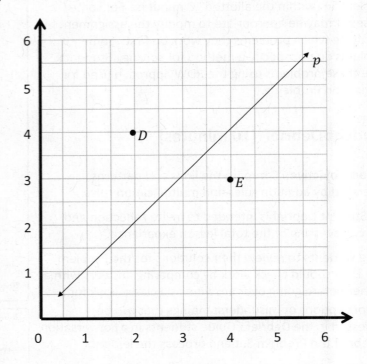

    g. Identify a rule to describe line **e**.

    h. Compare and contrast lines **d** and **e** in terms of their relationship to line **p**.

2. Write a rule for a fourth line that would be parallel to those above and would contain the point $(3\frac{1}{2}, 6)$.

    a. Explain how you know.

Lesson 10:	Compare with lines and patterns generated by addition rules and multiplication rules.
Date:	1/31/14

6.B.54

3. Use the coordinate plane below to complete the following tasks.

    a. Line p represents the rule *x and y are equal*.

    b. Construct a line, v, that contains the origin and point V.

    c. Name 3 points on line v.

    d. Identify a rule to describe line v.

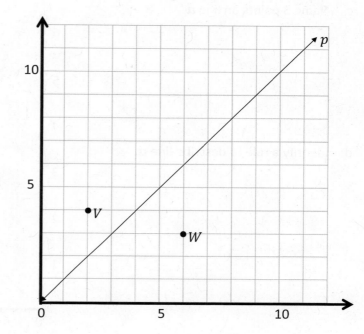

    e. Construct a line, w, that contains the origin and point W.

    f. Name 3 points on line w.

    g. Identify a rule to describe line w.

    h. Compare and contrast lines v and w in terms of their relationship to line p.

    i. What patterns do you see in lines that are generated by multiplication rules?

4. Circle the rules that generate lines that are parallel to each other.

    Add 5 to x   *Multiply x by* $\frac{2}{3}$ *x plus* $\frac{1}{2}$ *x times* $1\frac{1}{2}$

COMMON CORE™ | **Lesson 10:** Compare with lines and patterns generated by addition rules and multiplication rules.

Date: 1/31/14

6.B.55

Name _____ Date _____

1. Use the coordinate plane below to complete the following tasks.

    a. Line **p** represents the rule *x and y are equal*.

    b. Construct a line, **a**, that is parallel to line **p** and contains point A.

    c. Name 3 points on line **a**.

    d. Identify a rule to describe line **a**.

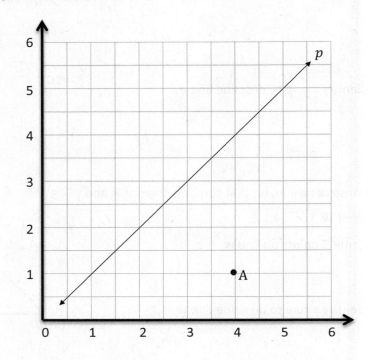

COMMON CORE™ | **Lesson 10:** Compare with lines and patterns generated by addition rules and multiplication rules.

Date: 1/31/14

6.B.56

Name 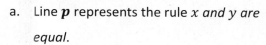   Date _____

1. Use the coordinate plane to complete the following tasks.

   a. Line **p** represents the rule *x and y are equal*.

   b. Construct a line, **d**, that is parallel to line **p** and contains point *D*.

   c. Name 3 coordinates pairs on line **d**.

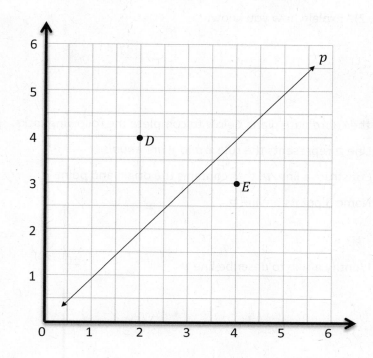

   d. Identify a rule to describe line **d**.

   e. Construct a line, **e**, that is parallel to line **p** and contains point *E*.

   f. Name 3 points on line **e**.

   g. Identify a rule to describe line **e**.

   h. Compare and contrast lines **d** and **e** in terms of their relationship to line **p**.

2. Write a rule for a fourth line that would be parallel to those above and that would contain the point

$(5\frac{1}{2}, 2)$. Explain how you know.

3. Use the coordinate plane below to complete the following tasks.

   a. Line **p** represents the rule *x and y are equal*.

   b. Construct a line, **v**, that contains the origin and point V.

   c. Name 3 points on line **v**.

   d. Identify a rule to describe line **v**.

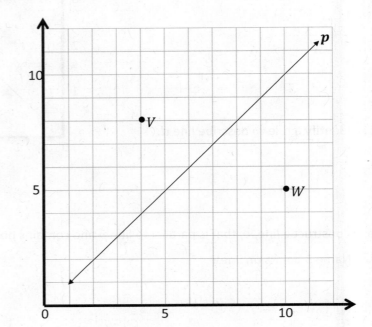

   e. Construct a line, **w**, that contains the origin and point W.

   f. Name 3 points on line **w**.

   g. Identify a rule to describe line **w**.

   h. Compare and contrast lines **v** and **w** in terms of their relationship to line **p**.

   i. What patterns do you see in lines that are generated by multiplication rules?

COMMON CORE™

Lesson 10: Compare with lines and patterns generated by addition rules and multiplication rules.

Date: 1/31/14

6.B.58

Line **p**

Rule: *y is 0 more than x*

x	y	(x, y)
0		
5		
10		
15		

Line **b**

Rule: _____

x	y	(x, y)
7		
10		
13		
18		

Line **c**

Rule: _____

x	y	(x, y)
2		
4		
8		
11		

Line **d**

Rule: _____

x	y	(x, y)
5		
7		
12		
15		

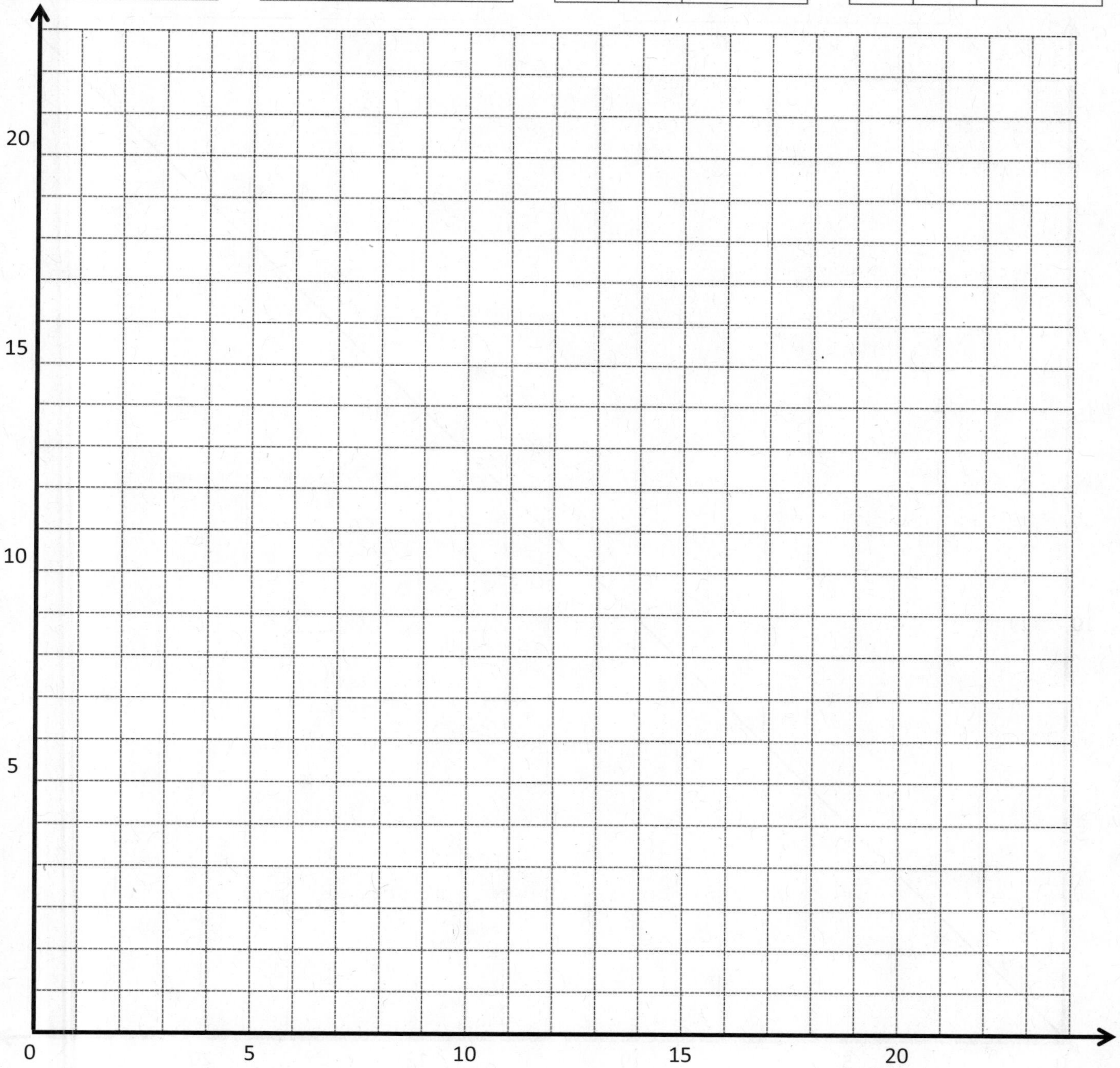

Line *g*

Rule: _____

x	y	(x, y)
1		
2		
5		
7		

Line *h*

Rule: _____

x	y	(x, y)
3		
6		
12		
15		

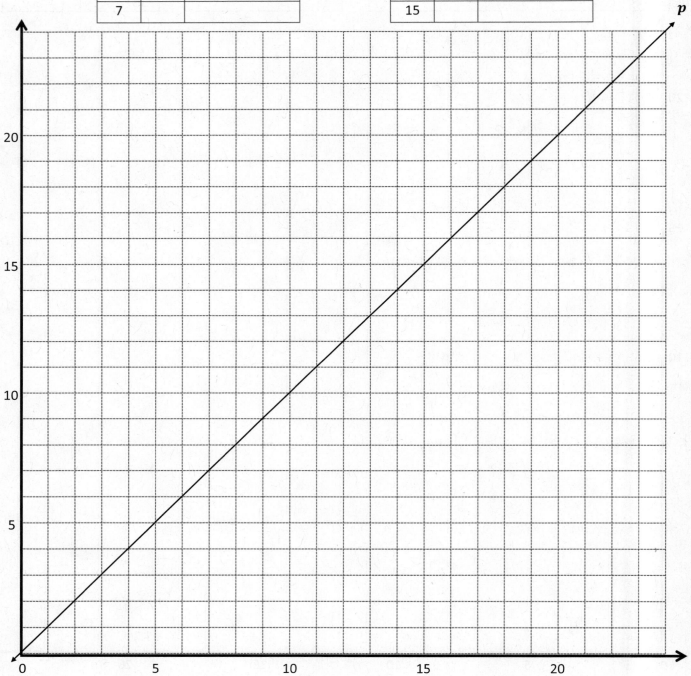

Lesson 10: Compare with lines and patterns generated by addition rules and multiplication rules.

Date: 1/31/14

6.B.60

Lesson 11

Objective: Analyze number patterns created from mixed operations.

Suggested Lesson Structure

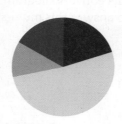

■ Fluency Practice   (12 minutes)
■ Application Problem   (7 minutes)
■ Concept Development   (31 minutes)
■ Student Debrief   (10 minutes)
     Total Time   **(60 minutes)**

Fluency Practice (12 minutes)

▪ Sprint: Round to the Nearest One **5.NBT.4**   (9 minutes)
▪ Add and Subtract Decimals **5.NBT.7**   (3 minutes)

Sprint: Round to the Nearest One (9 minutes)

Materials: (S) Round to the Nearest One Sprint

Note: This Sprint reviews G5–Module 1 concepts.

Add and Subtract Decimals (3 minutes)

Materials: (S) Personal white boards

Note: This fluency activity reviews G5–Module 1 concepts.

     T: (Write 5.634 + 1.) Write the number sentence.
     S: (Write 5.634 + 1 = 6.634.)
     T: (Write 5.634 – 1.) Write the number sentence.
     S: (Write 5.634 – 1 = 4.634.)

Continue the process with 5.634 – 0.1, 5.634 + 0.1, 5.937 + 0.02, 5.937 – 0.02, 7.056 – 0.003, 7.056 + 0.003, and 4.304 – 0.004.

Application Problem (7 minutes)

Michelle has 3 kg of strawberries that she divided equally into small bags with $\frac{1}{5}$ kg in each bag.

Lesson 11:   Analyze number patterns created from mixed operations.
Date: 1/31/14

6.B.61

a.   How many bags of strawberries did she make?

b.   She gave a bag to her friend, Sarah. Sarah ate half of her strawberries. How many grams of strawberries does Sarah have left?

Note: The Application Problem requires that students convert kilograms to grams and use fraction division and multiplication to answer this multi-step problem. Students may use decimals to solve.

a. $3 kg \div \frac{1}{5} = 3 \times 5 = 15$
15 bags of strawberries.

b. $\frac{1}{2} \times \frac{1}{5} kg = \frac{1}{10} kg$
   $= 100 g$
She had 100g left.

Concept Development (31 minutes)

Materials: (S) Personal white board, straightedge, coordinate plane template

Problem 1: Compare the lines and patterns generated by mixed operations rules.

T: (Distribute coordinate plane template to students. Display coordinate plane on board.) Say the rule for line ℓ.

S: Multiply x by 3.

T: What is the y-coordinate of the point whose x is 2?

S: 6.

T: Before you complete the chart, plot the points and draw line ℓ; tell your neighbor what you predict it will look like.

S: It's a multiplication rule, so it will pass through the origin. → The y-coordinates are 3 times the x-coordinates, so it will be pretty steep. (Draw line.)

S: (Draw line .)

T: Say the rule for line m.

S: Multiply x by 3; then, add 3.

T: How is the rule for line m different from the other rules we've used to describe lines? Turn and talk.

S: We've only had rules that showed lines for adding something to x or multiplying x by a number. → This rule has two operations.

T: Show me the coordinate pair for the point whose x-coordinate is 2.

S: (Show (2, 9).)

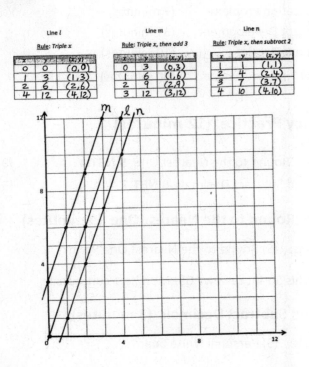

Line *l*
Rule: *Triple x*

x	y	(x, y)
0	0	(0,0)
1	3	(1,3)
2	6	(2,6)
4	12	(4,12)

Line *m*
Rule: *Triple x, then add 3*

x	y	(x, y)
0	3	(0,3)
1	6	(1,6)
2	9	(2,9)
3	12	(3,12)

Line *n*
Rule: *Triple x, then subtract 2*

x	y	(x, y)
1	1	(1,1)
2	4	(2,4)
3	7	(3,7)
4	10	(4,10)

NOTES ON MULTIPLE MEANS OF REPRESENTATION:

Students who are not yet finding the value of y mentally may benefit from writing equations. You may guide students working below grade level with the following frames:

For triple x,

___ ×3.

For triple x then add 3,

(___ ×3) + 3.

For triple x then subtract 2,

(___ ×3) − 2.

Lesson 11:   Analyze number patterns created from mixed operations.
Date: 1/31/14

6.B.62

T: Fill in the rest of the missing *y*-coordinates in the chart for line **m**.

S: (Fill in coordinates.)

T: Plot each point from the chart; then, use your straightedge to draw line **m**.

S: (Draw line.)

T: What do you notice about these lines? Turn and talk.

S: They are parallel lines. → Line **m** doesn't go through the origin. It's a multiplication rule that doesn't go through the origin. → The lines are equally steep, but line **m** is just farther from the *x*-axis. → The lines are identical, except line **m** doesn't pass through the origin. It passes through the *y*-axis at (0, 3).

T: Do lines **ℓ** and **m** intersect?

S: No, they're parallel.

T: Which line is steeper?

S: They're equally steep.

T: What is different about the lines?

S: The points on line **m** are farther from the *x*-axis than the point on line **ℓ**. → Line **m** does not pass through the origin.

Line *l*		
Rule: *Triple x*		
x	*y*	*(x, y)*
0	0	(0,0)
1	3	(1,3)
2	6	(2,6)
4	12	(4,12)

Line *m*		
Rule: *Triple x, then add 3*		
x	*y*	*(x, y)*
0	3	(0,3)
1	6	(1,6)
2	9	(2,9)
3	12	(3,12)

Line *n*		
Rule: *Triple x, then subtract 2*		
x	*y*	*(x, y)*
1	1	(1,1)
2	4	(2,4)
3	7	(3,7)
4	10	(4,10)

T: Let's look at another mixed operation rule. Say the rule for line **n**.

S: Triple *x*, then subtract 2.

T: Show me the coordinate pair for this rule when *x* is 1.

S: (Show (1, 1).)

T: Fill in the rest of the missing *y*-coordinates for line **n**.

MP.7 S: (Fill in missing coordinates.)

T: Based on the patterns we've seen, predict what line **n** will look like.

S: It won't go through the origin, because when *x* is 0, we get $0 - 2$, but I don't know what to do with that. → It's going to be parallel again, but this time it will fall below line **ℓ** because we're subtracting this time.

T: Plot each point and draw line **n**.

S: (Draw line **n**.)

NOTES ON
MULTIPLE MEANS OF
REPRESENTATION:

Depending on the level of English proficiency of English language learners, consider rephrasing questions for discussion or making them available in the students' first language, if possible.

Lesson 11:   Analyze number patterns created from mixed operations.
Date: 1/31/14

6.B.63

T: What have lines ℓ, m, and n taught you about lines generated from mixed operations? Turn and talk.

S: You can generate parallel lines involving multiplication, but you have to add or subtract after multiplying. → Not every rule with multiplication will produce a line that passes through the origin. → If the multiplication part of the rule is the same for both lines, adding after multiplying makes the points on the line shift up by whatever you are adding. → Subtracting after multiplying makes the points on the line shift down if the multiplication part of the rule is the same.

Problem 2: Identify coordinate pairs to satisfy mixed operation rules.

T: (Post rule, *multiply x by $\frac{1}{2}$, then add $\frac{3}{4}$* on the board.) Tell a neighbor what the line described by this rule would look like.

S: We'd have to add $\frac{3}{4}$ after multiplying by $\frac{1}{2}$; so, that means the points on this line would shift up $\frac{3}{4}$ more than the points on the line that you see when just multiplying by $\frac{1}{2}$. → The rule has you multiply by one-half first. Multiplying by a half will be a line that is less steep than multiplying by a whole number. → It's a mixed operation, so it won't go through the origin.

T: Tell your neighbor how you'll find the y-coordinate for this point if x is 1.

S: You have to multiply by $\frac{1}{2}$ first. So, 1 times $\frac{1}{2}$ is $\frac{1}{2}$. Then, you have to add $\frac{3}{4}$ to $\frac{1}{2}$. → I'll multiply first, and that's easy since any number times 1 is just that number. So, I'll end up adding $\frac{3}{4}$ to $\frac{1}{2}$, or $\frac{2}{4}$, which will be $\frac{5}{4}$. The y-coordinate is $\frac{5}{4}$.

T: Show me the coordinate pair for this rule when x is 1.

S: (Show $(1, \frac{5}{4})$ or $(1, 1\frac{1}{4})$.)

T: What is the first step in finding the y-coordinate when x is $1\frac{1}{2}$?

S: Multiply by $\frac{1}{2}$.

T: Show me the multiplication sentence.

S: (Show $1\frac{1}{2} \times \frac{1}{2} = \frac{3}{4}$ or $\frac{3}{2} \times \frac{1}{2} = \frac{3}{4}$.)

T: What is the next step in finding the y-coordinate?

S: Add 3 fourths.

T: Show me the addition sentence.

S: (Show $\frac{3}{4} + \frac{3}{4} = 1\frac{1}{2}$ or $\frac{3}{4} + \frac{3}{4} = \frac{6}{4} = \frac{3}{2}$.)

T: Show me the coordinate pair for this rule when x is $1\frac{1}{2}$.

S: (Show $(1\frac{1}{2}, 1\frac{1}{2})$.)

T: Work independently, and show me the coordinate pair for this rule when x is $\frac{3}{4}$.

S: (Work and show $(\frac{3}{4}, 1\frac{1}{8})$.)

T: Would the line for this rule contain the point $(3, 2\frac{1}{4})$? Turn and talk.

COMMON CORE™

Lesson 11: Analyze number patterns created from mixed operations.
Date: 1/31/14

6.B.64

S: It would. 3 times $\frac{1}{2}$ is 3 halves. And, 3 halves plus 3 fourths is equal to 9 fourths. 9 fourths is the same as $2\frac{1}{4}$. → Yes. If I take the x-coordinate and multiply it by one-half, then add 3 fourths to the product, I get 2 and one-fourth.

T: What about coordinate pair $(3\frac{1}{2}, 2\frac{1}{4})$?

S: (Work.) No.

T: Tell a neighbor how you know.

S: I tried it, and when I multiplied and then added, I found that when x is $3\frac{1}{2}$, the y-coordinate is $2\frac{1}{2}$. → I actually worked backwards. I subtracted $\frac{3}{4}$ from $2\frac{1}{4}$ and got $1\frac{1}{2}$. Then, I doubled $1\frac{1}{2}$ and got 3, but the coordinate pair we were given had an x-coordinate of $3\frac{1}{2}$, so I knew that this pair wouldn't be on the line.

T: Generate another coordinate pair that the line for rule *multiply x by $\frac{1}{2}$, then add $\frac{3}{4}$* would contain. Have a neighbor check your work when you're finished.

S: (Work, share, and check.)

Problem Set (10 minutes)

Students should do their personal best to complete the Problem Set within the allotted 10 minutes. For some classes, it may be appropriate to modify the assignment by specifying which problems they work on first. Some problems do not specify a method for solving. Students solve these problems using the RDW approach used for Application Problems.

Student Debrief (10 minutes)

Lesson Objective: Analyze number patterns created from mixed operations.

The Student Debrief is intended to invite reflection and active processing of the total lesson experience.

Invite students to review their solutions for the Problem Set. They should check work by comparing answers with a partner before going over answers as a class. Look for misconceptions or misunderstandings that can be addressed in the Debrief. Guide students in a conversation to debrief the Problem Set and process the lesson.

You may choose to use any combination of the questions below to lead the discussion.

- Make a statement that describes how the lines generated from mixed operations behave. How

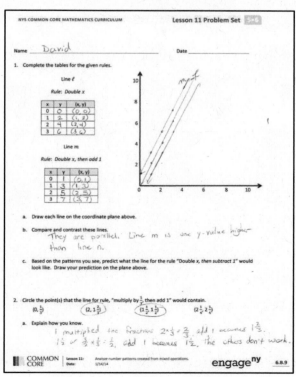

are they similar and different from *multiplication only* or *addition* or *subtraction only* rules?

- Share your answers to Problems 2(b) and 4(b) with a neighbor. Explain your thought process as you generated the coordinate pairs.

- Predict what line m would look like if you added first and then multiplied.

Exit Ticket (3 minutes)

After the Student Debrief, instruct students to complete the Exit Ticket. A review of their work will help you assess the students' understanding of the concepts that were presented in the lesson today and plan more effectively for future lessons. You may read the questions aloud to the students.

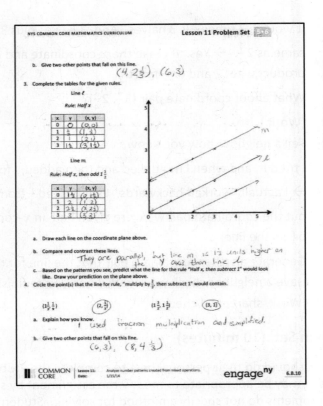

COMMON CORE

Lesson 11:   Analyze number patterns created from mixed operations.
Date: 1/31/14

6.B.66

A

Round to the nearest whole number.

Correct _____

#			#		
1	3.1 ≈		23	12.51 ≈	
2	3.2 ≈		24	16.61 ≈	
3	3.3 ≈		25	17.41 ≈	
4	3.4 ≈		26	11.51 ≈	
5	3.5 ≈		27	11.49 ≈	
6	3.6 ≈		28	13.49 ≈	
7	3.9 ≈		29	13.51 ≈	
8	13.9 ≈		30	15.51 ≈	
9	13.1 ≈		31	15.49 ≈	
10	13.5 ≈		32	6.3 ≈	
11	7.5 ≈		33	7.6 ≈	
12	8.5 ≈		34	49.5 ≈	
13	9.5 ≈		35	3.45 ≈	
14	19.5 ≈		36	17.46 ≈	
15	29.5 ≈		37	11.76 ≈	
16	89.5 ≈		38	5.2 ≈	
17	2.4 ≈		39	12.8 ≈	
18	2.41 ≈		40	59.5 ≈	
19	2.42 ≈		41	5.45 ≈	
20	2.45 ≈		42	19.47 ≈	
21	2.49 ≈		43	19.87 ≈	
22	2.51 ≈		44	69.51 ≈	

Lesson 11: Analyze number patterns created from mixed operations.
Date: 1/31/14

6.B.67

B

Improvement _____   # Correct _____

Round to the nearest whole number.

1	4.1 ≈		23	13.51 ≈	
2	4.2 ≈		24	17.61 ≈	
3	4.3 ≈		25	18.41 ≈	
4	4.4 ≈		26	12.51 ≈	
5	4.5 ≈		27	12.49 ≈	
6	4.6 ≈		28	14.49 ≈	
7	4.9 ≈		29	14.51 ≈	
8	14.9 ≈		30	16.51 ≈	
9	14.1 ≈		31	16.49 ≈	
10	14.5 ≈		32	7.3 ≈	
11	7.5 ≈		33	8.6 ≈	
12	8.5 ≈		34	39.5 ≈	
13	9.5 ≈		35	4.45 ≈	
14	19.5 ≈		36	18.46 ≈	
15	29.5 ≈		37	12.76 ≈	
16	79.5 ≈		38	6.2 ≈	
17	3.4 ≈		39	13.8 ≈	
18	3.41 ≈		40	49.5 ≈	
19	3.42 ≈		41	6.45 ≈	
20	3.45 ≈		42	19.48 ≈	
21	3.49 ≈		43	19.78 ≈	
22	3.51 ≈		44	59.51 ≈	

Lesson 11:   Analyze number patterns created from mixed operations.
Date: 1/31/14

6.B.68

Name _____   Date _____

1. Complete the tables for the given rules.

Line ℓ

Rule: *Double x*

x	y	(x, y)
0		
1		
2		
3		

Line m

Rule: *Double x, then add 1*

x	y	(x, y)
0		
1		
2		
3		

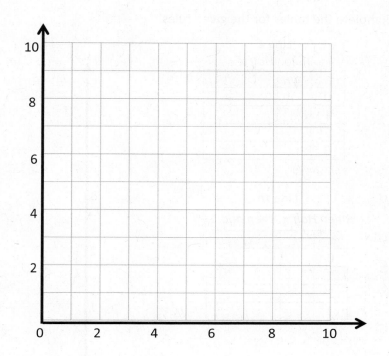

a. Draw each line on the coordinate plane above.

b. Compare and contrast these lines.

c. Based on the patterns you see, predict what the line for the rule *double x, then subtract 1* would look like. Draw the line on the plane above.

2. Circle the point(s) that the line for rule *multiply by $\frac{1}{3}$, then add 1* would contain.

$(0, \frac{1}{3})$ $(2, 1\frac{2}{3})$ $(1\frac{1}{2}, 1\frac{1}{2})$ $(2\frac{1}{4}, 2\frac{1}{4})$

a. Explain how you know.

    b.   Give two other points that fall on this line.

3.   Complete the tables for the given rules.

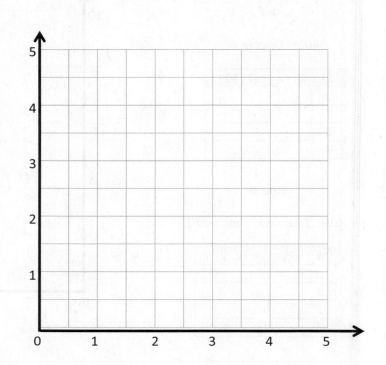

Line ℓ

Rule: *Half x*

x	y	(x, y)
0		
1		
2		
3		

Line m

Rule: *Half x, then add* $1\frac{1}{2}$

x	y	(x, y)
0		
1		
2		
3		

    a.   Draw each line on the coordinate plane above.

    b.   Compare and contrast these lines.

    c.   Based on the patterns you see, predict what the line for the rule *half x, then subtract 1* would look like. Draw the line on the plane above.

4.   Circle the point(s) that the line for rule *multiply by* $\frac{2}{3}$, *then subtract 1* would contain.

    $(1\frac{1}{3}, \frac{1}{9})$ $(2, \frac{1}{3})$ $(1\frac{3}{2}, 1\frac{1}{2})$ $(3, 1)$

    a.   Explain how you know.

    b.   Give two other points that fall on this line.

Name _____   Date _____

1. Complete the tables for the given rules.

Line ℓ

Rule: *Double x*

x	y	(x, y)
0		
1		
2		
3		

Line m

Rule: *Double x, then add 1*

x	y	(x, y)
0		
1		
2		
3		

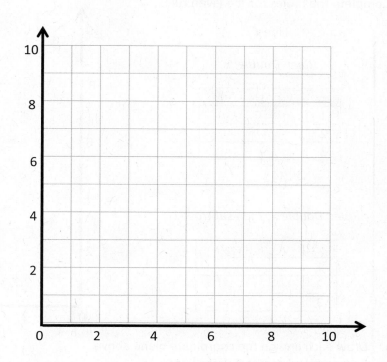

a. Draw each line on the coordinate plane above.

b. Compare and contrast these lines.

2. Circle the point(s) that the line for rule *multiply by $\frac{1}{3}$ then add 1* would contain.

$(0, \frac{1}{2})$ $(1, 1\frac{1}{3})$ $(2, 1\frac{2}{3})$ $(3, 2\frac{1}{2})$

Name _____   Date _____

1. Complete the tables for the given rules.

Line ℓ

Rule: Double x

x	y	(x, y)
1		
2		
3		

Line m

Rule: Double x, then subtract 1

x	y	(x, y)
1		
2		
3		

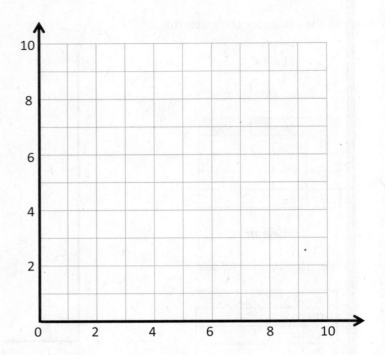

a. Draw each line on the coordinate plane above.
b. Compare and contrast these lines.

c. Based on the patterns you see, predict what the line for the rule *double x, then add 1* would look like. Draw your prediction on the plane above.

2. Circle the point(s) that the line for the rule *multiply by $\frac{1}{2}$ then add 1* would contain.

    $(0, \frac{1}{2})$ $(2, 1\frac{1}{4})$ $(2, 2)$ $(3, \frac{1}{2})$

a. Explain how you know.

b. Give two other points that fall on this line.

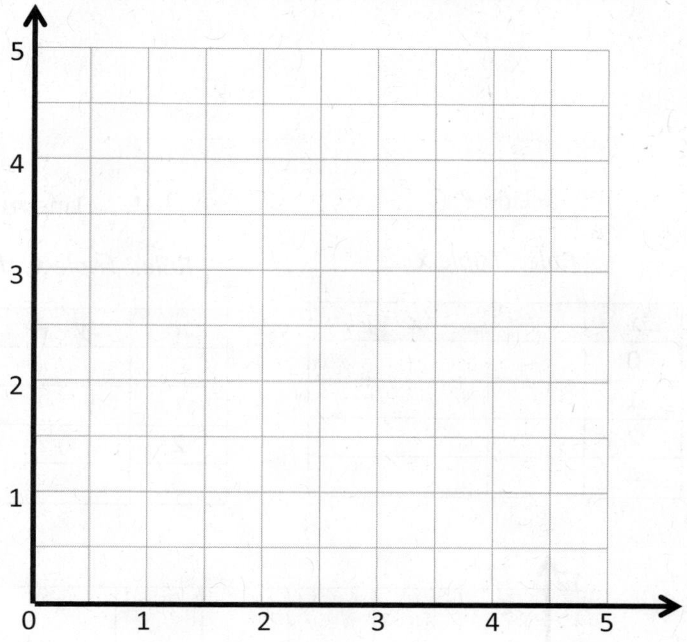

3.   Complete the tables for the given rules.

Line ℓ

Rule: Halve x, then add 1

x	y	(x, y)
0		
1		
2		
3		

Line m

Rule: Halve x, then add $1\frac{1}{4}$

x	y	(x, y)
0		
1		
2		
3		

d.
e.

a.   Draw each line on the coordinate plane above.

b.   Compare and contrast these lines.

c.   Based on the patterns you see, predict what the line for the rule *halve x, then subtract 1* would look like. Draw your prediction on the plane above.

4.   Circle the point(s) that the line for rule *multiply by $\frac{3}{4}$, then subtract $\frac{1}{2}$* would contain.

  $(1, \frac{1}{4})$ $(2, \frac{1}{4})$ $(3,\ 1\frac{3}{4})$ $(3, 1)$

a.   Explain how you know.

b.   Give two other points that fall on this line.

| **Lesson 11:** Analyze number patterns created from mixed operations.
| **Date:**   1/31/14

Line ℓ

Rule: Triple x

x	y	(x, y)
0		
1		
2		
4		

Line m

Rule: Triple x, then add 3

x	y	(x, y)
0		
1		
2		
3		

Line n

Rule: Triple x, then subtract 2

x	y	(x, y)
1		
2		
3		
4		

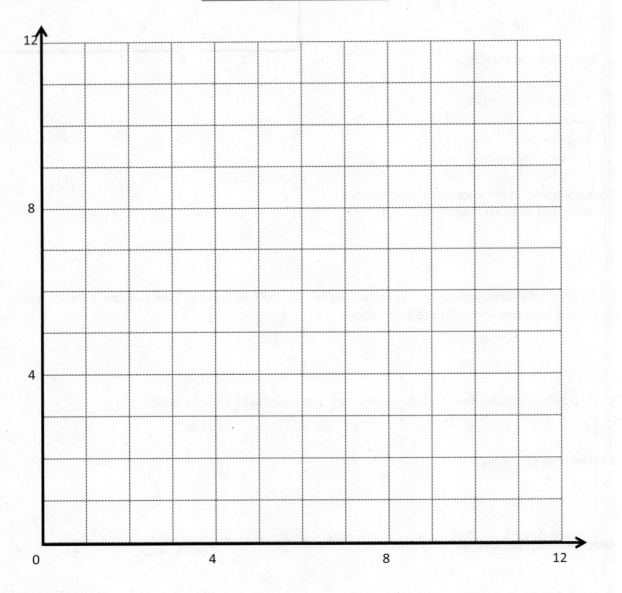

Lesson 12

Objective: Create a rule to generate a number pattern, and plot the points.

Suggested Lesson Structure

■ Application Problem   (7 minutes)
■ Fluency Practice   (12 minutes)
■ Concept Development   (31 minutes)
■ Student Debrief   (10 minutes)
  Total Time   **(60 minutes)**

Application Problem (7 minutes)

Mr. Jones had 640 books. He sold $\frac{1}{4}$ of them for $2.00 each in the month of September. He sold half of the remaining books in October. Each book he sold in October earned $\frac{3}{4}$ of what each book sold for in September. How much money did Mr. Jones earn selling books? Show your thinking with a tape diagram.

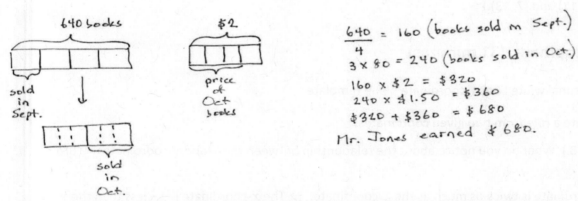

Note: This Application Problem reviews fraction skills taught in G5-Module 2 and opens the lesson, as the fluency activity's graphing flows well into the Concept Development. This problem is quite complex and given only seven minutes of instructional time. A simpler version of the problem can be used: Mr. Jones had 640 books. He sold $\frac{1}{4}$ of them in the month of September. He sold half of the remaining books in October. How many books did he sell in all?

Fluency Practice (12 minutes)

- Sprint: Subtract Decimals **5.NBT.7**   (9 minutes)
- Make a Number Pattern **5.OA.3**   (3 minutes)

Sprint: Subtract Decimals (9 minutes)

Materials: (S) Subtract Decimals Sprint

Note: This Sprint reviews G5–Module 1 concepts.

Make a Number Pattern (3 minutes)

Materials: (S) Personal white boards with coordinate grid insert

Note: This fluency activity reviews G5–M6–Lesson 11.

Rule: Double x, then subtract 1.

x	y	(x, y)
1	1	(1,1)
2	3	(2,3)
3	5	(3,5)
4	7	(4,7)
5	9	(5,9)

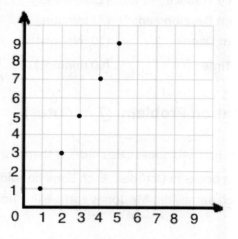

- T: (Project table with only the x-values filled in. Write *Rule: Double x, then subtract 1.*) Fill in the table and plot the points.
- S: (Complete the table and plot (1, 1), (2, 3), (3, 5), (4, 7), and (5, 9).)
- T: (Write the next two coordinates in the pattern.)
- S: (Write (6, 11) and (7, 13).)

Concept Development (31 minutes)

Materials: (S) Personal white board, coordinate plane template

Problem 1: Generate a rule from two given coordinates.

- T: (Plot $(1\frac{1}{2}, 3.)$ What do you notice about the relationship between the x-and y-coordinates? Turn and talk.
- S: The y-coordinate is twice as much as the x-coordinate. → The x-coordinate is $1\frac{1}{2}$ less than the y-coordinate.
- T: I'm visualizing line ℓ, which contains point A. Take a moment to think about what line ℓ might look like. (Pause.) Draw your line on the plane with your finger for your neighbor.
- S: (Draw line with finger.)
- T: The line you showed may or may not have been like your neighbor's. Why is knowing the location of one point that falls on the line not enough to name the rule for line ℓ? Turn and talk.

Lesson 12:	Create a rule to generate a number pattern, and plot the points.
Date:	1/31/14

6.B.76

S: It could be almost any line, as long as it goes through A. → The line could be horizontal, vertical, or a steep line. → With just one point, I could imagine drawing one line and then spinning it around like a propeller to get lots of lines.

T: (Display B: $(2, 3\frac{1}{2})$ on board.) Record the location of B in your chart; then, plot it on your plane. (Record and plot B.)

S: (Record and plot B.)

T: Line ℓ, the line I have been thinking of, also contains point B. What pattern do you notice in the coordinate pairs of line ℓ? Turn and talk.

S: The y-coordinate is always more than the x-coordinate. → At first, I thought we were going to be doubling x, but now I can see that we're adding $1\frac{1}{2}$ to x.

T: Use your finger again to show your neighbor what you think line ℓ looks like.

S: (Share with neighbor.)

T: Raise your hand if your neighbor's line was still different than yours.

S: (Hands should remain down.)

T: Once we know the location of 2 points on a line, we know exactly where the line falls. Line ℓ is here. (Drag your finger across the plane to show ℓ.) But, I still need you to tell me a rule to describe this line. Do you have enough information, *now*, to name a rule for line ℓ?

S: Yes.

T: Show me the rule for line ℓ.

S: (Add $1\frac{1}{2}$ to x. → y is $1\frac{1}{2}$ more than x. → y is x plus $1\frac{1}{2}$.)

T: Record the rule you created on the chart for line ℓ.

T: Identify the coordinates of two other points that line ℓ contains; then, plot them on your plane and use your straight edge to draw line ℓ.

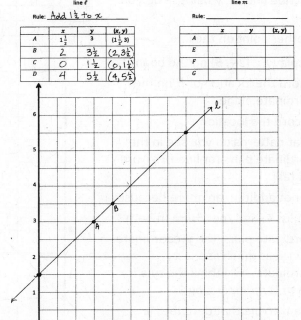

line ℓ

Rule: Add $1\frac{1}{2}$ to x

	x	y	(x, y)
A	$1\frac{1}{2}$	3	$(1\frac{1}{2}, 3)$
B	2	$3\frac{1}{2}$	$(2, 3\frac{1}{2})$
C	0	$1\frac{1}{2}$	$(0, 1\frac{1}{2})$
D	4	$5\frac{1}{2}$	$(4, 5\frac{1}{2})$

line m

Rule: _____

	x	y	(x, y)
A			
E			
F			
G			

NOTES ON MULTIPLE MEANS OF REPRESENTATION:

Scaffold finding the unknown rule for students working below grade level as follows:

Ask, "Write the two possible rules for $(1\frac{1}{2}, 3)$."

____ × 2

____ $+ 1\frac{1}{2}$

Problem 2: Generate rules that describe multiple lines that share a common point.

T: Line m also contains point A. Record the location of A in the chart for line m.

S: (Record the location.)

T: Is it possible that more than one line can contain point A? Turn and talk.

Lesson 12:   Create a rule to generate a number pattern, and plot the points.
Date: 1/31/14

6.B.77

S: (Discuss with partner.)

T: In order to name a rule to describe line m, what else do you need?

S: Another point on the line.

T: (Display E: $(2\frac{1}{2}, 5)$ on the board.) Record the location of E on the coordinate plane.

S: (Record the location.)

T: What patterns do you see in the coordinate pairs for line m? Turn and talk.

S: It's not addition anymore because $2\frac{1}{2}$ plus $1\frac{1}{2}$ is 4, not 5. → In both coordinate pairs, the y-coordinate is twice as much as the x-coordinate. → I think the rule for line m is *multiply x by 2.*

T: Give the rule that describes line m.

S: Multiply x by 2. → Double x. → y is twice as much as x.

T: Identify two more points that lie on line m and then draw the line on your plane. (Draw line m.)

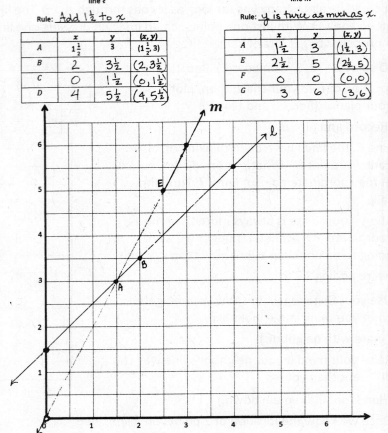

line ℓ

Rule: Add 1½ to x

	x	y	(x, y)
A	$1\frac{1}{2}$	3	$(1\frac{1}{2}, 3)$
B	2	$3\frac{1}{2}$	$(2, 3\frac{1}{2})$
C	0	$1\frac{1}{2}$	$(0, 1\frac{1}{2})$
D	4	$5\frac{1}{2}$	$(4, 5\frac{1}{2})$

line m

Rule: y is twice as much as x.

	x	y	(x, y)
A	$1\frac{1}{2}$	3	$(1\frac{1}{2}, 3)$
E	$2\frac{1}{2}$	5	$(2\frac{1}{2}, 5)$
F	0	0	$(0, 0)$
G	3	6	$(3, 6)$

S: (Draw line m.)

T: Do you think there are still other lines that could contain point A? Turn and talk.

S: I think that there could be a horizontal line that goes through point A. → We could have a line that's perpendicular to the x-axis and contains point A. → We learned about rules with mixed operations yesterday. Maybe there's a line with a mixed operation rule that could contain point A. → There are lots of lines that go through that point.

T: Use your arm to show what a line parallel to the y-axis would look like.

S: (Raise an arm vertically.)

T: Work with a neighbor to identify a rule that describes a line that is parallel to the y-axis and contains point A.

S: (Work and show rule *x is always $1\frac{1}{2}$*.)

T: A vertical line where x is always $1\frac{1}{2}$ would contain point A. (Drag your finger along plane to show the location of this line. Write on the board: *Rule for a line parallel to the y-axis: x is always $1\frac{1}{2}$.*) Show me another coordinate pair that this line would contain.

Lesson 12:   Create a rule to generate a number pattern, and plot the points.
Date: 1/31/14

6.B.78

S: (Show a coordinate pair with $1\frac{1}{2}$ as the x-coordinate and any value for the y-coordinate.)

T: Give a rule for a line that is perpendicular to the y-axis and contains point A.

S: (Work and show rule *y is always 3*.)

T: Show your neighbor another coordinate pair that this horizontal line would contain.

S: (Work and share.)

Problem 3: Generate a mixed operation rule from a coordinate pair.

T: Let's find a mixed operation rule that would contain point A. Let's begin by creating a rule with multiplication and addition. Let's write a sentence frame for our mixed operation rule. (Write *multiply x by _____, then add _____* on the board.)

T: If our rule is to include multiplication and addition, we need to make sure that *after* we multiply, the product is less than 3. Tell a neighbor why.

S: The product needs to be less than 3 so that we still have some room to add. → If the product were more than 3, then we would need to subtract to get the y-coordinate.

T: Tell your neighbor what we could multiply $1\frac{1}{2}$ by and get a product less than 3.

S: Well $1\frac{1}{2}$ times 2 is exactly 3, so it needs to be less than 2. → We could multiply by $\frac{1}{2}$; that will definitely be less than 3.

T: Let's see what happens if we multiply by $1\frac{1}{2}$. (Write $1\frac{1}{2}$ in sentence frame.) Work with a partner and show me the product of $1\frac{1}{2}$ times $1\frac{1}{2}$ as a fraction in its simplest form.

S: (Work and show $2\frac{1}{4}$.)

T: So far, our rule says, *multiply x by $1\frac{1}{2}$, then add….* What must we add to $2\frac{1}{4}$ so that our y-coordinate is 3?

S: $\frac{3}{4}$.

T: (Write $\frac{3}{4}$ in sentence frame.) Say the mixed operation rule for the line that contains point A.

S: Multiply x by $1\frac{1}{2}$, then add $\frac{3}{4}$.

T: Work with a neighbor to name 2 other coordinate pairs that this line would contain.

S: (Work and share.)

T: Work with a neighbor to see if you can identify another mixed operation rule that would contain point A. It may involve multiplication and addition again, or you can try one with multiplication and subtraction.

S: (Work and share.)

Circulate around room to check work and support struggling learners. After some time, allow students to share their mixed operation rules with the class. As rules are presented, students may identify other coordinate pairs that each line would contain.

Lesson 12:   Create a rule to generate a number pattern, and plot the points.
Date: 1/31/14

Problem Set (10 minutes)

Students should do their personal best to complete the Problem Set within the allotted 10 minutes. For some classes, it may be appropriate to modify the assignment by specifying which problems they work on first. Some problems do not specify a method for solving. Students solve these problems using the RDW approach used for Application Problems.

Student Debrief (10 minutes)

Lesson Objective: Create a rule to generate a number pattern, and plot the points.

The Student Debrief is intended to invite reflection and active processing of the total lesson experience.

Invite students to review their solutions for the Problem Set. They should check work by comparing answers with a partner before going over answers as a class. Look for misconceptions or misunderstandings that can be addressed in the Debrief. Guide students in a conversation to debrief the Problem Set and process the lesson.

You may choose to use any combination of the questions below to lead the discussion.

- Compare your rules from Problem 3 with a neighbor. Which rule is the only one that might be different from a neighbor? Why?

- In Problem 4, did Avi, Ezra, and Erik name all of the rules that contain the point (0.6, 1.8)? Name some other rules that would contain this point.

- In Problem 5, what was your thought process or strategy as you worked to identify a mixed operation rule? In order to create a rule for a line parallel to $\overleftrightarrow{OP}$, what part of the rule did you need to change?

- If you know the location of one point on the plane, how many lines contain that point? If you know the location of two points on the plane, how many lines contain both of those points?

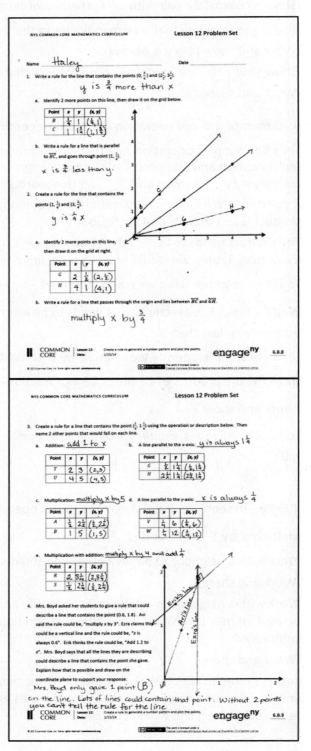

COMMON CORE   Lesson 12: Create a rule to generate a number pattern, and plot the points.
Date: 1/31/14

6.B.80

Exit Ticket (3 minutes)

After the Student Debrief, instruct students to complete the Exit Ticket. A review of their work will help you assess the students' understanding of the concepts that were presented in the lesson today and plan more effectively for future lessons. You may read the questions aloud to the students.

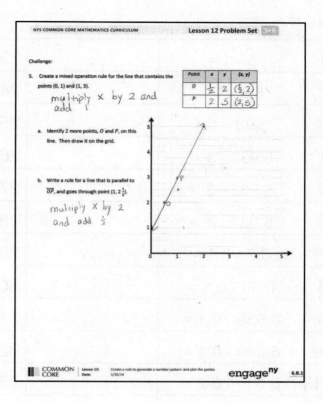

NYS COMMON CORE MATHEMATICS CURRICULUM   Lesson 12 Problem Set 5•6

Challenge:

5. Create a mixed operation rule for the line that contains the points (0, 1) and (1, 3).

Point	x	y	(x, y)
O	$\frac{1}{2}$	2	$(\frac{1}{2}, 2)$
P	2	5	(2,5)

multiply x by 2 and add 1

a. Identify 2 more points, O and P, on this line. Then draw it on the grid.

b. Write a rule for a line that is parallel to $\overline{OP}$, and goes through point $(1, 2\frac{1}{2})$.

multiply x by 2 and add $\frac{1}{2}$

COMMON CORE   Lesson 12:   Create a rule to generate a number pattern and plot the points.
                Date: 1/15/14

engage^ny   6.B.1

A

Correct _____

Subtract.

1	5 - 1 =	.	23	7.985 - 0.002 =	.
2	5.9 - 1 =	.	24	7.985 - 0.004 =	.
3	5.93 - 1 =	.	25	2.7 - 0.1 =	.
4	5.932 - 1 =	.	26	2.785 - 0.1 =	.
5	5.932 - 2 =	.	27	2.785 - 0.5 =	.
6	5.932 - 4 =	.	28	4.913 - 0.4 =	.
7	0.5 - 0.1 =	.	29	3.58 - 0.01 =	.
8	0.53 - 0.1 =	.	30	3.586 - 0.01 =	.
9	0.539 - 0.1 =	.	31	3.586 - 0.05 =	.
10	8.539 - 0.1 =	.	32	7.982 - 0.04 =	.
11	8.539 - 0.2 =	.	33	6.126 - 0.001 =	.
12	8.539 - 0.4 =	.	34	6.126 - 0.004 =	.
13	0.05 - 0.01 =	.	35	9.348 - 0.006 =	.
14	0.057 - 0.01 =	.	36	8.347 - 0.3 =	.
15	1.057 - 0.01 =	.	37	9.157 - 0.05 =	.
16	1.857 - 0.01 =	.	38	6.879 - 0.009 =	.
17	1.857 - 0.02 =	.	39	6.548 - 2 =	.
18	1.857 - 0.04 =	.	40	6.548 - 0.2 =	.
19	0.005 - 0.001 =	.	41	6.548 - 0.02 =	.
20	7.005 - 0.001 =	.	42	6.548 - 0.002 =	.
21	7.905 - 0.001 =	.	43	6.196 - 0.06 =	.
22	7.985 - 0.001 =	.	44	9.517 - 0.004 =	.

B

Subtract.

Improvement _____   # Correct _____

1	6 - 1 =	.	23	7.986 - 0.002 =	.
2	6.9 - 1 =	.	24	7.986 - 0.004 =	.
3	6.93 - 1 =	.	25	3.7 - 0.1 =	.
4	6.932 - 1 =	.	26	3.785 - 0.1 =	.
5	6.932 - 2 =	.	27	3.785 - 0.5 =	.
6	6.932 - 4 =	.	28	5.924 - 0.4 =	.
7	0.6 - 0.1 =	.	29	4.58 - 0.01 =	.
8	0.63 - 0.1 =	.	30	4.586 - 0.01 =	.
9	0.639 - 0.1 =	.	31	4.586 - 0.05 =	.
10	8.639 - 0.1 =	.	32	6.183 - 0.04 =	.
11	8.639 - 0.2 =	.	33	7.127 - 0.001 =	.
12	8.639 - 0.4 =	.	34	7.127 - 0.004 =	.
13	0.06 - 0.01 =	.	35	1.459 - 0.006 =	.
14	0.067 - 0.01 =	.	36	8.457 - 0.4 =	.
15	1.067 - 0.01 =	.	37	1.267 - 0.06 =	.
16	1.867 - 0.01 =	.	38	7.981 - 0.001 =	.
17	1.867 - 0.02 =	.	39	7.548 - 2 =	.
18	1.867 - 0.04 =	.	40	7.548 - 0.2 =	.
19	0.006 - 0.001 =	.	41	7.548 - 0.02 =	.
20	7.006 - 0.001 =	.	42	7.548 - 0.002 =	.
21	7.906 - 0.001 =	.	43	7.197 - 0.06 =	.
22	7.986 - 0.001 =	.	44	1.627 - 0.004 =	.

Name _____   Date _____

1. Write a rule for the line that contains the points $(0, \frac{3}{4})$ and $(2\frac{1}{2}, 2\frac{1}{4})$.

    a. Identify 2 more points on this line, then draw it on the grid below.

Point	x	y	(x, y)
B			
C			

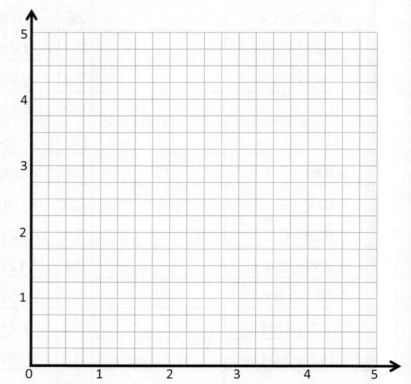

    b. Write a rule for a line that is parallel to $\overleftrightarrow{BC}$ and goes through point $(1, \frac{1}{4})$.

2. Create a rule for the line that contains the points $(1, \frac{1}{4})$ and $(3, \frac{3}{4})$.

    a. Identify 2 more points on this line, then draw it on the grid at right.

Point	x	y	(x, y)
G			
H			

    b. Write a rule for a line that passes through the origin and lies between $\overleftrightarrow{BC}$ and $\overleftrightarrow{GH}$.

3. Create a rule for a line that contains the point $(\frac{1}{4}, 1\frac{1}{4})$, using the operation or description below. Then, name 2 other points that would fall on each line.

a. Addition: _____

Point	x	y	(x, y)
T			
U			

b. A line parallel to the x-axis: _____

Point	x	y	(x, y)
G			
H			

c. Multiplication: _____

Point	x	y	(x, y)
A			
B			

d. A line parallel to the y-axis: _____

Point	x	y	(x, y)
V			
W			

e. Multiplication with addition: _____

Point	x	y	(x, y)
R			
S			

4. Mrs. Boyd asked her students to give a rule that could describe a line that contains the point (0.6, 1.8). Avi said the rule could be *multiply x by 3*. Ezra claims this could be a vertical line, and the rule could be *x is always 0.6*. Erik thinks the rule could be *add 1.2 to x*. Mrs. Boyd says that all the lines they are describing could describe a line that contains the point she gave. Explain how that is possible, and draw the lines on the coordinate plane to support your response.

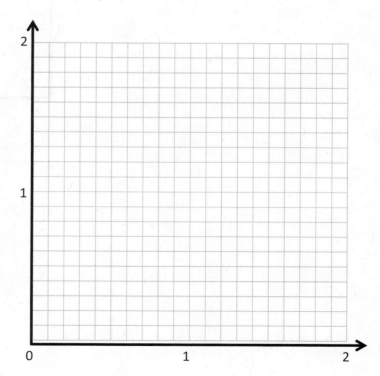

Lesson 12:   Create a rule to generate a number pattern, and plot the points.
Date: 1/31/14

Challenge:

5. Create a mixed operation rule for the line that contains the points (0, 1) and (1, 3).

Point	x	y	(x, y)
O			
P			

a. Identify 2 more points, O and P, on this line, and draw it on the grid.

b. Write a rule for a line that is parallel to $\overleftrightarrow{OP}$ and goes through point $(1, 2\frac{1}{2})$.

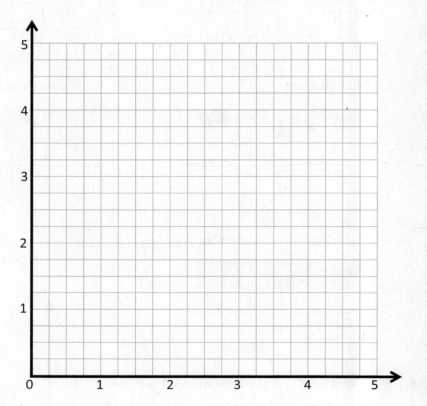

COMMON CORE™

Lesson 12:   Create a rule to generate a number pattern, and plot the points.
Date: 1/31/14

6.B.86

Name _____   Date _____

1. Write the rule for the line that contains the points $(0, 1\frac{1}{2})$ and $(1\frac{1}{2}, 3)$.

a. Identify 2 more points on this line,
    then draw it on the grid below.

Point	x	y	(x, y)
B			
C			

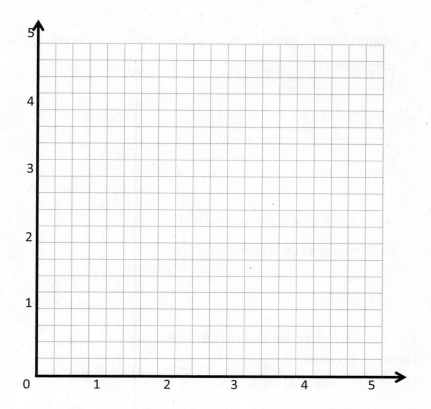

b. Write a rule for a line that is parallel
    to $\overleftrightarrow{BC}$ and goes through point $(1, \frac{1}{2})$.

Name _____   Date _____

1. Write a rule for the line that contains the points $(0, \frac{1}{4})$ and $(2\frac{1}{2}, 2\frac{3}{4})$.

    a. Identify 2 more points on this line, then draw it on the grid below.

Point	x	y	(x, y)
B			
C			

    b. Write a rule for a line that is parallel to $\overleftrightarrow{BC}$ and goes through point $(1, 2\frac{1}{4})$.

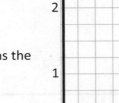

2. Give the rule for the line that contains the points $(1, 2\frac{1}{2})$ and $(2\frac{1}{2}, 2\frac{1}{2})$.

    a. Identify 2 more points on this line, then draw it on the grid above.

Point	x	y	(x, y)
G			
H			

    b. Write a rule for a line that is parallel to $\overleftrightarrow{GH}$.

3. Give the rule for a line that contains the point $(\frac{3}{4}, 1\frac{1}{2})$, using the operation or description below. Then, name 2 other points that would fall on each line.

a. Addition: _____

Point	x	y	(x, y)
T			
U			

b. A line parallel to the x-axis: _____

Point	x	y	(x, y)
G			
H			

c. Multiplication: _____

Point	x	y	(x, y)
A			
B			

d. A line parallel to the y-axis: _____

Point	x	y	(x, y)
V			
W			

e. Multiplication with addition:

_____

Point	x	y	(x, y)
R			
S			

4. On the grid, two lines intersect at (1.2, 1.2). If line *a* passes through the origin, and line *b* contains the point at (1.2,0), write a rule for line *a* and line *b*.

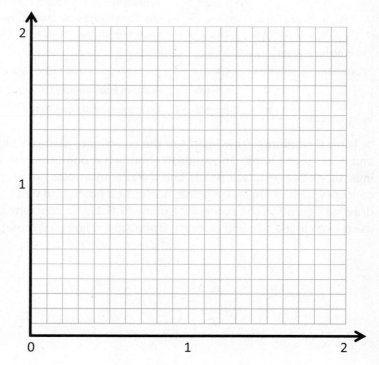

Lesson 12:   Create a rule to generate a number pattern, and plot the points.

Date: 1/31/14

COMMON CORE™

6.B.89

Topic C
Drawing Figures in the Coordinate Plane

5.G.1, 5.G.2

Focus Standard:	5.G.1	Use a pair of perpendicular number lines, called axes, to define a coordinate system, with the intersection of the lines (the origin) arranged to coincide with the 0 on each line and a given point in the plan located by using an ordered pair of numbers, called its coordinates. Understand that the first number indicates how far to travel from the origin in the direction of one axis, and the second number indicates how far to travel in the direction of the second axis, with the convention that the names of the two axes and the coordinates correspond (e.g., x-axis and x-coordinate, y-axis and y-coordinate).
	5.G.2	Represent real world and mathematical problems by graphing points in the first quadrant of the coordinate plane, and interpret coordinate values of points in the context of the situation.
Instructional Days:	5	
Coherence -Links from:	G4–M4	Angle Measure and Plane Figures
	G4–M5	Fraction Equivalence, Ordering, and Operations
-Links to:	G6–M4	Expressions and Equations

In Topic C, students draw figures in the coordinate plane by plotting points to create parallel, perpendicular, and intersecting lines. They reason about what points are needed to produce such lines and angles, and investigate the resultant points and their relationships. In preparation for Topic D, students recall Grade 4 concepts such as angles on a line, angles at a point, and vertical angles—all produced by plotting points and drawing figures on the coordinate plane (**5.G.1**). To conclude the topic, students draw symmetric figures using both angle size and distance from a given line of symmetry (**5.G.2**).

A Teaching Sequence Towards Mastery of Drawing Figures in the Coordinate Plane

Objective 1: Construct parallel line segments on a rectangular grid.
(Lesson 13)

Objective 2: Construct parallel line segments, and analyze relationships of the coordinate pairs.
(Lesson 14)

Objective 3: Construct perpendicular line segments on a rectangular grid.
(Lesson 15)

Objective 4: Construct perpendicular line segments, and analyze relationships of the coordinate pairs.
(Lesson 16)

Objective 5: Draw symmetric figures using distance and angle measure from the line of symmetry.
(Lesson 17)

Lesson 13

Objective: Construct parallel line segments on a rectangular grid.

Suggested Lesson Structure

■ Fluency Practice   (12 minutes)
■ Concept Development   (38 minutes)
■ Student Debrief   (10 minutes)
   Total Time   **(60 minutes)**

Fluency Practice (12 minutes)

- Multiply **5.NBT.5**   (5 minutes)
- Draw Angles **4.G.6**   (7 minutes)

Multiply (5 minutes)

Materials: (S) Personal white boards

Note: This drill reviews year-long fluency standards.

   T: Solve 43 × 23 using the standard algorithm.
   S: (Write 43 × 23 = 989 using the standard algorithm.)

Continue the process for 543 × 23, 49 × 32, 249 × 32, and 954 × 25.

Draw Angles (7 minutes)

Materials: (S) Blank paper, ruler, protractor

Note: This fluency activity reviews Grade 4
concepts and prepares students for today's
lesson.

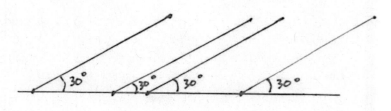

   T: Use your ruler to draw a 4-inch
        horizontal line on your paper.
   T: Plot four points at random on the line.
   T: Use each point as a vertex. Above the line, draw and label 30° angles that open to the right.

Repeat with 60° and 45° angles as time permits. Students should notice each set of lines is parallel.

	Lesson 13:	Construct parallel line segments on a rectangular grid.
	Date:	1/31/14

6.C.3

Concept Development (38 minutes)

Materials: (T) Triangle templates in various sizes (made from rectangle template) (S) Straightedge, rectangle template (used to make triangle templates), recording sheet, scissors, unlined paper

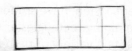

Note: An Application Problem is not included in this lesson in order to provide adequate time for the Concept Development.

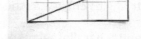

Problem 1: Construct parallel lines using a triangle template and straightedge.

Note: Demonstrate and give work time to the level your students need throughout this process.

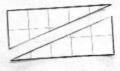

T: (Distribute 1 rectangle template and unlined paper to each student.)

T: Cut out the 5 unit by 2 unit rectangle.

T: (Allow students time to cut.) Position your rectangle on your paper so that the horizontal side is 5 units.

T: With your straightedge, draw the diagonal from the lower left to the upper right vertex.

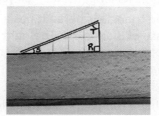

T: Cut along the diagonal.

T: Put one of the right triangles away. Tell your neighbor some things that you know about it.

S: One angle is a right angle and measures 90 degrees. → One side is 2 units long and the other side is 5 units. → The angles that aren't 90 degrees are acute.

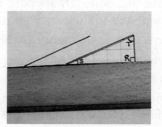

T: Place your triangle on your paper so that the horizontal side is 5 units and the 90-degree angle is to the right.

T: Label the right angle and name its vertex R.

T: Name the vertex of the angle at the top of the triangle as T and the vertex of the angle at left as S.

T: Place your straightedge horizontally across your paper, then place the base of the triangle along the straightedge. Trace a line across $\overline{ST}$.

T: Slide triangle RST to the right, about an inch, along your straightedge, without moving the straightedge. Trace a second line across $\overline{ST}$.

T: Remove the triangle and straightedge from your paper. What do you notice about the two line segments you've drawn? Turn and talk.

S: We traced the same segment twice, so they're the same length. → They are parallel because angle S is the same and comes out of the same line.

T: Let's try it again, but this time we'll arrange our straightedge so that it's oriented vertically on our paper.

Lesson 13:   Construct parallel line segments on a rectangular grid.
Date: 1/31/14

6.C.4

Repeat the same construction along a vertical straightedge, moving the triangle down about an inch before tracing the parallel segment. Then, have students work with a partner to cut out the remaining rectangles and bisect them on the diagonal to create a variety of right triangles.

T: Continue to construct parallel segments using a variety of angle templates. Place your straightedge in a variety of ways on your paper. Share your work with a neighbor as you work. Think about how the angles of your triangles change as the sides change.

Problem 2: Identify parallel segments on grid paper.

T: (Distribute parallel lines recording sheet to students. Display image of segments $\overline{AB}$ and $\overline{CD}$ on board.) Put your finger on line segment $\overline{AB}$.

S: (Put finger on line segment.)

T: Using the gridlines, visualize a right triangle that has $\overline{AB}$ as its longer side. Tell your neighbor what you see.

S: The triangle is here. It has a height of 2 units and a base of 3 units. → The right angle would be at the bottom and across from segment $\overline{AB}$. → I see a triangle that is above $\overline{AB}$. The right angle is on the top right across from $\overline{AB}$.

T: (Shade triangle.) The triangle has a height of 2 units and a base of 3 units. (Mark right angle with right angle symbol.) Shade the triangle on your paper.

T: Now look at segment $\overline{CD}$. Shade a right triangle that has $\overline{CD}$ as its longer side.

T: What do you notice about the two triangles that were used to construct each segment? Turn and talk.

S: They're the exact same triangle. → For $\overline{CD}$ the triangle just moved over to the right. → The triangles have the same side lengths and the angles look like they are the same size too.

T: This is the same as when we slid our triangles along the straightedge. Now the triangle is sliding along the grid lines. (Drag finger along the grid line to show the movement of the triangle.) Can we say then, that segment $\overline{AB}$ is parallel to $\overline{CD}$? Why or why not?

S: Yes, they're parallel because they intersect the grid line at the same angle.

Repeat the process with $\overline{EF}$ and $\overline{GH}$.

T: If $\overline{EF}$ was drawn first, how was the triangle moved before $\overline{GH}$ was constructed? Turn and talk.

S: The triangle moved to the right and then down. → I can see that the triangle moved 1 grid square down and 1 grid square to the right. So that means that the segment's endpoints moved the same way.

NOTES ON
MULTIPLE MEANS OF
ACTION AND
EXPRESSION:

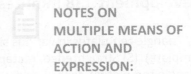

Cutting paper with scissors may be a challenge for some learners. Try the following tips:

- Provide rectangle template on cardstock or thicker paper.
- Darken and thicken the cutting lines.
- Provide left-handed, loop, spring, self-opening, or other adaptive scissors, if needed.
- Instruct students to turn the paper, not the scissors.
- Offer precut triangles.

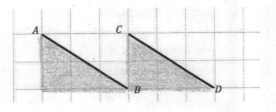

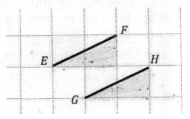

 Lesson 13:   Construct parallel line segments on a rectangular grid.
Date: 1/31/14

6.C.5

T: (Display segments $\overline{IJ}$ and $\overline{KL}$ on board.) Look at segments $\overline{IJ}$ and $\overline{KL}$. Shade the right triangles that have these segments as one of their longer sides.

T: Are the segments parallel? Turn and talk.

S: No. The triangle for $\overline{IJ}$ is taller. → $\overline{KL}$ has a height of 2 and $\overline{IJ}$ has a height of 3. → I can see that if we extend each segment, they intersect.

T: (Model extension of segments and their intersection.) As I extend these segments, are they parallel?

S: No, they intersect so they can't be parallel.

T: Let's consider something else about these segments. Imagine that we slid the longer segment over 1 unit to the right. Would the segments line up perfectly? Why or why not?

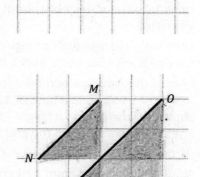

S: I can see the little one inside the big one. They are at different angles. They won't line up. → The acute angles in the triangles are different sizes so they don't have the same steepness which means they won't line up. → One segment is over 1 up 2 and the other one is over 1 up 4. That makes the angles in the triangles different sizes.

T: (Display segments $\overline{MN}$ and $\overline{OP}$ on board.) Look at segments $\overline{MN}$ and $\overline{OP}$. Are they parallel segments?

S: They look like they're parallel, but the triangle that includes $\overline{MN}$ has a height of 2 units and a base of 2 units, and the triangle for $\overline{OP}$ has a height of 4 units and a base of 4 units. → I extended segment $\overline{MN}$, and now it's the same length as $\overline{OP}$, and they are parallel.

T: The triangle that I can see for $\overline{MN}$ has a height of 2 units and a base of 2 units. (Shade triangle.) It looks like $\overline{OP}$ is the side of a triangle with a height and base of 4 units.

T: Look inside the larger triangle. Do you see two triangles like the one related to $\overline{MN}$? (Point out the two triangles.)

S: (Shade two separate triangles beneath $\overline{MN}$.) I can also see two triangles, each with heights and bases of 2 units, just like the triangle that includes $\overline{MN}$.

T: What do you think now? Are the segments parallel?

S: I see it now, they are parallel. $\overline{OP}$ is just longer. → We could have also just extended $\overline{MN}$ to make it longer, and then it could be part of a triangle with a height and base of 4 units.

Problem 3: Construct parallel segments on grid paper.

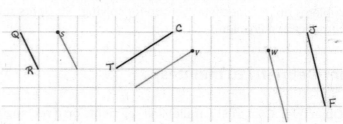

T: (Display image of segment $\overline{QR}$ on board.) Tell your neighbor about the triangle that you see that has segment $\overline{QR}$ as a side.

S: (Discuss triangle.)

T: Draw a segment parallel to $\overline{QR}$ that goes through point S. Tell your neighbor what you did.

S: I drew a triangle that's the same as the one that includes $\overline{QR}$ with a height of 2 units and a base of 1 unit directly below point S. Then, I put a point at the right end of the base, and connected it to point S. → I went down 2 units from Q and then right 1 unit to point R. So I went down 2 units from S and right 1 unit and made a point to connect to S.

T: Watch me. I visualized a triangle with a height of 2 and a base of 1 beneath segment $\overline{QR}$. (Demonstrate.) If I visualize the same triangle beneath point S, I can find a point to connect with point S, to make a parallel segment. (Demonstrate.)

T: Draw parallel segments for the other two examples on your paper. Share your work with a neighbor. (Allow students time to work.)

T: (Display image of line ℓ on board.) Look at line ℓ. Think about the triangle that you are visualizing for line ℓ. (Give students time to think.) Tell your neighbor about what you visualized.

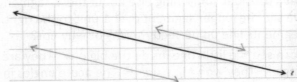

S: I can see a triangle with a height to 3 and a base of 12. → I see a triangle with a height of 2 and a base of 8. → I can see a bunch of triangles each with a height of 1 and a base of 4.

T: I heard that you saw several different triangles for line ℓ. Some of you saw a large triangle with a height of 3 units and a base of 12 units. (Use finger to show on board.) Others saw a series of smaller triangles with a height of 1 unit and a base of 4 units. Let's construct a line that is parallel to line ℓ. Draw a point on the grid somewhere above line ℓ. (Model on board.)

S: (Draw point.)

T: Now, plot a second point that creates the side of the triangle you visualized. For example, some of you visualized a triangle with a height of 2 units and a base of 8 units, so you'll move 2 units down and 8 units to the right, then plot a point. (Model on board.)

S: (Plot point.)

T: Use your straightedge to draw a line parallel to line ℓ through the two points you've plotted. (Allow students time to draw line.)

T: Do the same thing again, but this time, construct your line below line ℓ.

Note: The triangle templates the students created today will be used in future lessons. It may be helpful to keep them in individually labeled plastic bag.

Problem Set (10 minutes)

Students should do their personal best to complete the Problem Set within the allotted 10 minutes. For some classes, it may be appropriate to modify the assignment by specifying which problems they work on first. Some problems do not specify a method for solving. Students solve these problems using the RDW approach used for Application Problems.

Student Debrief (10 minutes)

Lesson Objective: Construct parallel line segments on a rectangular grid.

The Student Debrief is intended to invite reflection and active processing of the total lesson experience.

Lesson 13:   Construct parallel line segments on a rectangular grid.
Date: 1/31/14

6.C.7

Invite students to review their solutions for the Problem Set. They should check work by comparing answers with a partner before going over answers as a class. Look for misconceptions or misunderstandings that can be addressed in the Debrief. Guide students in a conversation to debrief the Problem Set and process the lesson.

You may choose to use any combination of the questions below to lead the discussion.

- In Problem 1, share your parallel lines with a partner. Explain how you drew the lines.

- Compare and share your solution for Problem 2 with a partner. Explain how you know the lines are parallel. For the segments that were not circled, how did you determine that they were not parallel?

- Compare and check your answers for Problem 3 with a partner. Do you have the same answer? (It is possible that two students may create different segments that lie on the same parallel line, perhaps on Problem 3(f). Be sure to point out that while the segments aren't the same, they do lie on the same line.)

- On Problem 4, did you draw the same lines as your neighbor? If your answers are different, are you both correct? How is that possible?

- Go back to $\overline{EF}$ and $\overline{GH}$. We draw $\overline{EF}$. We slide down 1 grid square and draw the same segment. That new segment is parallel to $\overline{EF}$. Then, slide over 1 grid square and draw $\overline{GH}$. $\overline{GH}$ is parallel to our new segment. $\overline{EF}$ is parallel to the new segment and $\overline{GH}$ is parallel to the new segment. Then what do we know about $\overline{EF}$ and $\overline{GH}$?

- How does drawing these parallel segments relate to our fluency activity with angles?

Exit Ticket (3 minutes)

After the Student Debrief, instruct students to complete the Exit Ticket. A review of their work will help you assess the students' understanding of the concepts that were presented in the lesson today and plan more effectively for future lessons. You may read the questions aloud to the students.

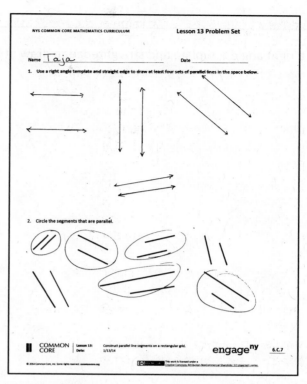

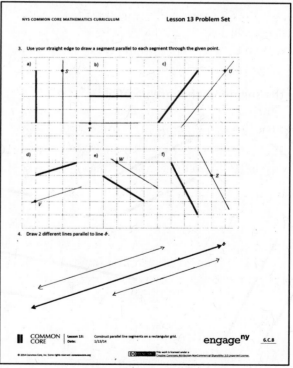

Lesson 13:   Construct parallel line segments on a rectangular grid.
Date: 1/31/14

6.C.8

Name _____ Date _____

1. Use a right angle template and straightedge to draw at least four sets of parallel lines in the space below.

2. Circle the segments that are parallel.

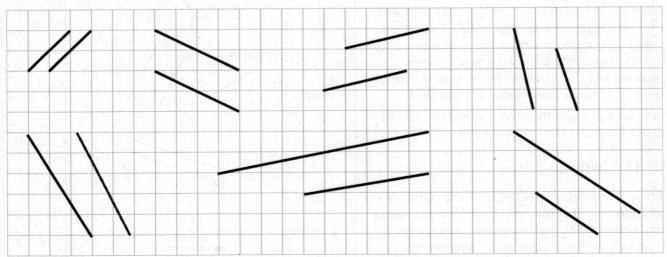

3. Use your straightedge to draw a segment parallel to each segment through the given point.

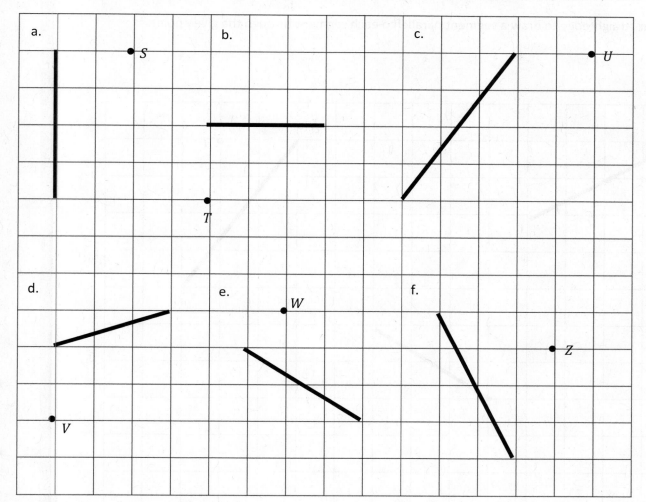

4. Draw 2 different lines parallel to line 𝑏.

COMMON CORE™

Lesson 13: Construct parallel line segments on a rectangular grid.
Date: 1/31/14

6.C.10

Name _____   Date _____

1.   Use your straightedge to draw a segment parallel to each segment through the given point.

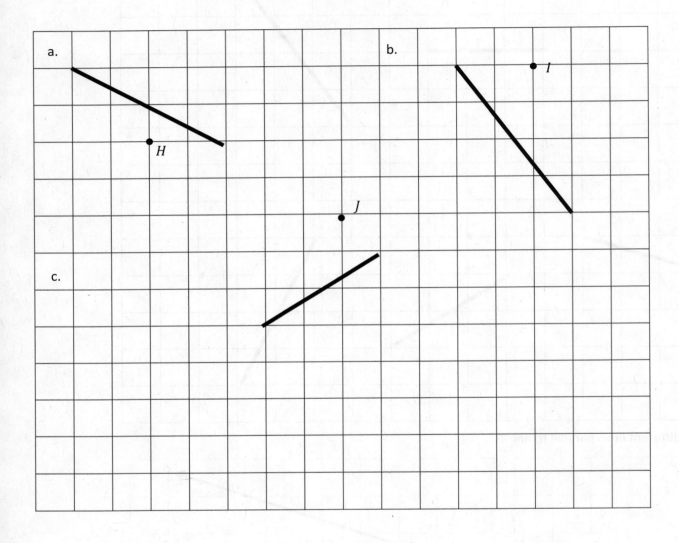

COMMON CORE™

Lesson 13:   Construct parallel line segments on a rectangular grid.
Date: 1/31/14

6.C.11

Name _____   Date _____

1. Use your right angle template and straightedge to draw at least three sets of parallel lines in the space below.

2. Circle the segments that are parallel.

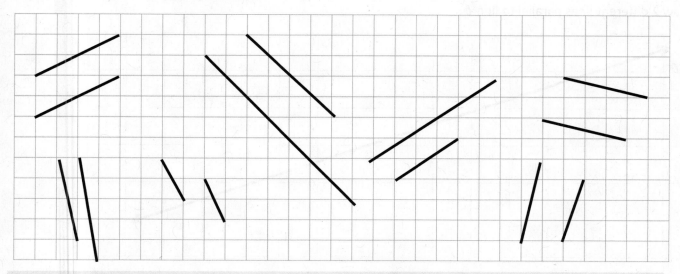

3. Use your straightedge to draw a segment parallel to each segment through the given point.

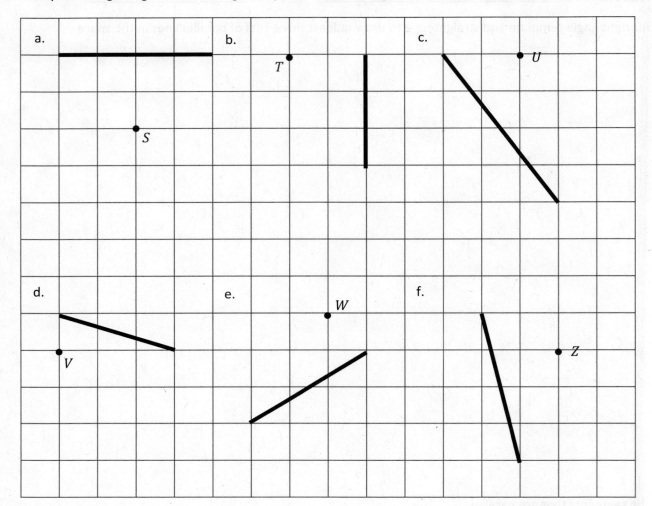

4. Draw 2 different lines parallel to line *b*.

a.↓   b.↓   c.↓   d.↓

e.→   f.↓   g.→   h.→

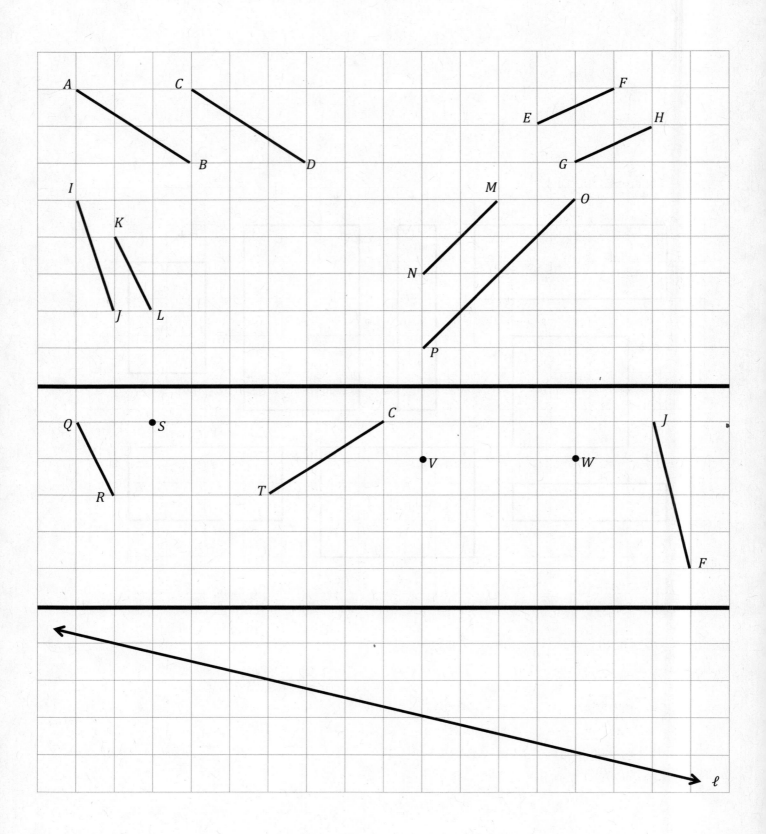

Lesson 14

Objective: Construct parallel line segments, and analyze relationships of the coordinate pairs.

Suggested Lesson Structure

■ Application Problem	(7 minutes)
■ Fluency Practice	(14 minutes)
■ Concept Development	(29 minutes)
■ Student Debrief	(10 minutes)
Total Time	**(60 minutes)**

Application Problem (7 minutes)

Drew's fish tank measures 32 cm by 22 cm by 26 cm. He pours 20 liters of water into it, and some water overflows the tank. Find the volume of water, in milliliters, that overflows.

Note: Today's Application Problem reviews volume concepts from G5–Module 5.

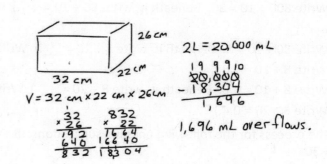

Fluency Practice (14 minutes)

- Multiply Multi-Digit Whole Numbers **5.NBT.5**   (4 minutes)
- Multiply and Divide Decimals **5.NBT.7**   (3 minutes)
- Draw Angles **4.G.1**   (7 minutes)

Multiply Multi-Digit Whole Numbers (4 minutes)

Materials: (S) Personal white boards

Note: This drill reviews year-long fluency standards.

T: Solve 45 × 25 using the standard algorithm.

S: (Write 45 × 25 = 1,125 using the standard algorithm.)

Continue process for 345 × 25, 59 × 23, 149 × 23, and 756 × 43.

COMMON CORE™

Lesson 14:   Construct parallel line segments, and analyze relationships of the coordinate pairs.
Date: 1/31/14

6.C.16

Multiply and Divide Decimals (3 minutes)

Materials: (S) Personal white boards

Note: This fluency activity reviews G5–Module 2 concepts.

NOTES ON
MULTIPLE MEANS FOR
ACTION AND
EXPRESSION:

Depending on the needs of students working below grade level, scaffold the Multiply and Divide Decimals fluency activity with visuals, such as arrays of number disks, that clearly illustrate the number patterns.

T: (Write 4 × 2 = ___.) What's 4 × 2?

S: 8.

T: (Write 4 × 2 = 8. Beneath it, write 0.4 × 2 = ___.) What's 0.4 × 2?

S: 0.4 × 2 = 0.8.

T: (Write 0.4 × 2 = 0.8. Beneath it, write 0.04 × 2 = ___.) Write the number sentence.

S: (Write 0.04 × 2 = 0.08.)

T: (Write 800 ÷ 10 = ___.) What's 800 ÷ 10?

S: 80.

T: (Write 800 ÷ 10 = 80. Beneath it, write 80 ÷ 10 = ___.) What's 80 ÷ 10?

S: 8.

T: (Write 80 ÷ 10 = 8. Beneath it, write 8 ÷ 10 = ___.) Write the number sentence.

S: (Write 8 ÷ 10 = 0.8.)

T: (Write 8 ÷ 10 = 0.8. Beneath it, write 8 ÷ 20 = ___.) Write the number sentence.

S: (Write 8 ÷ 20 = 0.4.)

Continue the process for the following possible suggestions: 8 ÷ 40, 15 ÷ 5, 15 ÷ 50, 2.5 ÷ 10, 2.5 ÷ 50, 0.12 ÷ 3, and 0.12 ÷ 30.

Draw Angles (7 minutes)

Materials: (S) Blank paper, ruler, protractor

Note: This fluency activity informally prepares students for today's lesson. Provide students time to work following each step.

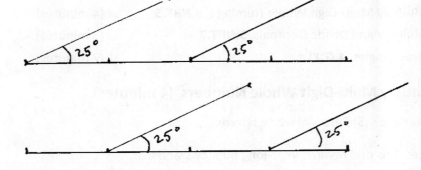

T: Use your ruler to draw two parallel 4-inch horizontal lines on your paper.

T: Plot 5 points, one at each inch, including 0 inches.

T: Use the points at 0 and 2 inches on the upper line as the vertices of two angles with the same measure.

T: Use the points at 1 inch and 3 inches on the lower line as the vertices of two angles with the same measure as those on the upper line.

Lesson 14:	Construct parallel line segments, and analyze relationships of the coordinate pairs.
Date:	1/31/14

6.C.17

Repeat as time allows. Take note as to whether the students observe which lines are parallel as they attempt to explain why.

Concept Development (29 minutes)

Materials: (T) Right angle template *RST* (with a base of 5 units and a height of 2 units) (S) Personal white board, coordinate plane template , straightedge, right angle template *RST* (created in G5–M6–Lesson 13)

Problem 1: Slide right triangle template parallel to the axes along coordinate plane to create parallel segments.

Note: Demonstrate and give work time to the level your students need throughout this process.

T: (Distribute coordinate plane template to students and display coordinate plane on board.) Plot points *A* and *B* at the following locations. (Display *A*: (2, 3) and *B*: (7, 5) on the board.)

T: Draw $\overline{AB}$.

T: Turn and tell your neighbor about a right triangle that you can see that has $\overline{AB}$ as its longest side. Use the grid lines to help you.

S: I see one with a base of 5 units and height of 2 units. → It has two acute angles. → The bottom left angle is less than the top right one because the triangle is going across more than it is going up.

MP.7 T: Find triangle *RST* that you cut out during yesterday's lesson. Remember that the letters name the vertices of the angles in this triangle.

T: Tell your neighbor how you can use triangle *RST* to draw a segment parallel to $\overline{AB}$.

S: It's just like we did yesterday. I can slide triangle *RST* to the right or to the left and trace the long side of the triangle. → I can move the triangle along the grid lines like yesterday. Up, down, left, right, or a combination of horizontal and vertical movements are ok as long as I keep the horizontal side parallel to the gridlines. → It's like we did in Fluency Practice: Because ∠*S* is the same as ∠*A* coming off the same base line, the lines will be parallel.

T: Yes, we can slide triangle *RST* along the grid lines, in a variety of directions, and then trace side $\overline{ST}$ to make parallel segments. (Demonstrate.)

T: Place your triangle back where it would be if you were first drawing $\overline{AB}$. (Show right triangle template *RST* on coordinate plane, just beneath $\overline{AB}$.)

T: Slide triangle *RST* to the right, one full grid square. (Model on the board.) Is side $\overline{ST}$ parallel to segment $\overline{AB}$?

S: Yes.

T: What coordinates does the vertex of ∠ *S* touch now?

S: (3, 3).

T: The vertex of ∠ *T*?

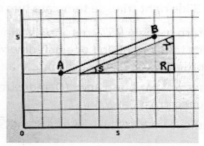

S: (8, 5).

T: Tell your neighbor how the x-coordinates of the endpoints changed when I slid the triangle one unit to the right.

S: They went from 2 to 3, and 7 to 8. → Both x-coordinates are 1 more than they were.

T: Do the y-coordinates of the endpoints change?

S: No.

T: As triangle RST slides one unit to the right, the x-coordinates of the vertices are increased by 1. (Move the triangle template back to original position.) Tell a neighbor how the x-coordinates would change if the triangle were slid along the gridlines 2 units to the *left*. (Slide the triangle template to the left.)

S: Both x-coordinates would be 2 less. → It's subtracting 2 from the x-coordinates of the vertices.

Repeat the process, moving 3 to the right and 3 to the left, asking students to analyze the change in the x-coordinate.

T: Position your triangle back at its original location. (Demonstrate.)

T: Watch as I slide the triangle up, along the grid lines two units. Is $\overline{ST}$ parallel to $\overline{AB}$? How do you know?

S: Yes. You kept the base parallel to the x-axis while you were sliding it up. → You slid it like there was a ruler on the left which is perpendicular to the x-axis, and you kept the triangle up against it the whole time.

T: What coordinates does the vertex of $\angle S$ touch ?

S: (2, 5).

T: The vertex of $\angle T$?

S: (7, 7).

T: Tell your neighbor how the y-coordinates of the vertices changed when I slid the triangle along the gridlines 2 units up. (Allow students time to share.)

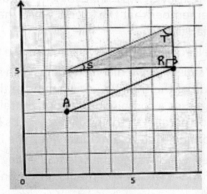

T: Did the x-coordinates of the vertices change?

S: No.

T: As triangle RST slides 2 units up parallel to the y-axis, the y-coordinates are increased by 2. (Move the triangle template back to the original position.)

Repeat the process, sliding the triangle both up and down and analyzing the change in the y coordinates.

Problem 2: Slide right triangle template two directions along coordinate plane to create parallel segments.

T: Return triangle RST to its original location. Slide your triangle 2 units to the right and one unit down. Tell your neighbor how the coordinates of the vertices of $\angle S$ and $\angle T$ have changed.

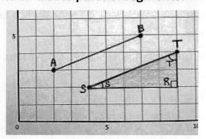

T: Trace $\overline{ST}$ on your plane. (Demonstrate.) Label the endpoints of your segment, as S and T.

T: Remove your triangle. Are $\overline{AB}$ and $\overline{ST}$ parallel? How do you

---

COMMON CORE™   Lesson 14:   Construct parallel line segments, and analyze relationships of the
                              coordinate pairs.   6.C.19
              Date: 1/31/14

know? Turn and talk.

S: They don't form a right angle, so they're not perpendicular. → They never touch, so they're parallel. → This is like yesterday. When we slide the triangle down, we can think about a parallel imaginary segment. Then, when we slide it over, we find a third segment that's parallel to the imaginary one and then we draw it.

T: $\overline{AB}$ and $\overline{ST}$ are parallel to each other because they are both parallel to the imaginary segment we found when we first slid the triangle down. We can also think about the angles in the triangles. $\angle A$ and $\angle S$ are the same measure because they were drawn from parallel baselines. So we can write, $\overline{AB}$ is parallel to $\overline{ST}$. (Write $\overline{AB}$ ∥ $\overline{ST}$ on the board.) Show me this statement on your personal board.

T: Record the coordinates of points S and T.

T: Compare the coordinates of points A and B to the coordinates of points S and T. Tell your neighbor why each x-coordinate in points S and T are 2 more than the x-coordinates in points A and B.

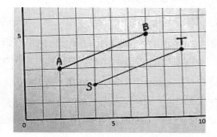

S: We shifted the triangle to the right, so the x-coordinate increased. → We slid the triangle over 2 units along the gridlines, so both x-coordinates are 2 more.

T: Tell your neighbor why the y-coordinates are 1 less.

S: We shifted the triangle to down, so the y-coordinate decreased. → We slid the triangle 1 grid squares down, so both y-coordinates are 1 less.

Problem 2: Identify coordinate pairs that create parallel lines.

T: (Display image of the second coordinate plane.) On the coordinate plane at the bottom of your page, plot the following points. (Write $C(1\frac{1}{2}, 2\frac{1}{2})$ and $D(3, 2)$ on the board.)

T: Use your straightedge to draw $\overline{CD}$.

T: Tell your neighbor about a right triangle that has $\overline{CD}$ as its long side and its right angle's vertex at $(1\frac{1}{2}, 2)$.

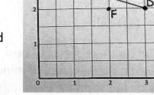

S: I see a triangle with a height of 1 unit and a length of 3 units. → The right angle is to the left, 1 unit beneath point C.

T: Focus for a moment on the vertex of the triangle that is at point C. Now, visualize that triangle moving 2 grid units to the left. Tell your neighbor the location of that vertex now.

S: $(\frac{1}{2}, 2\frac{1}{2})$.

T: Plot a point, E, at that location.

S: (Plot E.)

T: Plot another point, F, on the plane, that when connected to E will create a segment parallel to $\overline{CD}$. Tell your neighbor how you'll identify the location of point F.

S: It looks like point C slid 2 units to the left, so I can slide point D 2 units to the left also. → If I think of the triangle I saw with $\overline{CD}$, I can go down 1 unit from E and then right 3 units. That will be point F.

→ The x-coordinate of E is 1 less than C, so I can subtract 1 from D to find the x-coordinate of F.

T: Name the location of point F.

S: (2, 2).

T: Plot point F, then draw $\overline{EF}$ on your plane.

T: Imagine the lines that contain $\overline{CD}$ and $\overline{EF}$. If the part of these lines that we've drawn here are parallel to each other, we can say that the lines that contain them are also parallel. Write a statement naming the relationship between these two lines. (Draw arrows to show lines.)

S: Lines CD and EF are parallel. → (Write $\overleftrightarrow{CD}$ ∥ $\overleftrightarrow{EF}$.)

T: Plot a point, G, at $(3\frac{1}{2}, 2\frac{1}{2})$.

S: (Plot point.)

T: Compare the coordinates of point C to point G. Tell your neighbor how are they different.

S: (Discuss differences.)

T: Name the location of a point, H, that when connected to G, would create a segment parallel to line $\overleftrightarrow{CD}$.

S: (2, 3). → (5, 2). → $(\frac{1}{2}, 3\frac{1}{2})$.

T: Tell your neighbor how you identified the location of point H.

S: (Discuss with neighbor.)

T: Draw $\overleftrightarrow{GH}$ and write a statement about the relationship between these lines.

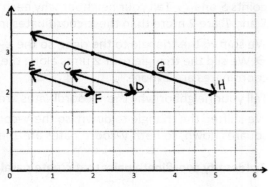

Problem Set (10 minutes)

Students should do their personal best to complete the Problem Set within the allotted 10 minutes. For some classes, it may be appropriate to modify the assignment by specifying which problems they work on first. Some problems do not specify a method for solving. Students solve these problems using the RDW approach used for Application Problems.

Student Debrief (10 minutes)

Lesson Objective: Construct parallel line segments, and analyze relationships of the coordinate pairs.

The Student Debrief is intended to invite reflection and active processing of the total lesson experience.

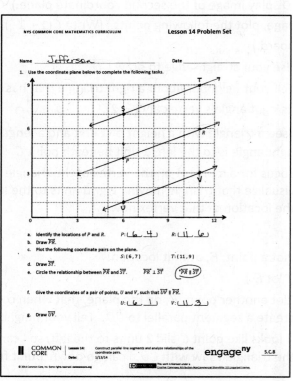

COMMON CORE™   **Lesson 14:**   Construct parallel line segments, and analyze relationships of the coordinate pairs.

Date: 1/31/14   6.C.21

© 2014 Common Core, Inc. All rights reserved. commoncore.org

Invite students to review their solutions for the Problem Set. They should check work by comparing answers with a partner before going over answers as a class. Look for misconceptions or misunderstandings that can be addressed in the Debrief. Guide students in a conversation to debrief the Problem Set and process the lesson.

You may choose to use any combination of the questions below to lead the discussion.

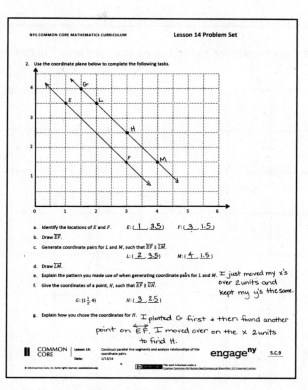

- Tell your neighbor about the triangle you visualized In Problem 1. Do the same for Problem 2.

- Show your coordinate pairs from Problem 1(g) to your neighbor. Can they identify how you manipulated the coordinates?

- Share the coordinate pairs you found for L and M in Problem 2(c). Explain how a triangle template could have been used to construct $\overleftrightarrow{LM}$ parallel to $\overleftrightarrow{EF}$. How many different ways would there be to slide the triangle template and get the same line?

- Explain your thought process as you identified the location of point H in Problem 2(f).

- Will any movement of a triangle on a grid produce parallel lines? Why or why not? What must we remember when we are using a triangle or set square to draw parallel lines either on a grid or off? (Students should mention the importance of keeping the movements parallel to one axis while perpendicular to the other.)

Exit Ticket (3 minutes)

After the Student Debrief, instruct students to complete the Exit Ticket. A review of their work will help you assess the students' understanding of the concepts that were presented in the lesson today and plan more effectively for future lessons. You may read the questions aloud to the students.

COMMON CORE™ | Lesson 14:   Construct parallel line segments, and analyze relationships of the coordinate pairs.   **6.C.22**

Date: 1/31/14

Name _____ Date _____

1. Use the coordinate plane below to complete the following tasks.

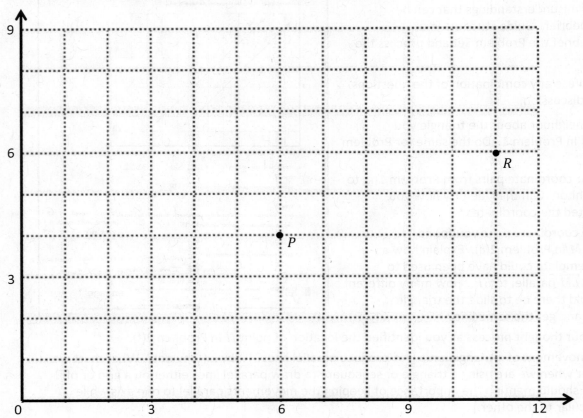

a. Identify the locations of *P* and *R*.   *P*: (_____, _____)   *R*: (_____, _____)

b. Draw $\overleftrightarrow{PR}$.

c. Plot the following coordinate pairs on the plane.

    S: (6, 7)   *T*: (11, 9)

d. Draw $\overleftrightarrow{ST}$.

e. Circle the relationship between $\overleftrightarrow{PR}$ and $\overleftrightarrow{ST}$. $\overleftrightarrow{PR} \perp \overleftrightarrow{ST}$ $\overleftrightarrow{PR} \parallel \overleftrightarrow{ST}$

f. Give the coordinates of a pair of points, *U* and *V*, such that $\overleftrightarrow{UV} \parallel \overleftrightarrow{PR}$.

    U: (_____, _____)   *V*: (_____, _____)

g. Draw $\overleftrightarrow{UV}$.

COMMON CORE™   **Lesson 14:**   Construct parallel line segments, and analyze relationships of the coordinate pairs.   **6.C.23**

    Date: 1/31/14

2.   Use the coordinate plane below to complete the following tasks.

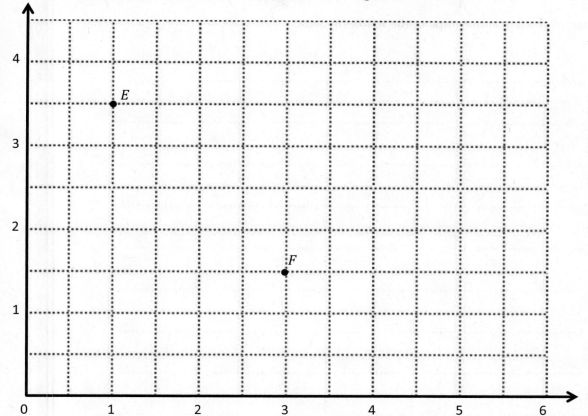

a.   Identify the locations of E and F. E: (_____, _____) F: (_____, _____)

b.   Draw $\overleftrightarrow{EF}$.

c.   Generate coordinate pairs for L and M, such that $\overleftrightarrow{EF} \parallel \overleftrightarrow{LM}$.

L: (____, ____) M: (____, ____)

d.   Draw $\overleftrightarrow{LM}$.

e.   Explain the pattern you made use of when generating coordinate pairs for L and M.

f.   Give the coordinates of a point, H, such that $\overleftrightarrow{EF} \parallel \overleftrightarrow{GH}$.

G: $(1\frac{1}{2}, 4)$ H: (____, ____)

g.   Explain how you chose the coordinates for H.

Name _____   Date _____

1. Use the coordinate plane below to complete the following tasks.

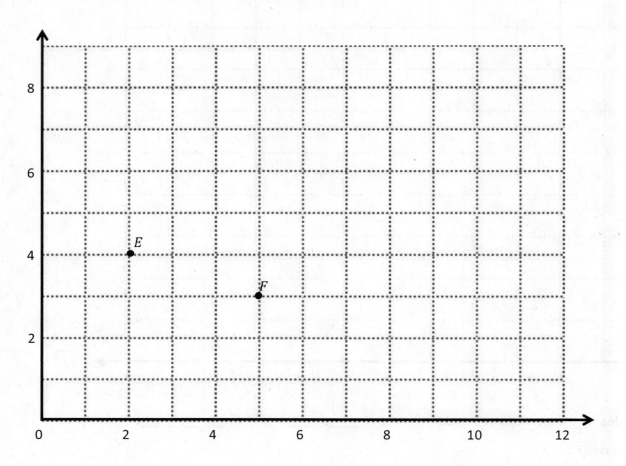

a. Identify the locations of E and F. E: (_____ , _____) F: (_____ , _____)

b. Draw $\overleftrightarrow{EF}$.

c. Generate coordinate pairs for L and M, such that $\overleftrightarrow{EF} \parallel \overleftrightarrow{LM}$.

L: (_____ , _____) M: (_____ , _____)

d. Draw $\overleftrightarrow{LM}$.

Name _____   Date _____

1. Use the coordinate plane below to complete the following tasks.

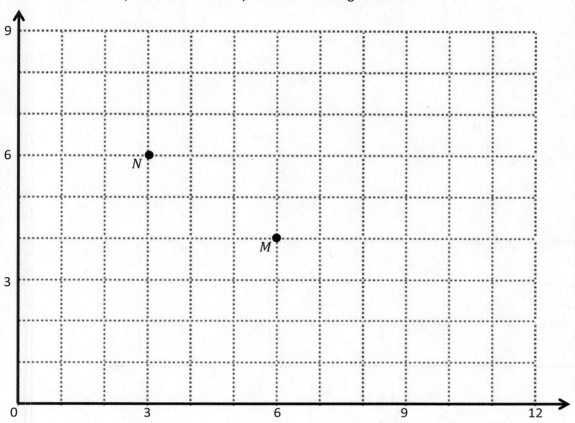

a. Identify the locations of M and N. M: (_____, _____) N: (_____, _____)

b. Draw $\overleftrightarrow{MN}$.

c. Plot the following coordinate pairs on the plane.

                          J: (5, 7) K: (8, 5)

d. Draw $\overleftrightarrow{JK}$.

e. Circle the relationship between $\overleftrightarrow{MN}$ and $\overleftrightarrow{JK}$. $\overleftrightarrow{MN} \perp \overleftrightarrow{JK}$ $\overleftrightarrow{MN} \parallel \overleftrightarrow{JK}$

f. Give the coordinates of a pair of points, F and G, such that $\overleftrightarrow{FG} \parallel \overleftrightarrow{MN}$.

                          F: (_____, _____) G: (_____, _____)

g. Draw $\overleftrightarrow{FG}$.

2. Use the coordinate plane below to complete the following tasks.

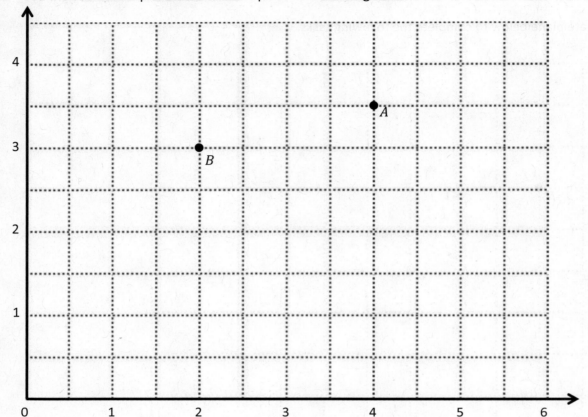

a. Identify the locations of A and B. A: (_____, _____) B: (_____, _____)

b. Draw $\overleftrightarrow{AB}$.

c. Generate coordinate pairs for C and D, such that $\overleftrightarrow{AB} \parallel \overleftrightarrow{CD}$.

C: (_____, _____) D: (_____, _____)

d. Draw $\overleftrightarrow{CD}$.

e. Explain the pattern you you used when generating coordinate pairs for C and D.

f. Give the coordinates of a point, F, such that $\overleftrightarrow{AB} \parallel \overleftrightarrow{EF}$.

E: $(2\frac{1}{2}, 2\frac{1}{2})$ F: (_____, _____)

g. Explain how you chose the coordinates for F.

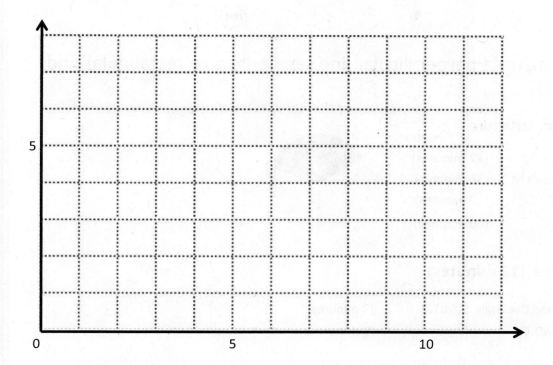

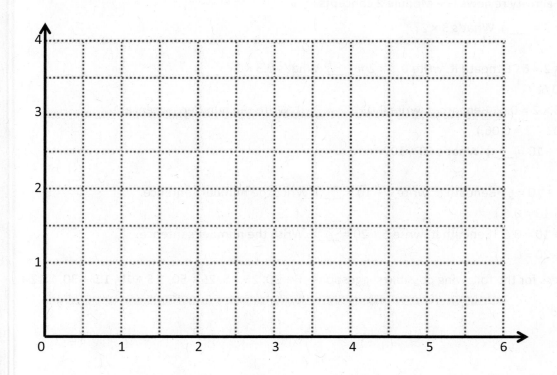

Lesson 15

Objective: Construct perpendicular line segments on a rectangular grid.

Suggested Lesson Structure

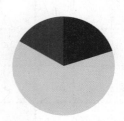

■ Fluency Practice   (12 minutes)
  Concept Development   (38 minutes)
■ Student Debrief   (10 minutes)
  Total Time   **(60 minutes)**

Fluency Practice (12 minutes)

▪ Multiply and Divide Decimals **5.NBT.7**   (3 minutes)
▪ Draw Angles **4.MD.6**   (9 minutes)

Multiply and Divide Decimals (3 minutes)

Materials: (S) Personal white boards

Note: This fluency activity reviews G5–Module 2 concepts.

> T: (Write 3 × 2 = ___.) What's 3 × 2?
> S: 6.
> T: (Write 3 × 2 = 6. Beneath it, write 0.3 × 2 = ___.) What's 0.3 × 2?
> S: 0.3 × 2 = 0.6.
> T: (Write 0.3 × 2 = 0.6. Beneath it, write 0.03 × 2 = ___.) Write the number sentence.
> S: (Write 0.03 × 2 = 0.06.)
> T: (Write 60 ÷ 10 = ___.) What's 60 ÷ 10?
> S: 6.
> T: (Write 60 ÷ 10 = 6. Beneath it, write 6 ÷ 10 = ___.) Write the number sentence.
> S: (Write 6 ÷ 10 = 0.6.)
> T: (Write 6 ÷ 10 = 0.6. Beneath it, write 6 ÷ 20 = ___.) Write the number sentence.
> S: (Write 6 ÷ 20 = 0.3.)

Continue the process for the following possible suggestions: 6 ÷ 30, 25 ÷ 5, 25 ÷ 50, 1.5 ÷ 10, 1.5 ÷ 30, 0.12 ÷ 4, and 0.12 ÷ 40.

COMMON CORE™

Lesson 15:   Construct perpendicular line segments on a rectangular grid.
Date: 1/31/14

Draw Angles (9 minutes)

Materials: (S) Blank paper, ruler, protractor

Note: This fluency activity informally prepares students for today's lesson.

Part 1:

T: Use your ruler to draw a 4-inch horizontal line
     about 3 inches down from the top of your paper.

T: Plot 5 points, one at each inch including 0 inches.

T: Turn to your partner and name pairs of angles
     whose sums are 90 degree.

S: 45° and 45°. → 30° and 60°. → 25° and 65°.

T: Use the points at zero and 1 inch as the vertices
     of 2 angles whose sum is 90°.

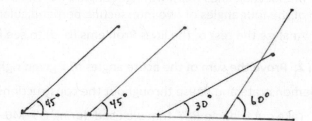

Part 2:

T: Use your ruler to draw another 4-inch horizontal line about 3 inches below your first one.

T: Plot 5 points, one at each inch including 0
     inches.

T: Draw the same angle you made on the top line
     at the first third inch.

T: Draw the same angle pair you made on the top
     line but this time, open the angles to the left
     and let the angle share a vertex with its pair.

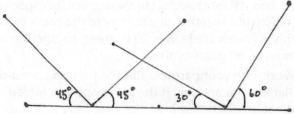

Repeat as time allows. Take note informally as to
whether the students observe which lines are perpendicular. Students will return to these lines in the Debrief
to more closely analyze.

Concept Development (38 minutes)

Materials: (T) Triangle *RST* template A (with a base of 5 units and a height of 2 units), triangle *RST* template
             B (with a height of 2 units and a base of 3 units), angle templates in other various sizes
             (S) Straightedge, perpendicular lines recording sheet, angle templates (in various sizes, from G5–
             M6–Lesson 13) unlined paper

Note: An Application Problem is not included in this lesson in order to provide adequate time for the Concept
Development.

Problem 1: Identify perpendicular lines on the grid.

T: (Distribute 1 copy of the perpendicular lines recording sheet to students and display image of
     Problem (a) on the board.) How do you know if the lines in Problem (a) are perpendicular? Turn and

Lesson 15:   Construct perpendicular line segments on a rectangular grid.
Date: 1/31/14

6.C.30

talk.

S: I can just see it, the lines intersect at the corner of these grid squares, so I know they're perpendicular. → They're perpendicular. I can put the corner of my paper at the vertex and I can see that it's 90 degrees. → I can use my set square to prove that they're perpendicular.

T: Talk to your partner about what you know about perpendicular lines.

S: Lines that intersect and create 90-degree angles are perpendicular. → Perpendicular lines are intersecting lines that form right angles. → The sides of right angles are perpendicular. → The sum of the four angles of two intersecting perpendicular lines is 360 degrees or 4 times 90 degrees.

T: Analyze the rest of the lines Problems (b–d) to see if they are perpendicular.

Problem 2: Prove the sum of the acute angles of a given right triangle is 90 degrees by folding.

Note: Demonstrate and pause throughout the constructions as necessary for your students.

T: Take out triangle RST that we used during G5–M6–Lesson 14. (Distribute an unlined piece of paper to each student.)

T: Fold the triangle so that vertex T and vertex S match up with vertex R.

T: What do you notice? Turn and talk.

S: $\angle S$ and $\angle T$ completely cover $\angle R$, with no overlap. → $\angle S$ and $\angle T$ must add up to 90 degrees, because when they're put together at $\angle R$, they're the same as $\angle R$. → I did this in fourth grade, R is 90 degrees, so the sum of S and T must be 90 degrees also.

T: Work with your partner. Cut the bottom corner off your blank paper and fold it the same way you folded $\triangle RST$. What do you notice?

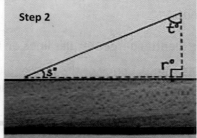

T: When one angle of a triangle is a right angle, the measures of the other two angles add up to 90 degrees. (Write $\angle S + \angle T = 90°$.) Keep this in mind as we work today.

Problem 3: Construct perpendicular line segments using the sum of the acute angles and a straightedge.

MP.1

T: Place your straightedge horizontally across your paper. Then, position triangle RST so that $\overline{SR}$ runs along your straightedge. (See images to the right.)

Step 1

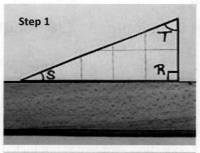

T: Use the triangle template to trace $\overline{ST}$. Then, trace the base and height of the triangle using a dashed line and label the interior angles as $r°, s° \, t°$.

T: Next, slide triangle RST to the left along your straightedge until $\angle R$ shares a vertex with angle $s°$.

T: Finally, rotate triangle RST 90 degrees clockwise, and arrange $\overline{RT}$ so that it forms a straight angle with $\overline{SR}$ along your straightedge.

Step 2

COMMON CORE Lesson 15:   Construct perpendicular line segments on a rectangular grid.
Date: 1/31/14

6.C.31

MP.1

T: A straight angle measures how many degrees?

S: 180°.

T: Trace $\overline{ST}$, then use dashed lines to trace the shorter sides of the triangle.

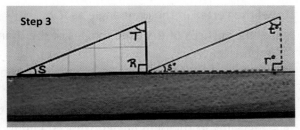

Step 3

T: Now, let's label the interior angles. (Point to the topmost angle.) This angle has the same measure as which angle in triangle RST?

S: ∠S.

T: Since it is equal in measure, let's label it as s° also.

Repeat with the other interior angles.

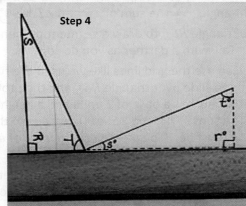

Step 4

T: Label the angle formed by the solid segments (as opposed to dashed lines) we've drawn as $u°$.

T: (Drag finger along straight line angle at base of figure.) What is the sum of angles on a straight line? In this case, the measures of angles $s°, t°,$ and $u°$?

S: 180 degrees.

T: What did we learn about the sum of $s°$ and $t°$?

S: They add up to 90 degrees.

T: So, if this straight angle measures 180°, and the sum of these measures (point to $s°$ and $t°$) is 90°, what do we know about the measure of the third angle (point to $u°$).

S: It's a right angle. → It measures 90 degrees.

T: (Draw right angle symbol on figure.) What is the name we use for segments that form right angles?

S: Perpendicular lines.

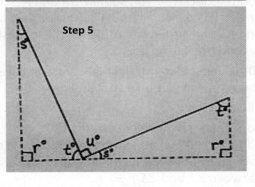

Step 5

T: After sliding and rotating △ RST, the two longest sides of triangles created perpendicular segments. Use some of the other triangle templates from G5–M6–Lesson 13, and work with a partner to draw other examples of perpendicular segments using this method.

Some students may be ready to work independently, while others may need another guided experience. As students are ready, encourage them to orient their straightedges in a variety of ways on their paper.

Problem 4: Construct perpendicular segments on grid paper.

T: Let's look again at the perpendicular lines sheet we used earlier. (Display segment (1).) Look at segment (1). Turn and tell your neighbor about a right triangle that has $\overline{ST}$ as its longest side.

T: I see a triangle with a height of 2 units and a base of 3 units. (Draw dashed lines to show this triangle.) Draw the base and height of this triangle on your paper too.

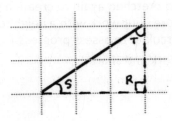

T: Label the vertex of the right angle as R.

T: Label the vertices of the acute angles of the triangle as S and T.

T: Remind your neighbor what you know about the measures of $\angle S$ and $\angle T$ and how you know it.

S: We found out when we folded the triangle that they are the same as the right angle. They add up to the right angle. → The sum of $\angle S$ and $\angle T$ is 90°.

T: Use triangle RST to draw a segment perpendicular to $\overline{ST}$. Talk with a partner as you do so.

S: We can use the grid lines like we used the ruler. I'm going to slide over triangle RST and then rotate it so that it now has a base of 2 units and a height of 3 units. → The sum of $\angle T$ and $\angle S$ is 90 degrees so the third angle must be 90 degrees since the sum of all three angles is 180.

T: (Allow students time to work.) Yes, you sketched a new triangle, the same as triangle RST, moved over 3 units and rotated clockwise 90°, so that $\overline{SR}$ and $\overline{RT}$ create a straight angle. (Slide and rotate.) I'll use a dashed line to sketch $\overline{RT}$ and $\overline{RS}$ and a solid line to sketch the longest side, $\overline{ST}$. (Sketch second triangle on board.)

T: (Drag finger along straight line angle at base of figure.) What is the sum of angles on a straight line?

S: 180 degrees.

T: So, if this straight line measures 180°, and $\angle S$ and $\angle T$ add up to 90°, what do we know about the angle that's formed by our solid segments? (Point to area of figure between $\angle T$ and $\angle S$.)

S: It's a right angle. → It measures 90 degrees. → The two longest sides of these triangles intersect to make perpendicular segments. (Display segment (2) on board.)

T: Continue to sketch a right triangle for each remaining segment. Then show how that triangle can be moved and sketched again to create a perpendicular segment. Share your work with a neighbor when you're through. (Circulate to assess progress.)

S: (Work and share.)

NOTES ON MULTIPLE MEANS OF ENGAGEMENT:

There may be a great disparity in the spatial reasoning abilities among students in the same classroom. Some students may be ready for independent practice rather quickly. If so, let them work independently while others work in a smaller group provided with another guided experience.

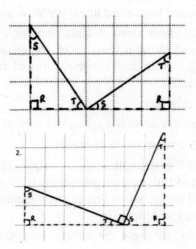

NOTES ON MULTIPLE MEANS OF REPRESENTATION:

The method used to construct the perpendicular segments in this lesson may, at first, seem to be an unnecessarily complicated process if the end result is simply to create perpendicular segments. After all, isn't that what a set square is for? However, taking the time to slide and draw the triangles gives students opportunity to reason about what's presented on the grid and its foreshadowing of slope which will form the basis of many concepts in future learning.

Lesson 15:   Construct perpendicular line segments on a rectangular grid.
Date: 1/31/14

6.C.33

Problem Set (10 minutes)

Students should do their personal best to complete the Problem Set within the allotted 10 minutes. For some classes, it may be appropriate to modify the assignment by specifying which

problems they work on first. Some problems do not specify a method for solving. Students solve these problems using the RDW approach used for Application Problems.

Student Debrief (10 minutes)

Lesson Objective: Construct perpendicular line segments on a rectangular grid.

The Student Debrief is intended to invite reflection and active processing of the total lesson experience.

Invite students to review their solutions for the Problem Set. They should check work by comparing answers with a partner before going over answers as a class. Look for misconceptions or misunderstandings that can be addressed in the Debrief. Guide students in a conversation to debrief the Problem Set and process the lesson.

You may choose to use any combination of the questions below to lead the discussion.

- In Problem 1, explain how you determined which sets of segments were perpendicular.

- In Problem 3, do your segments look like your neighbor's line segments? Are there other lines that are perpendicular to the given segments, or is your figure the only correct response?

- How is drawing perpendicular lines similar to and different from drawing parallel lines?

- How do the dimensions of the triangle affect the size of its interior angles?

- Think back on our fluency activity drawing angles. What can you say about the unmarked angles on the line? How was this similar to our work with the triangle templates?

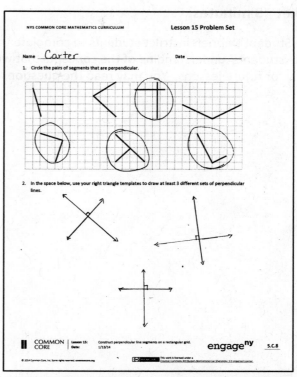

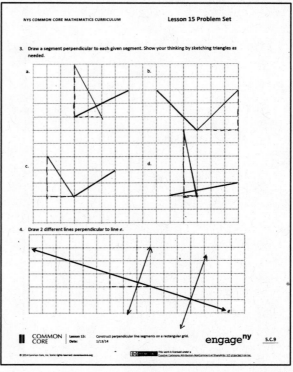

COMMON CORE™

Lesson 15:   Construct perpendicular line segments on a rectangular grid.
Date: 1/31/14

6.C.34

Exit Ticket (3 minutes)

After the Student Debrief, instruct students to complete the Exit Ticket. A review of their work will help you assess the students' understanding of the concepts that were presented in the lesson today and plan more effectively for future lessons. You may read the questions aloud to the students.

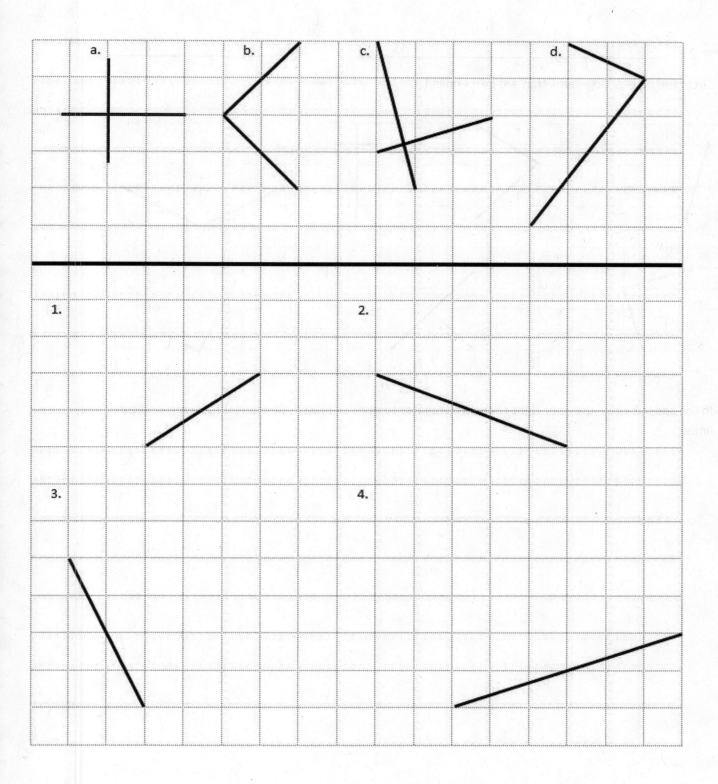

a.

b.

c.

d.

1.

2.

3.

4.

COMMON CORE | **Lesson 15:**   Construct perpendicular line segments on a rectangular grid.
                  | **Date:**   1/31/14

6.C.36

Name _____   Date _____

1. Circle the pairs of segments that are perpendicular.

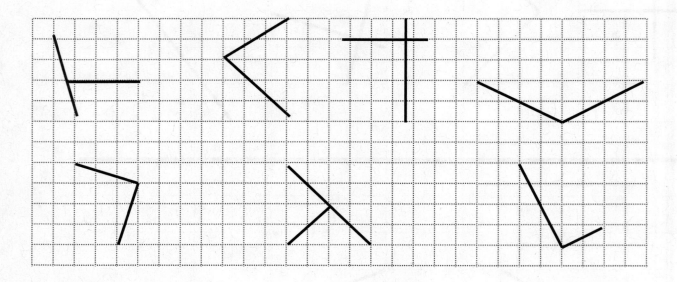

2. In the space below, use your right triangle templates to draw at least 3 different sets of perpendicular lines.

COMMON CORE™

Lesson 15:   Construct perpendicular line segments on a rectangular grid.
Date: 1/31/14

6.C.37

3. Draw a segment perpendicular to each given segment. Show your thinking by sketching triangles as needed.

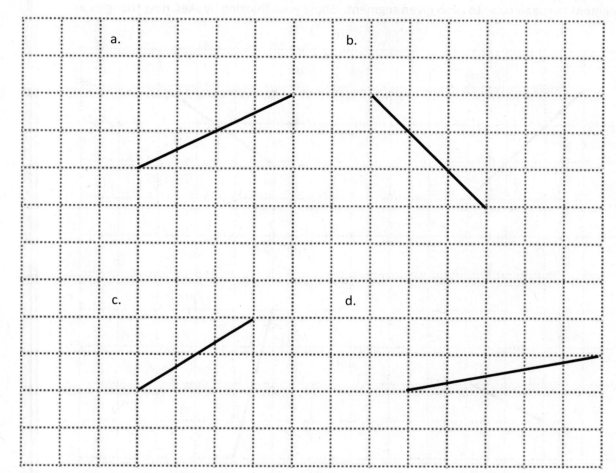

4. Draw 2 different lines perpendicular to line *e*.

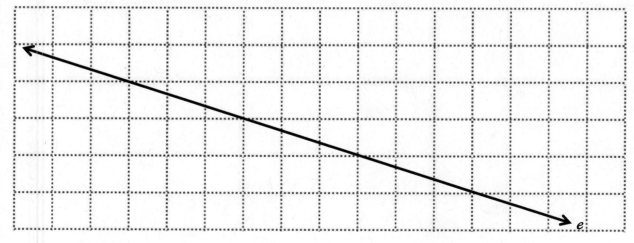

COMMON CORE™

Lesson 15:   Construct perpendicular line segments on a rectangular grid.
Date: 1/31/14

6.C.38

Name _____   Date _____

1. Draw a segment perpendicular to each given segment. Show your thinking by sketching triangles as needed.

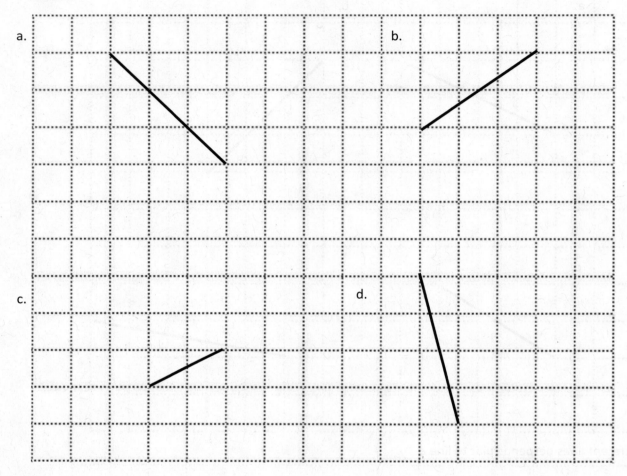

COMMON CORE

Lesson 15:   Construct perpendicular line segments on a rectangular grid.
Date: 1/31/14

6.C.39

© 2014 Common Core, Inc. All rights reserved. commoncore.org

Name _____ Date _____

1. Circle the pairs of segments that are perpendicular.

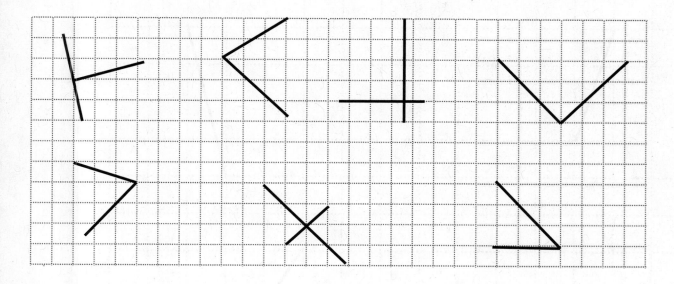

2. In the space below, use your right triangle templates to draw at least 3 different sets of perpendicular lines.

COMMON CORE

Lesson 15:   Construct perpendicular line segments on a rectangular grid.
Date: 1/31/14

6.C.40

3. Draw a segment perpendicular to each given segment. Show your thinking by sketching triangles as needed.

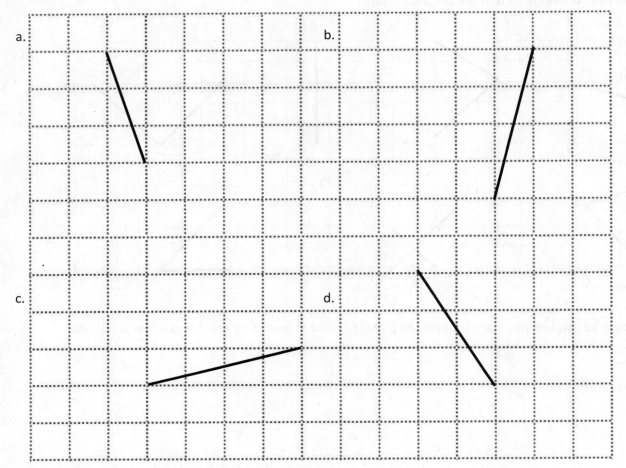

a.

b.

c.

d.

4. Draw 2 different lines perpendicular to line **b**.

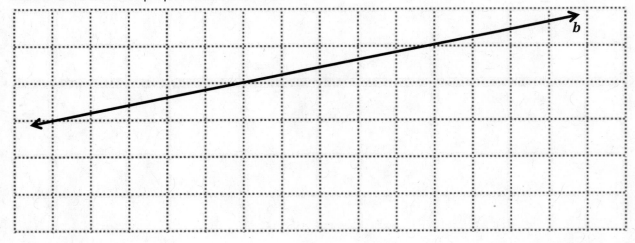

b

Triangle *RST* Template A

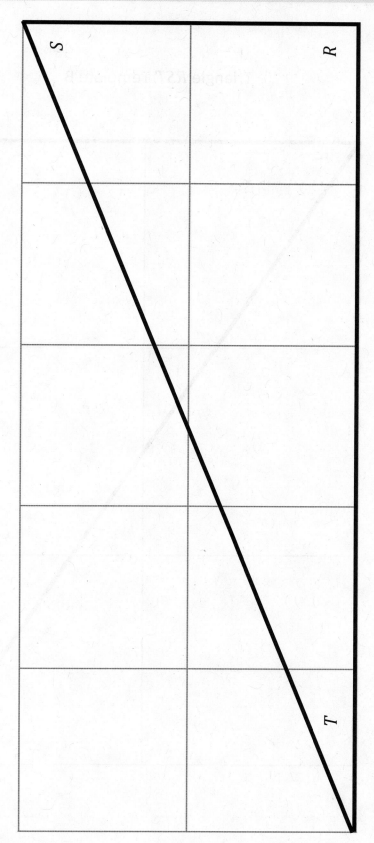

COMMON CORE

Lesson 15:
Date:

Construct perpendicular line segments on a rectangular grid.
1/31/14

6.C.42

Triangle *RST* Template B

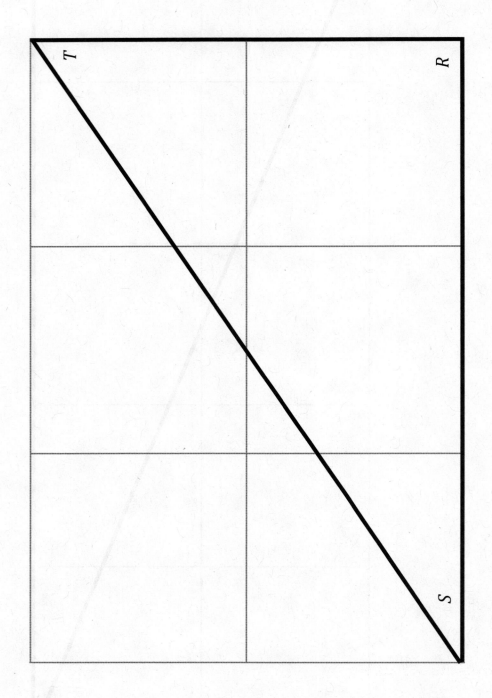

Lesson 15: Construct perpendicular line segments on a rectangular grid.
Date: 1/31/14

Lesson 16

Objective: Construct perpendicular line segments, and analyze relationships of the coordinate pairs.

Suggested Lesson Structure

■ Fluency Practice	(12 minutes)
■ Application Problem	(7 minutes)
■ Concept Development	(31 minutes)
■ Student Debrief	(10 minutes)
Total Time	**(60 minutes)**

Fluency Practice (12 minutes)

- Make Larger Units **4.NF.1**   (4 minutes)
- Draw Angles **4.NF.1**   (8 minutes)

Make Larger Units (4 minutes)

Materials: (S) Personal white boards

Note: This fluency activity reviews G5–Module 3 concepts.

T: (Write $\frac{2}{4}$ = ___.) Say 2 fourths in larger units.

S: 1 half.

T: (Write $\frac{2}{6}$ = ___.) Say 2 sixths in larger units.

S: 1 third.

T: (Write $\frac{2}{10}$ = ___.) Write 2 tenths in larger units.

S: (Write $\frac{2}{10}$ = $\frac{1}{5}$.)

Continue the process for $\frac{5}{10}, \frac{3}{9}, \frac{6}{9}, \frac{5}{15}, \frac{10}{15}, \frac{3}{12}, \frac{9}{12}, \frac{8}{24}, \frac{16}{24}, \frac{7}{28}$, and $\frac{21}{28}$.

Draw Angles (8 minutes)

Materials: (S) Blank paper, ruler, protractor

Note: This fluency activity informally prepares students for today's lesson.

Lesson 16:	Construct perpendicular line segments, and analyze relationships of the coordinate pairs.	6.C.44
Date:	1/31/14	

T: Use your ruler to draw a 4-inch segment, $\overline{AB}$.

T: Plot a point at the third inch from point A.

T: From that point, draw a 30° angle that opens to the left. Label its endpoint C.

T: From the same point and also opening to the left, draw a 60° angle below AB. Extend the angle's side so that it is at least 4 inches long. Label its endpoints D and E. (Demonstrate.)

T: Use any tool to draw a segment perpendicular to $\overline{AB}$ with endpoints at C that intersects $\overline{DE}$.

Have students label the intersection of $\overline{AB}$ and $\overline{CF}$ as point G. See if they notice that $\angle GCE$, $\angle GFE$ and $\angle FEC$ have angles that are the same measure.

Repeat with other angle pairs as time permits.

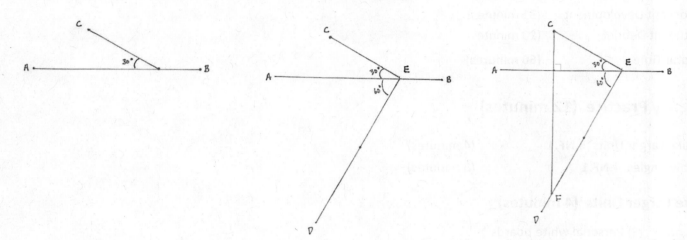

Application Problem (7 minutes)

a. Complete the table for the rule *y is 1 more than half x*, graph the coordinate pairs and draw a line to connect them.

b. Give the y coordinate for the point on this line whose x-coordinate is $42\frac{1}{4}$.

Bonus: Give the x-coordinate for the point on this line whose y-coordinate is $5\frac{1}{2}$.

Note: The Application Problem reviews coordinate graphing and fraction multiplication.

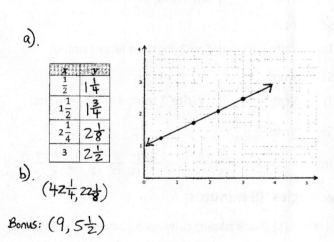

a).

x	y
$\frac{1}{2}$	$1\frac{1}{4}$
$1\frac{1}{2}$	$1\frac{3}{4}$
$2\frac{1}{4}$	$2\frac{1}{8}$
3	$2\frac{1}{2}$

b).

$\left(42\frac{1}{4}, 22\frac{1}{8}\right)$

Bonus: $\left(9, 5\frac{1}{2}\right)$

Lesson 16:	Construct perpendicular line segments, and analyze relationships of the coordinate pairs.	6.C.45
Date:	1/31/14	

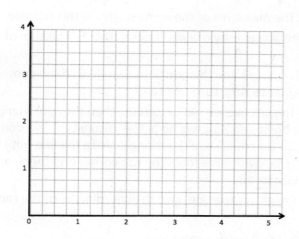

x	y
$\frac{1}{2}$	
$1\frac{1}{2}$	
$2\frac{1}{4}$	
3	

Concept Development (31 minutes)

Materials: (T) Triangle *RST* Template A (used in G5–M6–Lesson 15), images of coordinate plane with
A, B plotted for display (S) Personal white board, coordinate plane template, straightedge, right
angle template *RST* (from G5–M6–Lesson 13)

Problem 1: Slide and rotate right triangle template along coordinate plane to create perpendicular segments.

T: (Distribute coordinate plane template to students and display images of coordinate plane on board
with Point A plotted at (3, 1) and Point B plotted at (8, 3).) Say the coordinates of point *A*.

S: (3, 1.)

T: Record the coordinates of *A* in the
table. Then, plot *A* on your plane.

T: Tell your neighbor the coordinates
of *B*, record in the table, and plot.

S: (Share, record, and plot.)

MP.7 T: Use your straightedge to draw $\overline{AB}$.

T: Visualize a right triangle that has
$\overline{AB}$ as its longest side and follows
the grid lines on its other two
sides. Describe this triangle to
your partner.

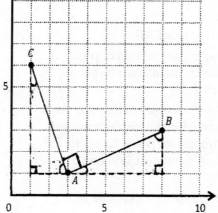

	(x, y)
A	(3,1)
B	(8,3)
C	(1,6)

S: I see a triangle below $\overline{AB}$. The
longer side is 5 units long and the shorter side is 2 units high. The right angle is directly below *B*. →
I see a triangle that is above $\overline{AB}$. The right angle is 2 units above *A*. The longer side is 5 units long.

T: Let's draw the triangle below the segment that you described. Use a dashed line to draw the other
sides of the right triangle that has $\overline{AB}$ as its long side and its right angle's vertex at (8, 1).
(Demonstrate.)

COMMON CORE | **Lesson 16:** | Construct perpendicular line segments, and analyze relationships of
the coordinate pairs.

Date: 1/31/14

6.C.46

T: Tell me what you know about the measures of the acute angles in this triangle.

S: If we folded them over the right angle, they'd cover it perfectly. → The sum of the two acute angles is 90 degrees.

T: Imagine how we could use this triangle and the grid lines to help us draw another segment whose endpoint is A and is perpendicular to $\overline{AB}$. Turn and talk.

S: We could slide the triangle to the left like we did yesterday, then turn the triangle up and mark the top vertex. If we connect that point and A, it will be perpendicular. → We don't have a ruler today, but the grid lines are straight, so we could slide the triangle along the line until the right angle touches A. Then, rotate it 90° clockwise. We mark the top corner and then connect it to A. That segment would be perpendicular to $\overline{AB}$.

T: After we slide and rotate our imaginary triangle, give the coordinates of the top vertex.

S: (1, 6).

T: Put these coordinates in your table, plot this point and label it C. Use your straightedge to connect C and A. What can we say about $\overline{CA}$ and $\overline{AB}$? How do you know?

S: It's what we did yesterday. The longer side of the first triangle and the shorter side of the second triangle form a straight angle at the bottom of the figure. We know the acute angles add up to 90°, so the angle between them, $\angle CAB$, must also be 90°.

T: Segments AB and CA are perpendicular segments. Write this in symbols on your personal board. (Write $\overline{AB} \perp \overline{CA}$ on the board.)

Problem 2: Analyze the differences in the coordinate pairs of the perpendicular segments.

T: Put your finger on A, the vertex of $\angle CAB$.

T: Use the table to compare the x-coordinates of points A and B. Tell your neighbor which point has a larger x-coordinate and why that is true.

S: B has the larger x because we traveled to the right on the coordinate plane to get to point B. → We traveled 5 units to the right on the coordinate plane to get to B. → The triangle that has $\overline{AB}$ as its longest side had a base of 5 units.

T: Now, compare the y-coordinate of points A and B. Tell your neighbor which point has a larger y-coordinate and why that is true.

S: B also has the larger y because we traveled up to get to point B. → We traveled 2 units up on the coordinate plane to get to B. → The triangle that was used to draw segment $\overline{AB}$, had a height of 2 units.

NOTES ON MULTIPLE MEANS OF ACTION AND EXPRESSION:

It may have been noted that the triangles that are visualized and drawn by the teacher are consistently those triangles "below" the segment being considered. These are by no means the only triangles that might be used to draw the perpendicular segments. Consider the following figure in which the upper triangles for each segment (drawn in red) are used to construct perpendicular segments (drawn in black).

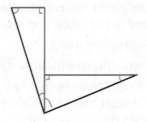

The use of the triangles below give rise to greater opportunity to reason about angles and their relationships, but students who visualize alternate triangles should not be discouraged from using them to produce the segments.

T: Put your finger back on A, the vertex of $\angle CAB$.

T: Think about how many units to the left the triangle was slid and how rotating the triangle located point C. Compare the way you moved your finger for each triangle. Turn and talk.

S: Instead of moving right and then up, this time we moved left and then up. → First, we moved over 5 then up 2, now we move over 2 then up 5. The number of units is the same but they're switched. →

   In both cases the y-coordinate is being increased, but this time we're moving left 2 units, and that will make the x-coordinate less. → That's because we rotated the triangle!

T: Compare the coordinates of A and C. How do they differ?

S: The x-coordinate of C is 2 less than A, but the y-coordinate is 5 more. → You have to move 2 to the left and 5 up from A to get to C.

T: What do you notice about how the coordinates of A and B differ, compared to how the coordinates of A and C differ? Turn and talk.

S: Both times there's a difference of 5 units and 2 units. → In A and B, the difference in the x-coordinates is 5, then 5 is the difference between the y-coordinates in A and C. → It all has to do with the triangles on the plane. They're the same triangle, but they're being moved and rotated so they change the coordinates by 5 units and 2 units.

T: What are the other side lengths of the triangle we used to construct the perpendicular lines?

S: 5 units and 2 units. → It's the base and height of the triangles that tell us the change in the coordinates!

T: Right, so in this case the coordinates change by 5 and 2 units. Since the same sized triangle is used to construct the perpendicular segments, the x-coordinates changes by 5 or by 2 and the y-coordinate changes by 5 or by 2. (Point to clarify.)

Repeat the process with DEF and GHI (as pictured below).

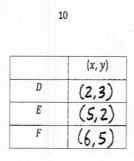

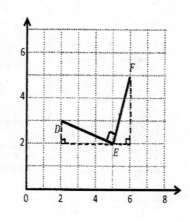

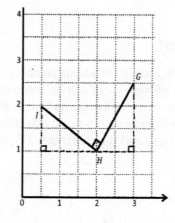

Problem Set (10 minutes)

Students should do their personal best to complete the Problem Set within the allotted 10 minutes. For some classes, it may be appropriate to modify the assignment by specifying which problems they work on first. Some problems do not specify a method for solving. Students solve these problems using the RDW approach used for Application Problems.

	Lesson 16:	Construct perpendicular line segments, and analyze relationships of the coordinate pairs.	
	Date:	1/31/14	6.C.48

Student Debrief (10 minutes)

Lesson Objective: Construct perpendicular line segments, and analyze relationships of the coordinate pairs.

The Student Debrief is intended to invite reflection and active processing of the total lesson experience.

Invite students to review their solutions for the Problem Set. They should check work by comparing answers with a partner before going over answers as a class. Look for misconceptions or misunderstandings that can be addressed in the Debrief. Guide students in a conversation to debrief the Problem Set and process the lesson.

You may choose to use any combination of the questions below to lead the discussion.

- Talk about the triangle that you see when you look at $\overline{AB}$ and $\overline{AC}$.
- Tell your neighbor about how visualizing the triangles helps you locate the points needed to draw a perpendicular line.
- In Problem 1, are there other segments that are perpendicular to $\overline{AB}$? Explain how you know.
- Explain your thought process as you solved Problem 3.

Exit Ticket (3 minutes)

After the Student Debrief, instruct students to complete the Exit Ticket. A review of their work will help you assess the students' understanding of the concepts that were presented in the lesson today and plan more effectively for future lessons. You may read the questions aloud to the students.

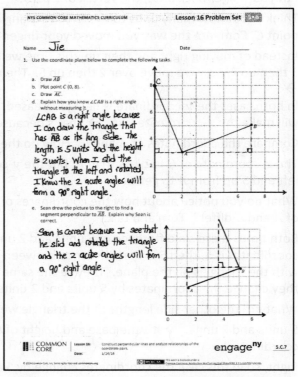

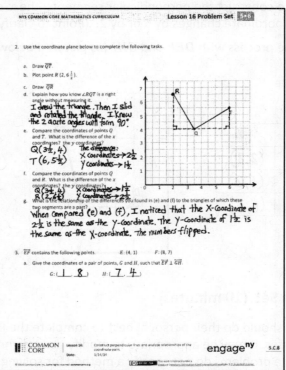

Lesson 16:   Construct perpendicular line segments, and analyze relationships of
Date: the coordinate pairs.
               1/31/14

6.C.49

Name _____   Date _____

1. Use the coordinate plane below to complete the following tasks.

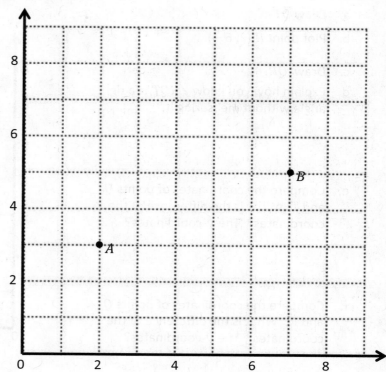

a. Draw $\overline{AB}$

b. Plot point C (0, 8).

c. Draw $\overline{AC}$.

d. Explain how you know ∠CAB is a right angle
    without measuring it.

e. Sean drew the picture to the right to find a
    segment perpendicular to $\overline{AB}$. Explain why Sean is
    correct.

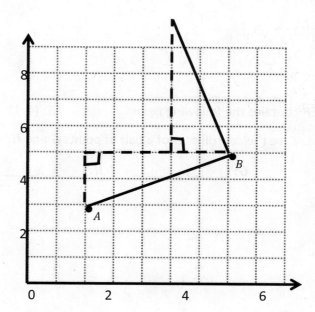

COMMON CORE™   Lesson 16:   Construct perpendicular line segments, and analyze relationships of
                                   the coordinate pairs.
                     Date: 1/31/14   6.C.50

2. Use the coordinate plane below to complete the following tasks.

   a. Draw $\overline{QT}$.

   b. Plot point R $(2, 6\frac{1}{2})$.

   c. Draw $\overline{QR}$.

   d. Explain how you know $\angle RQT$ is a right angle without measuring it.

   e. Compare the coordinates of points Q and T. What is the difference of the x-coordinates? The y-coordinates?

   f. Compare the coordinates of points Q and R. What is the difference of the x-coordinates? The y-coordinates?

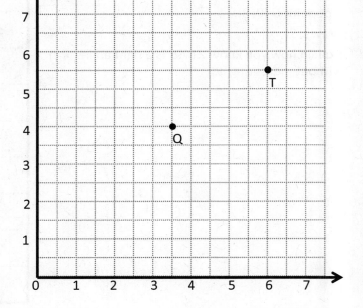

   g. What is the relationship of the differences you found in (e) and (f) to the triangles of which these two segments are a part?

3. $\overleftrightarrow{EF}$ contains the following points. E: (4, 1) F: (8, 7)

   a. Give the coordinates of a pair of points G and H, such that $\overleftrightarrow{EF} \perp \overleftrightarrow{GH}$.

   G: (_____ , _____) H: (_____ , _____)

COMMON CORE™

Lesson 16: Construct perpendicular line segments, and analyze relationships of the coordinate pairs.

Date: 1/31/14

6.C.51

Name _____   Date _____

1. Show your thinking on the plane.

    a. Draw $\overline{UV}$.

    b. Plot point W $(4\frac{1}{2}, 6)$.

    c. Draw $\overline{VW}$.

    d. Explain how you know that $\angle UVW$ is a right angle without measuring it.

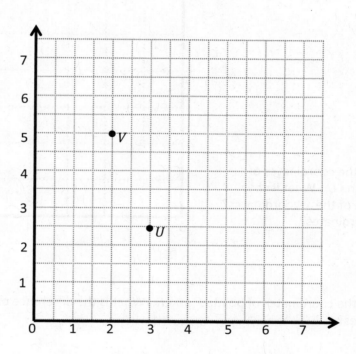

COMMON CORE™ | Lesson 16:   Construct perpendicular line segments, and analyze relationships of
                      | the coordinate pairs.
                      | Date: 1/31/14

6.C.52

Name _____   Date _____

1. Use the coordinate plane below to complete the following tasks.

    a. Draw $\overline{PQ}$.

    b. Plot point R (7, 7).

    c. Draw $\overline{PR}$.

    d. Explain how you know ∠PQR is a right angle without measuring it.

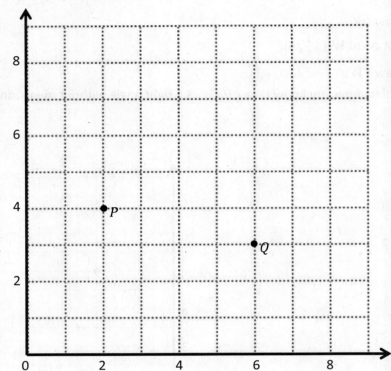

    e. Compare the coordinates of points P and Q. What is the difference of the x-coordinates? The y-coordinates?

    f. Compare the coordinates of points P and R. What is the difference of the x-coordinates? The y-coordinates?

    g. What is the relationship of the differences you found in (e) and (f) to the triangles of which these two segments area a part?

Lesson 16:	Construct perpendicular line segments, and analyze relationships of the coordinate pairs.
Date:	1/31/14

6.C.5

2. Use the coordinate plane below to complete the following tasks.

    a. Draw $\overline{BC}$.

    b. Plot point D (3, $2\frac{1}{2}$).

    c. Draw $\overline{BD}$.

    d. Explain how you know $\angle BCD$ is a right angle without measuring it.

    e. Compare the coordinates of points B and C. What is the difference of the x-coordinates? The y-coordinates?

    f. Compare the coordinates of points B and D. What is the difference of the x-coordinates? The y-coordinates?

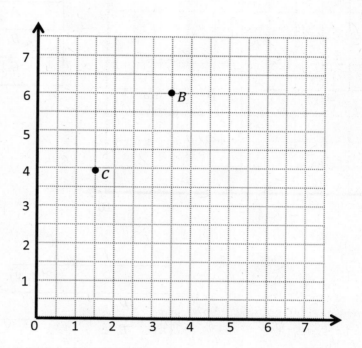

    g. What is the relationship of the differences you found in (e) and (f) to the triangles of which these two segments area a part?

3. $\overleftrightarrow{ST}$ contains the following points. S: (2, 3) T: (9, 6)

    a. Give the coordinates of a pair of points, U and V, such that $\overleftrightarrow{ST} \perp \overleftrightarrow{UV}$.

    S: (_____, _____) T: (_____, _____)

COMMON CORE™ | Lesson 16: | Construct perpendicular line segments, and analyze relationships of the coordinate pairs.

Date: | 1/31/14

6.C.54

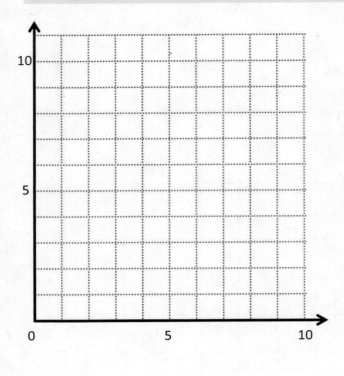

	(x, y)
A	
B	
C	

	(x, y)
D	
E	
F	

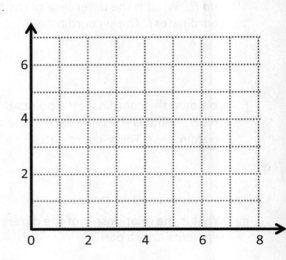

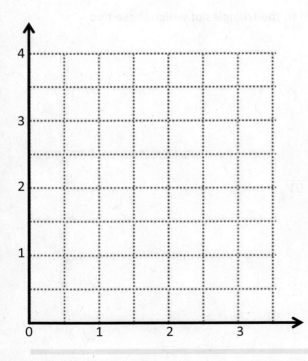

	(x, y)
G	
H	
I	

COMMON CORE™

Lesson 16: Construct perpendicular line segments, and analyze relationships of the coordinate pairs.

Date: 1/31/14

6.C.55

Lesson 17

Objective: Draw symmetric figures using distance and angle measure from the line of symmetry.

Suggested Lesson Structure

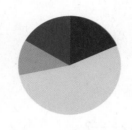

■ Fluency Practice   (11 minutes)
■ Application Problem   (7 minutes)
■ Concept Development   (32 minutes)
■ Student Debrief   (10 minutes)

    Total Time   **(60 minutes)**

Fluency Practice (11 minutes)

- Make Larger Units **4.NF.1**   (3 minutes)
- Subtract a Fraction from a Whole **4.NF.3**   (4 minutes)
- Draw Perpendicular Lines Using a Set Square **4.G.1**   (4 minutes)

Make Larger Units (3 minutes)

Materials: (S) Personal white boards

Note: This fluency activity reviews G5–Module 3 concepts.

    T: (Write $\frac{3}{6}$.) Say 3 sixths in larger units.

    S: 1 half.

    T: (Write $\frac{3}{9}$.) Say 3 ninths in larger units.

    S: 1 third.

    T: (Write $\frac{3}{15}$.) Write 3 fifteenths in larger units.

    S: (Write $\frac{3}{15} = \frac{1}{5}$.)

Continue the process for $\frac{4}{10}$, $\frac{4}{12}$, $\frac{5}{20}$, $\frac{15}{20}$, $\frac{3}{12}$, $\frac{6}{9}$, $\frac{7}{21}$, $\frac{14}{21}$, $\frac{8}{32}$, and $\frac{24}{32}$.

Subtract a Fraction from a Whole (4 minutes)

Materials: (S) Personal white boards

Note: This fluency activity reviews G5–Module 3 concepts.

T: What's $1 - \frac{2}{4}$?

S: $\frac{1}{2}$. → $\frac{2}{4}$.

T: What's $1\frac{1}{4} - \frac{1}{2}$?

S: $\frac{3}{4}$.

T: (Write $1\frac{1}{4} - \frac{1}{2} = \frac{3}{4}$.)

T: (Beneath $1\frac{1}{4} - \frac{1}{2} = \frac{3}{4}$, write $2\frac{1}{4} - \frac{1}{2}$.) What's $2\frac{1}{4} - \frac{1}{2}$?

S: $1\frac{3}{4}$.

T: (Write $1\frac{1}{4} - \frac{1}{2} = \frac{3}{4}$.)

T: (Beneath $1\frac{1}{4} - \frac{1}{2} = \frac{3}{4}$, write $6\frac{1}{4} - \frac{1}{2}$.) What's $6\frac{1}{4} - \frac{1}{2}$?

S: $5\frac{3}{4}$.

T: (Write $6\frac{1}{4} - \frac{1}{2} = 5\frac{3}{4}$.)

Continue the process for the following possible suggestions: $1\frac{1}{6} - \frac{1}{3}$, $2\frac{1}{6} - \frac{1}{3}$, $3\frac{1}{6} - \frac{1}{3}$, $7\frac{1}{6} - \frac{1}{3}$, $1\frac{1}{8} - \frac{3}{4}$, $2\frac{1}{8} - \frac{3}{4}$, $5\frac{1}{8} - \frac{3}{4}$, and $9\frac{1}{8} - \frac{3}{4}$.

Draw Perpendicular Lines using a Set Square (4 minutes)

Materials: (S) Set square, unlined paper

T: Draw a horizontal 4 inch segment $\overline{AB}$ on your paper.

T: Use your set square to draw a $1\frac{3}{4}$ inch segment $\overline{AD}$ perpendicular to $\overline{AB}$.

T: Extend that segment $1\frac{3}{4}$ inch on the other side of $\overline{AB}$.

T: What is the total length of the segment perpendicular to AB?

Repeat the sequence drawing other lines perpendicular to $\overline{AB}$ using the following suggested lengths: 2.5 cm, $1\frac{3}{8}$ cm, and $1\frac{7}{10}$ cm.

Lesson 17:	Draw symmetric figures using distance and angle measure from the line of symmetry.
Date:	1/31/14

6.C.5

Application Problem (7 minutes)

Materials: (S) Straightedge

Plot (10, 8) and (3, 3) on the coordinate plane, connect
with a straightedge, and label as C and D.

a. Draw a segment parallel to $\overline{CD}$.

b. Draw a segment perpendicular to $\overline{CD}$.

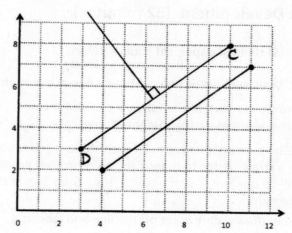

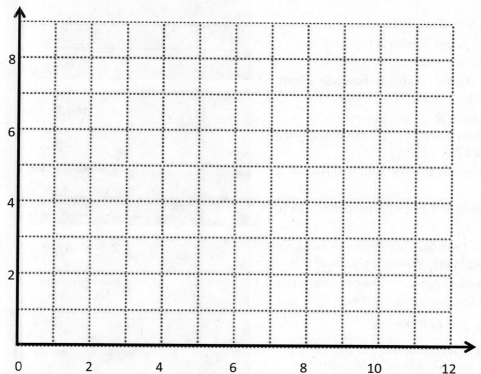

Note: This Application Problem applies plotting concepts from G5–M6–Lessons 14 and 16.

Concept Development (32 minutes)

Materials: (S) Unlined paper, set square, ruler

Problem 1: Draw symmetric points about a line of symmetry.

Note: Demonstrate each of the following steps for students giving the work time appropriate for students in the class.

Step 1

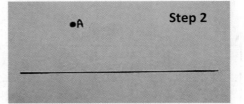
Step 2

- T: (Distribute unlined paper to each student.) Use your ruler as a straightedge to draw a segment on your paper. This will be our line of symmetry. (This is Step 1, as pictured to the right.)

- T: Next, draw a dark point off the line and label it A. F. (This is Step 2.)

- T: Fold the page along this line of symmetry.

- T: Then, rub the area of the paper behind A using some pressure with your finger or eraser. (This is Step 3.)

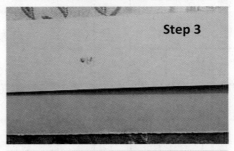
Step 3

- T: Unfold your paper. You should be able to now see a faint point on the other side of the line. (This is Step 4.)

- T: Darken this point and label it B. Then, use your straightedge to lightly draw a segment connecting these two points. (This is Step 5.)

- T: Measure the angles formed by the segment and $\overline{AB}$. What do you find?

- S: All the angles are 90°. → The segment is perpendicular to the line.

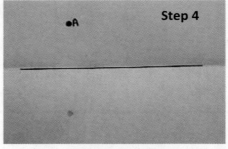
Step 4

- T: Use your ruler to measure the distance between each point and the line along the segment. What do you find?

- S: The segments are the same length. → The points are the same distance from the line along the segments.

Repeat this sequence for another point off the line.

- T: Using what we've just discovered about this pair of symmetric points, draw another pair of points without folding and rubbing our paper. Talk to your partner as you work.

- S: (Work and discuss.)

- T: Let's do another together. I'll guide you through. Draw another point off the line.

- T: Use your set square to draw a segment that crosses the line of symmetry at a 90 degree angle and includes your point. (Demonstrate.)

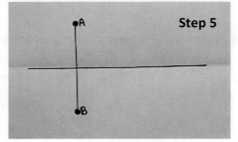
Step 5

Lesson 17:	Draw symmetric figures using distance and angle measure from the line of symmetry.
Date:	1/31/14

6.C.5?

T: Use your ruler to measure the distance from your point to the line of symmetry along the perpendicular segment that you drew.

T: Measure the same distance along the perpendicular segment on the opposite side of the line of symmetry and draw a point.

T: Since these points were drawn using a line perpendicular to the line of symmetry and are equidistant from the line of symmetry, we say they are symmetric about the line.

T: Practice drawing other sets of corresponding points about different lines of symmetry. Use any method that works for you.

Problem 2: Draw symmetric figures about a line of symmetry.

T: Draw a line of symmetry.

T: Draw a point, A, off the line.

T: Draw a second point, B, on the same side of the line as A.

T: Draw $\overline{AB}$.

T: How is this drawing different from the ones we did earlier?

S: We drew 2 points this time. → The other ones were just a point, but now we have a segment.

MP.7

T: Show your neighbor how you'll draw a point symmetric to A about the line. Name it C. (Allow students time to share.)

T: Work independently to draw a point symmetric to B. Name it D.

T: Draw $\overline{CD}$. Compare $\overline{AB}$ to $\overline{CD}$. What do you notice? Turn and talk.

S: They're the same length. → They're the same length, but they are mirror images of each other.

T: We can say that $\overline{AB}$ is symmetric to $\overline{CD}$ about the line symmetry.

T: Draw another line of symmetry.

T: Draw a point, E, off the line.

T: Draw a second point, F, **on** the line.

T: Draw $\overline{EF}$.

T: Draw a third point, G, **on** the line.

T: Draw $\overline{EG}$.

T: How is this figure different from the one we just did?

S: We drew 3 points this time. → This one is 2 segments. → This figure has 2 points on the line of symmetry, and 1 off of it.

T: You drew points F and G on the line of symmetry. Point E, is off the line. Draw a point, H, symmetric

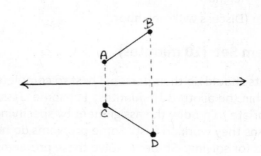

NOTES ON MULTIPLE MEANS OF ENGAGEMENT:

Students with fine motor deficits may benefit from being paired with another student for drawing the figures. One partner might draw while the other is responsible for measuring the segments in order to place the points.

Possible quadrilaterals:

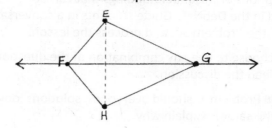

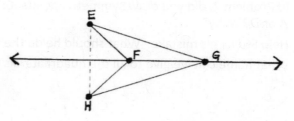

Lesson 17: Draw symmetric figures using distance and angle measure from the line of symmetry.

Date: 1/31/14

6.C.60

to E about $\overleftrightarrow{FG}$.

T: Draw segments $\overline{FH}$ and $\overline{GH}$.

T: (Allow students time to work.) Compare the figures on either side of $\overleftrightarrow{FG}$. What do you notice? Turn and talk.

S: They're symmetric. → They're the same size and the angles are all the same.

T: Yes, we can say that quadrilateral $EFHG$ is symmetric about $\overleftrightarrow{FG}$. Turn and share your quadrilateral with your neighbor.

S: (Discuss with neighbor.)

Problem Set (10 minutes)

Students should do their personal best to complete the Problem Set within the allotted 10 minutes. For some classes, it may be appropriate to modify the assignment by specifying which problems they work on first. Some problems do not specify a method for solving. Students solve these problems using the RDW approach used for Application Problems.

Student Debrief (10 minutes)

Lesson Objective: Draw symmetric figures using distance and angle measure from the line of symmetry.

The Student Debrief is intended to invite reflection and active processing of the total lesson experience.

Invite students to review their solutions for the Problem Set. They should check work by comparing answers with a partner before going over answers as a class. Look for misconceptions or misunderstandings that can be addressed in the Debrief. Guide students in a conversation to debrief the Problem Set and process the lesson.

You may choose to use any combination of the questions below to lead the discussion.

- In Problem 1, should everyone's solutions look the same? Explain why.
- In Problem 2, did you draw symmetric points for A or D? Why?
- Help Stu fix his mistake. What should he do the next time he draws a symmetric figure?
- What name can we give to all the quadrilaterals we drew in Problem 3? Explain your reasoning.

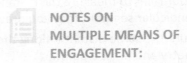

NOTES ON MULTIPLE MEANS OF ENGAGEMENT:

Drawing symmetric figures lends itself well to connections with art. Students might use these construction techniques to create symmetric figures by cutting and gluing colored strips of paper or through other media.

Students might also enjoy creating inkblots by placing paint in the center of paper, folding, and unfolding. Once the blots are dry, students might measure various parts of their creation from the line of symmetry to confirm the concepts developed in the lesson.

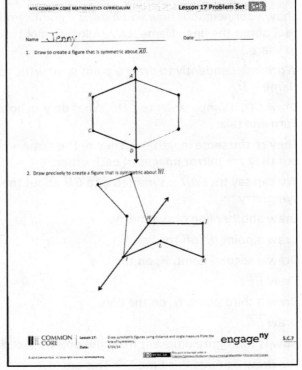

Lesson 17:   Draw symmetric figures using distance and angle measure from the line of symmetry.

Date: 1/31/14

6.C.61

Exit Ticket (3 minutes)

After the Student Debrief, instruct students to complete the Exit Ticket. A review of their work will help you assess the students' understanding of the concepts that were presented in the lesson today and plan more effectively for future lessons. You may read the questions aloud to the students.

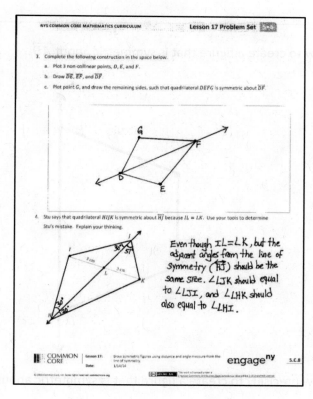

COMMON
CORE™

Lesson 17:   Draw symmetric figures using distance and angle measure from the
              line of symmetry.
Date: 1/31/14

6.C.62

© 2014 Common Core, Inc. All rights reserved. commoncore.org

Name _____   Date _____

1. Draw to create a figure that is symmetric about $\overleftrightarrow{AD}$.

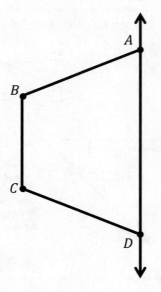

2. Draw precisely to create a figure that is symmetric about $\overleftrightarrow{HI}$.

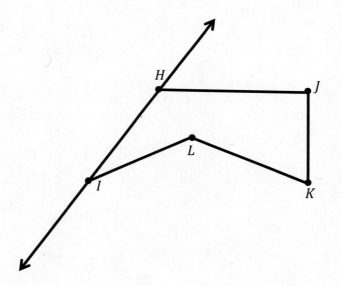

COMMON CORE™

Lesson 17:   Draw symmetric figures using distance and angle measure from the line of symmetry.

Date: 1/31/14

6.C.63

3. Complete the following construction in the space below.

   a. Plot 3 non-collinear points D, E, and F.

   b. Draw $\overline{DE}$, $\overline{EF}$, and $\overleftrightarrow{DF}$.

   c. Plot point G, and draw the remaining sides, such that quadrilateral $DEFG$ is symmetric about $\overleftrightarrow{DF}$.

4. Stu says that quadrilateral $HIJK$ is symmetric about $\overleftrightarrow{HJ}$ because $IL = LK$. Use your tools to determine Stu's mistake. Explain your thinking.

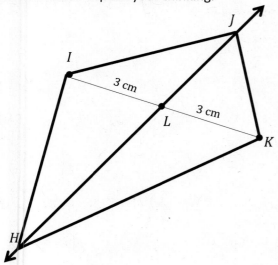

COMMON CORE™   Lesson 17:   Draw symmetric figures using distance and angle measure from the
                    line of symmetry.
                    Date: 1/31/14

6.C.64

Name _____ Date _____

1. Draw 2 points on one side of the line below and label them T and U.

2. Use your set square and ruler to draw symmetrical points about your line that correspond to T and U and label them V and W.

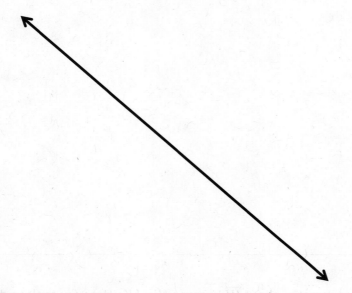

COMMON CORE

Lesson 17: Draw symmetric figures using distance and angle measure from the
line of symmetry.

Date: 1/31/14

6.C.65

Name _____ Date _____

1. Draw to create a figure that is symmetric about $\overleftrightarrow{DE}$.

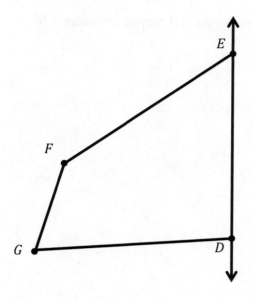

2. Draw to create a figure that is symmetric about $\overleftrightarrow{LM}$.

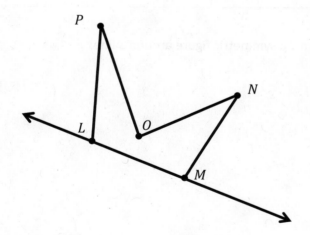

COMMON CORE™

Lesson 17:   Draw symmetric figures using distance and angle measure from the
             line of symmetry.
Date: 1/31/14

6.C.66

3. Complete the following construction in the space below.

   a. Plot 3 non-collinear points, G, H, and I.

   b. Draw $\overline{GH}$, $\overline{HI}$, and $\overleftrightarrow{IG}$.

   c. Plot point J, and draw the remaining sides, such that quadrilateral $GHIJ$ is symmetric about $\overleftrightarrow{IG}$.

4. In the space below, use your tools to draw a symmetric figure around a line.

Lesson 17:   Draw symmetric figures using distance and angle measure from the
             line of symmetry.
Date: 1/31/14

6.C.67

Topic D

Problem Solving in the Coordinate Plane

5.OA.3, 5.G.2

Focus Standard:	5.OA.3	Generate two numerical patterns using two given rules. Identify apparent relationships between corresponding terms. Form ordered pairs consisting of corresponding terms from the two patterns, and graph the ordered pairs on a coordinate plane. *For example, given the rule "Add 3" and the starting number 0, and given the rule "Add 6" and the starting number 0, generate terms in the resulting sequences, and observe that the terms in one sequence are twice the corresponding terms in the other sequence. Explain informally why this is so.*
	5.G.2	Represent real world and mathematical problems by graphing points in the first quadrant of the coordinate plane, and interpret coordinate values of points in the context of the situation.
Instructional Days:	3	
Coherence -Links from:	G4–M4	Angle Measure and Plane Figures
-Links to:	G6–M1	Ratios and Unit Rates

Applications of the coordinate plane in the real world are the focus of Topic D. Students use the coordinate plane to show locations, movement, and distance on maps. Line graphs are also used to explore patterns in the coordinate plane and make predictions based on those patterns (**5.G.2, 5.OA.3**). To close their work with the coordinate plane, students solve real world problems.

A Teaching Sequence Towards Mastery of Problem Solving in the Coordinate Plane

Objective 1: Draw symmetric figures on the coordinate plane.
(Lesson 18)

Objective 2: Plot data on line graphs and analyze trends.
(Lesson 19)

Objective 3: Use coordinate systems to solve real world problems.
(Lesson 20)

Lesson 18

Objective: Draw symmetric figures on the coordinate plane.

Suggested Lesson Structure

■ Application Problem   (6 minutes)
■ Fluency Practice   (11 minutes)
■ Concept Development   (33 minutes)
■ Student Debrief   (10 minutes)
   Total Time   **(60 minutes)**

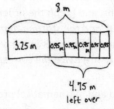

Application Problem (6 minutes)

Denis buys 8 m of ribbon. He uses 3.25 m for a gift. He uses the remaining ribbon equally to tie bows on 5 boxes. How much ribbon did he use on each box?

Note: This problem reviews subtracting decimals and dividing decimal numbers by single digit whole numbers, concepts from G5–Module 1.

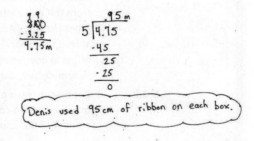

Fluency Practice (11 minutes)

▪ Make Larger Units **4.NF.1**   (4 minutes)
▪ Unknown Angles **4. MD.6**   (7 minutes)

Make Larger Units (4 minutes)

Materials: (S) Personal white boards

Note: This fluency activity reviews G5–Module 3 concepts.

T: (Write $\frac{5}{10}$.) Simplify the fraction by writing it using a larger fractional unit.

S: $\frac{1}{2}$.

T: (Write $\frac{5}{15}$.) Simplify.

NOTES ON MULTIPLE MEANS FOR ACTION AND EXPRESSION:

When giving directions for Simplify Fractions, challenge advanced learners to both simplify the fraction and write others that simplify to the same fraction with denominators greater than 144.

Lesson 18:	Draw symmetric figures on the coordinate plane.
Date:	1/31/14

6.D.2

S: $\frac{1}{3}$.

T: (Write $\frac{5}{25}$.) Simplify.

S: (Write $\frac{5}{25} = \frac{1}{5}$.)

Continue the process for $\frac{10}{25}, \frac{2}{6}, \frac{2}{8}, \frac{6}{8}, \frac{4}{12}, \frac{8}{12}, \frac{9}{27}, \frac{18}{27}, \frac{6}{24}$, and $\frac{18}{24}$.

Unknown Angles (7 minutes)

Materials: (S) Blank paper, ruler, protractor

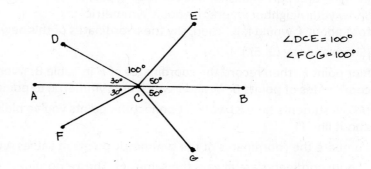

T: Draw a 4-inch segment AB.

T: Plot point C at the 2-inch mark.

T: Draw a 30° degree angle opening to the left from point C with $\overline{AB}$ as one side. Label its endpoint D.

T: Draw a segment symmetric to $\overline{CD}$ about $\overline{AB}$ and label its endpoint F

T: Draw an angle less than 90° opening to the right from point C with $\overline{AB}$ as one side. Label its endpoint E.

T: Draw segment symmetric to $\overline{CE}$ about $\overline{AB}$ and label its endpoint G.

T: What is the measure of angle $\angle DCE$?

T: What angle has the same measure?

T: Share your work with a partner. What is the measure of $\angle DCE$ in your partner's drawing?

Repeat as time permits possibly beginning with a 75° angle.

Note: This fluency activity reviews concepts from Grade 4 in preparation for today's lesson.

Concept Development (33 minutes)

Materials: (S) Coordinate plane template, ruler, protractor

Problem 1: Create symmetrical figures across a vertical line of symmetry.

Note: Demonstrate, give work time, and have students partner-share as needed to meet their needs.

T: (Distribute coordinate plane template and display image of plane with points A–E.) Record the coordinates of points A through E in Table A.

T: Use your ruler to connect these points in alphabetical order.

T: Use your ruler to construct a line of symmetry, ℓ, whose rule is *x is always 5.*

T: Remind your neighbor how we drew symmetric figures yesterday.

S: We used a set square to see a line perpendicular to the line of symmetry. → We measured to make sure the corresponding points were the same distance from the line of symmetry.

T: Imagine a line that is perpendicular to ℓ that goes through A. What is the distance from A to the line of symmetry along this perpendicular line?

S: 4 units.

T: Imagine that perpendicular line continuing past ℓ. Show your neighbor where the point symmetric to A about ℓ would fall. Then, say the coordinates of this new point, F.

S: (Share and say (9, 6).)

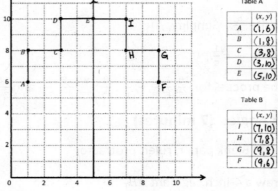

Table A

	(x, y)
A	$(1, 6)$
B	$(1, 8)$
C	$(3, 8)$
D	$(3, 10)$
E	$(5, 10)$

Table B

	(x, y)
I	$(7, 10)$
H	$(7, 8)$
G	$(9, 8)$
F	$(9, 6)$

T: Plot point F, then record the coordinates of F in Table B. Work with a partner to plot and record the coordinates of points G, H, and I which are symmetric to points B, C, and D about ℓ.

T: (Allow students time to work.) Connect the points you've plotted to create a figure that is symmetric about line ℓ.

T: Compare the coordinates of the symmetric points in Tables A and B. Turn and talk.

S: The y-coordinates are always the same. → The x-coordinate changes but the y-coordinates don't.

T: Why is this true?

S: We are moving across a vertical line to draw the points, so moving left and right changes x, but not y. → We are moving parallel to the x axis to find the symmetric points, so the points are on a line that is perpendicular to y. So, the points must have the same y-coordinate.

Problem 2: Create symmetrical figures across a horizontal line of symmetry.

T: Let's create a new line of symmetry. Use your ruler to construct a horizontal line, m, whose rule is y is always 6.

T: (Allow students time to draw.) Let's complete the drawing and create a figure that is symmetric about line m. Tell your neighbor how far point A is from line m.

S: It's on the line. → The distance is zero from A to line m.

T: Label the point symmetric to B. What are its coordinates?

S: (1, 4).

Table A

	(x, y)
A	$(1, 6)$
B	$(1, 8)$
C	$(3, 8)$
D	$(3, 10)$
E	$(5, 10)$

Table C

(x, y)
$(1, 4)$
$(3, 4)$
$(3, 2)$
$(5, 2)$

Table B

	(x, y)
I	$(7, 10)$
H	$(7, 8)$
G	$(9, 8)$
F	$(9, 6)$

Table D

(x, y)
$(7, 2)$
$(7, 4)$
$(9, 4)$

T: Plot and record the coordinates of each symmetric point in Table C. Check your work with a neighbor as you go.

T: Use your ruler to connect the points you plotted to draw the symmetric figure.

T: Compare the coordinates in Tables A and B, with their symmetric point in Table C. What do you

Lesson 18:   Draw symmetric figures on the coordinate plane.
Date: 1/31/14

6.D.4

notice about points when they're symmetric about a horizontal line? Turn and talk.

S: It's the opposite of a vertical line of symmetry. → The x-coordinates don't change, but the y-coordinates do. → The y-coordinates are the same amount greater than or less than 6.

T: When a figure is drawn about a horizontal line of symmetry, the x-coordinates remain constant, while the y-coordinates change.

Problem 3: Create symmetrical figures across a diagonal line of symmetry.

T: (Display image of second coordinate plane on board.) Plot the coordinate pairs in Table D.

T: Now use your ruler to connect the points in alphabetical order. Then connect H to A.

S/T: (Draw.)

T: Is this figure symmetrical? Turn and talk.

S: Yes it's kind of like a leaf and if I turn the plane at an angle the left and right are symmetrical. → Yes, if I drew a line from A to E, then that would make 2 symmetrical halves.

Table D

	(x, y)
A	$(1, 1)$
B	$(1\frac{1}{2}, 3\frac{1}{2})$
C	$(2, 3)$
D	$(2\frac{1}{2}, 3\frac{1}{2})$
E	$(2\frac{1}{2}, 2\frac{1}{2})$
F	$(3\frac{1}{2}, 2\frac{1}{2})$
G	$(3, 2)$
H	$(3\frac{1}{2}, 1\frac{1}{2})$

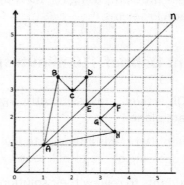

T: This figure is symmetrical about a diagonal line. It begins at the origin and goes through points $(1, 1)$, $(2, 2)$, $(3\frac{1}{2}, 3\frac{1}{2})$, and so on. (Draw line on board.) We'll name this line n.

T: Use your pencil to lightly connect the points that are symmetrical to one another about n. Predict the angle at which these segments intersect n.

S: They should intersect at 90-degree angles. → If the points are symmetric, the line and segments should intersect at right angles.

T: Test your prediction by measuring with your protractor.

S: (Measure.)

T: In order for these points to be symmetric, what else must be true?

S: They have to be the same distance from the line of symmetry. → The distance along the perpendicular must be the same from the line to the points that correspond to each other.

T: Measure the distances of these points to the line of symmetry to confirm that they are truly symmetric.

S: (Measure the distance of the points.)

T: If I wanted to plot another pair of points that were symmetric about n, what would I do? Turn and talk.

If time permits, ask students to compare the coordinates for the symmetric points. While the reversal of the coordinates is apparent for the line $y = x$, challenge students to test whether this pattern holds for other diagonal lines (e.g., *y is twice as much as x*).

Problem Set (10 minutes)

Students should do their personal best to complete the Problem Set within the allotted 10 minutes. For some classes, it may be appropriate to modify the assignment by specifying which problems they work on first. Some problems do not specify a method for solving. Students solve these problems using the RDW approach used for Application Problems.

Student Debrief (10 minutes)

Lesson Objective: Draw symmetric figures on the coordinate plane.

The Student Debrief is intended to invite reflection and active processing of the total lesson experience.

Invite students to review their solutions for the Problem Set. They should check work by comparing answers with a partner before going over answers as a class. Look for misconceptions or misunderstandings that can be addressed in the Debrief. Guide students in a conversation to debrief the Problem Set and process the lesson.

You may choose to use any combination of the questions below to lead the discussion.

- Compare drawing symmetric figures on the coordinate grid to drawing them on blank paper.

- Does the orientation of the line of symmetry change the way symmetric points must be drawn? Why or why not?

- What must be true for a pair of points to be symmetric about a line?

- When drawing figures about a vertical line of symmetry on a coordinate plane, explain why only the x-coordinate differs in symmetric coordinate pairs. Explain what happens to the coordinate pairs when drawing symmetric points about a horizontal line on the coordinate plane.

- In Problem 3, did your partner plot any points on line u? If so, did the pattern of how the x- and y-coordinates change continue for these fixed points?

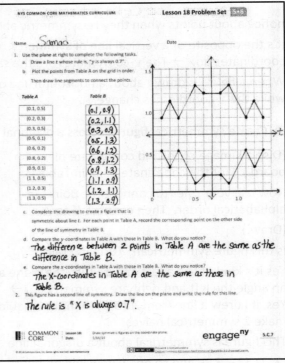

NOTES ON MULTIPLE MEANS OF ENGAGEMENT:

When asking questions, provide visuals to support understanding. For example, when asking the fourth question, draw before you speak.

Step 1: Draw a vertical line of symmetry on the coordinate plane.

Step 2: Say, "Here is a vertical line of symmetry on the coordinate plane."

Step 3: Draw two symmetric coordinate pairs.

Step 4: Say, "Explain why only the x-coordinate differs in symmetric pairs."

Lesson 18:   Draw symmetric figures on the coordinate plane.
Date: 1/31/14

6.D.6

Exit Ticket (3 minutes)

After the Student Debrief, instruct students to complete
the Exit Ticket. A review of their work will help you assess
the students' understanding of the concepts that were
presented in the lesson today and plan more effectively
for future lessons. You may read the questions aloud to
the students.

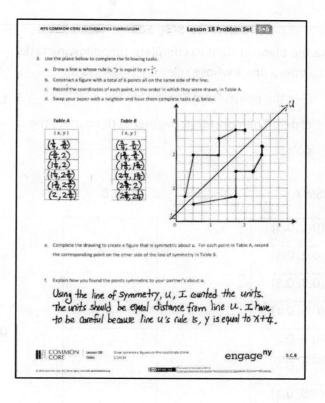

COMMON
CORE™

Lesson 18:   Draw symmetric figures on the coordinate plane.
Date: 1/31/14

6.D.7

Name _____   Date _____

1. Use the plane at right to complete the following tasks.

   a. Draw a line **t** whose rule is, *y is always 0.7*.

   b. Plot the points from Table A on the grid in order. Then draw line segments to connect the points.

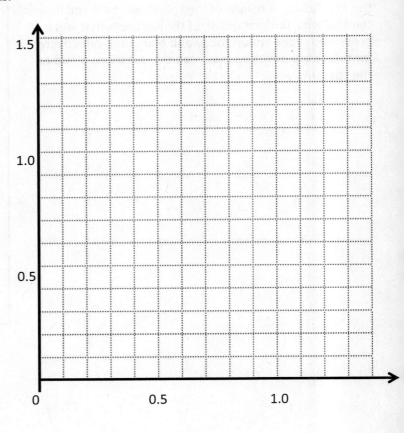

Table A

Table A
(0.1, 0.5)
(0.2, 0.3)
(0.3, 0.5)
(0.5, 0.1)
(0.6, 0.2)
(0.8, 0.2)
(0.9, 0.1)
(1.1, 0.5)
(1.2, 0.3)
(1.3, 0.5)

Table B

Table B

   c. Complete the drawing to create a figure that is symmetric about line **t**. For each point in Table A, record the corresponding point on the other side of the line of symmetry in Table B.

   d. Compare the *y*-coordinates in Table A with those in Table B. What do you notice?

   e. Compare the *x*-coordinates in Table A with those in Table B. What do you notice?

2. This figure has a second line of symmetry. Draw the line on the plane and write the rule for this line.

3. Use the plane below to complete the following tasks.

    a. Draw a line **u** whose rule is, *y is equal to x +* $\frac{1}{4}$*.*

    b. Construct a figure with a total of 6 points all on the same side of the line.

    c. Record the coordinates of each point, in the order in which they were drawn, in Table A.

    d. Swap your paper with a neighbor and have him or her complete Parts (e–f), below.

Table A

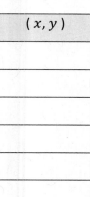

Table B

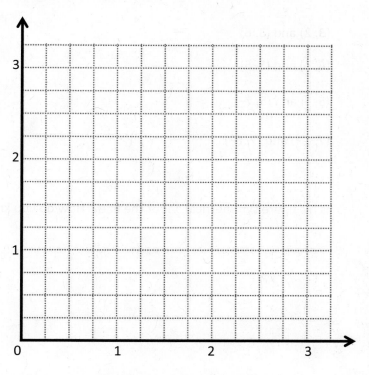

    e. Complete the drawing to create a figure that is symmetric about **u**. For each point in Table A, record

        the corresponding point on the other side of the line of symmetry in Table B.

    f. Explain how you found the points symmetric to your partner's about **u**.

COMMON
CORE ™

Lesson 18:
Date:

Draw symmetric figures on the coordinate plane.
1/31/14

6.D.9

Name _____   Date _____

1. Kenny plotted the following pairs of points and said they made a symmetric figure about a line with the rule:

$$y \text{ is always } 4.$$

(3, 2) and (3, 6)

(4, 3) and (5, 5)

$(5, \frac{3}{4})$ and $(5, 7\frac{1}{4})$

$(7, 1\frac{1}{2})$ and $(7, 6\frac{1}{2})$

Is his figure symmetrical about the line? How do you know?

Name _____   Date _____

1. Use the plane at right to complete the following tasks.

    a. Draw a line **s** whose rule is, *x is always 5*.

    b. Plot the points from Table A on the grid in order. Then draw line segments to connect the points in order.

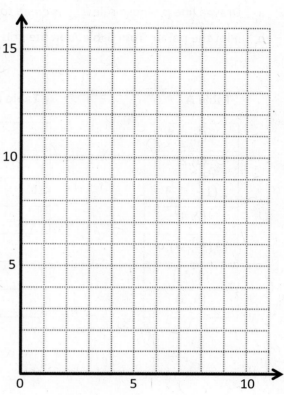

Table A   **Table B**

Table A
(1, 13)
(1, 12)
(2, 10)
(4, 9)
(4, 3)
(1, 2)
(5, 2)

    c. Complete the drawing to create a figure that is symmetric about line **s**. For each point in Table A, record the symmetric point on the other side of **s**.

    d. Compare the *y*-coordinates in Table A with those in Table B. What do you notice?

    e. Compare the *x*-coordinates in Table A with those in Table B. What do you notice?

2. Use the plane at right to complete the following tasks.

a. Draw a line **p** whose rule is, *y is equal to x*.

b. Plot the points from Table A on the grid in order. Then draw line segments to connect the points.

Table A

$(\frac{1}{2}, \frac{1}{2})$
$(1, 2)$
$(1\frac{1}{2}, 1\frac{1}{2})$
$(2, 4)$
$(3\frac{1}{2}, 3\frac{1}{2})$
$(4, 4\frac{1}{2})$
$(5, 5)$

Table B

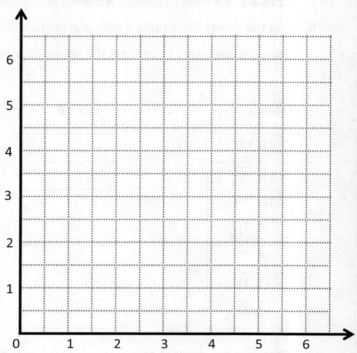

c. Complete the drawing to create a figure that is symmetric about line **p**. For each point in Table A, record the symmetric point on the other side of the line **p** in Table B.

d. Compare the *y*-coordinates in Table A with those in Table B. What do you notice?

e. Compare the *x*-coordinates in Table A with those in Table B. What do you notice?

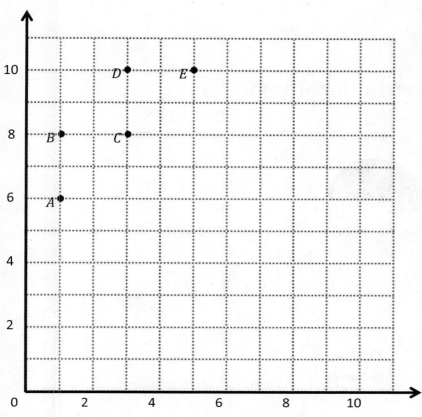

Table A

Point	(x, y)
A	
B	
C	
D	
E	

Table C

(x, y)

Table B

Point	(x, y)
I	
H	
G	
F	

Table D

(x, y)

Table D

Point	(x, y)
A	$(1, 1)$
B	$(1\frac{1}{2}, 3\frac{1}{2})$
C	$(2, 3)$
D	$(2\frac{1}{2}, 3\frac{1}{2})$
E	$(2\frac{1}{2}, 2\frac{1}{2})$
F	$(3\frac{1}{2}, 2\frac{1}{2})$
G	$(3, 2)$
H	$(3\frac{1}{2}, 1\frac{1}{2})$

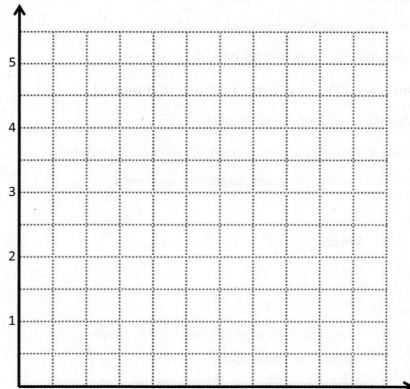

Lesson 18: Draw symmetric figures on the coordinate plane.
Date: 1/31/14

6.D.13

Lesson 19

Objective: Plot data on line graphs and analyze trends.

Suggested Lesson Structure

- ■ Fluency Practice   (13 minutes)
- ■ Application Problem   (6 minutes)
- ■ Concept Development   (31 minutes)
- ■ Student Debrief   (10 minutes)

  Total Time   **(60 minutes)**

Fluency Practice (13 minutes)

- ▪ Sprint: Make Larger Units **4.NF.1**   (9 minutes)
- ▪ Subtract a Fraction from a Whole **4.NF.3**   (4 minutes)

Sprint: Make Larger Units (9 minutes)

Materials: (S) Make Larger Units Sprint

Note: This Sprint reviews G5–Module 3 concepts.

Subtract a Fraction from a Whole (4 minutes)

Materials: (S) Personal white boards

Note: This fluency activity reviews G5–Module 3 concepts.

NOTES ON MULTIPLE MEANS FOR ACTION AND EXPRESSION:

If students need a bit more guidance in using strategies to solve the Subtract a Fraction from a Whole fluency activity, focus on one strategy at a time. Choose between compensation, break apart, convert to fractions, or another strategy. Guide students towards skillful mastery with repetition and practice using scaffolded questioning and choral response as modeled here.

T: Simplify $\frac{2}{10}$ by using larger fractional units.

S: $\frac{1}{5}$.

T: What's $1\frac{1}{10} - \frac{1}{5}$?

S: $\frac{9}{10}$.

T: (Write $1\frac{1}{10} - \frac{1}{5} = \frac{9}{10}$.)

T: There are many ways to solve $1\frac{1}{10} - \frac{1}{5}$. Maybe you used one of these strategies: (Write $1 - \frac{2}{10} + \frac{1}{10}$, $1\frac{1}{10} - \frac{1}{10} - \frac{1}{10}$, $\frac{11}{10} - \frac{2}{10} = \frac{9}{10}$.) Discuss the solution

---

COMMON CORE™

Lesson 19:   Plot data on line graphs and analyze trends.
Date: 1/31/14

6.D.14

methods with your partner.

S: (Discuss.)

T: Solve the following problems using any method.

T: (Beneath $1\frac{1}{10} - \frac{1}{5} = \frac{9}{10}$ write $2\frac{1}{10} - \frac{1}{5}$.) What's $2\frac{1}{10} - \frac{1}{5}$?

S: $1\frac{9}{10}$.

Continue with larger numbers of ones before switching to another set of related differences, such as $1\frac{1}{7} - \frac{1}{14}$ and $1\frac{1}{12} - \frac{1}{6}$.

Application Problem (6 minutes)

Three feet are equal to 1 yard. The following table shows the conversion. Use the information to complete the following tasks:

1. Plot each set of coordinates.

2. Use a straightedge to connect each point.

3. Plot one more point on this line and write its coordinates.

4. 27 feet can be converted to how many yards? _____

Feet	Yards
3	1
6	2
9	3
12	4

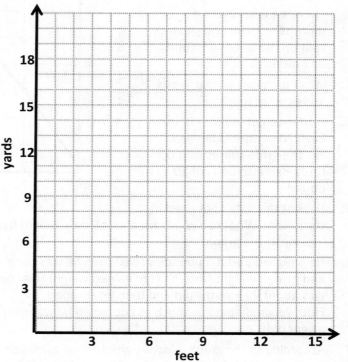

5. Write the rule that describes the line.

Note: This problem reviews concepts from the first topics in this module.

Concept Development (31 minutes)

Materials: (S) Line graph practice sheet

Read and interpret line graphs.

T: (Post image of Problem 1 from the line graph practice sheet on the board.) How are this coordinate plane and the one from our Application Problem different from others we've been looking at? Turn and talk.

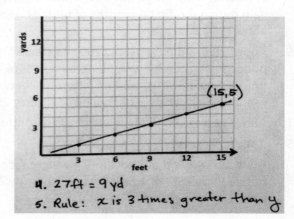

4. 27ft = 9 yd
5. Rule: x is 3 times greater than y

S: The x- and y-axes have labels and different units on them. → This new one isn't a straight line.

T: A coordinate plane can be used to show a set of data, like you see here, in the form of a line graph. What information is this line graph showing us?

S: How much Fido weighs on certain days. → Fido's weight.

T: Right, this graph shows a German Shepherd, Fido's, weight over a period of time. What information is shown on the x-axis?

S: Fido's age.

T: What unit is being used to show Fido's age?

S: There's a label every 4 months. → The grid squares split up the x-axis into units of 2 months.

T: What is shown on the y-axis and in what unit?

S: Fido's weight in pounds. → Each 20 pounds is labeled. → The grid squares split up the y-axis into units of 10 pounds.

T: Look at the data contained in the graph. What can you learn about Fido's weight by looking at the graph?

S: He weighed about a pound or two when he was born and gained weight fast! → Fido gained weight until he was about 20 months old and then he stopped. → Fido weighed about as much as I do when he was only a year old!

T: According to the graph, Fido weighed about 1, maybe 2, pounds at birth. About how much weight did Fido gain during the first 4 months of his life? How do you know?

MP.2

S: About 29 or 28 pounds, because he started at 1 or 2 pounds and then his weight increased. It reached 30 pounds at 4 months. → The difference between his 4-month weight and his birth-weight is 28 or 29 pounds.

T: About how much did Fido weigh at 8 months old?

S: About 55 pounds.

T: How can you find out how much weight Fido gained between the age of 4 months and 8 months? Turn and talk.

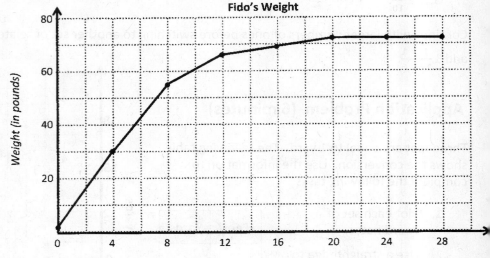

Fido's Weight

Age (in months)

NOTES ON
MULTIPLE MEANS OF
REPRESENTATION:

Support students working below grade level and others read the Fido's Weight line graph with the following modifications:

- Use color to outline the line and its points, as well as the information on the x- and y-axes.

- Add additional labeling to the x- and y- axes, or at least check that students accurately point and count units along each axis.

- Draw additional lines or labels for points that do not intersect a clearly labeled y-coordinate (such as 0,1).

Lesson 19:   Plot data on line graphs and analyze trends.
Date: 1/31/14

6.D.16

S: I can subtract 30 pounds from 55 pounds. → I could count up from 30 pounds. → I can find the difference between his weight at those ages. He gained 25 pounds between 4 and 8 months.

T: So, did Fido gain more weight in the first 4 months of his life, or the second 4 months?

S: The first 4 months.

T: About how much more?

MP.2

S: About 5 pounds more.

T: Compare the segment that shows the change from 0 to 4 months with the segment that shows the change from 4 months to 8 months.

S: They're a lot alike, because they both go up, but the line from 0 to 4 is a little steeper. → The triangles that have these segments as their longest sides are different. The one I see for 0 to 4 months has a height of 3 units and the one I see for 4 to 8 months has a height of $2\frac{1}{2}$.

T: Work with a partner to find out how much weight Fido gained during the remaining 4 month increments on the graph.

T: We know that Fido gained more weight from birth to 4 months than he did from 4 months to 8 months. What do you notice about the two segments joining those points?

S: The segment for the first 4 months is steeper, because he gained more weight then.

T: Explain what happens to Fido's weight and the line on the graph between months 20 and 28.

S: Fido's weight stays the same, and the line doesn't change, it just goes straight across. → Fido's weight remains constant so the line is horizontal.

T: The line becomes horizontal to show that his weight is unchanged during that time. In this case, Fido's weight stayed the same.

T: Can we make a prediction about what this line graph might look like if we could see the next 28 months of Fido's life? Why or why not? Turn and talk.

S: We can't really tell from this information. His weight might just keep staying the same. My dog was full-grown at 2 years old. → If Fido gets sick he might start losing weight a bit, but there's no way to know. → Well, a lot of things could happen. He might not exercise very much and gain weight. Or, he might run away, and have a hard time finding food and lose weight.

T: All of you could be right, but the truth is, we have no way of knowing. This line graph simply shows us what Fido's weight was at these specific times in his life. We can't predict how or if Fido's weight will change in the future without more information than what is contained in this graph.

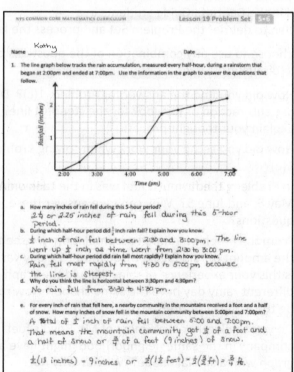

Lesson 19:   Plot data on line graphs and analyze trends.
Date: 1/31/14

6.D.17

Problem Set (10 minutes)

Students should do their personal best to complete the Problem Set within the allotted 10 minutes. For some classes, it may be appropriate to modify the assignment by specifying which problems they work on first. Some problems do not specify a method for solving. Students solve these problems using the RDW approach used for Application Problems.

Student Debrief (10 minutes)

Lesson Objective: Plot data on line graphs and analyze trends.

The Student Debrief is intended to invite reflection and active processing of the total lesson experience.

Invite students to review their solutions for the Problem Set. They should check work by comparing answers with a partner before going over answers as a class. Look for misconceptions or misunderstandings that can be addressed in the Debrief. Guide students in a conversation to debrief the Problem Set and process the lesson.

You may choose to use any combination of the questions below to lead the discussion.

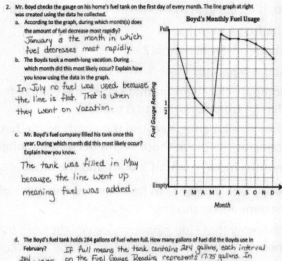

- ▪ How did you find the answer for Problem 1(c)? Did you use subtraction or just look for the steepest line? Explain your thought process.

- ▪ How did you setup your work when solving Problem 1(e)?

- ▪ In Problem 2, how much fuel was in the tank on April 5, May 5, and June 5? Why can't we answer these questions?

- ▪ From the graph on rainfall accumulation, we see that the amount of rain falling throughout the day varied. Is this your experience of rain? Would the graph of a different rainy day have the same shape? How might it be the same? Different?

- ▪ Do you think other customers of Mr. Boyd's fuel company in the same neighborhood might have a graph with a similar shape? Why or why not?

NOTES ON
LINE GRAPHS:

The third question uses Mr. Boyd's Fuel Usage graph to help students understand that the segments between each point on the graph serve to connect those data but do not communicate data. Mr. Boyd may have used much fuel on one day and very little on another day. There is no way of knowing. What is known is how much fuel was in his tank on the first of each month. The graph shows a sharp decrease between January and February, but perhaps if those 30 days each had a data point, the graph would look much different.

Exit Ticket (3 minutes)

After the Student Debrief, instruct students to complete the Exit Ticket. A review of their work will help you assess the students' understanding of the concepts that were presented in the lesson today and plan more effectively for future lessons. You may read the questions aloud to the students.

Lesson 19:   Plot data on line graphs and analyze trends.
Date: 1/31/14

6.D.19

A

Correct _____

Simplify.

1	$\frac{2}{4} =$		23	$\frac{9}{27} =$	
2	$\frac{2}{6} =$		24	$\frac{9}{63} =$	
3	$\frac{2}{8} =$		25	$\frac{8}{12} =$	
4	$\frac{5}{10} =$		26	$\frac{8}{16} =$	
5	$\frac{5}{15} =$		27	$\frac{8}{24} =$	
6	$\frac{5}{20} =$		28	$\frac{8}{64} =$	
7	$\frac{4}{8} =$		29	$\frac{12}{18} =$	
8	$\frac{4}{12} =$		30	$\frac{12}{16} =$	
9	$\frac{4}{16} =$		31	$\frac{9}{12} =$	
10	$\frac{3}{6} =$		32	$\frac{6}{8} =$	
11	$\frac{3}{9} =$		33	$\frac{10}{12} =$	
12	$\frac{3}{12} =$		34	$\frac{15}{18} =$	
13	$\frac{4}{6} =$		35	$\frac{8}{10} =$	
14	$\frac{6}{12} =$		36	$\frac{16}{20} =$	
15	$\frac{6}{18} =$		37	$\frac{12}{15} =$	
16	$\frac{6}{30} =$		38	$\frac{18}{27} =$	
17	$\frac{6}{9} =$		39	$\frac{27}{36} =$	
18	$\frac{7}{14} =$		40	$\frac{32}{40} =$	
19	$\frac{7}{21} =$		41	$\frac{45}{54} =$	
20	$\frac{7}{42} =$		42	$\frac{24}{36} =$	
21	$\frac{8}{12} =$		43	$\frac{60}{72} =$	
22	$\frac{9}{18} =$		44	$\frac{48}{60} =$	

Lesson 19: Plot data on line graphs and analyze trends.
Date: 1/31/14

6.D.20

B   Improvement _____   # Correct _____

1	$\frac{5}{10}=$		23	$\frac{8}{24}=$	
2	$\frac{5}{15}=$		24	$\frac{8}{56}=$	
3	$\frac{5}{20}=$		25	$\frac{8}{12}=$	
4	$\frac{2}{4}=$		26	$\frac{9}{18}=$	
5	$\frac{2}{6}=$		27	$\frac{9}{27}=$	
6	$\frac{2}{8}=$		28	$\frac{9}{72}=$	
7	$\frac{3}{6}=$		29	$\frac{12}{18}=$	
8	$\frac{3}{9}=$		30	$\frac{6}{8}=$	
9	$\frac{3}{12}=$		31	$\frac{9}{12}=$	
10	$\frac{4}{8}=$		32	$\frac{12}{16}=$	
11	$\frac{4}{12}=$		33	$\frac{8}{10}=$	
12	$\frac{4}{16}=$		34	$\frac{16}{20}=$	
13	$\frac{4}{6}=$		35	$\frac{12}{15}=$	
14	$\frac{7}{14}=$		36	$\frac{10}{12}=$	
15	$\frac{7}{21}=$		37	$\frac{15}{18}=$	
16	$\frac{7}{35}=$		38	$\frac{16}{24}=$	
17	$\frac{6}{9}=$		39	$\frac{24}{32}=$	
18	$\frac{6}{12}=$		40	$\frac{36}{45}=$	
19	$\frac{6}{18}=$		41	$\frac{40}{48}=$	
20	$\frac{6}{36}=$		42	$\frac{24}{36}=$	
21	$\frac{8}{12}=$		43	$\frac{48}{60}=$	
22	$\frac{8}{16}=$		44	$\frac{60}{72}=$	

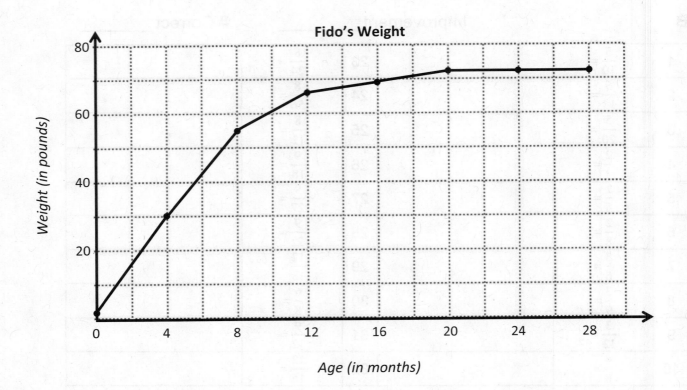

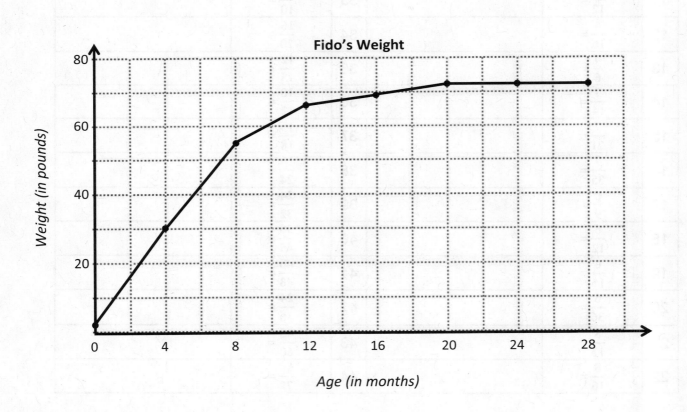

COMMON CORE™ | **Lesson 19:**   Plot data on line graphs and analyze trends.

                | **Date:**   1/31/14

6.D.2

Name _____   Date _____

1. The line graph below tracks the rain accumulation, measured every half hour, during a rainstorm that began at 2:00 p.m. and ended at 7:00 p.m. Use the information in the graph to answer the questions that follow.

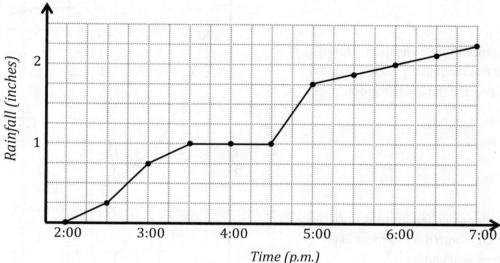

a. How many inches of rain fell during this five-hour period?

b. During which half-hour period did $\frac{1}{2}$ inch rain fall? Explain how you know.

c. During which half-hour period did rain fall most rapidly? Explain how you know.

d. Why do you think the line is horizontal between 3:30 p.m. and 4:30 p.m.?

e. For every inch of rain that fell here, a nearby community in the mountains received a foot and a half of snow. How many inches of snow fell in the mountain community between 5:00 p.m. and 7:00 p.m.?

COMMON CORE™

Lesson 19:   Plot data on line graphs and analyze trends.
Date: 1/31/14

6.D.23

2. Mr. Boyd checks the gauge on his home's fuel tank on the first day of every month. The line graph at right was created using the data he collected.

   a. According to the graph, during which month(s) does the amount of fuel decrease most rapidly?

   b. The Boyds took a month-long vacation. During which month did this most likely occur? Explain how you know using the data in the graph.

   c. Mr. Boyd's fuel company filled his tank once this year. During which month did this most likely occur? Explain how you know.

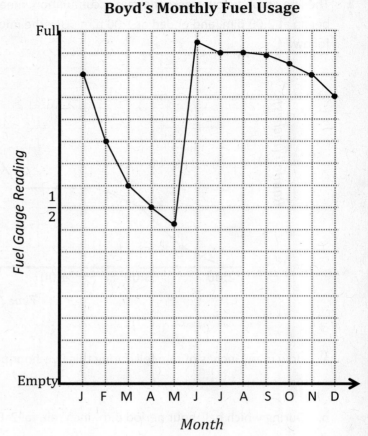

Boyd's Monthly Fuel Usage

   d. The Boyd family's fuel tank holds 284 gallons of fuel when full. How many gallons of fuel did the Boyds use in February?

   e. Mr. Boyd pays $3.54 per gallon of fuel. What is the cost of the fuel used in February and March?

COMMON CORE™

Lesson 19:   Plot data on line graphs and analyze trends.
Date: 1/31/14

6.D.24

Name _____   Date _____

1. The line graph below tracks the water level of Plainsview Creek, measured each Sunday, for 8 weeks. Use the information in the graph to answer the questions that follow.

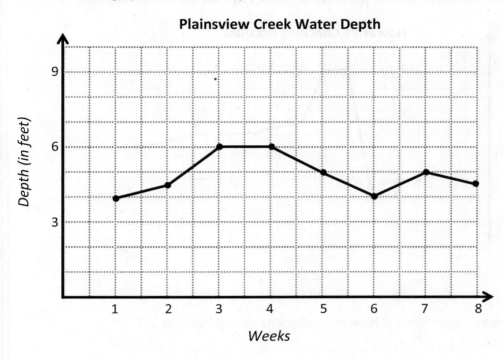

Plainsview Creek Water Depth

a. About how many feet deep was the creek in Week 1? _____

b. According to the graph, which week had the greatest change in water depth? _____

c. It rained hard throughout the sixth week. During what other weeks might it have rained? Explain why you think so.

d. What might have been another cause leading to an increase in the depth of the creek?

Name _____   Date _____

1. The line graph below tracks the balance of Howard's checking account, at the end of each day, between May 12 and May 26. Use the information in the graph to answer the questions that follow.

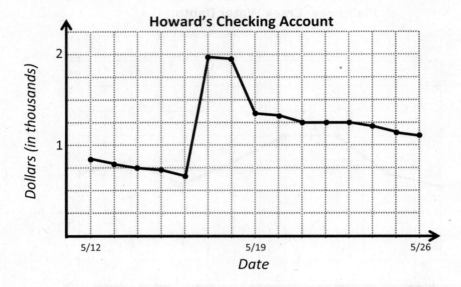

a. About how much money does Howard have in his checking account on May 21?

b. If Howard spends $250 from his checking account on May 26, about how much money will he have left in his account?

c. Explain what happened with Howard's money between May 21 and May 23.

d. Howard received a payment from his job that went directly into his checking account. On which day did this most likely occur? Explain how you know.

e. Howard bought a new television during the time shown in the graph. On which day did this most likely occur? Explain how you know.

Lesson 19:	Plot data on line graphs and analyze trends.
Date:	1/31/14

6.D.2●

2. The line graph below tracks Santino's time, at the beginning and end of each length of a triathlon. Use the information in the graph to answer the questions that follow.

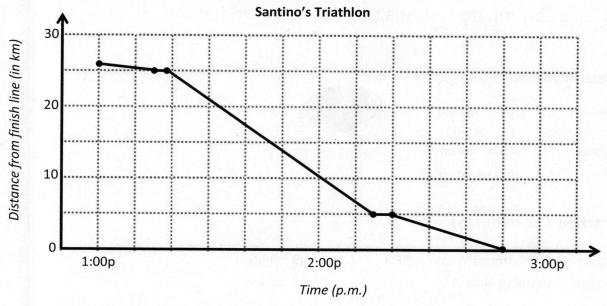

a. How long does it take Santino to finish the triathlon?

b. To complete the triathlon, Santino first swims across a lake, then bikes through the city, and finishes by running around the lake. According to the graph, what was the distance of the running portion of the race?

c. During the race Santino pauses to put on his biking shoes and helmet, and then later change into his running shoes. At what times did this most likely occur? Explain how you know.

d. Which part of the race does Santino finish most quickly? How do you know?

e. During which part of the triathlon is Santino racing most quickly? Explain how you know.

Lesson 20

Objective: Use coordinate systems to solve real world problems.

Suggested Lesson Structure

■ Fluency Practice   (12 minutes)
  Concept Development   (38 minutes)
■ Student Debrief   (10 minutes)
  Total Time   **(60 minutes)**

Fluency Practice (12 minutes)

▪ Sprint: Subtract a Fraction from a Whole **4.NF.3**   (9 minutes)
▪ Express Fractions as Decimals **4.NF.3**   (3 minutes)

Sprint: Subtract a Fraction from a Whole (9 minutes)

Materials: (S) Subtract a Fraction from a Whole Sprint

Note: This Sprint reviews G5–Module 3 concepts.

Express Fractions as Decimals (3 minutes)

Materials: (S) Personal white boards

Note: This fluency activity reviews G5–Module 4 content.

T: (Write $\frac{1}{2}$ on board.) Express the fraction in hundredths.

S: 50 hundredths.

T: Write this number as a decimal.

S: (Write 0.50.)

T: (Write $\frac{1}{20}$ on board.) Express the fraction in hundredths.

S: 5 hundredths.

T: Write this number as a decimal.

S: (Write 0.05.)

Repeat the process with the following possible sequence: $\frac{3}{2}, \frac{1}{4}, \frac{6}{20}, \frac{8}{20}, \frac{3}{5}, \frac{7}{5}, \frac{3}{50}, \frac{9}{50}, \frac{101}{50}, \frac{3}{4}, \frac{4}{4}, \frac{1}{25}, \frac{4}{25}$, and $\frac{7}{25}$.

Lesson 20:   Use coordinate systems to solve real world problems.
Date: 1/31/14

Concept Development (38 minutes)

Materials: (S) Problem Set

Note: An Application Problem is not included in this lesson in order to provide adequate time for the Concept Development.

Suggested Delivery of Instruction for Solving Lesson 20's Word Problems. (All times are approximate.)

1. Read the graph or scenario. (3 minutes)

Review the following questions and have students discuss the answers before beginning the first problem.

- What data is the graph or scenario communicating?
- What information and what units are shown on the axes?

As students discuss, circulate. Reiterate the questions above. After a minute or so, have the pairs of students share their thoughts.

2. Solve the problems. (9 minutes)

Give everyone five minutes of quiet work time to answer the questions. After four minutes, invite them to work together if they so choose in order to complete all components of the problem. All students should write their equations and statements for each question.

3. Assess the solution for reasonableness and review the answers. (4 minutes)

Give students the opportunity to explain the reasonableness of their solutions with a peer. Review the answers with the whole class.

4. Debrief. (3 minutes)

Each question is followed by a set of questions to support you in guiding students to think more deeply about the data.

Problem 1

The line graph below tracks the total tomato production for one tomato plant. The total tomato production is plotted at the end of each of 8 weeks. Use the information in the graph to answer the questions that follow.

    a. How many pounds of tomatoes did this plant produce at the end of 13 weeks?

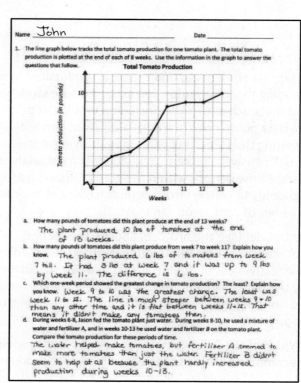

Lesson 20:   Use coordinate systems to solve real world problems.
Date: 1/31/14

6.D.29

b. How many pounds of tomatoes did this plant produce between Week 7 and Week 11? Explain how you know.

c. Which one-week period shows the greatest change in tomato production? The least? Explain how you know.

d. During weeks 6–8, Jason fed the tomato plant just water. During Weeks 8–10, he used a mixture of water and Fertilizer A, and in Weeks 10–13, he used water and Fertilizer B on the tomato plant. Compare the tomato production for these periods of time.

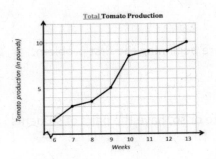

Total Tomato Production

Tomato production (in pounds)

Weeks

a. The plant produced 10 lbs of tomatoes

b. The plant produced 6 lbs of tomatoes from week 7 to 11. It had made 3 lbs at week 7 + it was up to 9 pounds by week 11. The difference is 6 lbs.

c. Week 9 to 10 was the greatest change. The least was week 11 to 12. The line is much steeper between weeks 9 + 10 than any other time + it is flat between weeks 11 + 12. That means it didn't make any tomatoes then.

d. The water helped make tomatoes, but fertilizer A seemed to make more tomatoes than just the water. Fertilizer B didn't seem to help at all because the plant hardly increased production during weeks 10–13.

Problem 1(a) asks students to find the total production, assuring they are reading the information correctly. Be sure students understand that each data point (including Week 6) is a cumulative data point, not a starting value. Problem 1(b), requires relating the steepness of a segment to greater production. To answer Problem 1(c), students must analyze three separate time periods within the graph. Problem 1(d) requires students to convert from pounds to ounces in order to find the number of cans Jason can make.

During the Debrief (see the protocol above), the second question challenges assumptions students may have made about the effectiveness of the fertilizers. We can speculate about why the data changed the way it did, but the line graph alone does not provide enough information to know the truth of what happened.

- Which of the feeding methods used by Jason would you recommend he use to increase his tomato production next year? Why?

NOTES ON MULTIPLE MEANS OF ENGAGEMENT:

Students may find data plotting and analysis more engaging if the data is self-generated. Consider allowing students to develop and administer simple surveys or grow and measure their own plants.

Such data might be plotted and analyzed on paper or could be entered into simple spreadsheets in a spreadsheet program and plotted using the graph features contained therein.

Lesson 20: Use coordinate systems to solve real world problems.
Date: 1/31/14

6.D.3(

- Would your answer change if you learned that during Weeks 10–13, the temperature dropped dramatically in Jason's town?
- What other factors may have had an impact on the tomato plant's production?
- Why might this information be helpful? Who might be interested in seeing it?

Problem 2

Use the story context below to sketch a line graph. Then answer the questions that follow.

The number of fifth-grade students attending Magnolia School has changed over time. The school opened in 2006, with 156 students in the fifth grade. The student population grew the same amount each year before reaching its largest class of 210 students in 2008. The following year, Magnolia lost one-seventh of its fifth-graders. In 2010, the enrollment dropped to 154 students and remained constant in 2011. For the next two years, the enrollment grew by 7 students each year.

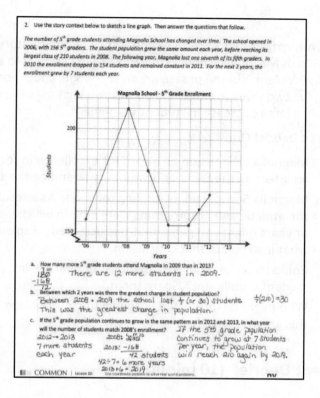

a. How many more fifth-grade students attended Magnolia in 2009 than in 2013?

b. Between which two consecutive years was there the greatest change in student population?

c. If the fifth-grade population continues to follow the same growth pattern as in 2012 and 2013, in what year will the number of students match 2008's enrollment?

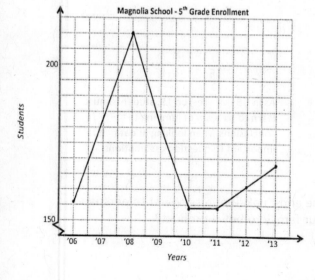

a) $\begin{array}{r} 1\overset{7}{8}\overset{10}{0} \\ -\ 168 \\ \hline 1\ 2 \end{array}$ There are 12 more students in 2009.

b) Between 2008 & 2009 the school lost $\frac{1}{7}$ of (or 30 students) its population. This was the greatest change in population.

c) 2012 → 2013:
    7 students more each year

    2008: $\overset{1}{2}\overset{10}{1}\overset{10}{6}$
    2013: $-\ 168$
    $\overline{\qquad 42\ students}$

    $42 \div 7 = 6$
    $2013 + 6\ years = 2019$

    If the 5th grade population continues to grow in the same pattern, the population will reach 210 again by 2019.

COMMON CORE

Lesson 20:   Use coordinate systems to solve real world problems.
Date: 1/31/14

6.D.31

In this problem, students are given the task of reading a story context about the changing fifth-grade population of Magnolia School. They must read carefully to extract the necessary data and complete the line graph. In Problem 2(b) the phrase *greatest change*, could pose a challenge as students may be tempted to look for the two years in which the population increases the most. However, in this case, the greatest change is actually a large decrease in student enrollment.

Suggested Debrief Questions:

- Magnolia School won an award for excellence in teaching in 2011. Do you think that the award had an affect on the number of students attending the school? Explain.

- Magnolia School had its funding reduced. As a result, the athletic and art programs were cut. In which year or years might you guess that this occurred? Explain what lead you to that conclusion.

- Could there be other explanations for changes in student enrollment? Share them.

- Who might be interested in seeing the information in this graph? Why?

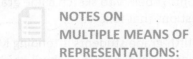

NOTES ON MULTIPLE MEANS OF REPRESENTATIONS:

Creating line graphs may pose a challenge to students with fine-motor skill deficits. Consider providing larger-scale graph paper (such as 1 inch) to scaffold their efforts.

Student Debrief (10 minutes)

Lesson Objective: Use coordinate systems to solve real world problems.

The Student Debrief is intended to invite reflection and active processing of the total lesson experience.

Invite students to review their solutions for the Problem Set. They should check work by comparing answers with a partner before going over answers as a class. Look for misconceptions or misunderstandings that can be addressed in the Debrief. Guide students in a conversation to debrief the Problem Set and process the lesson.

You may choose to use any combination of the questions below to lead the discussion.

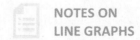

NOTES ON LINE GRAPHS

As in G5–M6–Lesson 19, students must learn to be wary of jumping to conclusions when looking at data. It is important to question assumptions.

- How are the line graphs alike and different?

- How did your solutions differ from your neighbor's solutions?

- What other scenarios might be interesting to graph?

- Can you see ways in which the data could be used to misrepresent the effectiveness of the fertilizer or the reasons for changes in the enrollment?

- When we see data used in advertisements we need to pause and think about its power to persuade us. Can you think of any ways data is used to get you or your family to buy a product?

Exit Ticket (4 minutes)

After the Student Debrief, instruct students to complete the Exit Ticket.

	Lesson 20:	Use coordinate systems to solve real world problems.
	Date:	1/31/14

6.D.3

A

Subtract. Give each answer as a mixed number in its simplest form.

Correct _____

1	$4 - \frac{1}{2} =$		23	$3 - \frac{1}{8} =$	
2	$3 - \frac{1}{2} =$		24	$3 - \frac{3}{8} =$	
3	$2 - \frac{1}{2} =$		25	$3 - \frac{5}{8} =$	
4	$1 - \frac{1}{2} =$		26	$3 - \frac{7}{8} =$	
5	$1 - \frac{1}{3} =$		27	$2 - \frac{7}{8} =$	
6	$2 - \frac{1}{3} =$		28	$4 - \frac{1}{7} =$	
7	$4 - \frac{1}{3} =$		29	$3 - \frac{6}{7} =$	
8	$4 - \frac{2}{3} =$		30	$2 - \frac{3}{7} =$	
9	$2 - \frac{2}{3} =$		31	$4 - \frac{4}{7} =$	
10	$2 - \frac{1}{4} =$		32	$3 - \frac{5}{7} =$	
11	$2 - \frac{3}{4} =$		33	$4 - \frac{3}{4} =$	
12	$3 - \frac{3}{4} =$		34	$2 - \frac{5}{8} =$	
13	$3 - \frac{1}{4} =$		35	$3 - \frac{3}{10} =$	
14	$4 - \frac{3}{4} =$		36	$4 - \frac{2}{5} =$	
15	$2 - \frac{1}{10} =$		37	$4 - \frac{3}{7} =$	
16	$3 - \frac{9}{10} =$		38	$3 - \frac{7}{10} =$	
17	$2 - \frac{7}{10} =$		39	$3 - \frac{5}{10} =$	
18	$4 - \frac{3}{10} =$		40	$4 - \frac{2}{8} =$	
19	$3 - \frac{1}{5} =$		41	$2 - \frac{9}{12} =$	
20	$3 - \frac{2}{5} =$		42	$4 - \frac{2}{12} =$	
21	$3 - \frac{4}{5} =$		43	$3 - \frac{2}{6} =$	
22	$3 - \frac{3}{5} =$		44	$2 - \frac{8}{12} =$	

Lesson 20: Use coordinate systems to solve real world problems.
Date: 1/31/14

6.D.33

B Subtract. Give each answer as a mixed number in its simplest form.

Improvement _____   # Correct _____

1	$1 - \frac{1}{2} =$		23	$2 - \frac{1}{8} =$	
2	$2 - \frac{1}{2} =$		24	$2 - \frac{3}{8} =$	
3	$3 - \frac{1}{2} =$		25	$2 - \frac{5}{8} =$	
4	$4 - \frac{1}{2} =$		26	$2 - \frac{7}{8} =$	
5	$1 - \frac{1}{4} =$		27	$4 - \frac{7}{8} =$	
6	$2 - \frac{1}{4} =$		28	$3 - \frac{1}{7} =$	
7	$4 - \frac{1}{4} =$		29	$2 - \frac{6}{7} =$	
8	$4 - \frac{3}{4} =$		30	$4 - \frac{3}{7} =$	
9	$2 - \frac{3}{4} =$		31	$3 - \frac{4}{7} =$	
10	$2 - \frac{1}{3} =$		32	$2 - \frac{5}{7} =$	
11	$2 - \frac{2}{3} =$		33	$3 - \frac{3}{4} =$	
12	$3 - \frac{2}{3} =$		34	$4 - \frac{5}{8} =$	
13	$3 - \frac{1}{3} =$		35	$2 - \frac{3}{10} =$	
14	$4 - \frac{2}{3} =$		36	$3 - \frac{2}{5} =$	
15	$3 - \frac{1}{10} =$		37	$3 - \frac{3}{7} =$	
16	$2 - \frac{9}{10} =$		38	$2 - \frac{7}{10} =$	
17	$4 - \frac{7}{10} =$		39	$2 - \frac{5}{10} =$	
18	$3 - \frac{3}{10} =$		40	$3 - \frac{6}{8} =$	
19	$2 - \frac{1}{5} =$		41	$4 - \frac{3}{12} =$	
20	$2 - \frac{2}{5} =$		42	$3 - \frac{10}{12} =$	
21	$2 - \frac{4}{5} =$		43	$2 - \frac{4}{6} =$	
22	$3 - \frac{3}{5} =$		44	$4 - \frac{4}{12} =$	

Lesson 20: Use coordinate systems to solve real world problems.
Date: 1/31/14

6.D.3

Name _____   Date _____

1. The line graph below tracks the total tomato production for one tomato plant. The total tomato production is plotted at the end of each of 8 weeks. Use the information in the graph to answer the questions that follow.

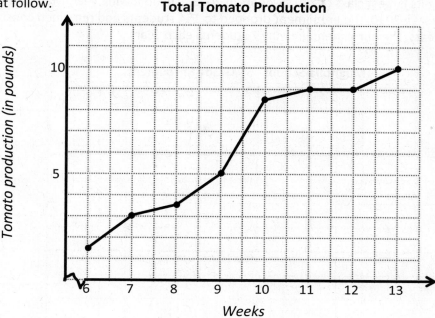

Total Tomato Production

a. How many pounds of tomatoes did this plant produce at the end of 13 weeks?

b. How many pounds of tomatoes did this plant produce from Week 7 to Week 11? Explain how you know.

c. Which one-week period showed the greatest change in tomato production? The least? Explain how you know.

d. During Weeks 6–8, Jason fed the tomato plant just water. During Weeks 8–10, he used a mixture of water and Fertilizer A, and in Weeks 10–13 he used water and Fertilizer B on the tomato plant. Compare the tomato production for these periods of time.

2. Use the story context below to sketch a line graph. Then answer the questions that follow.

The number of fifth-grade students attending Magnolia School has changed over time. The school opened in 2006, with 156 students in the fifth grade. The student population grew the same amount each year before reaching its largest class of 210 students in 2008. The following year, Magnolia lost one-seventh of its fifth-graders. In 2010, the enrollment dropped to 154 students and remained constant in 2011. For the next two years, the enrollment grew by 7 students each year.

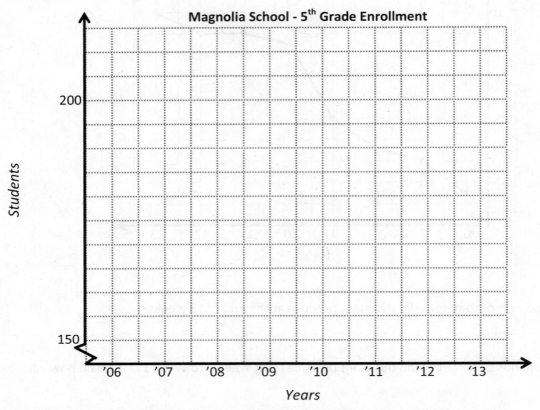

a. How many more fifth-grade students attend Magnolia in 2009 than in 2013?

b. Between which two years was there the greatest change in student population?

c. If the fifth-grade population continues to grow in the same pattern as in 2012 and 2013, in what year will the number of students match 2008's enrollment?

COMMON CORE™

Lesson 20:   Use coordinate systems to solve real world problems.
Date: 1/31/14

6.D.3

Name _____   Date _____

1. Use the following information to complete the line graph below. Then answer the questions that follow.

   Harry runs a hot dog stand at the county fair. When he arrived on Wednesday, he had 38 dozen hot dogs on his stand. The graph shows the number of hot dogs (in dozens) that remained unsold at the end of each day of sales.

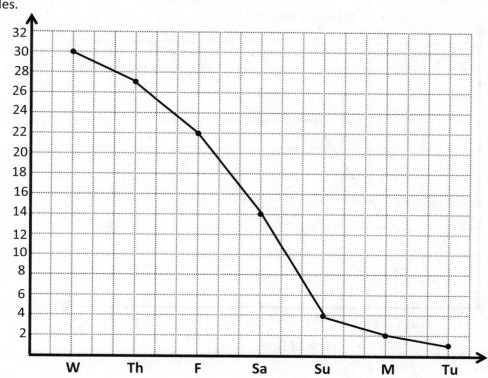

   a. How many dozen hot dogs did Harry sell on Wednesday? How do you know?

   b. Between which two-day period did the number of hot dogs sold change the most? Explain how you determined your answer.

   c. During which three days did Harry sell the most hot dogs?

   d. How many dozens of hot dogs were sold on these three days?

Name _____   Date _____

1. Use the graph to answer the questions.

   Johnny left his home at 6 a.m. and kept track of the number of kilometers he traveled at the end of each hour of his trip. He recorded the data in a line graph.

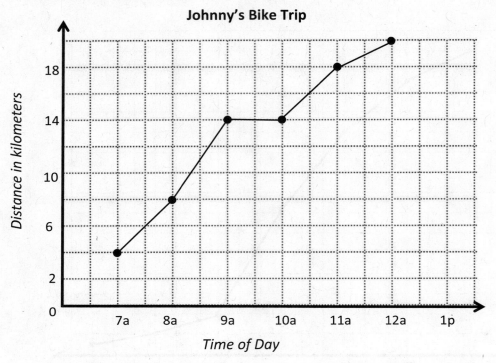

   Johnny's Bike Trip

   a. How far did Johnny travel in all? How long did it take?

   b. Johnny took a one-hour break to have a snack and take some pictures. What time did he stop? How do you know?

c. Did Johnny cover more distance before his break or after? Explain.

d. Between which two hours did Johnny ride 4 kilometers?

e. Which hour did Johnny ride the fastest? Explain how you know.

 Lesson 20:   Use coordinate systems to solve real world problems.
Date: 1/31/14

6.D.39

Name _____   Date _____

1. Give the coordinates of each point.

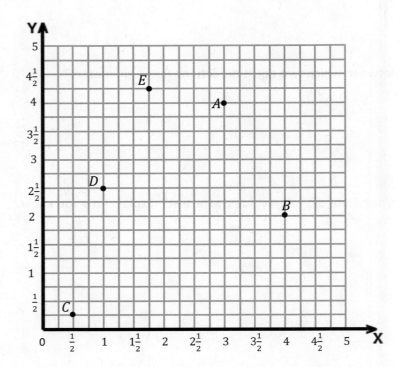

A _____

B _____

C _____

D _____

E _____

2. Plot each point in the coordinate plane above, and label each point with F, G, or H.

    F (0, 4) G (2, 1) H $(4\frac{3}{4}, 3\frac{3}{4})$

3.
   a. Give coordinates for three points that are on the same vertical line. Include at least one point that has a mixed number as a coordinate.

   b. Give coordinates for three points that are on the same horizontal line. Include at least one point that has a fraction as a coordinate.

4. Garrett and Jeffrey are planning a treasure hunt. They decide to place a treasure at a point that is a distance of 5 units from the x-axis and 3 units from the y-axis. Jeffrey places a treasure at point J and Garrett places one at point G. Who put the treasure in the right place? Explain how you know.

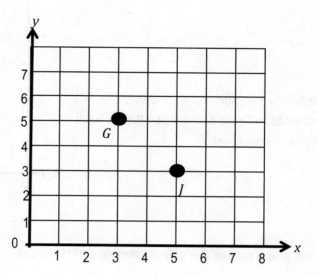

5.

a. Find the y-coordinates by following the rules given for each table.

Table A: Multiply by $\frac{1}{2}$ **Table B:**   Multiply by $\frac{1}{4}$

x	y
0	
1	
2	
3	

x	y
0	
1	
2	
3	

b. Graph and label the coordinate pairs from Table A. Connect the points and label the line *a*. Graph and label the coordinate pairs from Table B. Connect the points and label the line *b*.

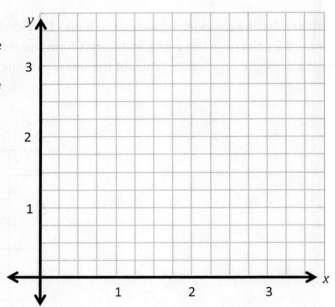

c. Describe the relationship between the *y*-coordinates in Table A and Table B that have the same *x*-coordinate.

6.

a. Use the graph to give the coordinate pairs of the points marked on the line.

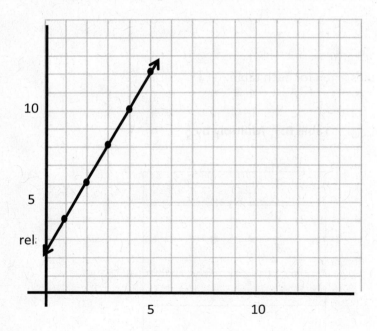

x	*y*

b. Using this rule, generate three more points that would be on this line but lie beyond the portion of the coordinate plane that is pictured.

COMMON CORE™ | **Module 6:**   Problem Solving with the Coordinate Plane
                       | **Date:**   1/31/14   6.S.

© 2014 Common Core, Inc. All rights reserved. **commoncore.org**

Mid-Module Assessment Task	Topics A–B
Standards Addressed	

Write and interpret numerical expressions.

5.OA.2   Write simple expressions that record calculations with numbers, and interpret numerical expressions without evaluating them. *For example, express the calculation "add 8 and 7, then multiply by 2" as 2 × (8 + 7). Recognize that 3 × (18932 + 921) is three times as large as 18932 + 921, without having to calculate the indicated sum or product.*

Analyze patterns and relationships.

5.OA.3   Generate two numerical patterns using two given rules. Identify apparent relationships between corresponding terms. Form ordered pairs consisting of corresponding terms from the two patterns, and graph the ordered pairs on a coordinate plane. *For example, given the rule "Add 3" and the starting number 0, and given the rule "Add 6" and the starting number 0, generate terms in the resulting sequences, and observe that the terms in one sequence are twice the corresponding terms in the other sequence. Explain informally why this is so.*

Graph points on the coordinate plane to solve real-world and mathematical problems.

5.G.1   Use a pair of perpendicular number lines, called axes, to define a coordinate system, with the intersection of the lines (the origin) arranged to coincide with the 0 on each line and a given point in the plane located by using an ordered pair of numbers, called its coordinates. Understand that the first number indicates how far to travel from the origin in the direction of one axis, and the second number indicates how far to travel in the direction of the second axis, with the convention that the names of the two axes and the coordinates correspond (e.g., x-axis and x-coordinate, y-axis and y-coordinate).

Evaluating Student Learning Outcomes

A Progression Toward Mastery is provided to describe steps that illuminate the gradually increasing understandings that students develop *on their way to proficiency.* In this chart, this progress is presented from left (Step 1) to right (Step 4). The learning goal for each student is to achieve Step 4 mastery. These steps are meant to help teachers and students identify and celebrate what the student CAN do now and what they need to work on next.

	Module 6:	Problem Solving with the Coordinate Plane	
	Date:	1/31/14	6.S.4

A Progression Toward Mastery

Assessment Task Item and Standards Assessed	STEP 1 Little evidence of reasoning without a correct answer. (1 Point)	STEP 2 Evidence of some reasoning without a correct answer. (2 Points)	STEP 3 Evidence of some reasoning with a correct answer or evidence of solid reasoning with an incorrect answer. (3 Points)	STEP 4 Evidence of solid reasoning with a correct answer. (4 Points)
1 **5.G.1**	The student gives the coordinates for one point on the plane and uses correct notation, including parentheses and a comma.	The student gives the coordinates for two points on the plane and uses correct notation, including parentheses and a comma.	The student gives the coordinates for three points on the plane and uses correct notation, including parentheses and a comma.	The student correctly gives the coordinates for four or five points using correct notation as: A (3, 4) B (4, 2) C $(\frac{1}{2}, \frac{1}{4})$ D $(1, 2\frac{1}{2})$ E $(1\frac{3}{4}, 4\frac{1}{4})$
2 **5.G.1**	The student plots one point, but does not label it.	The student plots one point with label or two points without labels.	The student is able to correctly plot three points, but does not label them.	The student correctly: • Plots three points • Labels the points on the grid.
3 **5.G.1** **5.OA.3**	The student is unable to give coordinates for points on the same vertical line or horizontal line.	The student gives coordinates for two points on the same vertical line *or* horizontal line.	The student gives two coordinates on the same vertical line and two coordinates on the same horizontal line.	The student: • Gives three collinear points on a vertical line (all three points have the same x-coordinate). • Gives three collinear points on a horizontal line (all three points have the same y-coordinate).
4 **5.G.1**	The student is neither able to identify Garrett's placement as correct nor able to explain the reasoning used.	The student is unable to identify Garrett's placement as correct, but does explain the reasoning used.	The student identifies Garrett's placement as correct, but the explanation lacks clarity.	The student: • Identifies Garrett's placement as correct. • Clearly explains the reasoning used.

Module 6:   Problem Solving with the Coordinate Plane
Date: 1/31/14

6.S.

A Progression Toward Mastery

5 **5.G.1** **5.OA.2** **5.OA.3**	The student: • Partially completes the tables in Part (a). • Plots a few points in Part (b), but does not connect the points with a line. • Makes no attempt to describe the relationship between the corresponding terms.	The student: • Correctly completes the tables in Part (a). • Plots some points in Part (b), but does not connect the points with a line. • Incorrectly describes the relationship between corresponding terms.	The student: • Correctly completes the tables in Part (a) • Plots all points in Part (b), connecting the points with a line. • Describes the relationship between corresponding terms, but the explanation lacks clarity.	The student: • Correctly completes the tables in Part (a). Table A: $(0, 0)$; $(1, \frac{1}{2})$; $(2, 1)$; $(3, 1\frac{1}{2})$ Table B: $(0,0)$; $(1, \frac{1}{4})$; $(2, \frac{1}{2})$; $(3, \frac{3}{4})$ • Plots all points in Part (b), connecting the points with a line. • Correctly describes the relationship between corresponding terms such that terms in Table A are twice the terms in Table B, or that B is half of A using words or notation (e.g., Multiply A by 2, A is twice as much as B, B is half of A, $2 \times A = B$ or $\frac{1}{2} B = A$).
6 **5.G.1** **5.OA.3**	The student is able to identify some of the ordered pairs from the graph, but is unable to generate other collinear points.	The student either correctly identifies the ordered pairs from the graph or generates other collinear points.	The student correctly identifies the ordered pairs from the graph, but generates collinear points that lie on the portion of the grid that is pictured.	The student: • Correctly identifies the ordered pairs from the graph as $(1,4)$; $(2,6)$; $(3,8)$; $(4,10)$; $(5,12)$. • Generates three collinear points whose y-coordinates are greater than 14 and/or whose x-coordinates are greater than 30.

Name ___Allison___ Date _____

1. Give the coordinates of each point.

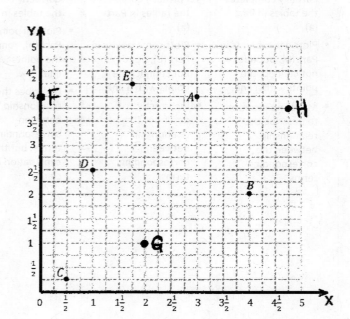

A ___(3,4)___

B ___(4,2)___

C ___$(\frac{1}{2}, \frac{1}{4})$___

D ___$(1, 2\frac{1}{2})$___

E ___$(1\frac{3}{4}, 4\frac{1}{4})$___

2. Plot each point in the coordinate plane above, and label each point with F, G, or H.

   F (0,4)   G (2, 1)   H $(4\frac{3}{4}, 3\frac{3}{4})$

3.

   a. Give coordinates for three points that are on the same vertical line. Include at least one point that has a mixed number as a coordinate.

   (1,2) $(1, 3\frac{1}{2})$ (1,4)

   b. Give coordinates for three points that are on the same horizontal line. Include at least one point that has a fraction as a coordinate.

   $(\frac{3}{4}, 2)$ (2,2) (9,2)

4. Garrett and Jeffrey are planning a treasure hunt. They decide to place a treasure at a point that is a distance of 5 units from the x-axis and 3 units from the y-axis. Jeffrey places a treasure at point J and Garrett places one at point G. Who put the treasure in the right place? Explain how you know.

Garrett put the treasure in the right place. When you measure out to point G from the y-axis it is 3 units. Point G is 5 units up from the x-axis.

Jeffrey's treasure is 3 units from the x-axis and 5 units from the y-axis.

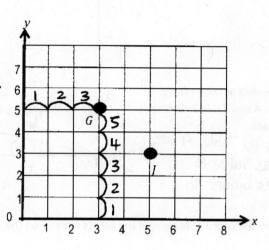

5.
   a. Find the y coordinates by following the rules given for each table.

Table A: Multiply by $\frac{1}{2}$

x	y
0	0
1	$\frac{1}{2}$
2	1
3	$1\frac{1}{2}$

Table B: Multiply by $\frac{1}{4}$

x	y
0	0
1	$\frac{1}{4}$
2	$\frac{1}{2}$
3	$\frac{3}{4}$

b. Graph and label the coordinate pairs from Table A. Connect the points and label the line *a*. Graph and label the coordinate pairs from Table B. Connect the points and label the line *b*.

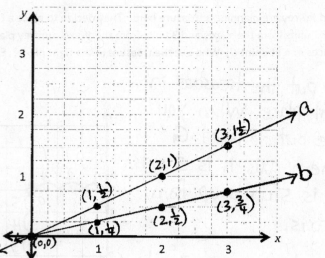

c. Describe the relationship between the *y*-coordinates in Table A and Table B that have the same *x* coordinate.

The y-coordinates in Table A are twice as much as Table B. They are 2 times bigger in Table A.

6.

a. Use the graph to give the coordinate pairs of the points marked on the line.

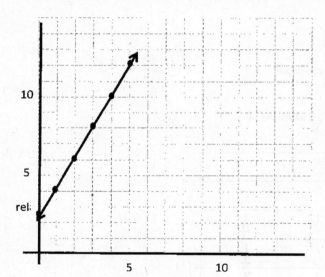

x	y
1	4
2	6
3	8
4	10
5	12

b. Using this rule, generate three more points that would be on this line but lie beyond the portion of the coordinate plane that is pictured.

The rule is multiply by 2 then add 2 to get the y-coordinates.
(15, 32) (16, 34) (17, 36)

Name _____   Date _____

1. Follow the directions.

    a. Draw a ray that starts at point L at $(1\frac{1}{2}, 3)$ and includes point K at $(5, 3)$. Label points K and L.

    b. Give the coordinates of three other points on the ray.

    c. Draw a second ray with the same initial point and containing point M with coordinates $(3\frac{1}{2}, 4\frac{1}{4})$. Label point M.

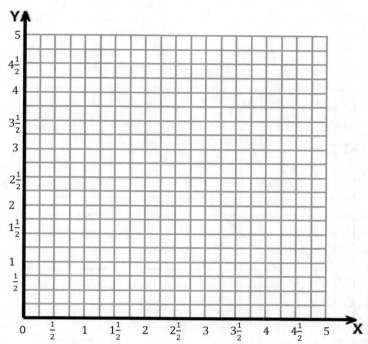

2. David draws a line segment from point Q $(\frac{1}{4}, \frac{7}{8})$ to point R $(\frac{5}{8}, \frac{1}{2})$. He then draws a line perpendicular to the first segment that intersects segment $\overline{QR}$ and includes point S $(\frac{3}{4}, 1)$.

    a. Draw $\overline{QR}$ and label the endpoints on the grid.

    b. Draw the perpendicular line and label point S.

    c. Name another point that lies on the perpendicular line whose x-coordinate is between 1 and $1\frac{1}{2}$.

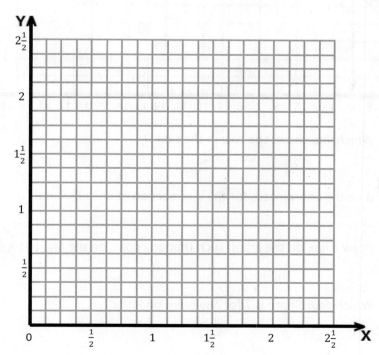

3. Complete the table for the rule *multiply by 2 then add 2* for the values of x from 0 to 4.   Then use the coordinate plane to answer the questions.

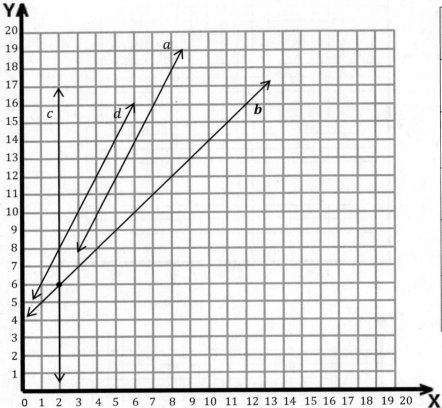

x	y	(x, y)
0		
1		
2		
3		
4		

a. Which line shows the rule in the table?

b. Give the coordinates for the intersection of lines b and c.

c. Draw a line on the graph such that any point on the line has a y-coordinate of 2. Label your line as e.

d. Which coordinate is 2 for any point on line c?

e. Write a rule that that tells how to find the y-coordinate when the x-coordinate is given for the points on line *b*.

f. Kim and Lacy want to draw a line on the coordinate plane that is parallel to line *a*. Kim uses the rule, *multiply by 4 and add 2* to generate her y-coordinates. Lacy uses the rule *multiply by 2 and add 4* to generate her y-coordinates. Which girl's line will be parallel to line *a*? Without graphing the lines, explain how you know.

4. An airplane is descending into an airport. When its altitude is 5 miles, it is 275 miles from the airport. When its altitude is 4 miles, it is 200 miles from the airport. At 3 miles, it is 125 miles from the airport.

a. If the pilot follows the same pattern, what will the plane's altitude be at 50 miles from the airport?

b. For the plane to land at the airport, the altitude will need to be 0 and the distance from the airport will need to be 0. Should the pilot continue this pattern? Why or why not?

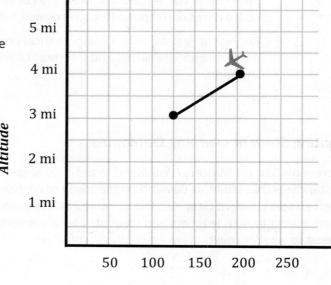

Miles from Airport

End-of-Module Assessment
Standards Addressed   Topics A–D

Write and interpret numerical expressions.

5.OA.2   Write simple expressions that record calculations with numbers, and interpret numerical expressions without evaluating them. *For example, express the calculation "add 8 and 7, then multiply by 2" as 2 × (8 + 7). Recognize that 3 × (18932 + 921) is three times as large as 18932 + 921, without having to calculate the indicated sum or product.*

Analyze patterns and relationships.

5.OA.3   Generate two numerical patterns using two given rules. Identify apparent relationships between corresponding terms. Form ordered pairs consisting of corresponding terms from the two patterns, and graph the ordered pairs on a coordinate plane. *For example, given the rule "Add 3" and the starting number 0, and given the rule "Add 6" and the starting number 0, generate terms in the resulting sequences, and observe that the terms in one sequence are twice the corresponding terms in the other sequence. Explain informally why this is so.*

Graph points on the coordinate plane to solve real-world and mathematical problems.

5.G.1   Use a pair of perpendicular number lines, called axes, to define a coordinate system, with the intersection of the lines (the origin) arranged to coincide with the 0 on each line and a given point in the plane located by using an ordered pair of numbers, called its coordinates. Understand that the first number indicates how far to travel from the origin in the direction of one axis, and the second number indicates how far to travel in the direction of the second axis, with the convention that the names of the two axes and the coordinates correspond (e.g., x-axis and x-coordinate, y-axis and y-coordinate).

5.G.2   Represent real world and mathematical problems by graphing points in the first quadrant of the coordinate plane, and interpret coordinate values of points in the context of the situation.

Evaluating Student Learning Outcomes

A Progression Toward Mastery is provided to describe steps that illuminate the gradually increasing understandings that students develop *on their way to proficiency.* In this chart, this progress is presented from left (Step 1) to right (Step 4). The learning goal for each student is to achieve Step 4 mastery. These steps are meant to help teachers and students identify and celebrate what the student CAN do now and what they need to work on next.

| Module 6: | Problem Solving with the Coordinate Plane |
| Date: | 1/31/14 |

A Progression Toward Mastery

Assessment Task Item and Standards Assessed	STEP 1 Little evidence of reasoning without a correct answer. (1 Point)	STEP 2 Evidence of some reasoning without a correct answer. (2 Points)	STEP 3 Evidence of some reasoning with a correct answer or evidence of solid reasoning with an incorrect answer. (3 Points)	STEP 4 Evidence of solid reasoning with a correct answer. (4 Points)
1 **5.G.1**	The student accurately completes at least three of the tasks embedded in the question.	The student accurately completes at least four of the tasks embedded in the question.	The student accurately completes at least five of the tasks embedded in the question.	The student accurately completes each task embedded in the question. ▪ Draws a ray with points at coordinates $(1\frac{1}{2}, 3)$ and $(5, 3)$. ▪ Labels point L. ▪ Labels point K. ▪ Gives the coordinates of three other points on the ray. (Correct answers are any two coordinates with the y-coordinate of 3.) ▪ Draws a second ray with one point at the coordinates $(1\frac{1}{2}, 3)$ and point M at $(3\frac{1}{2}, 4\frac{1}{4})$. ▪ Labels point M.
2 **5.G.1** **5.G.2**	The student accurately completes at least two of the tasks embedded in the question.	The student accurately completes at least three of the tasks embedded in the question.	The student accurately completes at least four of the tasks embedded in the question.	The student accurately completes all of the tasks embedded in the question: ▪ Draws $\overline{QR}$. ▪ Labels $\overline{QR}$. ▪ Draws a line perpendicular to

A Progression Toward Mastery

				$\overline{QR}$. • Labels point S. • Names one of the following coordinates: $1\frac{1}{8}, 1\frac{3}{8}$ $1\frac{1}{4}, 1\frac{1}{2}$ or equivalent $1\frac{3}{8}, 1\frac{5}{8}$.
3 **5.G.1** **5.OA.2** **5.OA.3**	The student accurately completes at least two of the tasks embedded in the question. The table counts as one task.	The student accurately completes at least three of the tasks embedded in the question. The table counts as one task.	The student accurately completes at least five of the tasks embedded in the question. The table counts as one task.	The student accurately completes all of the tasks embedded in the question and gives correct responses. • Completes the table: | x	y	(x, y)
---	---	---
0	2	(0,2)
1	4	(1,4)
2	6	(2,6)
3	8	(3,8)
4	10	(4,10)	 a. Line a. b. (2, 6). c. Draws and labels line e parallel to the x-axis, y coordinate 2. d. The x-coordinate. e. *Add 4 or plus 4.* f. Lacy's rule will make a line parallel to line a. The rule for line a is *multiply x by 2, add 2.* The rule for Lacy's line is *multiply x-coordinate by 2 and add 4.* Lacy's line is parallel

A Progression Toward Mastery

				because the steepness of the line is the same. (That is, the multiplication part of the rule is the same.) The adding part of the rule will make the y-coordinates two more than those in line a.)
4 **5.G.1** **5.G.2** **5.OA.3**	The student has no correct answers for either Part (a) or Part (b).	The student has correctly answered either Part (a) or Part (b), but may not have a clear answer of *why* for Part (b).	The student has correctly answered both Part (a) and Part (b), but lacks a clear answer of *why* for Part (b).	The student has accurately completed Part (a) and Part (b), including a clear explanation of *why* for Part (b). a. The plane's altitude will be 2 miles. b. No, the pilot should not continue this pattern. If he continues this pattern, his plane will have 0 altitude between 1 and 2 miles past the airport (or other correct response).

Name __Julian__   Date _____

1. Follow the directions.

   a. Draw a ray that starts at point L at $(1\frac{1}{2}, 3)$ and includes point K at $(5, 3)$. Label points K and L.

   b. Give the coordinates of three other points on the ray.

   $(2\frac{1}{3}, 3) \quad (4, 3) \quad (4\frac{3}{4}, 3)$

   c. Draw a second ray with the same initial point and containing point M with coordinates $(3\frac{1}{2}, 4\frac{1}{4})$. Label point M.

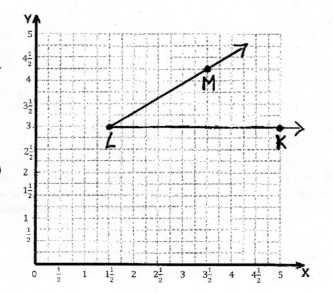

2. David draws a line segment from point Q $(\frac{1}{4}, \frac{7}{8})$ to point R $(\frac{5}{8}, \frac{1}{2})$. He then draws a line perpendicular to the first segment that intersects segment $\overline{QR}$ and includes point S $(\frac{3}{4}, 1)$.

   a. Draw $\overline{QR}$ and label the endpoints on the grid.

   b. Draw the perpendicular line and label point S.

   c. Name another point that lies on the perpendicular line whose x-coordinate is between 1 and $1\frac{1}{2}$.

   $(1\frac{1}{8}, 1\frac{3}{8})$

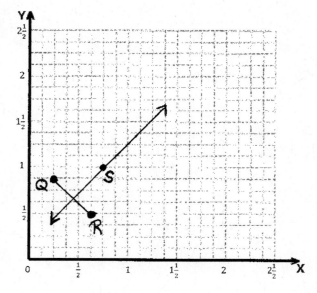

3. Complete the table for the rule *multiply by 2 then add 2* for the values of x from 0 to 4.   Then use the coordinate plane to answer the questions.

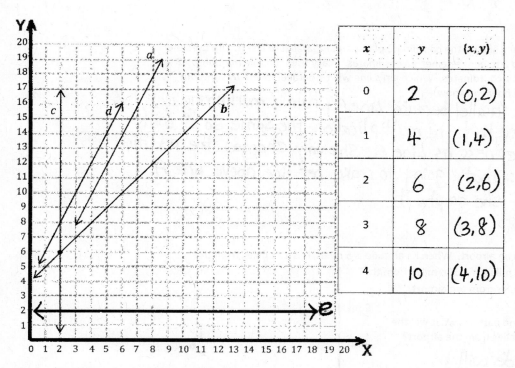

x	y	(x, y)
0	2	(0,2)
1	4	(1,4)
2	6	(2,6)
3	8	(3,8)
4	10	(4,10)

a. Which line shows the rule in the table?

Line a

b. Give the coordinates for the intersection of lines *b* and *c*.

(2,6)

c. Draw a line on the graph such that any point on the line has a y-coordinate of 2. Label your line as *e*.

d. Which coordinate is 2 for any point on line *c*?

X-coordinate

e. Write a rule that that tells how to find the y-coordinate when the x-coordinate is given for the points on line *b*.

(1,5)
(2,6)
(3,7)

Add 4 to x-coordinate to get y-coordinate

f. Kim and Lacy want to draw a line on the coordinate plane that is parallel to line *a*. Kim uses the rule, *multiply by 4 and add 2* to generate her y-coordinates. Lacy uses the rule *multiply by 2 and add 4* to generate her y-coordinates. Which girl's line will be parallel to line *b*? Without graphing the lines, explain how you know.

Lacy's line will be parallel because Line A's rule is multiplying by 2, then add 2. Lacy kept the multiplication the same so it will be the same steepness as Line A. She only changed the addition part of the rule. That's going to make her line above line A on the plane if she graphs it.

4. An airplane is descending into an airport. When its altitude is 5 miles, it is 275 miles from the airport. When its altitude is 4 miles, it is 200 miles from the airport. At 3 miles, it is 125 miles from the airport.

a. If the pilot follows the same pattern, what will the plane's altitude be at 50 miles from the airport?

The plane's altitude will be 2 miles when it is 50 miles from airport.

b. For the plane to land at the airport, the altitude will need to be 0 and the distance from the airport will need to be 0. Should the pilot continue this pattern? Why or why not?

He should **not** keep this pattern. He would be way past the airport when his altitude is 0 miles.

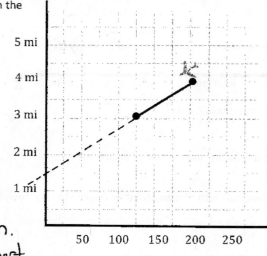

Miles from Airport

Topic E
Multi-Step Word Problems

5.NF.2, 5.NF.3, 5.NF.6, 5.NF.7c, 5.MD.1, 5.MD.5, 5.G.2

Instructional Days:	5		
Coherence	-Links from:	G4–M1	Place Value, Rounding, and Algorithms for Addition and Subtraction
		G4–M3	Multi-Digit Multiplication and Division
		G4–M5	Fraction Equivalence, Ordering, and Operations
		G4–M6	Decimal Fractions
		G4–M7	Exploring Measurement with Multiplication
	-Links to:	G6–M1	Ratios and Unit Rates
		G6–M2	Arithmetic Operations Including Division of Fractions
		G6–M5	Area, Surface Area, and Volume Problems

Topic E provides an opportunity for students to encounter complex, multi-step problems requiring the application of the concepts and skills mastered throughout the Grade 5 curriculum. Students use all four operations with both whole and fractional numbers in varied contexts. The problems in Topic E are designed to be non-routine problems that require students to persevere in order to solve them.

While wrestling with complexity is an important part of Topic E, the true strength of this topic is derived from the time allocated for students to construct arguments and critique the reasoning of their classmates. After students have been given adequate time to ponder and solve the problems, two lessons are devoted to sharing of approaches and solutions. Students will partner to justify their conclusions, communicate them to others, and respond to the arguments of their peers.

A Teaching Sequence Towards Mastery of Multi-Step Word Problems
Objective 1: Make sense of complex, multi-step problems and persevere in solving them. Share and critique peer solutions.   (Lessons 21–25)

Lesson 21

Objective: Make sense of complex, multi-step problems and persevere in solving them. Share and critique peer solutions.

Suggested Lesson Structure

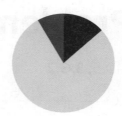

■ Fluency Practice   (8 minutes)

   Concept Development   (47 minutes)

■ Student Debrief   (5 minutes)

   Total Time   **(60 minutes)**

Fluency Practice (8 minutes)

- Change Mixed Numbers to Improper Fractions **5.NF.3**   (4 minutes)
- Add Unlike Denominators **5.NF.1**   (4 minutes)

Change Mixed Numbers to Improper Fractions (4 minutes)

Materials: (S) Personal white boards

Note: This fluency activity reviews G5–Module 3 concepts.

T: (Write $1\frac{1}{2}$.) How many halves are in 1?

S: 2 halves.

T: (Write $1\frac{1}{2} = \frac{2}{2} + \frac{1}{2}$.) What is $\frac{2}{2} + \frac{1}{2}$?

S: 3 halves.

T: (Write $1\frac{1}{2} = \frac{3}{2}$.)

T: (Write $3 + \frac{1}{2}$.) Write the answer as a mixed number.

S: (Write $3\frac{1}{2}$.)

T: How many halves are in 1?

S: 2 halves.

T: How many halves are in 2?

S: 4 halves.

T: How many halves are in 3?

NOTES ON LESSONS 21–25:

Lesson Sequence for M6–Topic E:

- Lessons 21–22 use a protocol to solve problems within teams of four. The number of problems solved will vary between teams.
- Lesson 23 uses a protocol to share and critique student solutions from Lessons 21–22.
- Lesson 24 resumes the problem solving begun in Lessons 21–22.
- Lesson 25 uses the protocol from Lesson 23 to again share and critique student solutions.

COMMON CORE™

Lesson 21:   Make sense of complex, multi-step problems and persevere in solving them. Share and critique peer solutions.

Date: 1/31/14

6.E.3

S: 6 halves.

T: (Write $3\frac{1}{2} = \frac{}{2} + \frac{1}{2} = \frac{}{2}$.) Write the addition sentence, filling in the missing numerators.

S: (Write $3\frac{1}{2} = \frac{6}{2} + \frac{1}{2} = \frac{7}{2}$.)

Continue the process for the following possible suggestions: $2\frac{1}{3}$, $2\frac{2}{3}$, $3\frac{1}{5}$, $3\frac{3}{5}$, and $4\frac{3}{4}$.

Add Unlike Denominators (4 minutes)

Materials: (S) Personal white boards

Note: This activity reviews content from G5–Module 3.

T: (Write $\frac{1}{2} + \frac{1}{3}$.) Add the fractions. Simplify the sum, if possible.

S: (Add.)

Repeat the process for $\frac{1}{4} + \frac{1}{3}$, $\frac{1}{5} + \frac{1}{3}$, $\frac{1}{4} + \frac{1}{6}$, $\frac{1}{5} + \frac{1}{7}$, $\frac{1}{8} + \frac{1}{7}$.

Concept Development (47 minutes)

Note: This topic culminates the year with five days dedicated to problem solving. The problems solved in G5–M6–Lessons 21, 22, and 24 and then shared and critiqued in G5–M6–Lessons 23 and 25 are non-routine and multi-step. The intent is to encourage students to integrate cross-modular knowledge, to strategize, and to persevere.

In G5–M6–Lessons 21, 22, and 24, a protocol is suggested to allow for teams (level-alike or student-selected as per the teacher's professional discretion) to work at their own pace through the nine problems with the understanding that one group may complete two problems while another group completes them all.

Problems are handed out one at a time to each team individually as they complete work on each problem to the best of their ability. (Notes on an approach to this system are included in the UDL box to the right.)

There are no Exit Tickets for these lessons, shortening the Student Debrief. This is to allow more time for problem solving. The Homework includes one story problem similar to the problems worked in class, and one brainteaser meant to provide a fun challenge for families. Student work samples and a full Debrief are included in G5–M6–Lessons 24–25.

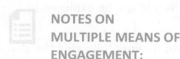

NOTES ON MULTIPLE MEANS OF ENGAGEMENT:

Students will offer solutions that are less than perfect. Use your professional discretion when deciding whether to move a team forward to the next problem.

Reasons for persisting:

▪ Do they need to learn perseverance? (Will this help them to be more attentive to detail, to show their work more effectively, or to work until they get it right?)

Reasons for moving on:

▪ Will another return to the same problem crush their enthusiasm?

▪ Does the team's current solution offer a great share and critique moment for G5–M6–Lessons 24–25?

Lesson 21:   Make sense of complex, multi-step problems and persevere in solving
               them. Share and critique peer solutions.
Date: 1/31/14

6.E.4

Materials: (S) Problem Set

Note: Print the Problem Set single-sided. Cut the problems apart, one problem per half page. As this limits the work space, consider pasting the smaller papers onto a larger 8½" × 11" sheet.

Process for G5–M6–Lessons 21, 22, and 23: Solving Word Problems in Teams of Four

1. Establish the intention of G5–M6–Lessons 21–25 with teams.

Let students know that over the next five days, they will be working in teams to solve some great problems and share their solutions with peers. Each team will work at its own pace to solve as many problems as possible. The object is not to compete with other groups, but for each team to do its personal best.

Introduce this protocol to the students: Think, pair, share, and complete.

Think: Work independently to begin each problem. Read the problem through quietly.

Pair: Work together with a partner from within the team to complete the problem.

Share: Share with the other pair of the team of four, giving each pair an opportunity to share. (A more in-depth analysis and share and critique will be explored in G5–M6–Lessons 23 and 25.)

Complete: Return to work following the sharing in order to incorporate ideas that came from the collaboration. Finalize the solution.

2. Establish a system for teams to communicate the completion of a problem.

Throughout the session, circulate and check solutions prior to giving teams the next problem in the sequence. Celebrate success when appropriate.

3. Let students know that completed work will be collected, organized, and analyzed.

NOTES ON
MULTIPLE MEANS OF
ENGAGEMENT:

For G5–M6–Lessons 23 and 25, consider reconfiguring students into new groups of four for a more in-depth share and critique process. Possible alternatives to this arrangement are given below:

- Solve the problems for three days consecutively. Share and critique for two days consecutively.

- Solve problems for four days, closing each session with a share and critique. Day 5 might be used for a museum walk.

All materials are housed here in G5–M6–Lesson 21, so that whatever structure is chosen, this lesson will be the home base.

To prepare for the share and critique protocol in G5–M6–Lessons 23 and 25, compile student work for the same problem from various teams. For example, after the first day, all sets of student solutions from Problem 1 would be housed in a dedicated folder as would sets of solutions from Problem 2, and so on. This organization will allow for efficient re-distribution of solutions as students work with members from different teams to analyze and critique the solution strategies.

Following this lesson's Debrief are analyses and possible solution strategies for each of the nine problems. The problem masters are included at the end of this lesson. The analyses and possible solutions are positioned after the Debrief to emphasize the fact that students will progress through these problems at different rates as they work within their groups.

Lesson 21: Make sense of complex, multi-step problems and persevere in solving them. Share and critique peer solutions.

Date: 1/31/14

6.E.5

Student Debrief (5 Minutes)

Lesson Objective: Make sense of complex, multi-step problems and persevere in solving them. Share and critique peer solutions.

- If you encountered a difficulty while solving the problem, what strategies did you use to keep going?
- What advice would you give a classmate who was having trouble with a difficult problem?
- What did you learn about yourself as a problem solver today that will help you to be a better problem solver tomorrow?

Note: There is no Exit Ticket for this lesson.

| Lesson 21: | Make sense of complex, multi-step problems and persevere in solving them. Share and critique peer solutions. | 6.E.6 |
| Date: | 1/31/14 | |

Analysis and Solution Strategies for Problems 1–9

Problem 1: Pierre's Paper

Pierre folded a square piece of paper vertically to make two rectangles. Each rectangle had a perimeter of 39 inches. How long is each side of the original square? What is the area of the original square? What is the area of one of the rectangles?

This problem calls on student knowledge of the properties of squares and rectangles as well as their knowledge of area and perimeter. Understanding the relationships between the lengths of the rectangle's sides is the key to solving it.

If students are having difficulty moving forward, the following questions may help them:

- How does knowing that this figure is a square help us know about the dimensions of the rectangle? How are the dimensions of the rectangle related to each other?
- What is the unit we are counting?
- Think of the rectangle's shorter side (or longer side) as 1 unit.

Below, Solution A solves for the longer side of the rectangle and uses a more abstract representation of the thinking, while Solution B solves for the shorter side of the rectangle.

Solution A

Each side length = l
$l + l + \frac{1}{2}l + \frac{1}{2}l = 39"$
$3l = 39"$
Each side of the square is 13".
Square's area is $13 \times 13 = 169\,in^2$.
The area of the rectangle is
$13 \times 6\frac{1}{2} = (13 \times 6) + (13 \times \frac{1}{2}) =$
$78 + 6.5 = 84.5\,in^2$.

Solution B

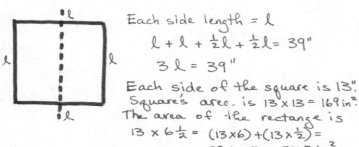

Rectangle $p = 39\,in$

Rectangle length $ \times 2$
rectangle width $ \times 2$ $\Big\}\,39$

$6\,units = 39$
$1\,unit = 6\frac{1}{2}$

Square's sides $\quad 6\frac{1}{2} + 6\frac{1}{2} = 13$
Square's area $\quad 13 \times 13 = 169$
Rectangle area $\quad 169 \div 2 = 84.5$

The square's sides are 13 inches long.
The area of the square is $169\,in^2$.
The area of the rectangle is $84.5\,in^2$.

COMMON CORE ™

Lesson 21:   Make sense of complex, multi-step problems and persevere in solving them. Share and critique peer solutions.
Date: 1/31/14

6.E.7

Problem 2: Shopping with Elise

Elise saved $184. She bought a scarf, a necklace, and a notebook. After her purchases, she still had $39.50. The scarf cost three-fifths the cost of the necklace, and the notebook was one-sixth as much as the scarf. What was the cost of each item? How much more did the necklace cost than the notebook?

This problem is fairly straightforward mathematically. However, students will need to find a common unit for all three items in order to determine the cost of the notebook. Once this is established, the costs of the other items may be found easily. Students may attempt to find a solution through fraction multiplication. This approach may stall when trying to determine the fraction of the money spent on the necklace. The following may provide scaffolding for students experiencing difficulty:

- Which item's tape should be the longest? The shortest?
- How can we make these units the same size?
- Begin with the notebook as 1 unit. If the notebook is 1 sixth the cost of the scarf, then how many times as much is the scarf's cost to the cost of the notebook?

Both solutions below begin by finding the amount spent on the three items. While both use the cost of the notebook as 1 unit, Solution A begins with the necklace and uses the fraction information to subdivide the other tapes. Solution B uses a multiplicative approach thinking of the scarf's cost as 6 times as much as the cost of the notebook.

Solution A

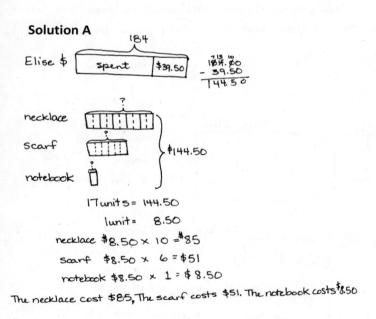

Solution B

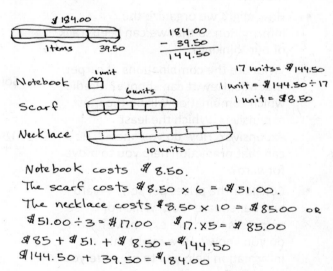

COMMON CORE™

Lesson 21:   Make sense of complex, multi-step problems and persevere in solving
Date: 1/31/14   them. Share and critique peer solutions.

6.E.8

Problem 3: The Hewitt's Carpet

The Hewitt family is buying carpet for two rooms. The dining room is a square that measures 12 feet on each side. The den is 9 yards by 5 yards. Mrs. Hewitt has budgeted $2,650 for carpeting both rooms. The green carpet she is considering costs $42.75 per square yard, and the brown carpet's price is $4.95 per square foot. What are the ways she can carpet the rooms and stay within her budget?

While the calculations for solving this problem are simple multiplication and addition, the path to finding the appropriate numbers on which to operate requires a high degree of organization. Students must attend not only to finding the various combinations that are possible, but they must also attend to the units in which the areas and prices are given. Students may choose to use only one unit of measure for the areas and prices, or they may use a combination. The following scaffolds may support struggling students:

MP.2

- Are the areas expressed in the same unit? Can we use them as they are or must we convert?

- How might we organize the information so that we can keep track of our thinking?

- What are the combinations of carpet that Mrs. Hewitt can choose? Predict which combination will be the most expensive? Which the least expensive? How do you know? How can that prediction help you to move forward?

- Consider the prices per square yard and per square foot. Which of these carpets is the more expensive? How do you know? How might this information help you to organize your thoughts?

Both of the solutions to the right show good organization of the calculations used to solve. Solution A converts the carpet prices to match the area units of the rooms. Solutions B converts the dimensions of the rooms to match the units of the prices.

Solution A

Green $42.75 yd²   Brown $44.55 yd²
        4.75 ft² $4.95 ft²

Dining	Den	Total
144 ft² × $4.75 = $684. Green	45yd² × 42.75 = $1,923.75 Green	$2,607.75
Green $684.00	Brown 45 yd² × $44.55 = $2004.75	$2,688.75
Brown 144 ft² × $4.95 = $712.80	Green $1,923.75	$2,636.55
Brown $712.80	Brown 2,004.75	$2,717.55

Mrs. Hewitt has 2 choices: both rooms in green, or the den in green and the dining room in brown.

Solution B

12ft.   9yds = 27ft   Budget $2650
                                Green: $42.75/yd²
12ft   5yds   Brown: $4.95/ft²
= 4yds   = 15ft

DR Green → 16yd² × $42.75 = $684.00
    Brown → 144ft² × $4.95 = $712.80

Den Green → 45yd² × $42.75 = $1923.75
     Brown → 405ft² × $4.95 = $2004.75

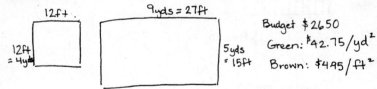

Den	G $1923.75	G $1923.75	B $2004.75	B $2004.75
Dining Rm	G⁺ 684.00	B⁺ 712.80	B⁺ 712.80	G⁺ 684.00
	$2607.75	$2636.55	$2717.55	2688.75

Mrs. Hewitt can have both rooms green or the den green + the dining room brown.

Problem 4: AAA Taxi

AAA Taxi charges $1.75 for the first mile and $1.05 for each additional mile. How far could Mrs. Leslie travel for $20 if she tips the cab driver $2.50?

Students encounter a part–part–whole problem with varying unit size in the AAA Taxi Problem. They must first consider the cost of the first mile and tip, and then determine how many groups of $1.05 can be made from the remaining $15.75.

To scaffold, consider the following:

- Will all of the $20 be used to pay for the mileage? Why not?
- Do all the miles cost the same? How do we account for that in our model?
- How would you solve this if all the miles cost the same? What if the tip was the same as the cost for the miles?

Solution A begins by counting on from the first mile. Solution B chooses to represent the problem with a tape diagram and divides to find how many units with a value of $1.05 there are once the sum of the tip and first mile are subtracted from the $20.

Solution A

mile
1   $ 1.75 + 2.50 (tip) = $ 4.25
2   $ 4.25 + 1.05 = $ 5.30
3   $ 5.30 + 1.05 = $ 6.35
6   $ 6.35 + 3.15 = $ 9.50
9   $ 9.50 + 3.15 = $ 12.65
12 $ 12.65 + 3.15 = $ 15.80
15 $ 15.80 + 3.15 = $ 18.95
16 $ 18.95 + 1.05 = $ 20.00

Mrs. Leslie can travel 16 miles for $20.

Solution B

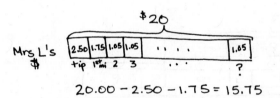

$20

Mrs L's $ | 2.50 | 1.75 | 1.05 | 1.05 | · · · · | 1.05
tip 1ˢᵗ mi 2 3 · · · ?

20.00 − 2.50 − 1.75 = 15.75

1.05 × ? units = 15.75

```
        15
105 | 1575
     −105
      525
     −525
        0
```

Mrs. Leslie can go 16 miles.

COMMON CORE

Lesson 21: Make sense of complex, multi-step problems and persevere in solving them. Share and critique peer solutions.
Date: 1/31/14

6.E.10

Problem 5: Pumpkins and Squash

Three pumpkins and two squash weigh 27.5 pounds. Four pumpkins and three squash weigh 37.5 pounds. Each pumpkin weighs the same as the other pumpkins, and each squash weighs the same as the other squash. How much does each pumpkin weigh? How much does each squash weigh?

This problem is a departure from the routine problems in most of Grade 5 in that students must unitize two different variables (1 pumpkin and 1 squash) as a single unit. Once the difference is found between the quantities, students have several avenues for finding the weights of the individual pumpkin and squash.

- Draw the tapes to represent the weights for the two situations. Which tape is longer? How much longer?
- How many more pumpkins are in the second tape? How many more squash?
- Outline the difference with a red pen. Can you find this same combination in the rest of the tape? How many can you find?

Both solutions below use tape diagrams to show that the difference between the two known facts is a combination of one pumpkin and one squash. Next, they reason that the sum of the weights of a pumpkin and squash is 10 pounds. From there, they can see two of those pumpkin and squash units in relationship to the 27.5 pound group. It is clear then that the weight of the pumpkin has to be 7.5 pounds.

Solution A

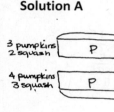

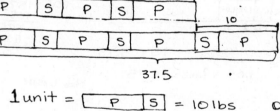

Solution B

$$1 \text{ unit} = \boxed{P \;\; S} = 10 \text{ lbs}$$

$$2 \text{ units} + \boxed{P} = 27.5 \text{ lbs}$$

$$20 + \boxed{P} = 27.5 \text{ lbs}$$

$$1 \text{ pumpkin} = 7.5 \text{ lbs}$$

$$10 - 7.5 = 2.5$$

One pumpkin weighs 7.5 pounds + one squash weighs 2.5 pounds.

COMMON CORE™

Lesson 21: Make sense of complex, multi-step problems and persevere in solving them. Share and critique peer solutions.

Date: 1/31/14

6.E.11

Problem 6: Toy Cars and Trucks

Henry had 20 convertibles and 5 trucks in his miniature car collection. After Henry's aunt bought him some more miniature trucks, Henry found that one-fifth of his collection consisted of convertibles. How many trucks did his aunt buy?

This problem requires students to process a before-and-after scenario. The larger quantity in the *before* situation becomes the smaller quantity in the *after* situation. This change in fractional relationship may be depicted in various ways. Students should be careful to model only 5 fifths in the *after* model—1 fifth for the convertibles and 4 fifths for the trucks. Use the following to scaffold student understanding:

- Draw Henry's convertibles and trucks before his aunt gave him more trucks. Draw the convertibles and trucks after his aunt gave him more.

- What amount stayed the same?

- Which is more, the cars or trucks? (Ask for both before and after. Have students simply draw the bars longer and shorter.)

- Refer to the convertibles tape in the after model. Ask, "If this is 1 fifth, what is the whole?"

Solution A combines the before and after models into one tape. The numbering on the top represents the *before* while the numbering below represents the *after*. Solution B also uses fraction division to determine the whole. Solution C uses a unit approach, with the number of trucks in the beginning as 1 unit.

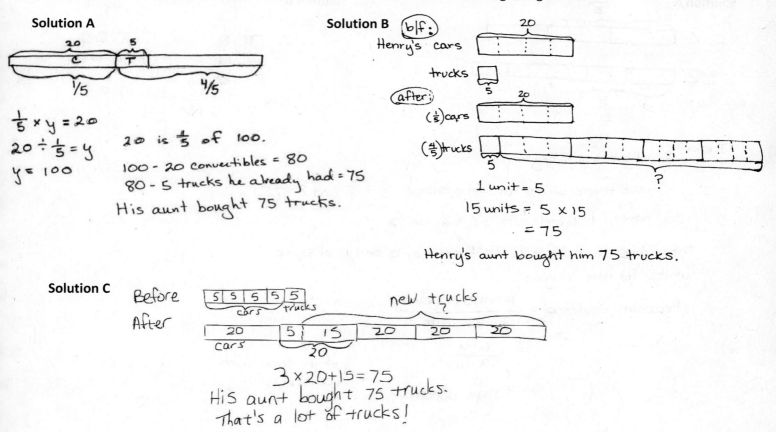

Lesson 21:	Make sense of complex, multi-step problems and persevere in solving them. Share and critique peer solutions.	6.E.12
Date:	1/31/14	

© 2014 Common Core, Inc. All rights reserved. commoncore.org

Problem 7: Pairs of Scouts:

Some girls in a Girl Scout troop are pairing up with some boys in a Boy Scout troop to practice square dancing. Two-thirds of the girls are paired with three-fifths of the boys. What fraction of the scouts is square dancing?

This problem challenges students to consider what they know about fraction equivalence. The key to this problem lies in recognizing the need for equal numbers of units. That is, equal numerators must be found! Once students can visualize that 6 of the girls' units are the same as 6 of the boys' units, a fraction of the total number of units can be found. Scaffold with the following:

- We know the same number of girls as boys are dancing. Are these units the same size? How can we make them the same size?

- How can 2 units be the same amount as 3 units? Only if one unit is larger than the other. For example, 2 yards equals 6 feet if we consider 1 larger unit and a smaller unit.

- Make sure that once students make 6 units in each tape for the dancing scouts, they also subdivide the remaining units in each bar. This will create the 19 total units.

Solution A uses a tape diagram to model the equal amounts and then decompose to make the boy and girls units equal. Solution B uses an array approach to match up girls and boys.

Solution A

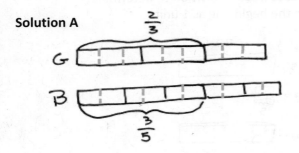

Solution B

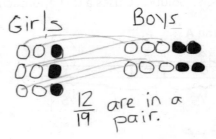

I know: 2 girl units = 3 boy units

I can make these units the same size! $\frac{2}{3} = \frac{6}{9}$ and $\frac{3}{5} = \frac{6}{10}$

So, now... 6 girl units = 6 boy units

There are 9 of these units for the girls and 10 of these units for the boys.

Fraction dancing $= \dfrac{\text{\# units dancing}}{\text{total units}}$

$\qquad = \dfrac{6+6}{9+10}$

$\qquad = \dfrac{12}{19}$ dancing

$\frac{12}{19}$ of the scouts are dancing.

Lesson 21:	Make sense of complex, multi-step problems and persevere in solving them. Share and critique peer solutions.	**6.E.1**
Date:	1/31/14	

Problem 8: Sandra's Measuring Cups

Sandra is making cookies that require $5\frac{1}{2}$ cups of oatmeal. She has only two measuring cups: a one-half cup and a three-fourths cup. What is the smallest number of scoops that she could make in order to get $5\frac{1}{2}$ cups?

Recognizing that using a larger unit will require fewer scoops is the beginning of understanding this problem. Students may try to name the total using all halves or all fourths, but will find that neither measure can be used exclusively. Using the larger measure first to scoop as much as possible, then moving to scoop the remainder with the smaller cup is the more efficient method of solving. To scaffold, ask the following questions:

- Which measuring cup is larger? How does knowing which is larger help you?
- Predict which measuring cup will do the job more quickly? How do you know?
- How many scoops will it take using just the half-cup measure? How many if only the larger cup is used? Is it possible to scoop all the oatmeal and fill the three-fourths cup every time?

All three solutions pictured below use the strategy of beginning with the larger cup measure. However, Solution A uses a unitary approach, decomposing the fourths into a multiple of 3 and a multiple of 2. Solution B counts on by three-fourths and then by halves. Solution C works at the numerical level to guess and check.

Solution A

$5\frac{1}{2}$

oatmeal

11 halves in $5\frac{1}{2}$
22 fourths in $5\frac{1}{2}$

X all $\frac{1}{2}$ c = 11 scoops
X all $\frac{3}{4}$ c = 7 scoops w/ $\frac{1}{4}$ left

22 fourths = 18 fourths + 4 fourths
$(6 \times 3 \text{ fourths}) + (2 \times 2 \text{ fourths})$

8 scoops (6 with $\frac{3}{4}$ c. and 2 with $\frac{1}{2}$ c) will be the fewest.

Solution B

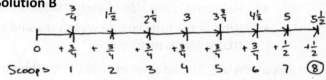

$\frac{3}{4}$ $1\frac{1}{2}$ $2\frac{1}{4}$ 3 $3\frac{3}{4}$ $4\frac{1}{2}$ 5 $5\frac{1}{2}$

0   $+\frac{3}{4}$ $+\frac{3}{4}$ $+\frac{3}{4}$ $+\frac{3}{4}$ $+\frac{3}{4}$ $+\frac{3}{4}$ $+\frac{1}{2}$ $+\frac{1}{2}$

Scoops   1   2   3   4   5   6   7   ⑧

The least number of scoops is 8.

Solution C

$\frac{3}{4} > \frac{1}{2}$

$5\frac{1}{2} = \frac{11}{2} = \frac{22}{4}$

$7 \times \frac{3}{4} = \frac{21}{4}$ but only $\frac{1}{4}$ left

$6 \times \frac{3}{4} = \frac{18}{4}$ with $\frac{4}{4}$ or $\frac{2}{2}$ left

So 6 $\frac{3}{4}$-scoops and 2 $\frac{1}{2}$-scoops

8 total scoops minimum

COMMON CORE™   **Lesson 21:**   Make sense of complex, multi-step problems and persevere in solving them. Share and critique peer solutions.   **6.E.14**

Date: 1/31/14

Problem 9: Blue Squares

The dimensions of each successive blue square pictured to the right are half that of the previous blue square. The lower left blue square measures 6 inches by 6 inches.

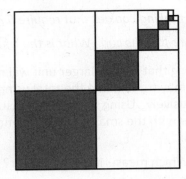

    a. *Find the area of the shaded part.*

    b. *Find the total area of the shaded and unshaded parts.*

    c. *What fraction of the figure is shaded?*

There are multiple ways to visualize this graphic, each leading to a different approach to solving. Students may see that there are 3 identical sets of graduated squares. Out of these 3 identical sets, only 1 set is shaded. Students may also do the work to find the fraction of the whole that the smallest shaded square represents and use an additive approach to finding the shaded area. The shaded area might then be used to find the total area. In contrast, the fraction that is shaded might be used in conjunction with the total area to name the area of the shaded parts. Scaffolds could include the following:

- Can you find the shaded area of just the first three squares (or L's)?
- Cut the graphic apart into separate L's or separate squares. What can you say about the fraction that is shaded in each one?
- How long is the side of each shaded square?
- What if the little square wasn't missing? What would be the area of the whole square? What part of that whole is missing?

Solution A uses the additive approach mentioned above to find the shaded area, which is multiplied by 3 to find the total. Solution B works backwards to name the fraction that is shaded, then finds the total area by using subtraction from a 12 by 12 square's area. These two pieces of information are then used to find the area of the shaded region in square inches.

Solution A

a) Shaded Area: $(6 \times 6) + (3 \times 3) + (1\frac{1}{2} \times 1\frac{1}{2}) + (\frac{3}{4} \times \frac{3}{4}) + (\frac{3}{8} \times \frac{3}{8})$

$= 36 + 9 + 2\frac{1}{4} + \frac{9}{16} + \frac{9}{64}$

$= 47 + \frac{16}{64} + \frac{36}{64} + \frac{9}{64}$

$= 47 + \frac{61}{64}$

$= 47\frac{61}{64}$

b) Total Area: $47\frac{61}{64} \times 3$

$= 141\frac{183}{64}$

$\begin{array}{r} 55 \\[-2pt] 64\overline{\smash{)}183} \\ \underline{-128} \\ 55 \end{array}$ $\;2\frac{55}{64}$

$= 141 + 2\frac{55}{64}$

$= 143\frac{55}{64}$

c) Fraction shaded: 1 out of 3 = $\frac{1}{3}$
       sets of squares

Shaded area is $47\frac{61}{64}$ in².
Total area is $143\frac{55}{64}$ in².
Fraction shaded is $\frac{1}{3}$.

Solution B

This is easier if you do the fraction first. There are 3 sets of graduated squares. 1 out of 3 sets is shaded.

c) Fraction shaded = $\frac{1}{3}$

b) Total area = $(12 \text{ in} \times 12 \text{ in}) - (\frac{3}{8} \text{ in} \times \frac{3}{8} \text{ in})$

$= 144 \text{ in}^2 - \frac{9}{64} \text{ in}^2$

$= 143\frac{55}{64} \text{ in}^2$

a) area shaded = $\frac{1}{3} \times 143\frac{55}{64} \text{ in}^2$

$= 47\frac{2}{3} \text{ in}^2 + \frac{55}{192} \text{ in}^2$

$= 47\frac{128}{192} \text{ in}^2 + \frac{55}{192} \text{ in}^2$

$= 47\frac{183}{192} \text{ in}^2$

$= 47\frac{61}{64} \text{ in}^2$

Lesson 21: Make sense of complex, multi-step problems and persevere in solving them. Share and critique peer solutions.

Date: 1/31/14

6.E.15

Student_____Team _____Date _____P1

Pierre's Paper

Pierre folded a square piece of paper vertically to make two rectangles. Each rectangle had a perimeter of 39 inches. How long is each side of the original square? What is the area of the original square? What is the area of one of the rectangles?

Student_____Team _____Date _____P2

Shopping with Elise

Elise saved $184. She bought a scarf, a necklace, and a notebook. After her purchases, she still had $39.50. The scarf cost three-fifths the cost of the necklace, and the notebook was one-sixth as much as the scarf. What was the cost of each item? How much more did the necklace cost than the notebook?

COMMON CORE

Lesson 21: Make sense of complex, multi-step problems and persevere in solving them. Share and critique peer solutions.

Date: 1/31/14

6.E.16

Student_____Team _____Date _____P3

The Hewitt's Carpet

The Hewitt family is buying carpet for two rooms. The dining room is a square that measures 12 feet on each side. The den is 9 yards by 5 yards. Mrs. Hewitt has budgeted $2,650 for carpeting both rooms. The green carpet she is considering costs $42.75 per square yard, and the brown carpet's price is $4.95 per square foot. What are the ways she can carpet the rooms and stay within her budget?

Student_____Team _____Date _____P4

AAA Taxi

AAA Taxi charges $1.75 for the first mile and $1.05 for each additional mile. How far could Mrs. Leslie travel for $20 if she tips the cab driver $2.50?

COMMON CORE™

Lesson 21: Make sense of complex, multi-step problems and persevere in solving them. Share and critique peer solutions.

Date: 1/31/14

6.E.17

Student_____Team _____Date _____P5

Pumpkins and Squash

Three pumpkins and two squash weigh 27.5 pounds. Four pumpkins and three squash weigh 37.5 pounds. Each pumpkin weighs the same as the other pumpkins, and each squash weighs the same as the other squash. How much does each pumpkin weigh? How much does each squash weigh?

Student_____Team _____Date _____P6

Toy Cars and Trucks

Henry had 20 convertibles and 5 trucks in his miniature car collection. After Henry's aunt bought him some more miniature trucks, Henry found that one-fifth of his collection consisted of convertibles. How many trucks did his aunt buy?

Date: 1/31/14

Student_____Team _____Date _____P7

Pairs of Scouts:

Some girls in a Girl Scout troop are pairing up with some boys in a Boy Scout troop to practice square dancing. Two-thirds of the girls are paired with three-fifths of the boys. What fraction of the scouts is square dancing?

(Each pair is one Girl Scout and one Boy Scout. The pairs are only from these two troops.)

Student_____Team _____Date _____P8

Sandra's Measuring Cups

Sandra is making cookies that require $5\frac{1}{2}$ cups of oatmeal. She has only two measuring cups: a one-half cup and a three-fourths cup. What is the smallest number of scoops that she could make in order to get $5\frac{1}{2}$ cups?

Student_____Team _____Date _____P9

Blue Squares

The dimensions of each successive blue square pictured to the right are half that of the previous blue square. The lower left blue square measures 6 inches by 6 inches.

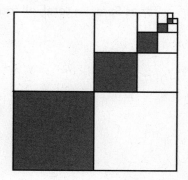

    a.   Find the area of the shaded part.

    b.   Find the total area of the shaded and unshaded parts.

    c.   What fraction of the figure is shaded?

Lesson 21:	Make sense of complex, multi-step problems and persevere in solving them. Share and critique peer solutions.
Date:	1/31/14

6.E.20

Name _____   Date _____

Sara travels twice as far as Eli when going to camp. Ashley travels as far as Sara and Eli together. Hazel travels 3 times as far as Sara. In total, all four travel a total of 888 miles to camp. How far do each of them travel?

Lesson 21:	Make sense of complex, multi-step problems and persevere in solving them. Share and critique peer solutions.
Date:	1/31/14

6.E.21

The following problem is a brainteaser for your enjoyment. It is intended to encourage working together and family problem solving fun. It is not a required element of this homework assignment.

A man wants to take a goat, a bag of cabbage, and a wolf over to an island. His boat will only hold him and one animal or item. If the goat is left with cabbage, he'll eat it. If the wolf is left with the goat, he'll eat it. How can the man transport all three to the island without anything being eaten?

COMMON CORE

Lesson 21: Make sense of complex, multi-step problems and persevere in solving them. Share and critique peer solutions.
Date: 1/31/14

6.E.22

Lesson 22

Objective: Make sense of complex, multi-step problems and persevere in solving them. Share and critique peer solutions.

Suggested Lesson Structure

■ Fluency Practice   (10 minutes)
  Concept Development   (45 minutes)
■ Student Debrief   (5 minutes)
  Total Time   **(60 minutes)**

Fluency Practice (10 minutes)

- Multiply **5.NBT.5**   (4 minutes)
- Change Improper Fractions to Mixed Numbers **5.NF.3**   (3 minutes)
- Add Unlike Fractions **5.NF.1**   (3 minutes)

Multiply (4 minutes)

Materials: (S) Personal white boards

Note: This drill reviews year-long fluency standards.

> T: Solve 34 × 24 using the standard algorithm.
>
> S: (Write 34 × 24 = 816 using the standard algorithm.)

Continue the process for 134 × 24, 46 × 42, 346 × 42, and 768 × 37.

Change Mixed Numbers to Improper Fractions (3 minutes)

Materials: (S) Personal white boards

Note: This fluency activity reviews G5–Module 3 concepts.

> T: (Write $1 + \frac{1}{3}$.) Say the sum as a mixed number.
>
> S: $1\frac{1}{3}$.
>
> T: (Write $1\frac{1}{3}$.) How many thirds are in 1?

**NOTES ON
LESSONS 21–25:**

Lesson Sequence for M6–Topic E:

- Lessons 21–22 use a protocol to solve problems within teams of four. The number of problems solved will vary between teams.
- Lesson 23 uses a protocol to share and critique student solutions from Lessons 21–22.
- Lesson 24 resumes the problem solving begun in Lessons 21–22.
- Lesson 25 uses the protocol from Lesson 23 to again share and critique student solutions.

Lesson 22:	Make sense of complex, multi-step problems and persevere in solving them. Share and critique peer solutions.
Date:	1/31/14

6.E.2

S: 3 thirds.

T: (Beneath $1\frac{1}{3}$, write $\frac{3}{3} + \frac{1}{3}$.) What's $\frac{3}{3} + \frac{1}{3}$?

S: 4 thirds.

T: (Write $1\frac{1}{3} = \frac{4}{3}$.)

T: (Write $3 + \frac{1}{3}$.) Write the sum as a mixed number.

S: (Write $3\frac{1}{3}$.)

T: How many thirds are in 1?

S: 3.

T: How many thirds are in 2?

S: 6.

T: How many thirds are in 3?

S: 9.

T: (Write $3\frac{1}{3}$. Beneath it, write $\frac{}{3} + \frac{1}{3} = \frac{}{3}$.) Beneath your mixed number, write the addition sentence, filling in the missing numbers.

S: (Beneath $3\frac{1}{3}$, write $\frac{9}{3} + \frac{1}{3} = \frac{10}{3}$.)

Continue the process for the following possible sequence: $3\frac{2}{3}$, $1\frac{3}{4}$, $2\frac{3}{4}$, $4\frac{1}{10}$, $4\frac{7}{10}$, and $3\frac{5}{6}$.

Add Unlike Denominators (3 minutes)

Materials: (S) Personal white boards

Note: This fluency activity reviews content from G5–Module 3.

T: (Write $\frac{2}{3} + \frac{1}{6}$.) Add the fractions. Simplify the sum, if possible.

S: (Add.)

Repeat the process for $\frac{3}{4} + \frac{2}{3}$ and $\frac{3}{8} + \frac{5}{6}$.

COMMON CORE™ | **Lesson 22:**   Make sense of complex, multi-step problems and persevere in solving them. Share and critique peer solutions.
   Date: 1/31/14

6.E.24

Concept Development (45 minutes)

Materials: (S) G5–M6–Lesson 21 Problem Set

Students continue work through the Problem Set presented in
G5–M6–Lesson 21.

**1. Re-establish the intention of G5–M6–Lessons 21–22: to give
students the opportunity to solve challenging, multi-step
problems.**

**2. Remind students of the *think, pair, share, and complete*
protocol.**

After having spent G5–M6–Lesson 21 using the protocol, students may now realize that different teams will
need quiet at different times. You may want to establish a system for lowered voices when necessary.

3. Remind teams of how they advance to the next problem.

Re-establish the way for teams to communicate that they have completed a problem and adjust the system
from the first day if it was flawed.

4. Remind students that completed solutions will be collected, organized, and analyzed.

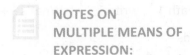

**NOTES ON
MULTIPLE MEANS OF
EXPRESSION:**

An engaging extension is to offer teams
the opportunity to videotape a solution
strategy to one of the problems. The
videos could be used as part of the
share and critique in G5–M6–Lessons
23 and 25.

Student Debrief (5 Minutes)

Lesson Objective: Make sense of complex, multi-step problems and persevere in solving them. Share and
critique peer solutions.

The Student Debrief is intended to invite reflection and active processing of the total lesson experience.

- If you encountered a difficulty while solving the problem, what strategies did you use to keep going?
- Did you apply what you learned yesterday to today's problems?
- What advice would you give a classmate who was having trouble with a hard problem?
- What did you learn about yourself today as a problem solver that will help you to be a better
  problem solver tomorrow?

Note: There is no Exit Ticket for this lesson.

COMMON CORE™ | Lesson 22:   Make sense of complex, multi-step problems and persevere in solving
them. Share and critique peer solutions.
Date: 1/31/14   6.E.2

Name _____   Date _____

Solve using any method. Show all your thinking.

1. Study this diagram showing all squares. Fill in the table.

Figure	Area in Square Feet
1	1 ft^2
2	
3	
4	9 ft^2
5	
6	1 ft^2
7	
8	

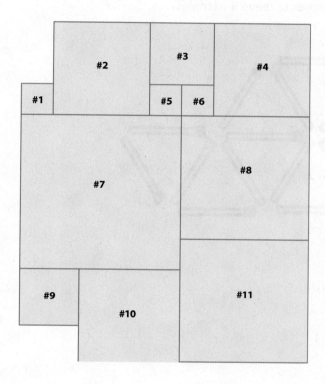

COMMON CORE

Lesson 22:   Make sense of complex, multi-step problems and persevere in solving
             them. Share and critique peer solutions.
Date: 1/31/14

6.E.26

The following problem is a brainteaser for your enjoyment. It is intended to encourage working together and family problem solving fun. It is not a required element of this homework assignment.

Remove 3 matches to leave 3 triangles.

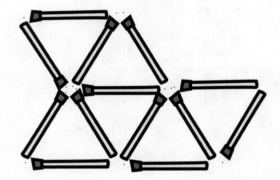

Lesson 23

Objective: Make sense of complex, multi-step problems and persevere in solving them. Share and critique peer solutions.

Suggested Lesson Structure

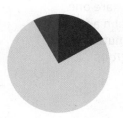

■ Fluency Practice   (10 minutes)
  Concept Development   (45 minutes)
■ Student Debrief   (5 minutes)
  Total Time   **(60 minutes)**

Fluency Practice (10 minutes)

▪ Sprint: Change Mixed Numbers into Improper Fractions **5.NF.3**   (10 minutes)

Sprint: Change Mixed Numbers into Improper Fractions (10 minutes)

Materials: (S) Change Mixed Numbers into Improper Fractions Sprint

Note: This Sprint reviews G5–Module 3 concepts.

Concept Development (45 minutes)

Materials: (S) G5–M6–Lesson 21 Problem Set

1. Establish the intention and structure of today's lesson.

Advise students that today they will revisit their solutions
completed in G5–M6–Lessons 21–22 with a new team of three
who also solved that problem. Depending on the class, consider
doing a whole-group guided example using a simple problem
such as, "Mrs. Peterson harvested 500 apples. She gave 1
seventh to her brother and 2 thirds of the remainder to the
food pantry. How many apples does she have left?"

2. Organize new teams of three.

Based upon an analysis of the solutions, students' strengths,
weaknesses, and inter-relationships, organize teams of three to
present solutions to the same problem.

**NOTES ON
LESSONS 21–25:**

Lesson Sequence for M6–Topic E:
▪ Lessons 21–22 use a protocol to
  solve problems within teams of
  four. The number of problems
  solved will vary between teams.
▪ Lesson 23 uses a protocol to share
  and critique student solutions
  from Lessons 21–22.
▪ Lesson 24 resumes the problem
  solving begun in Lessons 21–22.
▪ Lesson 25 uses the protocol from
  Lesson 23 to again share and
  critique student solutions.

Lesson 23:   Make sense of complex, multi-step problems and persevere in solving
Date: them. Share and critique peer solutions.
               1/31/14

6.E.28

3. Introduce the following suggested protocol to the students. (See box to the right.)

Step 1 Student A presents her solution step by step to the others in the group. (Allow two minutes.)

Step 2 Students B and C discuss and make sense of the solution while Student A listens without intervening. (Allow two minutes.)

Step 3 Students B and C each ask one question or share one thought directly related to the written solution and explanation. (Allow six minutes or three minutes per question.) Student A responds and whole-group dialogue follows.

Suggested stems:
- Can you explain why you chose to____?
- What did you mean when you wrote (or said) ___?
- I think you omitted _____.
- It might have been easier to understand your solution if you ____.
- I would argue that ____.

Step 4 Student A explains to the group what has been learned from the process and what changes would be made to the solution, if any. (Allow one minute.)

Step 5 Repeat Steps 1–4 for each student on the team.

4. Give students about seven minutes to either revise their solution based on their peers' input, support a peer's revision, or continue work on a problem from the set.

A NOTE ON MULTIPLE MEANS OF REPRESENTATION:

To clarify the *share and critique* protocol for the students, you might post the process listed step by step.

1. Student A presents her solution to the group.

2. Students B and C analyze and discuss the solution as Student A listens.

3. Students B and C each ask a question or share a thought about the solution. Student A responds first.

4. Student A explains to the group what has been learned and specific changes to improve the solution.

5. Repeat the process with Students B and C.

Student Debrief (5 minutes)

Lesson Objective: Make sense of complex, multi-step problems and persevere in solving them. Share and critique peer solutions.

The Student Debrief is intended to invite reflection and active processing of the total lesson experience.

- How did sharing and critiquing each other's work improve your solution?

- What emotions did you experience during the share and critique process? (Follow up with additional questions based on the responses.) When did you experience nervousness? Annoyance? Surprise? Confusion? Did those emotions change as you went through the process? Why?

- How can we improve our sharing and critiquing process, which we will be using again the day after tomorrow? (Possibly edit the steps together.)

- What did you learn today that will make you a better problem solver tomorrow?

Note: There is no Exit Ticket for this lesson.

Lesson 23:	Make sense of complex, multi-step problems and persevere in solving them. Share and critique peer solutions.
Date:	1/31/14

6.E.2

A

Correct_____

Express as an improper fraction.

1	$1\frac{1}{5} =$		23	$2\frac{7}{10} =$	
2	$2\frac{1}{5} =$		24	$4\frac{9}{10} =$	
3	$3\frac{1}{5} =$		25	$1\frac{1}{8} =$	
4	$4\frac{1}{5} =$		26	$1\frac{5}{6} =$	
5	$1\frac{1}{4} =$		27	$4\frac{5}{6} =$	
6	$1\frac{3}{4} =$		28	$4\frac{5}{8} =$	
7	$1\frac{2}{5} =$		29	$1\frac{5}{8} =$	
8	$1\frac{3}{5} =$		30	$2\frac{3}{8} =$	
9	$1\frac{4}{5} =$		31	$3\frac{3}{10} =$	
10	$2\frac{4}{5} =$		32	$4\frac{7}{10} =$	
11	$3\frac{4}{5} =$		33	$4\frac{4}{5} =$	
12	$2\frac{1}{4} =$		34	$4\frac{1}{8} =$	
13	$2\frac{3}{4} =$		35	$4\frac{3}{8} =$	
14	$3\frac{1}{4} =$		36	$4\frac{7}{8} =$	
15	$3\frac{3}{4} =$		37	$1\frac{5}{12} =$	
16	$4\frac{1}{3} =$		38	$1\frac{7}{12} =$	
17	$4\frac{2}{3} =$		39	$2\frac{1}{12} =$	
18	$2\frac{3}{5} =$		40	$3\frac{1}{12} =$	
19	$3\frac{3}{5} =$		41	$2\frac{7}{12} =$	
20	$4\frac{3}{5} =$		42	$3\frac{5}{12} =$	
21	$2\frac{1}{6} =$		43	$3\frac{11}{12} =$	
22	$3\frac{1}{8} =$		44	$4\frac{7}{12} =$	

B

Correct_____

Express as an improper fraction.

1	$1\frac{1}{2} =$		23	$2\frac{3}{10} =$	
2	$2\frac{1}{2} =$		24	$3\frac{1}{10} =$	
3	$3\frac{1}{2} =$		25	$1\frac{1}{6} =$	
4	$4\frac{1}{2} =$		26	$1\frac{3}{8} =$	
5	$1\frac{1}{3} =$		27	$3\frac{5}{6} =$	
6	$1\frac{2}{3} =$		28	$3\frac{5}{8} =$	
7	$1\frac{3}{10} =$		29	$2\frac{5}{8} =$	
8	$1\frac{7}{10} =$		30	$1\frac{7}{8} =$	
9	$1\frac{9}{10} =$		31	$4\frac{3}{10} =$	
10	$2\frac{9}{10} =$		32	$3\frac{7}{10} =$	
11	$3\frac{9}{10} =$		33	$2\frac{5}{6} =$	
12	$2\frac{1}{3} =$		34	$2\frac{7}{8} =$	
13	$2\frac{2}{3} =$		35	$3\frac{7}{8} =$	
14	$3\frac{1}{3} =$		36	$4\frac{1}{6} =$	
15	$3\frac{2}{3} =$		37	$1\frac{1}{12} =$	
16	$4\frac{1}{4} =$		38	$1\frac{11}{12} =$	
17	$4\frac{3}{4} =$		39	$4\frac{1}{12} =$	
18	$2\frac{2}{5} =$		40	$2\frac{5}{12} =$	
19	$3\frac{2}{5} =$		41	$2\frac{11}{12} =$	
20	$4\frac{2}{5} =$		42	$3\frac{7}{12} =$	
21	$3\frac{1}{6} =$		43	$4\frac{5}{12} =$	
22	$2\frac{1}{8} =$		44	$4\frac{11}{12} =$	

Lesson 23: Make sense of complex, multi-step problems and persevere in solving them. Share and critique peer solutions.

Date: 1/31/14

6.E.3

Name _____   Date _____

In the diagram, the length of S is $\frac{2}{3}$ the length of T. If S has an area of 368 cm², find the perimeter of the figure.

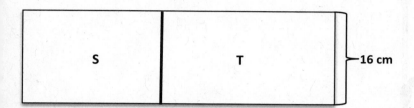

COMMON CORE™

Lesson 23:	Make sense of complex, multi-step problems and persevere in solving
	them. Share and critique peer solutions.
Date:	1/31/14

6.E.32

The following problems are puzzles for your enjoyment. They are intended to encourage working together and family problem solving fun and are not a required element of this homework assignment.

Take 12 matchsticks arranged in a grid as shown below, and remove 2 matchsticks so 2 squares remain. How can you do this? Draw the new arrangement.

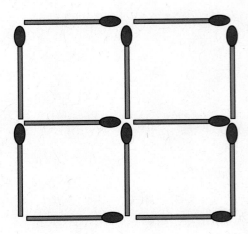

Moving only 3 matchsticks, make the fish turn around and swim the opposite way. Which matchsticks did you move? Draw the new shape.

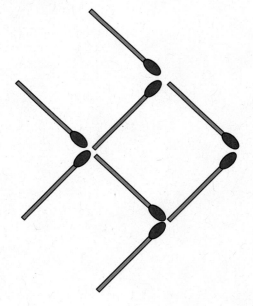

COMMON CORE™

Lesson 23:	Make sense of complex, multi-step problems and persevere in solving them. Share and critique peer solutions.
Date:	1/31/14

6.E.3

Lesson 24

Objective: Make sense of complex, multi-step problems and persevere in solving them. Share and critique peer solutions.

Suggested Lesson Structure

■ Fluency Practice   (10 minutes)

▨ Concept Development   (45 minutes)

■ Student Debrief   (5 minutes)

   Total Time   **(60 minutes)**

Fluency Practice (10 minutes)

- Subtract Unlike Denominators **5.NF.1**   (4 minutes)
- Order of Operations **5.OA.1**   (3 minutes)
- Multiply by Multiples of 10 **5.NBT.2**   (3 minutes)

Subtract Unlike Denominators (4 minutes)

Materials: (S) Personal white boards

Note: This drill reviews G5–Module 3 content.

  T: (Write $\frac{1}{2} - \frac{1}{3}$.) Add the fractions. Simplify the difference if possible.

  S: (Subtract.)

Repeat the process for $\frac{1}{5} - \frac{1}{10}$, $\frac{1}{3} - \frac{1}{4}$, and $\frac{1}{4} - \frac{1}{5}$.

Order of Operations (3 minutes)

Materials: (S) Personal white boards

Note: This fluency prepares students for today's lesson.

  T: (Write 12 ÷ 3 + 1.) On your boards, write the complete number sentence.

  S: (Write 12 ÷ 3 + 1 = 5.)

  T: (Write 12 ÷ (3 + 1).) On your boards, copy the expression.

  S: (Write 12 ÷ (3 + 1).)

NOTES ON
LESSONS 21–25:

Lesson Sequence for M6–Topic E:

- Lessons 21–22 use a protocol to solve problems within teams of four. The number of problems solved will vary between teams.
- Lesson 23 uses a protocol to share and critique student solutions from G5–M6–Lessons 21–22.
- Lesson 24 resumes the problem solving begun in Lessons 21–22.
- Lesson 25 uses the protocol from Lesson 23 to again share and critique student solutions.

COMMON CORE™ | Lesson 24: Make sense of complex, multi-step problems and persevere in solving them. Share and critique peer solutions.
Date: 1/31/14

6.E.34

T: Write the complete number sentence, performing the operation inside the parentheses.

S: (Beneath 12 ÷ (3 + 1) = _____, write 12 ÷ 4 = 3.)

Continue this process with the following possible sequence: 20 − 6 ÷ 2, (20 − 6) ÷ 2, 7 × 4 + 3, and 7 × (4 + 3).

Multiply by Multiples of 10 (3 minutes)

Note: This review fluency drill will help preserve skills students learned and mastered in G5–Module 1 and lay the groundwork for future concepts.

Materials: (S) Personal white boards

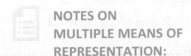

T: (Write 41 × 10.) Say the complete multiplication sentence.

S: 41 × 10 = 410.

T: (Write 410 × 2 beside 41 × 10 = 410.) Say the complete multiplication sentence.

S: 410 × 2 = 820.

T: (Write 410 × 20 below 410 × 2 = 820.) Write 410 × 20 as a three-factor multiplication sentence, using a number bond to factor out 10 from 20.

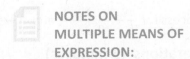

S: 410 × 10 × 2 = 8,200.

T: Show your board. (Check for accuracy.)

Direct students to solve using the same method for 32 × 30 and 43 × 30.

Concept Development (45 minutes)

Students continue work progressing through the set of nine problems presented in G5–M6–Lesson 21.

1. Re-establish the intention of G5–M6–Lessons 21–25 to give students time and support to solve some great problems. Remind them that tomorrow will again be devoted to sharing and critiquing each other's' work as they did in G5–M6–Lesson 23.

2. Remind students of the *think, pair, share, and complete* process. Invite students to share ways to make their workspace more effective and joyful.

3. Remind students that it is not the number of the problems completed but rather quality of the work that is of most importance.

4. Remind students that solutions will be collected, organized, and analyzed.

> **NOTES ON MULTIPLE MEANS OF REPRESENTATION:**
>
> If drawing or modeling is not working for a team when solving a given problem, suggest acting it out or modeling it with concrete materials. Using small balls of clay can be very empowering to represent a problem.

> **NOTES ON MULTIPLE MEANS OF EXPRESSION:**
>
> As students reflect on their growth as problem solvers, initiate the conversation using a personal example, "At first, when solving the Hewitt's Carpet, I felt overwhelmed by all the information. But, once I made a table, I relaxed and was able to solve it. I learned that making a table gave me the support I needed to persevere."

Lesson 24: Make sense of complex, multi-step problems and persevere in solving them. Share and critique peer solutions.

Date: 1/31/14

6.E.3!

Student Debrief (5 Minutes)

Lesson Objective: Make sense of complex, multi-step problems and persevere in solving them. Share and critique peer solutions.

The Student Debrief is intended to invite reflection and active processing of the total lesson experience.

- Did you apply what you learned yesterday to today's problems? How?
- What did you learn about yourself today as a problem solver that will help you to be a better problem solver tomorrow?

Note: There is no Exit Ticket for this lesson.

	Lesson 24:	Make sense of complex, multi-step problems and persevere in solving them. Share and critique peer solutions.	**6.E.36**
	Date:	1/31/14	

Name _____   Date _____

Pat's Potato Farm grew 490 pounds of potatoes. Pat delivered $\frac{3}{7}$ of the potatoes to a vegetable stand. The owner of the vegetable stand delivered $\frac{2}{3}$ of the potatoes he bought to a local grocery store which packaged half of the potatoes that were delivered into 5-pound bags. How many 5-pound bags did the grocery store package?

Lesson 24:	Make sense of complex, multi-step problems and persevere in solving them. Share and critique peer solutions.
Date:	1/31/14

6.E.37

The following problems are for your enjoyment. They are intended to encourage working together and family problem solving fun. They are not a required element of this homework assignment.

Six matchsticks are arranged into an equilateral triangle. How can you arrange them into 4 equilateral triangles without breaking or overlapping any of them? Draw the new shape.

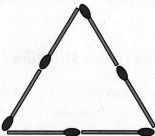

Kenny's dog, Charlie, is really smart! Last week, Charlie buried 7 bones in all. He buried them in 5 straight lines and put 3 bones in each line. How is this possible? Sketch how Charlie buried the bones.

Lesson 24:	Make sense of complex, multi-step problems and persevere in solving them. Share and critique peer solutions.	6.E.38
Date:	1/31/14	

Lesson 25

Objective: Make sense of complex, multi-step problems and persevere in solving them. Share and critique peer solutions.

Suggested Lesson Structure

■ Fluency Practice   (11 minutes)
■ Concept Development   (44 minutes)
■ Student Debrief   (5 minutes)
Total Time   **(60 minutes)**

Fluency Practice (11 minutes)

- Multiply **5.NBT.5**   (4 minutes)
- Order of Operations **5.OA.1**   (3 minutes)
- Subtract Unlike Denominators **5.NF.1**   (4 minutes)

Multiply (4 minutes)

Materials: (S) Personal white boards

Note: This drill reviews year-long fluency standards.

    T: (Write 4 tens 9 ones × 4 ten 3 ones = __ × __.) Write
       the multiplication sentence in standard form.
    S: (Write 49 × 43.)
    T: Solve 49 × 43 using the standard algorithm.
    S: (Write 49 × 43 = 2,107 using the standard algorithm.)

Continue the process for 249 × 43, 67 × 32, 867 × 32, and 938 × 27.

Order of Operations (3 minutes)

Materials: (S) Personal white boards

Note: This fluency prepares students for today's lesson.

    T: (Write 24 ÷ 3 + 1.) On your boards, write the complete number sentence.
    S: (Write 24 ÷ 3 + 1 = 9.)
    T: (Write 24 ÷ (3 + 1).) On your boards, copy the expression.

NOTES ON LESSONS 21–25:

Lesson Sequence for M6–Topic E:
- Lessons 21–22 use a protocol to solve problems within teams of four. The number of problems solved will vary between teams.
- Lesson 23 uses a protocol to share and critique student solutions from Lessons 21–22.
- Lesson 24 resumes the problem solving begun inLessons 21–22.
- Lesson 25 uses the protocol from Lesson 23 to again share and critique student solutions.

Lesson 25: Make sense of complex, multi-step problems and persevere in solving them. Share and critique peer responses.
Date: 1/31/14

6.E.39

S: (Write 24 ÷ (3 + 1).)

T: Write the complete number sentence, performing the operation inside the parentheses.

S: (Beneath 24 ÷ (3 + 1) = _____, write 24 ÷ 4 = 6.)

Continue this process with the following possible sequence: 5 × 4 − 2, 5 × (4 − 2), 36 ÷ 6 − 2, and 36 ÷ (6 − 2).

Subtract Unlike Denominators (4 minutes)

Materials: (S) Personal white boards

Note: This drill reviews G5–Module 3 content.

T: (Write $\frac{3}{5} - \frac{1}{2}$.) Add the fractions. Simplify the difference, if possible.

S: (Subtract.)

Repeat the process for $\frac{3}{4} - \frac{3}{8}$, $1\frac{5}{8} - \frac{2}{5}$, and $2\frac{1}{4} - \frac{2}{3}$.

Concept Development (44 minutes)

Materials: (S) Student work from G5–M6–Lessons 21, 22, and 24

1. Establish the intention and structure of today's lesson: to construct arguments, share, and critique peer solutions.

Advise students that today, they will revisit their solutions completed in G5–M6–Lessons 21, 22, and 24 and discuss their answers with students who also solved that problem.

2. Re-organize new teams of three (or keep those from G5–M6– Lesson 23) based upon an analysis of the solutions, students' strengths, weaknesses, and inter-relationships.

3. Re-introduce the protocol to the students, which may have been edited during the Debrief of G5–M6–Lesson 23. (See box to the right.)

Step 1   Student A presents his/her solution step by step to the others in the group. (Allow two minutes.)

Step 2   Students B and C discuss and make sense of the solution while Student A listens without intervening. (Allow two minutes.)

Step 3   Students B and C each ask one question or share one thought directly related to the written solution and explanation. (Allow six minutes or three minutes per question.) Student A responds and whole-group dialogue follows.

> ### A NOTE ON MULTIPLE MEANS OF REPRESENTATION:
>
> To clarify the *share and critique* protocol for the students, you might post the process listed step by step.
>
> 1. Student A presents her solution to the group.
> 2. Students B and C analyze and discuss the solution as Student A listens.
> 3. Students B and C each ask a question or share a thought about the solution. Student A responds first.
> 4. Student A explains to the group what has been learned and specific changes to improve the solution.
> 5. Repeat the process with Students B and C.

Lesson 25:	Make sense of complex, multi-step problems and persevere in solving them. Share and critique peer responses.
Date:	1/31/14

6.E.40

Suggested stems:

- Can you explain why you chose to_____?
- What did you mean when you wrote (or said) ____?
- I think you omitted _____.
- It might have been easier to understand your solution if you _____.
- I would argue that _____.

NOTES ON MULTIPLE MEANS OF EXPRESSION:

One way to have shy students share solution strategies or critique is through the use of puppets. Have the students put hand puppets as they explain their solution.

Step 4 Student A explains to the group what has been learned from the process and what changes would be made to the solution, if any. (Allow one minute.)

Step 5 Repeat Steps 1–4 for each student on the team.

4. Give students time to either revise their solution based on their peers' input or support a peer's revision. (7 minutes)

5. File all student solutions in their work portfolio.

Student Debrief (5 minutes)

Lesson Objective: Make sense of complex, multi-step problems and persevere in solving them. Share and critique peer solutions.

The Student Debrief is intended to invite reflection and active processing of the total lesson experience.

- Did your sharing and critiquing experience improve since the last time? How?
- What emotions did you experience during the share and critique process? (Follow up with additional questions based on the responses.) When did you experience nervousness? Annoyance? Surprise? Confusion?
- Did those emotions change as you went through the process? How? Why?
- What is the value of seeing other solutions and arguing about ways of solving problems?
- What did you learn today that will make you a better problem solver in the future?

Note: There is no Exit Ticket for this lesson.

Lesson 25:   Make sense of complex, multi-step problems and persevere in solving them. Share and critique peer responses.

Date: 1/31/14

6.E.41

Name _____   Date _____

Fred and Ethyl had 132 flowers altogether at first. After Fred sold $\frac{1}{4}$ of his flowers and Ethyl sold 48 of her flowers, they had the same number of flowers left. How many flowers did each of them have at first?

Lesson 25:   Make sense of complex, multi-step problems and persevere in solving
               them. Share and critique peer responses.
Date: 1/31/14

6.E.42

The following problems are puzzles for your enjoyment. They are intended to encourage working together and family problem solving fun. They are not a required element of this homework assignment.

Without removing any, move 2 matchsticks to make 4 identical squares. Which matchsticks did you move? Draw the new shape.

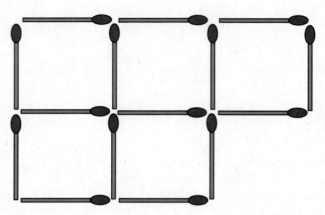

Move 3 matchsticks to form exactly (and only) 3 identical squares. Which matchsticks did you move? Draw the new shape.

Lesson 25: Make sense of complex, multi-step problems and persevere in solving them. Share and critique peer responses.
Date: 1/31/14

6.E.4

© 2014 Common Core, Inc. All rights reserved. **commoncore.org**

Topic F

The Years in Review: A Reflection on *A Story of Units*

In this final topic of Module 6, and in fact, the final topic of *A Story of Units*, students spend time producing a compendium of their learning. They not only reach back to recall learning from the very beginning of Grade 5, but also expand their thinking by exploring such concepts as the Fibonacci sequence. Students solidify the year's learning by creating and playing games and exploring patterns as they reflect back on their elementary years. All materials for the games and activities are then housed for summer use in boxes created by students in the final two lessons of the year.

The Years in Review: A Reflection on *A Story of Units*	
Objective 1:	Solidify writing and interpreting numerical expressions. (Lessons 26–27)
Objective 2:	Solidify fluency with Grade 5 skills. (Lesson 28)
Objective 3:	Solidify the vocabulary of geometry. (Lessons 29–30)
Objective 4:	Explore the Fibonacci sequence. (Lesson 31)
Objective 5:	Explore patterns in saving money. (Lesson 32)
Objective 6:	Design and construct boxes to house materials for summer use. (Lessons 33–34)

Topic F:	The Years in Review: A Reflection on *A Story of Units*	
Date:	1/31/14	6.F.1

Lesson 26

Objective: Solidify writing and interpreting numerical expressions.

Suggested Lesson Structure

- ■ Fluency Practice   (10 minutes)
- ■ Application Problem   (5 minutes)
- ■ Concept Development   (35 minutes)
- ■ Student Debrief   (10 minutes)
- **Total Time**   **(60 minutes)**

Fluency Practice (10 minutes)

- Order of Operations **5.OA.1**   (3 minutes)
- Multiply a Fraction and a Whole Number **5.NF.4**   (3 minutes)
- Multiply Decimals **5.NBT.7**   (4 minutes)

Order of Operations (3 minutes)

Materials: (S) Personal white boards

Note: This fluency activity prepares students for today's lesson.

  T: (Write (6 × 3) + 2.) Write the complete number sentence.
  S: (Write (6 × 3) + 2 = 20.)
  T: (Write 6 × (3 + 2).) Write the complete number sentence.
  S: (Write 6 × 5 = 30.)
  T: (Write 28 − (8 ÷ 2).) Write the complete number sentence.
  S: (Write 28 − (8 ÷ 2) = 24.)
  T: (Write (28 − 8) ÷ 2.) Write the complete number sentence.
  S: (Write (28 − 8) ÷ 2 = 10.)
  T: When there are no parentheses, we put imaginary parentheses around multiplication and division and do them first. We don't need the parentheses in these two expressions: (6 × 3) + 2 and 28 − (8 ÷ 2). We would solve them the same way even without the parentheses.

Continue the process with the following possible suggestions: 5 × 3 + 4 and 5 × (3 + 4).

Lesson 26:	Solidify writing and interpreting numerical expressions.
Date:	1/31/14

6.F.2

Multiply a Fraction and a Whole Number (3 minutes)

Materials: (S) Personal white boards

Note: This fluency activity reviews G5–M4–Lesson 8.

T: ($\frac{1}{2} \times 6 = \frac{\times}{2}$.) On your board, complete the number sentence.

S: (Write $\frac{1}{2} \times 6 = \frac{1 \times 6}{2}$.)

T: (Write $\frac{1}{2} \times 6 = \frac{1 \times 6}{2} = - = $ ___.) Complete the number sentence.

S: (Write $\frac{1}{2} \times 6 = \frac{1 \times 6}{2} = \frac{6}{2} = 3$.)

T: (Write $\frac{1}{2} \times 6 = \frac{1 \times 6}{2} = $ ___.) Find a common factor to simplify. Then multiply.

S: (Write $\frac{1}{2} \times 6 = \frac{1 \times \overset{3}{\cancel{6}}}{\underset{1}{\cancel{2}}} = \frac{3}{1} = 3$.)

Continue with the following possible suggestions: $6 \times \frac{1}{3}$, $12 \times \frac{2}{3}$, $\frac{3}{4} \times 12$, and $18 \times \frac{5}{6}$.

Multiply Decimals (4 minutes)

Materials: (S) Personal white boards

Note: This fluency activity reviews G5–M4–Lessons 17–18.

T: (Write $3 \times 2 = $ ___.) Say the number sentence.

S: $3 \times 2 = 6$.

T: (Write $3 \times 0.2 = $ ___.) On your board, write the number sentence.

S: (Write $3 \times 0.2 = 0.6$.)

T: (Write $0.3 \times 0.2 = $ ___.) On your board, write the number sentence.

S: (Write $0.3 \times 0.2 = 0.06$.)

$3 \times 2 = 6$	$3 \times 0.2 = 0.6$	$0.3 \times 0.2 = 0.06$	$0.03 \times 0.2 = 0.006$
$2 \times 7 = 14$	$2 \times 0.7 = 1.4$	$0.2 \times 0.7 = 0.14$	$0.02 \times 0.7 = 0.014$
$5 \times 3 = 15$	$0.5 \times 3 = 1.5$	$0.5 \times 0.3 = 0.15$	$0.5 \times 0.03 = 0.015$

Continue the process for the following possible suggestions: 2×7, 2×0.7, 0.2×0.7, 0.02×0.7, 5×3, 0.5×3, 0.5×0.3, and 0.5×0.03.

COMMON CORE

Lesson 26:   Solidify writing and interpreting numerical expressions.
Date: 1/31/14

6.F.3

Application Problem (5 minutes)

The market sells watermelons for $0.39 per pound and apples for $0.43 per pound. Write an expression that shows how much Carmen spends for a watermelon that weighs 11.5 pounds and a bag of apples that weigh 3.2 pounds.

$$\underbrace{(\$0.39 \times 11.5)}_{\text{cost of WM}} + \underbrace{(\$0.43 \times 3.2)}_{\text{cost of apples}}$$

Note: This problem reviews writing and interpreting numerical expressions within the context of money and previews the objective for today's lesson.

Concept Development (35 minutes)

This lesson is meant to be a review. Play one or both of the following games to review both writing numerical expressions and comparing expressions without calculating their values.

Game A: Writing Expressions Using the Properties Game

Materials: (S) Personal white boards, expression cards template (pictured below), timer

Description:

Students work with a partner to compete against another team of two students. Teams work together to write numerical expressions representing the written phrase. The game follows these steps:

Step 1   Turn over an expression card and start the timer.

Step 2   Teams work together to write as many numerical expressions as they can that represent the written phrase using the properties.

Step 3   When the timer sounds, a member from each team shows their expressions to the opposing team.

Step 4   The team analyzes the expressions to make sure they represent the given written phrase on the expression card.

Step 5   Teams work together to find the value of the expression.

Teams earn a point for each numerical expression they write

Expression Cards

six sevenths of nine	two thirds the sum of twenty-three and fifty-seven	forty-three less than three fifths of the product of ten and twenty	five sixths of the difference of three hundred twenty-nine and two hundred eighty-one
three times as much as the sum of three fourths and two thirds	the difference between thirty thirties and twenty-eight thirties	twenty-seven more than half the sum of four and one eighth and six and two thirds	the sum of eighty-eight and fifty-six divided by twelve
the product of nine and eight divided by four	one sixth the product of twelve and four	six copies of the sum of six twelfths and three fourths	double three fourths of eighteen

Lesson 26:   Solidify writing and interpreting numerical expressions.
Date: 1/31/14

6.F.4

that represents the written phrase on the expression card, and an additional point if they find the correct value of the expression. Play continues until all expression cards have been used, or until one team reaches a predetermined score.

Prepare the students:

Discuss how using the commutative, distributive, and associative properties can help teams write expressions.

For example, two-thirds the sum of twenty-three and fifty-seven can be written as $\frac{2}{3} \times (23 + 57)$ or using the

commutative property: $(23 + 57) \times \frac{2}{3}$.

distributive property: $\frac{2}{3} \times 23 + \frac{2}{3} \times 57$.

associative property: $\frac{1}{3} \times \left(2 \times (23 + 57)\right)$.

Remind students to respectfully analyze each other's work.

Game B: Comparing Expressions Game

Materials: (S) Comparing expressions cards template (pictured at right), personal white board, piece of paper

Description:

Students race a partner to write the symbol that makes the number sentences true. The game follows these steps:

- Cover all but the top expression with a hiding paper.
- Players race to write the symbol to make the number sentence true on their personal board.
- The first player to write the symbol explains her reasoning to the other player *without calculating*.
- If the first player is correct, she gets a point. If she is incorrect, the other player has a chance to explain and win the point instead.

MP.7

The partner with the most points when the game ends wins.

Prepare the students:

Review how to compare expressions without calculating their value.

**NOTES ON
MULTIPLE MEANS OF
ENGAGEMENT:**

Depending on the needs of the students, instead of a competition between teams, place emphasis on improvement and effort. For example, invite students to make a class goal for number of equivalent expressions written within a certain time frame. Celebrate efficiency, teamwork, problem solving, critical thinking, and communication.

Comparing Expressions Game Board

$96 \times \left(63 + \frac{17}{12}\right)$	$\bigcirc$	$(96 \times 63) + \frac{17}{12}$
$\left(437 \times \frac{9}{15}\right) \times \frac{6}{8}$	$\bigcirc$	$\left(437 \times \frac{9}{15}\right) \times \frac{7}{8}$
$4 \times 8.35 + 4 \times 6.21$	$\bigcirc$	4×15.87
$\frac{6}{7} \times (3{,}065 + 4{,}562)$	$\bigcirc$	$(3{,}065 + 4{,}562) + \frac{6}{7}$
$(8.96 \times 3) + (5.07 \times 8)$	$\bigcirc$	$(8.96 \times 3) \times (5.07 \times 8)$
$\left(297 \times \frac{16}{15}\right) + \frac{8}{3}$	$\bigcirc$	$\left(297 \times \frac{13}{15}\right) + \frac{8}{3}$
$\frac{12}{7} \times \left(\frac{5}{4} + \frac{5}{9}\right)$	$\bigcirc$	$\frac{12}{7} \times \frac{5}{4} + \frac{12}{7} \times \frac{5}{9}$

**NOTES ON
MULTIPLE MEANS OF
ENGAGEMENT:**

Every student needs to be challenged, but not necessarily in the same way. Differentiate the degree of difficulty or complexity of the Comparing Expressions game by adjusting the numbers. Students working below grade level may benefit from scaffolded practice in which they begin with simpler expressions and work towards more complex expressions. As an alternative to competition, place emphasis on effort, collaboration, and improvement.

COMMON CORE™

Lesson 26: Solidify writing and interpreting numerical expressions.
Date: 1/31/14

6.F.5

Problem Set (10 minutes)

Students should do their personal best to complete the Problem Set within the allotted 10 minutes. For some classes, it may be appropriate to modify the assignment by specifying which problems they work on first.

For this particular Problem Set consider pairing students to work on Problems 1(a)–1(d) together, asking them to share their strategies and explain their reasoning to one another before recording. To create an additional challenge for some pairs, add the requirement of recording two different, equivalent numerical expressions for each problem. Ask them to then choose only one and record their solution and reasoning. Students may need a separate piece of paper so that they have enough room to write.

Student Debrief (10 minutes)

Lesson Objective: Solidify writing and interpreting numerical expressions.

The Student Debrief is intended to invite reflection and active processing of the total lesson experience.

Invite students to review their solutions for the Problem Set. They should check work by comparing answers with a partner before going over answers as a class. Look for misconceptions or misunderstandings that can be addressed in the Debrief. Guide students in a conversation to debrief the Problem Set and process the lesson.

You may choose to use any combination of the questions below to lead the discussion.

- Compare your answers to Problem 1 to a partner's answers. How are the strategies that you used similar? How are they different?

- Share answers to Problem 2. How is writing equivalent expressions useful?

- Which strategies did you use to help you compare the expressions in Problem 3 without calculating their values?

- Which expressions in Problem 3 were most difficult to compare without calculating the values of the expressions? Why?

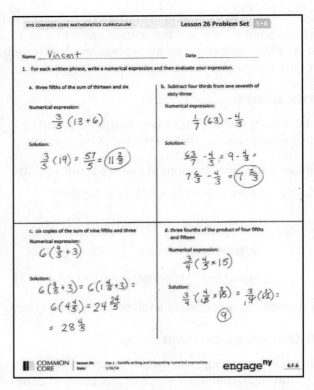

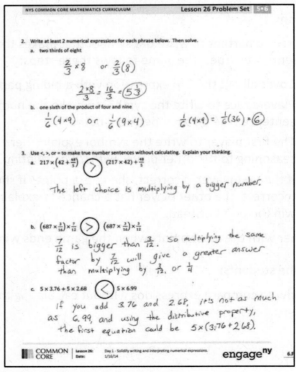

COMMON CORE

Lesson 26:   Solidify writing and interpreting numerical expressions.
Date: 1/31/14

6.F.6

- What mathematical properties were useful for completing today's Problem Set? How were they useful?
- How did the games we played prepare you to work independently on the Problem Set?

Reflection (3 minutes)

In G5–M6–Topic F, to close their elementary experience, the Exit Ticket is set aside and replaced by a brief opportunity to reflect on the mathematics done that day as it relates to their broader experience of math.

Name _____ Date _____

1. For each written phrase, write a numerical expression, and then evaluate your expression.

    a. Three-fifths of the sum of thirteen and six

       Numerical expression:

       Solution:

    b. Subtract four thirds from one seventh of sixty-three

       Numerical expression:

       Solution:

    c. Six copies of the sum of nine-fifths and three

       Numerical expression:

       Solution:

    d. Three-fourths of the product of four-fifths and fifteen

       Numerical expression:

       Solution:

2. Write at least 2 numerical expressions for each phrase below. Then solve.

   a. Two-thirds of eight

   b. One-sixth of the product of four and nine

3. Use <, >, or = to make true number sentences without calculating. Explain your thinking.

   a. $217 \times \left(42 + \frac{48}{5}\right)$ ◯ $(217 \times 42) + \frac{48}{5}$

   b. $\left(687 \times \frac{3}{16}\right) \times \frac{7}{12}$ ◯ $\left(687 \times \frac{3}{16}\right) \times \frac{3}{12}$

   c. $5 \times 3.76 + 5 \times 2.68$ ◯ 5×6.99

Name _____   Date _____

How did the games we played today prepare you to practice writing, solving, and comparing expressions this summer? Why do you think these are important skills to work on over the summer? Will you teach someone at home how to play these games with you? What math skills will you need to teach in order for someone at home to be able to play with you?

Name _____   Date _____

1. For each written phrase, write a numerical expression, and then evaluate your expression.

    a. Forty times the sum of forty-three and fifty-seven

        Numerical expression:

        Solution:

    b. Divide the difference between one thousand, three hundred, and nine hundred fifty by four

        Numerical expression:

        Solution:

    c. Seven times the quotient of five and seven

        Numerical expression:

        Solution:

    d. One-fourth the difference of four-sixths and three-twelfths

        Numerical expression:

        Solution:

2. Write at least 2 numerical expressions for each written phrase below. Then solve.

    a. Three fifths of seven

    b. One-sixth the product of four and eight

3. Use <, >, or = to make true number sentences without calculating. Explain your thinking.

    a. 4 tenths + 3 tens + 1 thousandth   30.41

    b. $\left(5 \times \frac{1}{10}\right) + \left(7 \times \frac{1}{1000}\right)$ ◯   0.507

    c. 8×7.20 ◯ $8 \times 4.36 + 8 \times 3.59$

six-sevenths of nine	two-thirds the sum of twenty-three and fifty-seven	forty-three less than three-fifths of the product of ten and twenty	five-sixths the difference of three hundred twenty-nine and two hundred eighty-one
three times as much as the sum of three-fourths and two-thirds	the difference between thirty thirties and twenty-eight thirties	twenty-seven more than half the sum of four and one-eighth and six and two-thirds	the sum of eighty-eight and fifty-six divided by twelve
the product of nine and eight divided by four	one-sixth the product of twelve and four	six copies of the sum of six-twelfths and three-fourths	double three-fourths of eighteen

COMMON CORE™   Lesson 26:   Solidify writing and interpreting numerical expressions.
Date: 1/31/14

6.F.13

$96 \times \left(63 + \dfrac{17}{12}\right)$ $(96 \times 63) + \dfrac{17}{12}$

$\left(437 \times \dfrac{9}{15}\right) \times \dfrac{6}{8}$ $\left(437 \times \dfrac{9}{15}\right) \times \dfrac{7}{8}$

$4 \times 8.35 + 4 \times 6.21$ 4×15.87

$\dfrac{6}{7} \times (3{,}065 + 4{,}562)$ $(3{,}065 + 4{,}562) + \dfrac{6}{7}$

$(8.96 \times 3) + (5.07 \times 8)$ $(8.96 + 3) \times (5.07 + 8)$

$\left(297 \times \dfrac{16}{15}\right) + \dfrac{8}{3}$ $\left(297 \times \dfrac{13}{15}\right) + \dfrac{8}{3}$

$\dfrac{12}{7} \times \left(\dfrac{5}{4} + \dfrac{5}{9}\right)$ $\dfrac{12}{7} \times \dfrac{5}{4} + \dfrac{12}{7} \times \dfrac{5}{9}$

COMMON CORE   Lesson 26:   Solidify writing and interpreting numerical expressions.   6.F.14
                         Date: 1/31/14

Lesson 27

Objective: Solidify writing and interpreting numerical expressions.

Suggested Lesson Structure

■ Fluency Practice	(12 minutes)
Concept Development	(38 minutes)
■ Student Debrief	(10 minutes)
Total Time	**(60 minutes)**

Fluency Practice (12 minutes)

- Multiply a Fraction and a Whole Number **5.NF.4**   (4 minutes)
- Multiply Decimals **5.NBT.7**   (4 minutes)
- Multiply Mentally **5.NBT.5**   (4 minutes)

Multiply a Fraction and a Whole Number (4 minutes)

Materials: (S) Personal white boards

Note: This fluency activity reviews G5–M4–Lessons 9–11.

> T: (Write $9 \div 3 =$ ___.) Say the division sentence.
>
> S: $9 \div 3 = 3$.
>
> T: (Write $\frac{1}{3} \times 9 =$ ___.) Say the multiplication sentence.
>
> S: $\frac{1}{3} \times 9 = 3$.
>
> T: (Write $\frac{2}{3} \times 9 =$ ___.) On your boards, write the multiplication sentence.
>
> S: (Write $\frac{2}{3} \times 9 = 6$.)
>
> T: (Write $9 \times \frac{2}{3} =$ ___.) On your boards, write the multiplication sentence.
>
> S: (Write $9 \times \frac{2}{3} = 6$.)

> **NOTES ON**
> **MULTIPLE MEANS OF**
> **REPRESENTATION:**
>
> The Multiply a Fraction and a Whole Number fluency activity can be scaffolded for students working below grade level by coupling written equations with models, such as a tape diagram for $\frac{2}{3} \times 9$, or by extending the equation to find a common factor, simplify, and then multiply. For example, $\frac{2}{3} \times 9 = \frac{2 \times 9}{3} = \frac{6}{1} = 6$.

Continue the process with the following possible sequence: $18 \div 6$, $\frac{1}{6} \times 18$, $\frac{5}{6} \times 12$, $12 \times \frac{5}{6}$, $\frac{1}{8} \times 16$, $16 \times \frac{1}{8}$, $32 \times \frac{3}{8}$, $\frac{2}{3} \times 15$, and $16 \times \frac{3}{4}$.

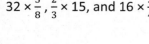

Lesson 27:   Solidify writing and interpreting numerical expressions.
Date: 1/31/14

6.F.15

Multiply Decimals (4 minutes)

Materials: (S) Personal white boards

Note: This fluency activity reviews G5–M4–Lessons 17–18.

T: (Write 3 × 3 = _____.) Say the
multiplication sentence.

S: 3 × 3 = 9.

T: (Write 3 × 0.3 = _____.) On your
boards, write the number
sentence.

S: (Write 3 × 0.3 = 0.9.)

T: (Write 0.3 × 0.3 = _____.) On your boards, write the number sentence.

S: (Write 0.3 × 0.3 = 0.09.)

3 × 3 = 9	3 × 0.3 = 0.9	0.3 × 0.3 = 0.09	0.03 × 0.3 = 0.009
2 × 6 = 12	2 × 0.6 = 1.2	0.2 × 0.6 = 0.12	0.02 × 0.6 = 0.012
7 × 5 = 35	0.7 × 5 = 3.5	0.7 × 0.5 = 0.35	0.7 × 0.05 = 0.035

Continue the process for the following possible suggestions: 2 × 6, 2 × 0.6, 0.2 × 0.6, 0.02 × 0.6, 7 × 5, 0.7 × 5, 0.7 × 0.5, and 0.7 × 0.05.

Multiply Mentally (4 minutes)

Materials: (S) Personal white boards

Note: This fluency activity will help bolster the students' understanding of and automaticity with the distributive property of multiplication.

T: (Write 8 × 10 = ____.) Say the multiplication sentence.

S: 8 × 10 = 80.

T: (Write 8 × 9 = 80 − _____ below 8 × 10 = 80.) On your personal boards, write the number sentence, filling in the blank.

S: (Write 8 × 9 = 80 − 8.)

T: What is 8 × 9?

S: 72.

Repeat the process for 8 × 100, 8 × 99, 12 × 10, 12 × 9, 25 × 100, and 25 × 99.

Concept Development (38 minutes)

Materials: (S) Blank paper, personal white boards

Write and solve word problems from a given expression.

Description:

Students work in pairs to create a word problem for a given expression, plan how to teach their word problem and solution to another pair, and then teach their solution to another pair of students.

Lesson 27:   Solidify writing and interpreting numerical expressions.
Date: 1/31/14

6.F.16

The process is as follows:

Step 1   Give each pair of students an expression. (Suggestions are given to the right.)

Step 2   Pairs work together to write a word problem that might be solved using the given expression.

Step 3   Pairs work together to develop a plan to teach another pair of students how to solve their word problem using the RDW process.

Step 4   Pairs teach their word problem and solution to another pair of students. The student pair asks questions of the teaching pair:
   - Why are we using that model to solve?
   - Could I solve it this way instead?
   - Can you be more specific?
   - I do not understand that step. Can you please explain it?

P.3

After the presentations, the teaching pair might discuss the effectiveness of their solution and make changes if necessary. Then, they can present their word problem and solution to a new pair. End the lesson with a class discussion about the changes the students made to their solutions between rounds and the reasoning behind these changes.

Suggestions for expressions:

- $65 \times \frac{4}{5}$
- $(27 + 33) \times \frac{2}{3}$
- $9 - \left(\frac{3}{8} + \frac{1}{2}\right)$
- $\left(\frac{5}{6} + \frac{7}{12}\right) \times 48$
- $7 + \left(\frac{3}{4} + \frac{7}{16}\right)$

NOTES ON MULTIPLE MEANS OF REPRESENTATION:

Depending on the level of English proficiency of English language learners, try inviting students to discuss, plan, write, and teach in their first language. Alternatively, provide extra time, reduce the amount of work, or provide sentence frames for discussion.

Problem Set (10 minutes)

Students should do their personal best to complete the Problem Set within the allotted 10 minutes. For some classes, it may be appropriate to modify the assignment by specifying which problems they work on first. Some problems do not specify a method for solving. Students solve these problems using the RDW approach used for Application Problems.

Student Debrief (10 minutes)

Lesson Objective: Solidify writing and interpreting numerical expressions.

The Student Debrief is intended to invite reflection and active processing of the total lesson experience.

Invite students to review their solutions for the Problem Set. They should check work by comparing answers with a partner before going over answers as a class. Look for

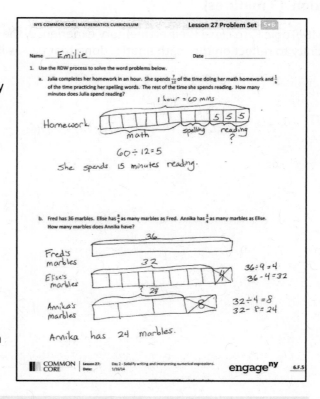

misconceptions or misunderstandings that can be addressed in the Debrief. Guide students in a conversation to debrief the Problem Set and process the lesson.

You may choose to use any combination of the questions below to lead the discussion.

- Compare your solutions for Problem 1 to a partner's solutions. Is one of your methods for solving more efficient? How do you know?

- Share the word problems that you wrote for Problem 2.

- In Problem 2, which expression was most challenging to represent with a word problem? Why?

- What did you find more challenging today, planning how to teach a word problem solution to your classmates or writing a word problem for a given expression? Why?

- What did you learn about your problem solving skills by teaching other students how to solve a word problem?

Reflection (3 minutes)

In G5–M6–Topic F, to close their elementary experience, the Exit Ticket is set aside and replaced by a brief opportunity to reflect on the mathematics done that day as it relates to their broader experience of math.

Name _____   Date _____

1. Use the RDW process to solve the word problems below.

    a. Julia completes her homework in an hour. She spends $\frac{7}{12}$ of the time doing her math homework and $\frac{1}{6}$ of the time practicing her spelling words. The rest of the time she spends reading. How many minutes does Julia spend reading?

    b. Fred has 36 marbles. Elise has $\frac{8}{9}$ as many marbles as Fred. Annika has $\frac{3}{4}$ as many marbles as Elise. How many marbles does Annika have?

Lesson 27:   Solidify writing and interpreting numerical expressions.
Date: 1/31/14

6.F.19

2. Write and solve a word problem that might be solved using the expressions in the chart below.

Expression	Word Problem	Solution
$\frac{2}{3} \times 18$		
$(26 + 34) \times \frac{5}{6}$		
$7 - \left(\frac{5}{12} + \frac{1}{2}\right)$		

Name _____   Date _____

How did teaching other students how to solve a word problem strengthen your skills as a problem solver? What did you learn about your problem solving skills? What are your strengths and weaknesses as a problem solver?

Lesson 27:   Solidify writing and interpreting numerical expressions.
Date: 1/31/14

6.F.21

Name _____   Date _____

1. Use the RDW process to solve the word problems below.

a. There are 36 students in Mr. Meyer's class. Of those students, $\frac{5}{12}$ played tag at recess, $\frac{1}{3}$ played kickball, and the rest played basketball. How many students in Mr. Meyer's class played basketball?

b. Julie brought 24 apples to school to share with her classmates. Of those apples, $\frac{2}{3}$ are red and the rest are green. Julie's classmates ate $\frac{3}{4}$ of the red apples and $\frac{1}{2}$ of the green apples. How many apples are left?

2. Write and solve a word problem for each expression in the chart below.

Expression	Word Problem	Solution
$144 \times \dfrac{7}{12}$		
$9 - \left(\dfrac{4}{9} + \dfrac{1}{3}\right)$		
$\dfrac{3}{4} \times (36 + 12)$		

COMMON CORE

Lesson 27:   Solidify writing and interpreting numerical expressions.
Date: 1/31/14

6.F.23

Lesson 28

Objective: Solidify fluency with Grade 5 skills.

Suggested Lesson Structure

■ Fluency Practice   (50 minutes)
■ Student Debrief   (10 minutes)
Total Time   **(60 minutes)**

Fluency Practice (50 minutes)

Mixed Review Fluency Activities

Materials: (S) Fluency activity template, Problem Set, personal white board

Part 1: Reflect on fluency.

T: This year, we devoted time each day to practicing different skills. Think about these fluency activities as you answer the questions in Problem 1.

S: (Answer the six components of Problem 1 listed below.)

Problem 1: Answer the following questions about fluency.

   a. What does being fluent with a math skill mean to you?

   b. Why is fluency with certain math skills important?

   c. With which math skills do you think you should be fluent?

   d. With which math skills do you feel most fluent? Least fluent?

   e. How can you continue to improve your fluency?

Part 2: Select and engage in fluency activities.

▪ Pass out the fluency activity templates. (There are a total of 16 activities. An example is shown to the right.)

▪ In pairs or small groups, students alternate the role of teacher and engage in the activities of their choice.

▪ As they play, students complete Problems 2 and 3 from the Problem Set.

NOTES ON
MULTIPLE MEANS OF
ACTION AND
EXPRESSION:

Students benefit from practicing fluency areas of both strength and weakness. As they get stronger at what they are good at, they can start to see connections that empower them in their areas of weakness. Encourage them to balance their practice.

Part 3: Create reference cards.

- Students cut out the 16 cards.
- On the back of the fluencies they have chosen for intensive summer practice, students make examples of expressions, equations, models, diagrams, and/or figures that represent the skill.

Students will store these fluency reference cards in the summer activity boxes that they create in G5–M6–Lessons 33–34.

Student Debrief (10 minutes)

Lesson Objective: Solidify fluency with Grade 5 skills.

The Student Debrief is intended to invite reflection and active processing of the total lesson experience.

Invite students to review their Problem Sets. Guide students in a conversation to debrief the Problem Set and process the lesson.

You may choose to use any combination of the questions below to lead the discussion.

- What is something you did today that you could not do before fifth grade?
- What did you learn about your fluency with different math skills today? What do you feel confident about? What do you need to continue to work on?
- Tell your partners some activities from today's lesson that you would like to include in your summer activity box to help you maintain and build your fluency.
- Read your responses to the questions in Problem 1. Now that you have had some time to practice different fluency activities, have your answers to any of the questions changed? Which ones? Why? Be as specific as possible.

NOTES ON MULTIPLE MEANS OF ACTION AND EXPRESSION:

Provide the following scaffolds for learners who may need more visual support:

For Find the Volume, provide a rectangular prism template to ease the task of drawing.

For Compare Decimal Fractions, have students represent numbers in a place value chart before comparing.

For Divide Whole Numbers by Unit Fractions, have students model with a tape diagram, number line, or another model.

For Unit Conversions, have students model using a tape diagram.

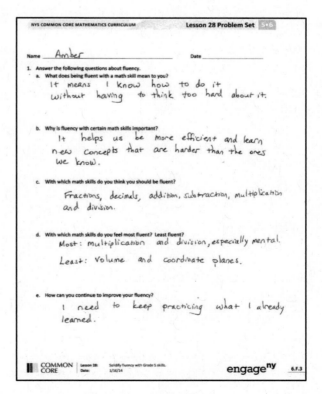

COMMON CORE™

Lesson 28:   Solidify fluency with Grade 5 skills.
Date: 1/31/14

6.F.25

Reflection (3 minutes)

In G5–M6–Topic F, to close their elementary experience, the Exit Ticket is set aside and replaced by a brief opportunity to reflect on the mathematics done that day as it relates to their broader experience of math.

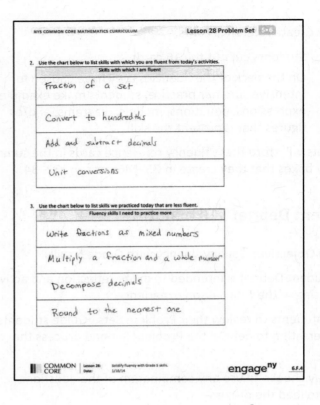

Lesson 28:   Solidify fluency with Grade 5 skills.
Date: 1/31/14

6.F.26

© 2014 Common Core, Inc. All rights reserved. commoncore.org

Name _____   Date _____

1. Answer the following questions about fluency.

    a. What does being fluent with a math skill mean to you?

    b. Why is fluency with certain math skills important?

    c. With which math skills do you think you should be fluent?

    d. With which math skills do you feel most fluent? Least fluent?

    e. How can you continue to improve your fluency?

Lesson 28:   Solidify fluency with Grade 5 skills.
Date: 1/31/14

6.F.27

2. Use the chart below to list skills with which you are fluent from today's activities.

Fluent Skills

3. Use the chart below to list skills we practiced today with which you are less fluent.

Skills to Practice More

Name _____   Date _____

What math skills have you improved through our fluency practice this year? How do you know you've improved? What math skills do you need to continue to practice this summer? Why?

Name _____   Date _____

1. Use what you learned about your fluency skills today to answer the questions below.
    a. Which skills should you practice this summer to maintain and build your fluency? Why?

    b. Write a goal for yourself about a skill that you want to work on this summer.

    c. Explain the steps you can take to reach your goal.

    d. How will reaching this goal help you as a math student?

2. In the chart below, plan a new fluency activity that you can play at home this summer to help you build or maintain a skill that you listed in Problem 1(a). When planning your activity, be sure to think about the factors listed below:

    - The materials that you'll need.
    - Who can play with you (if more than 1 player is needed).
    - The usefulness of the activity for building your skills.

Skill:	
Name of Activity:	
Materials Needed:	
Description:	

Lesson 28:   Solidify fluency with Grade 5 skills.
Date: 1/31/14

6.F.31

Write Fractions as Mixed Numbers

Materials: (S) Personal white boards

T: (Write $\frac{13}{2}$ = ＿＿ ÷ ＿＿ = ＿＿.) Write the fraction as a division problem and mixed number.

S: (Write $\frac{13}{2}$ = 13 ÷ 2 = $6\frac{1}{2}$.)

More practice!

$\frac{11}{2}, \frac{17}{2}, \frac{44}{2}, \frac{31}{10}, \frac{23}{10}, \frac{47}{10}, \frac{89}{10}, \frac{8}{3}, \frac{13}{3}, \frac{26}{3}, \frac{9}{4}, \frac{13}{4}, \frac{15}{4}$, and $\frac{35}{4}$.

Fraction of a Set

Materials: (S) Personal white boards

T: (Write $\frac{1}{2}$ × 10.) Draw a tape diagram to model the whole number.

S: (Draw tape diagram and label it 10.)

T: Draw a line to split the tape diagram in half.

S: (Draw line.)

T: What is the value of each part of your tape diagram?

S: 5.

T: So, what is $\frac{1}{2}$ of 10?

S: 5.

More practice!

$8 \times \frac{1}{2}$, $8 \times \frac{1}{4}$, $6 \times \frac{1}{3}$, $30 \times \frac{1}{6}$, $42 \times \frac{1}{7}$, $42 \times \frac{1}{6}$, $48 \times \frac{1}{8}$, $54 \times \frac{1}{9}$, and $54 \times \frac{1}{6}$.

Convert to Hundredths

Materials: (S) Personal white boards

T: (Write $\frac{3}{4} = \frac{}{100}$.) 4 times what factor equals 100?

S: 25.

T: Write the equivalent fraction.

S: (Write $\frac{3}{4} = \frac{75}{100}$.)

More practice!

$\frac{3}{4} = \frac{}{100}$, $\frac{1}{50} = \frac{}{100}$, $\frac{3}{50} = \frac{}{100}$, $\frac{1}{20} = \frac{}{100}$, $\frac{3}{20} = \frac{}{100}$, $\frac{1}{25} = \frac{}{100}$, and $\frac{2}{25} = \frac{}{100}$.

Multiply a Fraction and a Whole Number

Materials: (S) Personal white boards

T: (Write $\frac{8}{4}$.) Write the corresponding division sentence.

S: 8 ÷ 4 = 2.

T: (Write $\frac{1}{4}$ × 8 =.) Write the complete multiplication sentence.

S: (Write $\frac{1}{4}$ × 8 = 2.)

More practice!

$\frac{18}{6}, \frac{15}{3}, \frac{18}{6}, \frac{27}{9}, \frac{54}{6}, \frac{51}{3}, \frac{63}{7}$.

Lesson 28: Solidify fluency with Grade 5 skills.
Date: 1/31/14

6.F.3?

Multiply Mentally

Materials: (S) Personal white boards

T: (Write 9 × 10.) Write the complete multiplication sentence
S: 9 × 10 = 90.
T: (Write 9 × 9 = 90 – ____ below 9 × 10 = 90.) On your personal boards, write the number sentence, filling in the blank.
S: (Write 9 × 9 = 90 – 9.)
T: 9 × 9 is?
S: 81.

More practice!

9 × 99, 15 × 9, and 29 × 99.

One Unit More

Materials: (S) Personal white boards

T: (Write 5 tenths.) Write the decimal that's one-tenth more than 5 tenths.
S: 0.6

More practice!

5 hundredths, 5 thousandths, 8 hundredths, 2 thousandths. Specify the unit of increase.

T: (Write 0.052.) On your boards, write one more thousandth.
S: 0.053

More practice!

1 tenth more than 35 hundredths,
1 thousandth more than 35 hundredths, and
1 hundredth more than 438 thousandths.

Find the Product

Materials: (S) Personal white boards

T: (Write 4 × 3.) Complete the multiplication sentence giving the second factor in unit form.
S: 4 × 3 ones = 12 ones.
T: (Write 4 × 0.2.) Complete the multiplication sentence giving the second factor in unit form.
S: 4 × 2 tenths = 8 tenths.
T: (Write 4 × 3.2.) Complete the multiplication sentence giving the second factor in unit form.
S: 4 × 3 ones 2 tenths = 12 ones 8 tenths.
T: Write the complete multiplication sentence.
S: (Write 4 × 3.1 = 12.8.)

More practice!

4 × 3.21, 9 × 2, 9 × 0.1, 9 × 0.03, 9 × 2.13, 4.012 × 4, and 5 × 3.2375.

Add and Subtract Decimals

Materials: (S) Personal white boards

T: (Write 7258 thousandths + 1 thousandth = ____.) Write the addition sentence in decimal form.
S: 7.258 + 0.001 = 7.259.

More practice!

7 ones + 258 thousandths + 3 hundredths,
6 ones + 453 thousandths + 4 hundredths,
2 ones + 37 thousandths + 5 tenths, and
6 ones + 35 hundredths + 7 thousandths.

T: (Write 4 ones + 8 hundredths – 2 ones = ____ ones ____ hundredths.) Write the subtraction sentence in decimal form.
S: (Write 4.08 – 2 = 2.08.)

More practice!

9 tenths + 7 thousandths – 4 thousandths,
4 ones + 582 thousandths – 3 hundredths,
9 ones + 708 thousandths – 4 tenths, and
4 ones + 73 thousandths – 4 hundredths.

Lesson 28:   Solidify fluency with Grade 5 skills.
Date: 1/31/14

6.F.33

Decompose Decimals

Materials: (S) Personal white boards

T: (Project 7.463.) Say the number.
S: 7 and 463 thousandths.
T: Represent this number in a two-part number bond with ones as one part and thousandths as the other part.

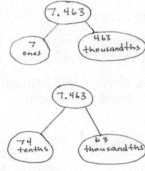

S: (Draw.)
T: Represent it again with tenths and thousandths.

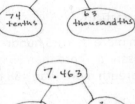

T: Represent it again with hundredths and thousandths.

More practice!

8.972 and 6.849.

Find the Volume

Materials: (S) Personal white boards

T: On your boards, write the formula for finding the volume of a rectangular prism.
S: (Write V = l × w × h.)
T: (Draw and label a rectangular prism with a length of 5 cm, width of 6 cm, and height of 2 cm.) On your boards, write a multiplication sentence to find the volume this rectangular prism.
S: (Beneath V = l × w × h, write V = 5 cm × 6 cm × 2 cm. Beneath it, write V = 60 cm³.)

More practice!

w = 9 ft, l = 7 ft, h = 3 ft

w = 6 in, l = 6 in, h = 5 in

w = 8 cm, l = 4 cm, h = 2 cm

Make a Like Unit

Materials: (S) Personal white boards

T: I'll say two unit fractions. You make the like unit and write it on your board. Show your board at the signal.
T: $\frac{1}{3}$ and $\frac{1}{2}$. (Pause. Signal.)
S: (Show sixths.)

More practice!

$\frac{1}{4}$ and $\frac{1}{3}$, $\frac{1}{2}$ and $\frac{1}{4}$, $\frac{1}{6}$ and $\frac{1}{2}$, $\frac{1}{3}$ and $\frac{1}{12}$, $\frac{1}{6}$ and $\frac{1}{8}$, and $\frac{1}{3}$ and $\frac{1}{9}$.

Unit Conversions

Materials: (S) Personal white boards

T: (Write 12 in = ___ ft.) 12 inches is the same as how many feet?
S: 1 foot.

More practice!

24 in, 36 in, 54 in, and 76 in.

T: (Write 1 ft = ___ in.) 1 foot is the same as how many inches?
S: 12 inches.

More practice!

2 ft, 2.5 ft, 3 ft, 3.5 ft, 4 ft 4.5 ft 9 ft, and 9.5 ft

Lesson 28: Solidify fluency with Grade 5 skills.
Date: 1/31/14

6.F.3

Compare Decimal Fractions

Materials: (S) Personal white boards

T: (Write 13.78 ___ 13.86.) On your personal boards, compare the numbers using the greater than, less than, or equal sign.

S: (Write 13.78 < 13.76.)

More practice!

0.78 ___ $\frac{78}{100}$, 439.3 ___ 4.39, 5.08 ___ fifty-eight tenths, and thirty-five and 9 thousandths ___ 4 tens.

Round to the Nearest One

Materials: (S) Personal white boards

T: (Write 3 ones 2 tenths.) Write 3 ones and 2 tenths as a decimal.

S: (Write 3. 2.)

T: (Write 3.2 ≈ ___.) Round 3 and 2 tenths to the nearest whole number.

S: (Write 3.2 ≈ 3.)

More practice!

3.7, 13.7, 5.4, 25.4, 1.5, 21.5, 6.48, 3.62, and 36.52.

Multiplying Fractions

Materials: (S) Personal white boards

T: (Write $\frac{1}{2} \times \frac{1}{3}$ = ___.) Write the complete multiplication sentence.

S: (Write $\frac{1}{2} \times \frac{1}{3} = \frac{1}{6}$.)

T: (Write $\frac{1}{2} \times \frac{3}{4}$ = ___.) Write the complete multiplication sentence.

S: (Write $\frac{1}{2} \times \frac{3}{4} = \frac{3}{8}$.)

T: (Write $\frac{2}{5} \times \frac{2}{3}$ = ___.) Write the complete multiplication sentence.

S: (Write $\frac{2}{5} \times \frac{2}{3} = \frac{4}{15}$.)

More practice!

$\frac{1}{2} \times \frac{1}{5}$, $\frac{1}{2} \times \frac{3}{5}$, $\frac{3}{4} \times \frac{3}{5}$, $\frac{4}{5} \times \frac{2}{3}$, and $\frac{3}{4} \times \frac{5}{6}$.

Divide Whole Numbers by Unit Fractions

Materials: (S) Personal white boards

T: (Write $1 \div \frac{1}{2}$.) How many halves are in 1?

S: 2.

T: (Write $1 \div \frac{1}{2}$ = 2. Beneath it, write $2 \div \frac{1}{2}$.) How many halves are in 2?

S: 4.

T: (Write $2 \div \frac{1}{2}$ = 4. Beneath it, write $3 \div \frac{1}{2}$.) How many halves are in 3?

S: 6.

T: (Write $3 \div \frac{1}{2}$ = 6. Beneath it, write $7 \div \frac{1}{2}$.) Write the complete division sentence.

S: (Write $7 \div \frac{1}{2}$ = 14.)

More practice!

$1 \div \frac{1}{3}$, $2 \div \frac{1}{5}$, $9 \div \frac{1}{4}$, and $3 \div \frac{1}{8}$.

Lesson 29

Objective: Solidify the vocabulary of geometry.

Suggested Lesson Structure

■ Fluency Practice   (12 minutes)
■ Concept Development   (38 minutes)
■ Student Debrief   (10 minutes)
  Total Time   **(60 minutes)**

Fluency Practice (12 minutes)

- Sprint: Multiply Decimals **5.NBT.7**   (9 minutes)
- Multiply Mentally **5.NBT.5**   (3 minutes)

Sprint: Multiply Decimals (9 minutes)

Materials: (S) Multiply Decimals Sprint

Note: This fluency activity reviews G5–Module 4 concepts.

Multiply Mentally (3 minutes)

Materials: (S) Personal white boards

Note: This fluency activity drill helps bolster students'
understanding of and automaticity with the distributive
property of multiplication.

T: (Write $7 \times 10 =$ ____.) Say the multiplication sentence.
S: $7 \times 10 = 70$.
T: (Write $7 \times 9 = 70 -$ ____ below $7 \times 10 = 70$.) On your
     personal boards, write the complete number sentence.
S: (Write $7 \times 9 = 70 - 7$.)
T: 7×9 is...?
S: 63.

Repeat the process and procedure for 7×99, 15×9, and 31×99.

**NOTES ON
MULTIPLE MEANS OF
ENGAGEMENT:**

To make the Multiply Mentally fluency
activity directions clear to English
language learners, give an example
before asking students to respond.
Differentiate for students working
above grade level by challenging
learners to respond without writing.
Also, encourage them to analyze the
strategy and present multiplication
sentences that best suits it, such as
using the distributive property to solve
7×99.

Lesson 29:	Solidify the vocabulary of geometry.
Date:	1/31/14

6.F.3

Concept Development (38 minutes)

Materials: (S) Chart paper or personal white board, scissors, Problem Set (copied on card stock), Math Pictionary directions (shown below), small envelope, 30-second timer

Today, students use the vocabulary terms of the Problem Set to play Math Pictionary.

Part 1: Match terms to definitions.

Students begin by cutting out the vocabulary terms and matching them to the intact card of definitions on the Problem Set by placing the correct term on top of its matching definition (pictured to the right). Let them review terms with each other and argue until a consensus is reached. Possibly review answers.

The definitions can then be collected and saved for use in G5–M6–Lesson 30 (later to be stored in the summer activity box).

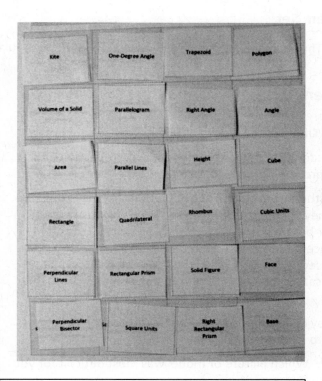

Part 2: Play Pictionary.

Students can play using the rules in the directions to the right. Demonstrating a round of the game as a whole class, then moving to play in small groups may maximize engagement.

Note on game directions: The first wrong guess from a team passes play to the other team. The purpose of this is two-fold. First of all, it encourages students to be as specific as possible when drawing to represent each vocabulary term. Secondly, it discourages teams from just running through a list of vocabulary words until they say the correct word.

After the session, students can put the vocabulary terms in a small envelope. The terms will be used in G5–M6–Lesson 30 and will be stored in the summer activity box. Each student should also receive a copy of the game directions to put in his/her summer activity box.

Math Pictionary:

Number of players: 4–8

Materials: Blank paper, timer, pencils

- Players divide into 2 teams. The vocabulary term cards are placed face down in a pile.
- A player from Team A chooses a card, silently reads the card, and draws a picture to represent the term on the card.
- As soon as the player reads the card, Team B starts the 30-second timer.
- Team A players use the drawing to figure out the term before the timer sounds.
- If the members of Team A correctly guess the term, they score a point for their team.
- However, the *first* wrong guess from Team A passes play to Team B. Team B then draws a picture to steal the point from Team A.
- Play continues with teams taking turns drawing until all cards have been used. The team with the most points wins.

Problem Set

Note: The Problem Set for G5–M6–Lesson 29 is the vocabulary definitions and terms.

Student Debrief (10 minutes)

Lesson Objective: Solidify the vocabulary of geometry.

The Student Debrief is intended to invite reflection and active processing of the total lesson experience.

Invite students to review their solutions for the Problem Set. They should check work by comparing answers with a partner before going over answers as a class. Look for misconceptions or misunderstandings that can be addressed in the Debrief. Guide students in a conversation to debrief the Problem Set and process the lesson.

You may choose to use any combination of the questions below to lead the discussion.

- Which picture or model was most difficult for you to draw? Why?
- How does drawing pictures and models help you understand and review these geometry terms?
- How can you use your pictorial vocabulary cards during the summer to review these geometry terms?
- Which terms go together? Why? (Students will have many ways of sorting these concepts.)

Reflection (3 minutes)

In G5–M6–Topic F, to close their elementary experience, the Exit Ticket is set aside and replaced by a brief opportunity to reflect on the mathematics done that day as it relates to their broader experience of math.

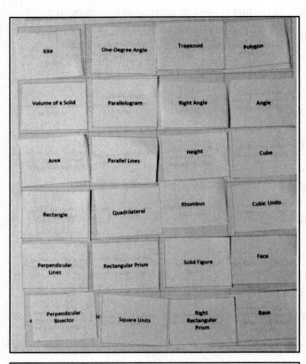

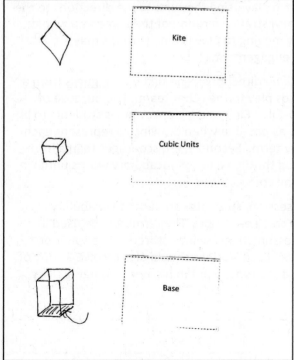

A

Multiply.   # Correct _____

1	$3 \times 2 =$		23	$0.6 \times 2 =$	
2	$3 \times 0.2 =$		24	$0.6 \times 0.2 =$	
3	$3 \times 0.02 =$		25	$0.6 \times 0.02 =$	
4	$3 \times 3 =$		26	$0.2 \times 0.06 =$	
5	$3 \times 0.3 =$		27	$5 \times 7 =$	
6	$3 \times 0.03 =$		28	$0.5 \times 7 =$	
7	$2 \times 4 =$		29	$0.5 \times 0.7 =$	
8	$2 \times 0.4 =$		30	$0.5 \times 0.07 =$	
9	$2 \times 0.04 =$		31	$0.7 \times 0.05 =$	
10	$5 \times 3 =$		32	$2 \times 8 =$	
11	$5 \times 0.3 =$		33	$9 \times 0.2 =$	
12	$5 \times 0.03 =$		34	$3 \times 7 =$	
13	$7 \times 2 =$		35	$8 \times 0.03 =$	
14	$7 \times 0.2 =$		36	$4 \times 6 =$	
15	$7 \times 0.02 =$		37	$0.6 \times 7 =$	
16	$4 \times 3 =$		38	$0.7 \times 0.7 =$	
17	$4 \times 0.3 =$		39	$0.8 \times 0.06 =$	
18	$0.4 \times 3 =$		40	$0.09 \times 0.6 =$	
19	$0.4 \times 0.3 =$		41	$6 \times 0.8 =$	
20	$0.4 \times 0.03 =$		42	$0.7 \times 0.9 =$	
21	$0.3 \times 0.04 =$		43	$0.08 \times 0.8 =$	
22	$6 \times 2 =$		44	$0.9 \times 0.08 =$	

B

Improvement _____   # Correct _____

Multiply.

1	4 x 2 =		23	0.8 x 2 =	
2	4 x 0.2 =		24	0.8 x 0.2 =	
3	4 x 0.02 =		25	0.8 x 0.02 =	
4	2 x 3 =		26	0.2 x 0.08 =	
5	2 x 0.3 =		27	5 x 9 =	
6	2 x 0.03 =		28	0.5 x 9 =	
7	3 x 3 =		29	0.5 x 0.9 =	
8	3 x 0.3 =		30	0.5 x 0.09 =	
9	3 x 0.03 =		31	0.9 x 0.05 =	
10	4 x 3 =		32	2 x 6 =	
11	4 x 0.3 =		33	7 x 0.2 =	
12	4 x 0.03 =		34	3 x 8 =	
13	9 x 2 =		35	9 x 0.03 =	
14	9 x 0.2 =		36	4 x 8 =	
15	9 x 0.02 =		37	0.7 x 6 =	
16	5 x 3 =		38	0.6 x 0.6 =	
17	5 x 0.3 =		39	0.6 x 0.08 =	
18	0.5 x 3 =		40	0.06 x 0.9 =	
19	0.5 x 0.3 =		41	8 x 0.6 =	
20	0.5 x 0.03 =		42	0.9 x 0.7 =	
21	0.3 x 0.05 =		43	0.07 x 0.7 =	
22	8 x 2 =		44	0.8 x 0.09 =	

Lesson 29:	Solidify the vocabulary of geometry.
Date:	1/31/14

6.F.4

A quadrilateral with two pairs of equal sides that are also adjacent.	An angle that turns through $\frac{1}{360}$ of a circle.	A quadrilateral with at least one pair of parallel lines.	A closed figure made up of line segments.
Measurement of space or capacity.	A quadrilateral with opposite sides that are parallel.	An angle measuring 90 degrees.	The union of two different rays sharing a common vertex.
The number of square units that covers a two-dimensional shape.	Two lines in a plane that do not intersect.	The number of adjacent layers of the base that form a rectangular prism.	A three-dimensional figure with six square sides.
A quadrilateral with four 90-degree angles.	A polygon with 4 sides and 4 angles.	A parallelogram with all equal sides.	Cubes of the same size used for measuring.
Two intersecting lines that form 90-degree angles.	A three-dimensional figure with six rectangular sides.	A three-dimensional figure.	Any flat surface of a 3-D figure.
A line that cuts a line segment into two equal parts at 90 degrees.	Squares of the same size, used for measuring.	A rectangular prism with only 90-degree angles.	One face of a 3-D solid, often thought of as the surface upon which the solid rests.

COMMON CORE™

Lesson 29:   Solidify the vocabulary of geometry.
Date: 1/31/14

6.F.41

Base	Volume of a Solid	Cubic Units	Kite
Height	One-Degree Angle	Face	Trapezoid
Right Rectangular Prism	Perpendicular Bisector	Cube	Area
Perpendicular Lines	Rhombus	Parallel Lines	Angle
Polygon	Rectangular Prism	Parallelogram	Rectangle
Right Angle	Quadrilateral	Solid Figure	Square Units

COMMON CORE™

Lesson 29: Solidify the vocabulary of geometry.
Date: 1/31/14

6.F.4

Name _____ Date _____

It is said that the true measure of knowing something is being able to teach it to someone else. Who can you teach these terms to this summer? How will you teach these terms to your summer student?

Name _____   Date _____

1. Use your ruler, protractor, and set square to help you give as many names as possible for each figure below. Then, explain your reasoning for how you named each figure.

Figure	Names	Reasoning for Names
a. 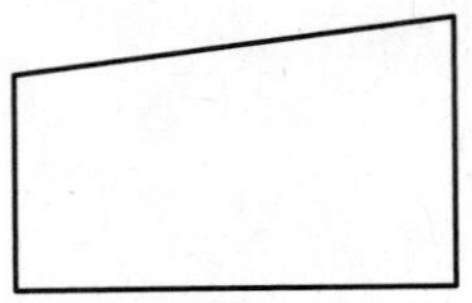		
b. 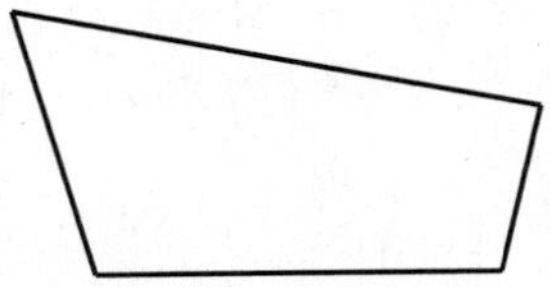		
c. 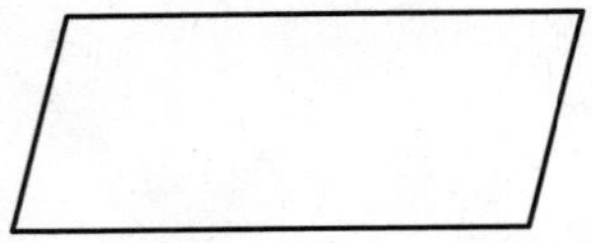		
d. 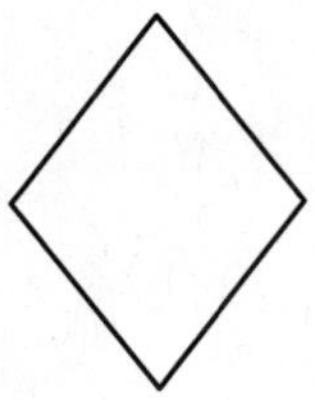		

COMMON CORE   Lesson 29:   Solidify the vocabulary of geometry.
Date: 1/31/14

6.F.4

2. Mark draws a figure that has the following characteristics:
   - Exactly 4 sides that are each 7 centimeters long
   - Two sets of parallel lines
   - Exactly 4 angles that measure 35 degrees, 145 degrees, 35 degrees, and 145 degrees

   a. Draw and label Mark's figure below.

   b. Give as many names of quadrilaterals as possible for Mark's figure. Explain your reasoning for the names of Mark's figure.

   c. List the names of Mark's figure in Problem 2(b) in order from least specific to most specific. Explain your thinking.

Lesson 29:   Solidify the vocabulary of geometry.
Date: 1/31/14

6.F.45

Math Pictionary:

Number of players: 4–8

Materials: Blank paper, timer, pencils

- Players divide into two teams. The vocabulary term cards are placed face down in a pile.
- A player from Team A chooses a card, silently reads the card, and draws a picture to represent the term on the card.
- As soon as the player reads the card, Team B starts the 30-second timer.
- Team A players use the drawing to figure out the term before the timer sounds.
- If the members of Team A correctly guess the term, they score a point for their team.
- However, the *first* wrong guess from Team A passes play to Team B. Team B then draws a picture to steal the point from Team A.
- Play continues with teams taking turns drawing until all cards have been used. The team with the most points wins.

Math Pictionary:

Number of players: 4–8

Materials: Blank paper, timer, pencils

- Players divide into two teams. The vocabulary term cards are placed face down in a pile.
- A player from Team A chooses a card, silently reads the card, and draws a picture to represent the term on the card.
- As soon as the player reads the card, Team B starts the 30-second timer.
- Team A players use the drawing to figure out the term before the timer sounds.
- If the members of Team A correctly guess the term, they score a point for their team.
- However, the *first* wrong guess from Team A passes play to Team B. Team B then draws a picture to steal the point from Team A.
- Play continues with teams taking turns drawing until all cards have been used. The team with the most points wins.

Math Pictionary:

Number of players: 4–8

Materials: Blank paper, timer, pencils

- Players divide into two teams. The vocabulary term cards are placed face down in a pile.
- A player from Team A chooses a card, silently reads the card, and draws a picture to represent the term on the card.
- As soon as the player reads the card, Team B starts the 30-second timer.
- Team A players use the drawing to figure out the term before the timer sounds.
- If the members of Team A correctly guess the term, they score a point for their team.
- However, the *first* wrong guess from Team A passes play to Team B. Team B then draws a picture to steal the point from Team A.
- Play continues with teams taking turns drawing until all cards have been used. The team with the most points wins.

COMMON CORE

Lesson 29: Solidify the vocabulary of geometry.
Date: 1/31/14

6.F.4

Lesson 30

Objective: Solidify the vocabulary of geometry.

Suggested Lesson Structure

■ Fluency Practice   (10 minutes)
▢ Concept Development   (40 minutes)
■ Student Debrief   (10 minutes)
Total Time   **(60 minutes)**

Fluency Practice (10 minutes)

▪ Multiply **5.NBT.5**   (5 minutes)
▪ Unit Conversions **5.MD.1**   (5 minutes)

Multiply (5 minutes)

Materials: (S) Personal white boards

Note: This fluency activity reviews year-long fluency standards.

    T: Solve 57 × 37 using the standard algorithm.
    S: (Write 57 × 37 = 2,109 using the standard algorithm.)

Continue the process for 457 × 37, 68 × 43, 568 × 43, and 749 × 72.

Unit Conversions (5 minutes)

Materials: (S) Personal white boards

Note: This fluency activity reviews G5–Module 4 concepts.

    T: (Write $\frac{1}{2}$ ft = ___ in.) How many inches are in 1 foot?
    S: 12 inches.
    T: (Write $\frac{1}{2}$ × 1 ft.) Write an equivalent expression using inches and convert.
    S: (Write $\frac{1}{2}$ × 12 in = 6 in.)
    T: $\frac{1}{2}$ ft is how many inches?
    S: 6 inches.

COMMON
CORE™

| Lesson 30: | Solidify the vocabulary of geometry. |
| Date: | 1/31/14 |

6.F.47

Repeat the process for the following possible sequence: $\frac{1}{3}$ ft, $\frac{3}{4}$ ft, and $5\frac{1}{4}$ ft.

T: (Write 40 cm = ____ m.) How many centimeters in a meter?

S: 100 centimeters.

T: (Write 40 × 1 cm.) Write an equivalent expression using meters and convert.

S: (Write $40 \times \frac{1}{100}$ m $= \frac{40}{100}$ m.)

T: Fill in the blank with a decimal number.

S: 0.40 meters.

T: Fill in the blank with a simplified fraction.

S: $\frac{2}{5}$ meters.

Repeat the process and procedure for 25 cm, 70 cm, 90 cm, 57 cm, and 9 cm.

Concept Development (40 minutes)

Materials: (S) Geometry pictorial vocabulary cards from G5–M6–Lesson 29, Problem Set of card stock game directions

Students use the term and definition description cards created in G5–M6–Lesson 29 to play the following games. The definition and description cards must be cut out to play Concentration. Game directions and cards should be cut out and housed in the summer activity boxes to be made in G5–M6–Lessons 33 and 34.

Game A: Three Questions to Guess my Term!

Number of players: 2–4

Description: A player selects and secretly views a term card. Other players take turns asking yes or no questions about the term.

- Players can keep track of what they know about the term on paper.
- Only yes or no questions are allowed (e.g., "What kind of angles do you have?" is not allowed).
- A final guess must be made after 3 questions, but may be made sooner. Once a player says, "This is my guess," no more questions may be asked by that player.
- If the term is guessed correctly after 1 or 2 questions, 2 points are earned. If all 3 questions are used, only 1 point is earned.
- If the no player guesses correctly, the card holder receives the point.
- The game continues as the player to the card holder's left selects a new card and questioning begins again.

The game ends when a player reaches a predetermined score.

Game B: Concentration

Number of players: 2–6

Description: Players persevere to match term cards with their definition and description cards.

- Create two identical arrays side by side, one of term cards and one of definition and description cards.

- Players take turns flipping over pairs of cards to find a match. A match is a vocabulary term and its definition or description card. Cards keep their precise location in the array if not matched. Remaining cards are not reconfigured into a new array.

- After all cards are matched, the player with the most pairs is the winner.

Game C: Attribute Buzz

Number of players: 2

Description: Players place geometry vocabulary cards face down in a pile and, as they select cards, name the attributes of each figure within 1 minute.

- Player A flips the first card and says as many attributes as possible within 30 seconds.

- Player B says, "Buzz," when or if Player A states an incorrect attribute or time is up.

- Player B explains why the attribute is incorrect (if applicable), and can then start listing attributes about the figure for 30 seconds.

- Players score a point for each correct attribute.

Play continues until students have exhausted the figure's attributes. A new card is selected and play continues. The player with the most points at the end of the game wins.

Game D: Bingo

Number of players: 4–whole class

Materials: Bingo cards

Description: Players match definitions to terms to be the first to fill a row, column, or diagonal.

- Players write a vocabulary term in each box of the math bingo game template. Each term should be used only once. The box that says math bingo is a free space.

- Players place the filled-in math bingo template in their personal boards.

Concentration

NOTES ON
MULTIPLE MEANS OF
ENGAGEMENT:

Smaller groups of players allow for more students to participate in games simultaneously. This reduces wait time and also helps to keep students on task.

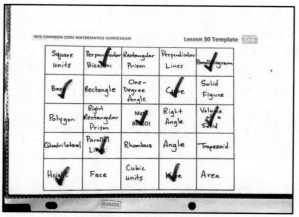

Bingo Game Example

Lesson 30:   Solidify the vocabulary of geometry.
Date: 1/31/14

6.F.49

- One person is the caller and reads the definition on a vocabulary card.
- Players cross off or cover the term that matches the definition.
- "Bingo!" is called when 5 vocabulary terms in a row are crossed off diagonally, vertically, or horizontally. The free space counts as 1 box towards the needed 5 vocabulary terms.
- The first player to have 5 in a row reads each crossed off word, states the definition, and gives a description or an example of each word. If all words are reasonably explained as determined by the caller, the player is declared the winner.

Student Debrief (10 minutes)

Lesson Objective: Solidify the vocabulary of geometry.

Invite students to review their solutions for the Problem Set. They should check work by comparing answers with a partner before going over answers as a class. Look for misconceptions or misunderstandings that can be addressed in the Debrief. Guide students in a conversation to debrief the Problem Set and process the lesson.

You may choose to use any combination of the questions below to lead the discussion.

- Which games did you choose to include in your summer activity box? Why?
- Which game did you enjoy the most? Why?
- Which game was most challenging? Why?
- How will playing these games during the summer help you prepare for Grade 6?

Reflection (3 minutes)

In G5–M6–Topic F, to close their elementary experience, the Exit Ticket is set aside and replaced by a brief opportunity to allow students to reflect on the mathematics done that day as it relates to their broader experience of math.

Attribute Buzz:

Number of players: 2

Description: Players place geometry vocabulary cards face down in a pile and, as they select cards, name the attributes of each figure within 1 minute.

- Player A flips the first card and says as many attributes as possible within 30 seconds.
- Player B says, "Buzz," when or if Player A states an incorrect attribute or time is up.
- Player B explains why the attribute is incorrect (if applicable), and can then start listing attributes about the figure for 30 seconds.
- Players score a point for each correct attribute.

Play continues until students have exhausted the figure's attributes. A new card is selected and play continues. The player with the most points at the end of the game wins.

Concentration:

Number of players: 2–6

Description: Players persevere to match term cards with their definition and description cards.

- Create two identical arrays side by side, one of term cards and one of definition and description cards.
- Players take turns flipping over pairs of cards to find a match. A match is a vocabulary term and its definition or description card. Cards keep their precise location in the array if not matched. Remaining cards are not reconfigured into a new array.
- After all cards are matched, the player with the most pairs is the winner.

Three Questions to Guess my Term!

Number of players: 2–4

Description: A player selects and secretly views a term card. Other players take turns asking yes or no questions about the term.

- Players can keep track of what they know about the term on paper.
- Only yes or no questions are allowed (e.g., "What kind of angles do you have?" is not allowed.)
- A final guess must be made after 3 questions, but may be made sooner. Once a player says, "This is my guess," no more questions may be asked by that player.
- If the term is guessed correctly after 1 or 2 questions, 2 points are earned. If all 3 questions are used, only 1 point is earned.
- If no player guesses correctly, the card holder receives the point.
- The game continues as the player to the card holder's left selects a new card and questioning begins again.
- The game ends when a player reaches a predetermined score.

Bingo:

Number of players: 4–whole class

Description: Players match definitions to terms to be the first to fill a row, column or diagonal.

- Players write a vocabulary term in each box of the math bingo game template. Each term should be used only once. The box that says Math Bingo is a free space.
- Players place the filled-in math bingo template in their personal boards.
- One person is the caller and reads the definition on a vocabulary card.
- Players cross off or cover the term that matches the definition.
- "Bingo!" is called when 5 vocabulary terms in a row are crossed off diagonally, vertically, or horizontally. The free space counts as 1 box towards the needed 5 vocabulary terms.
- The first player to have 5 in a row, reads each crossed off word, states the definition, and gives a description or an example of each word. If all words are reasonably explained as determined by the caller, the player is declared the winner.

Lesson 30:	Solidify the vocabulary of geometry.	
Date:	1/31/14	**6.F.51**

Name _____   Date _____

Playing math games can be a fun way to practice math skills. How will you use the games to retain these terms over the summer? Who will play with you? How can you change the games to play alone? How often will you play the games?

Name _____ Date _____

Teach someone at home how to play one of the games you played today with your pictorial vocabulary cards. Then answer the questions below.

1. What games did you play?

2. Who played the games with you?

3. What was it like to teach someone at home how to play?

4. Did you have to teach the person who played with you any of the math concepts before you could play? Which ones? What was that like?

5. When you play these games at home again, what changes will you make? Why?

6.F.53

		Math BINGO!		

		Math BINGO!		

Lesson 30:   Solidify the vocabulary of geometry.
Date: 1/31/14

6.F.54

Lesson 31

Objective: Explore the Fibonacci sequence.

Suggested Lesson Structure

- Application Problem   (10 minutes)
- Fluency Practice   (10 minutes)
- Concept Development   (30 minutes)
- Student Debrief   (10 minutes)

  Total Time   **(60 minutes)**

Application Problem (10 minutes)

Materials: (S) Protractor, white paper, ruler

Step 1   Draw $\overline{AB}$ 3 inches long centered near the bottom of a blank piece of paper.

Step 2   Draw $\overline{AC}$ 3 inches long, such that $\angle BAC$ measures 108°.

Step 3   Draw $\overline{CD}$ 3 inches long, such that $\angle ACD$ measures 108°.

Step 4   Draw $\overline{DE}$ 3 inches long, such that $\angle CDE$ measures 108°.

Step 5   Draw $\overline{EB}$.

Step 6   Measure $\overline{EB}$.

  T: What is the length of $\overline{EB}$?

  S: 3 inches.

  T: What shape have you drawn?

  S: Pentagon.

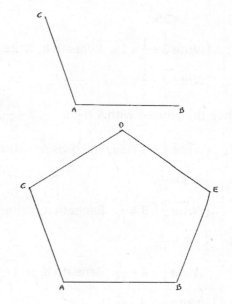

Note: Students apply their skill with angle measurement from G5–Module 5 to further explore polygons and experience the beauty and joy of geometry.

Fluency Practice (10 minutes)

- Divide Whole Numbers by Unit Fractions and Unit Fractions by Whole Numbers **5.NF.7**   (4 minutes)
- Quotients as Mixed Numbers **5.NBT.6**   (6 minutes)

NOTES ON MULTIPLE MEANS OF EXPRESSION:

Have early finishers or those enamored of drawing try to create other regular polygons by repeating other angle measures such as 60°, 90°, 120°, 135° in a similar, systematic way. Challenge them to construct triangles, squares, hexagons, and octagons. Some students simply love to draw. Challenge them to try constructing other shapes at home.

Lesson 31:   Explore the Fibonacci sequence.
Date: 1/31/14

6.F.55

Divide Whole Numbers by Unit Fractions and Unit Fractions by Whole Numbers (4 minutes)

Materials: (S) Personal white boards

Note: This fluency activity reviews G5–Module 4 concepts.

T: (Write $2 \div \frac{1}{5}$.) Say the division sentence.

S: $2 \div \frac{1}{5} = 10$.

T: (Write $2 \div \frac{1}{5} = 10$. Beneath it, write $3 \div \frac{1}{5}$.) Say the division sentence.

S: $3 \div \frac{1}{5} = 15$.

T: (Write $3 \div \frac{1}{5} = 15$. Beneath it, write $7 \div \frac{1}{5}$.) On your boards, complete the division sentence.

S: (Write $7 \div \frac{1}{5} = 35$.)

Continue the process with $4 \div \frac{1}{4}$, $8 \div \frac{1}{3}$, $1 \div \frac{1}{10}$, $2 \div \frac{1}{10}$, $9 \div \frac{1}{10}$, and $10 \div \frac{1}{10}$.

T: (Write $\frac{1}{5} \div 3$.) Say the division sentence.

S: $\frac{1}{5} \div 3 = \frac{1}{15}$.

T: (Write $\frac{1}{5} \div 3 = \frac{1}{15}$. Beneath it, write $\frac{1}{4} \div 4$.) Say the division sentence.

S: $\frac{1}{4} \div 4 = \frac{1}{16}$.

T: (Write $\frac{1}{4} \div 4 = \frac{1}{16}$. Beneath it, write $\frac{1}{8} \div 6$.) On your boards, write the division sentence.

S: (Write $\frac{1}{8} \div 6 = \frac{1}{48}$.)

T: (Write $\frac{1}{6} \div 3$.) Say the division sentence.

S: $\frac{1}{6} \div 3 = \frac{1}{18}$.

Continue the process with $9 \div \frac{1}{4}$, $\frac{1}{4} \div 9$, $5 \div \frac{1}{8}$, $\frac{1}{8} \div 5$, $\frac{1}{6} \div 9$, and $8 \div \frac{1}{9}$.

Quotients as Mixed Numbers (6 minutes)

Materials: (S) Personal white board, calculator

Note: This fluency activity reviews G5–Module 2 content and directly leads into today's lesson where students use a calculator to find quotients in order to see patterns.

T: (Write $\frac{61}{19}$.) On your boards, demonstrate how to estimate the quotient.

$$19\overline{)61} \quad \begin{array}{r} 3\frac{4}{19} \\ \hline 61 \\ 57 \\ \hline 4 \end{array} \qquad \left(3 \times 19\right) + 4 = 61$$

S: (Write $\frac{60}{20} = 3$.)

T: Solve. Express the quotient as a mixed number.

T: Check the answer.

S: (Solve and check as exemplified in the illustration.)

Repeat the process using the following possible sequence: 79 ÷ 22 and 97 ÷ 31.

Concept Development (30 minutes)

Materials: (T) Collection of pine cones, flowers, "Doodling in Math: Spirals, Fibonacci, and Being a Plant" by
             Vi Hart (http://youtu.be/ahXIMUkSXX0) (S) Problem Set, red crayon, ruler or straightedge,
             calculator per student or pair

Note: The Problem Set will be used for the construction of the Fibonacci spiral in today's lesson.

Part 1: Construct a spiral of squares on grid paper.

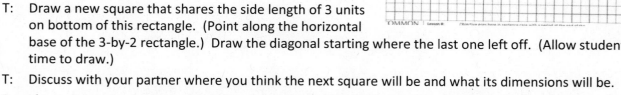

T: (Distribute Problem Set [grid paper with grey square].) Let's create a beautiful pattern of squares.
     Draw another square that shares a side length above the
     grey square. (Allow students time to draw.)

T: Draw a diagonal across the first square from the bottom,
     left to the top right vertex. Next, draw a diagonal across
     your new square from the bottom, right to the top left
     vertex. (Allow students time to draw.)

T: This 2 by 1 rectangle has a longer side length of…?

S: 2 units.

T: Draw a new square that shares the side length of 2 units
     on the left of this rectangle. (Point up and down the left
     vertical side length of the 2 by 1 rectangle. Allow
     students time to draw.)

T: Draw a diagonal across your new 2-by-2 square starting
     where the last one left off—at the top right vertex and
     going to the bottom left vertex. (Allow students time to
     draw.)

T: What is the length of the longer side of this rectangle
     that we've now drawn?

S: 3 units.

T: Draw a new square that shares the side length of 3 units
     on bottom of this rectangle. (Point along the horizontal
     base of the 3-by-2 rectangle.) Draw the diagonal starting where the last one left off. (Allow students
     time to draw.)

T: Discuss with your partner where you think the next square will be and what its dimensions will be.

S: I know it is going to start where the diagonal left off. → That is the side length of the 5-by-3

| Lesson 31: | Explore the Fibonacci sequence. |
| Date: | 1/31/14 |

6.F.57

rectangle it will share, so the new square is going to be 5 by 5. → Its side length is found by adding 3 + 2 = 5. → The side length of the new square is going to be the sum of the last two squares' side lengths.

T: Yes, it is going to the right. Go ahead and draw your new square and its diagonal.

S: (Draw.)

Continue through the squares, supporting as necessary. Many students will see the pattern and be able to work in partners or independently. It is suggested that students use rulers to draw the diagonals starting with the 8-by-8 square.

Part 2: Analyze the sequence of a square's dimensions to generate the Fibonacci sequence.

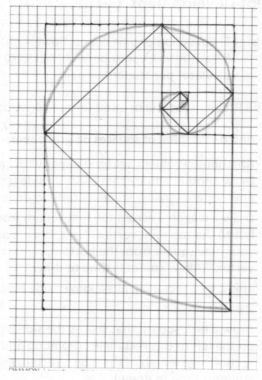

T: Below your grid, write down the sequence of side lengths of the squares. Work with your partner to see if you can figure out what the next numbers in the sequence would be if we had a really large piece of graph paper.

S: (Write and talk.) 1, 1, 2, 3, 5, 8, 13, 21, 34, 55, 89, 144, 233, 377, 610, 987….

T: Stop. Check your sequence with another pair and explain your thinking.

S: We realized that the sum of the last two side lengths was the new length. → The next number in the pattern was the sum of the two numbers right before it in the pattern.

T: This pattern is called the Fibonacci sequence.

T: Do you see the spiral you started to draw formed by the diagonals? Let's round that out a bit more so that the lines are no longer straight. Use a red crayon. (Model as shown to the right.)

T: What would happen to this spiral if we continued our sequence?

Part 3: Watch a short video on the Fibonacci sequence, at http://youtu.be/ahXIMUkSXX0.

Have students discuss the video and analyze any pine cones, flowers, or materials brought to the session, counting the spirals and looking for patterns.

Lesson 31:   Explore the Fibonacci sequence.
Date: 1/31/14

6.F.58

Student Debrief (10 minutes)

Lesson Objective: Explore the Fibonacci sequence.

The Student Debrief is intended to invite reflection and active processing of the total lesson experience.

Invite students to review their solutions for the Problem Set. They should check work by comparing answers with a partner before going over answers as a class. Look for misconceptions or misunderstandings that can be addressed in the Debrief. Guide students in a conversation to debrief the Problem Set and process the lesson.

You may choose to use any combination of the questions below to lead the discussion.

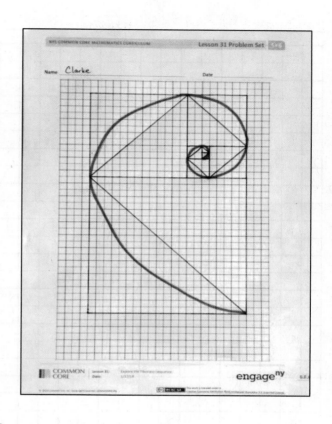

- The numerical sequence we studied today is called the Fibonacci sequence. Summarize to your partner the rule that generated the sequence.

- Do you remember the first few Fibonacci numbers? Try to tell the sequence to a partner.

- What surprised you most when you looked at the video?

- If you have access to the Internet, you can find a lot of interesting material about the Fibonacci numbers found in art and nature. What other questions do you still have about the Fibonacci numbers?

- Compare drawing the pentagon earlier and drawing the spiral using the Fibonacci sequence.

Reflection (3 minutes)

In G5–M6–Topic F, to close their elementary experience, the Exit Ticket is set aside and replaced by a brief opportunity to reflect on the mathematics done that day as it relates to the students' broader experience of math.

**NOTES ON
MULTIPLE MEANS OF
REPRESENTATION:**

Students can make art based on the spiral such as the simple design below. They can use the art to decorate the summer boxes they create in G5–M6–Lessons 33–34.

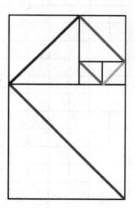

| Lesson 31: | Explore the Fibonacci sequence. |
| Date: | 1/31/14 |

6.F.59

Name _____   Date _____

Lesson 31:   Explore the Fibonacci sequence.
Date: 1/31/14

6.F.60

Name _____   Date _____

Today when we saw a video on the Fibonacci sequence in the spiral and in nature it may have felt a bit like "math magic." Have you ever felt math magic in your elementary school years? If so, when did you experience it? If not, did you experience it today? Explain.

Name _____   Date _____

1. List the Fibonacci numbers up to 21, and create a spiral of squares corresponding to each of the numbers you write on the graph paper below.

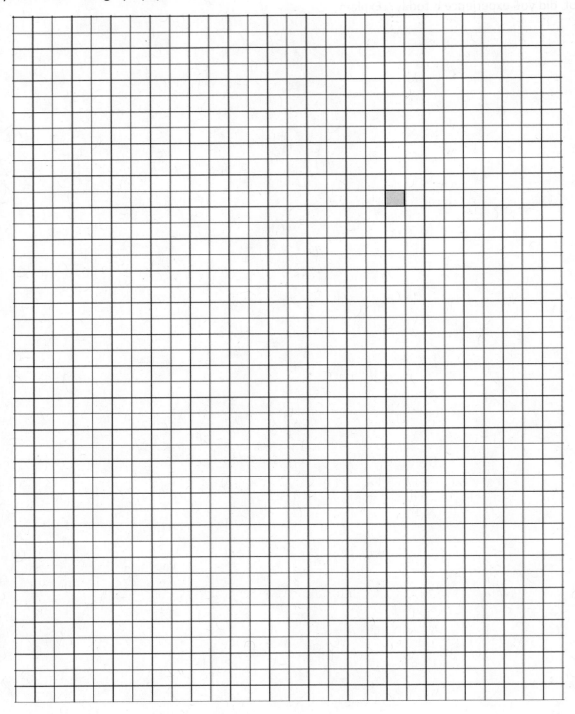

Lesson 31:   Explore the Fibonacci sequence.
Date: 1/31/14

6.F.62

2. In the space below, write a rule that generates the Fibonacci sequence.

3. Write at least the first 15 numbers of the Fibonacci sequence.

COMMON CORE™

Lesson 31:   Explore the Fibonacci sequence.
Date: 1/31/14

6.F.63

Lesson 32

Objective: **Explore patterns in saving money.**

Suggested Lesson Structure

■ Fluency Practice   (12 minutes)
■ Application Problem   (6 minutes)
■ Concept Development   (32 minutes)
■ Student Debrief   (10 minutes)

   Total Time   **(60 minutes)**

Fluency Practice (12 minutes)

- Multiply **5.NBT.5**   (4 minutes)
- Quotients as Mixed Numbers **5.NBT.6**   (4 minutes)
- The Fibonacci Sequence **5.NBT.7**   (4 minutes)

Multiply (4 minutes)

Materials: (S) Personal white boards

Note: This fluency activity reviews year-long fluency standards.

   T: (Write 6 tens 8 ones × 4 ten 3 ones = ___ × ___ = ___.) Write the multiplication sentence in standard
        form.
   S: (Write 68 × 43 = ___.)
   T: Solve 68 × 43 using the standard algorithm.
   S: (Write 68 × 43 = 2,924 using the standard algorithm.)

Continue the process for 368 × 43, 76 × 54, 876 × 54, and 978 × 86.

Quotients as Mixed Numbers (4 minutes)

Materials: (S) Personal white boards, calculator

Note: This fluency activity reviews G5–Module 2 content and directly leads into today's lesson, in which
students use calculators to find quotients and uncover patterns.

   T: (Write $\frac{87}{31}$.) On your boards, demonstrate how to estimate the quotient.

S: (Write $\frac{90}{30} = 3$.)

T: Solve. Express the quotient as a mixed number.

T: Check the answer.

S: (Solve and check as shown to the right.)

$$31\overline{)87} \quad 2\frac{25}{31}$$
$$-62$$
$$\ \ 25$$

$(2 \times 31) + 25 = 87$

Repeat the process using the following possible sequence: $82 \div 23$ and $95 \div 27$.

The Fibonacci Sequence (4 minutes)

Materials: (S) Personal white boards

Note: This fluency activity reviews G5–M6–Lesson 31 and leads into today's lesson.

T: For 90 seconds, write as many numbers in the Fibonacci sequence as you can. Take your mark, get set, go.

S: (Write.)

T: Stop! Check your sequence with a partner for one minute.

S: (Check.)

T: Write down the last number you wrote at the top of your board. Now, see if you can get farther than you did before. Take 90 seconds to write the sequence again. Take your mark, get set, go!

S: (Write.)

T: Raise your hand if you were able to write more numbers in the sequence this time.

Application Problem (6 minutes)

Look at the Fibonacci sequence you just wrote. Analyze which numbers are even. Is there a pattern to the even numbers? Why? Think about the spiral of squares that you made yesterday.

Note: This Application Problem allows students the opportunity to analyze the sequence further.

Concept Development (32 minutes)

Materials: (T/S) Problem Set

Note: Today's Problem Set is completed during instruction.

Problem 1: Ashley decides to save money, but she wants to build it up over a year. She starts with $1.00 and adds 1 more dollar each week. Complete the table to show how much she will have saved after a year.

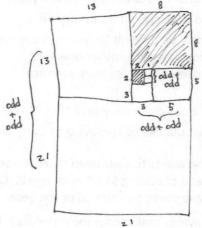

Lesson 32:   Explore patterns in saving money.
Date: 1/31/14

6.F.65

T: Let's read the problem together.

Read the problem chorally, or select a student to read the problem.

T: This is an interesting strategy for saving money. Have you ever tried to save money toward a goal?

S: Yes, but not with a number pattern. → My parents pay for everything. → No, but I want to try.

T: Work with a partner to fill in the table. When you are finished, answer the question at the top.

Circulate as students work. Ensure students participate equally and that each fill in their own tables. Have students who finish early check their numbers with other pairs.

NOTES ON MULTIPLE MEANS OF ENGAGEMENT:

Some students may not have a realistic sense of what this amount of money can buy. Take the opportunity to discuss the cost of a car, for example, if that is one that comes up. If the class has Internet access, show or assign students to look prices up online.

T: How much will Ashley have saved?

S: $1,378!

T: Are you surprised? That seems like a lot of money, doesn't it? What are some things Ashley could do with her savings?

S: She could buy a computer. → She could go to Disney World. → She could save it up to help with college.

T: Let's see what happens in this next situation where Carly saves a little less at a time.

Problem 2: Carly wants to save money too, but she has to start with the smaller denomination of quarters. Complete the second chart to show how much she will have saved by the end of the year if she adds a quarter more each week.

Have students complete the table as in Problem 1. When they have finished working, ask questions such as those suggested below:

- Do you think it's worth it to save $344.50 in a year?
- What would you do if you saved that money?
- At what point might it be difficult for you to increase the daily amount you save by another quarter? (Amount of allowance and money they earn are possible limitations.)
- How much more money did Ashley save than Carly?
- How many of you would like to try saving as Carly did?

NOTES ON MULTIPLE MEANS OF EXPRESSION:

As students see varied growth patterns related to saving money, their number sense is supported. To expedite Problem 3, have students use a calculator. This will allow them to get to the finish line more quickly and compare the results of the three options of increasing the amount saved.

Problem 3: David decides he wants to save even more money than Ashley did. He does so by adding the next Fibonacci number instead of adding $1.00 each week. Use your calculator to fill in the chart and find out how much money he will have saved by the end of the year.

T: Is this amount of savings realistic for most people? Explain your answer.

If students are unable to finish this page, they may pack the charts into their summer boxes to finish later and to motivate their personal savings program.

Student Debrief (10 minutes)

Lesson Objective: Explore patterns in saving money.

The Student Debrief is intended to invite reflection and active processing of the total lesson experience.

Invite students to review their solutions for the Problem Set. They should check work by comparing answers with a partner before going over answers as a class. Look for misconceptions or misunderstandings that can be addressed in the Debrief. Guide students in a conversation to debrief the Problem Set and process the lesson.

You may choose to use any combination of the questions below to lead the discussion.

- Why were the differences between the three totals so extreme?

- Which pattern is most realistic for fifth-grade students to do?

- What changes might you have to make in order to save like Carly did?

- Why is David's approach not realistic for most people?

- What pattern did you notice between the total amount David has saved and the Fibonacci numbers?

- At which point did you have to start using a calculator to figure out David's money?

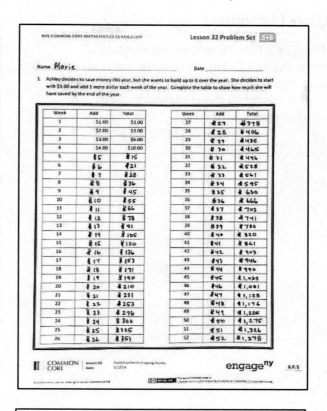

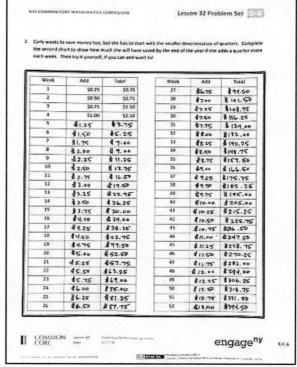

Lesson 32:   Explore patterns in saving money.
Date: 1/31/14

6.F.67

Reflection (3 minutes)

In G5–M6–Topic F, to close their elementary experience, the Exit Ticket is set aside and replaced by a brief opportunity to reflect on the mathematics done that day as it relates to the students' broader experience of math.

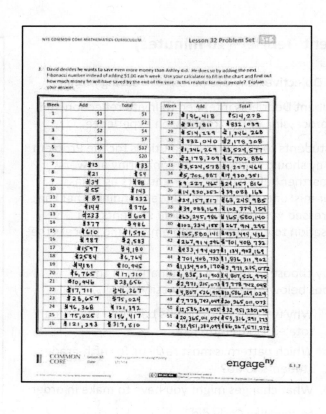

Name _____   Date _____

1. Ashley decides to save money this year, but she wants to build it up over the year. She decides to start with $1.00 and add 1 more dollar each week of the year. Complete the table to show how much she will have saved by the end of the year.

Week	Add	Total
1	$1.00	$1.00
2	$2.00	$3.00
3	$3.00	$6.00
4	$4.00	$10.00
5		
6		
7		
8		
9		
10		
11		
12		
13		
14		
15		
16		
17		
18		
19		
20		
21		
22		
23		
24		
25		
26		

Week	Add	Total
27		
28		
29		
30		
31		
32		
33		
34		
35		
36		
37		
38		
39		
40		
41		
42		
43		
44		
45		
46		
47		
48		
49		
50		
51		
52		

COMMON CORE™

Lesson 32:   Explore patterns in saving money.
Date: 1/31/14

6.F.69

2. Carly wants to save money too, but she has to start with the smaller denomination of quarters. Complete the second chart to show how much she will have saved by the end of the year if she adds a quarter more each week. Try it yourself, if you can and want to!

Week	Add	Total		Week	Add	Total
1	$0.25	$0.25		27		
2	$0.50	$0.75		28		
3	$0.75	$1.50		29		
4	$1.00	$2.50		30		
5				31		
6				32		
7				33		
8				34		
9				35		
10				36		
11				37		
12				38		
13				39		
14				40		
15				41		
16				42		
17				43		
18				44		
19				45		
20				46		
21				47		
22				48		
23				49		
24				50		
25				51		
26				52		

Lesson 32:   Explore patterns in saving money.
Date: 1/31/14

6.F.70

3. David decides he wants to save even more money than Ashley did. He does so by adding the next Fibonacci number instead of adding $1.00 each week. Use your calculator to fill in the chart and find out how much money he will have saved by the end of the year. Is this realistic for most people? Explain your answer.

Week	Add	Total	Week	Add	Total
1	$1	$1	27		
2	$1	$2	28		
3	$2	$4	29		
4	$3	$7	30		
5	$5	$12	31		
6	$8	$20	32		
7			33		
8			34		
9			35		
10			36		
11			37		
12			38		
13			39		
14			40		
15			41		
16			42		
17			43		
18			44		
19			45		
20			46		
21			47		
22			48		
23			49		
24			50		
25			51		
26			52		

Name _____   Date _____

Today, we watched how savings can grow over time, but we didn't discuss how the money saved was earned. Have you ever thought about how math skills might help you to earn money?   If so, what are some jobs that might require strong math skills? If not, think about it now. How might you make a living using math skills?

Name _____ Date _____

1. Jonas played with the Fibonacci sequence he learned in class. Complete the table he started.

1	2	3	4	5	6	7	8	9	10
1	1	2	3	5	8				

11	12	13	14	15	16	17	18	19	20

2. As he looked at the numbers, Jonas realized he could play with them. He took two consecutive numbers in the pattern and multiplied them by themselves, then added them together. He found they made another number in the pattern. For example, $(3 \times 3) + (2 \times 2) = 13$, another number in the pattern. Jonas said this was true for any two consecutive Fibonacci numbers. Was Jonas correct? Show your reasoning by giving at least two examples of why he was or was not correct.

3. Fibonacci numbers can be found in many places in nature. For example, the number of petals in a daisy, the number of spirals in a pine cone or a pineapple, and even the way branches grow on a tree. Find an example of something natural where you can see a Fibonacci number in action and sketch it here.

COMMON CORE™

Lesson 32: Explore patterns in saving money.
Date: 1/31/14

6.F.73

Lesson 33

Objective: Design and construct boxes to house materials for summer use.

Suggested Lesson Structure

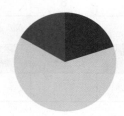

- ■ Fluency Practice   (12 minutes)
- ■ Concept Development   (38 minutes)
- ■ Student Debrief   (10 minutes)
- **Total Time**   **(60 minutes)**

Fluency Practice (12 minutes)

- ▪ Sprint: Divide Decimals **5.NBT.7**   (9 minutes)
- ▪ Find the Volume **5.MD.3**   (3 minutes)

Sprint: Divide Decimals (9 minutes)

Materials: (S) Divide Decimals Sprint

Note: This Sprint reviews G5–Module 4 concepts.

Find the Volume (3 minutes)

Materials: (S) Personal white boards

Note: This fluency activity reviews G5–Lesson 5.

- T: On your boards, write the formula for finding
       the volume of a rectangular prism.
- S: (Write $V = l \times w \times h$.)
- T: (Write $V = l \times w \times h$. Project rectangular prism
       with a length of 5 cm, width of 2 cm, and
       height of 3 cm. Point to the length.) Say the
       length.
- S: 5 cm.
- T: (Point to the width.) Say the width.
- S: 2 cm.
- T: (Point to the height.) Say the height.
- S: 3 cm.

**NOTES ON
MULTIPLE MEANS OF
ENGAGEMENT:**

Have four different students call out
the solutions to the Sprint, one
quadrant at a time or have all students
call out the solutions to the problems.
As the end of the year is approaching,
let the students release some energy
during the Sprint! In this way,
excitement and academics become
associated.

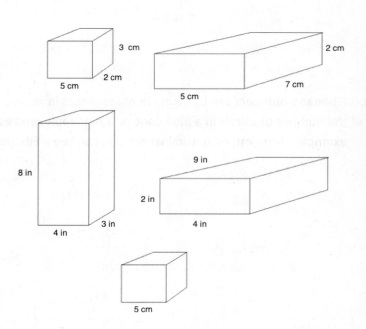

T: On your boards, write a multiplication sentence to express the volume of the rectangular prism.

S: (Beneath V = l × w × h, write V = 5 cm × 2 cm × 3 cm.   Beneath it, write V = 30 cm³.)

Continue the process for other rectangular prisms.

T: (Project cube with side lengths equal to 5 cm.)   Name the prism.

S: Cube.

T: What's the length of the each side of the cube?

S: 5 cm.

T: On your boards, write a multiplication sentence to show the volume of the cube.

S: (Write V = 5 cm × 5 cm × 5 cm.   Beneath it, write V = 125 cm³.)

Concept Development   (38 minutes)

Materials: (S) Problem Set, 3 pieces of 8½" × 11" cardstock paper trimmed to 27 cm by 21 cm, scissors, tape, ruler, summer practice materials

Note: In this lesson the time for the Application Problem has been allocated to the Concept Development.

Part 1: Establish the criteria for the boxes, and model constructing Box 1.

T: Today you'll put your math sense and geometric skills to work as you design and create two different size boxes and one lid to house your summer fluency materials.   These are the criteria:

- Boxes must store all summer materials.
- Box 1's base must measure 19 cm by 13 cm.
- Box 2 must fit inside Box 1 when Box 1 is closed.
- The lid for Box 1 must fit snugly to protect the contents.

T: (Distribute one piece of card stock.)   Here is the paper you will use to make Box 1.   What are its measurements?   (Allow students time to measure.)

S: 21 centimeters by 27 centimeters.

T: Talk to your partner.   Since the base of Box 1 is 19 centimeters by 13 centimeters, what does that mean about the height of Box 1?

Sample Base

S: The height has to be the same all the way around the base or the sides won't match up. → If the sides are 3 centimeters high that means adding 6 centimeters to 19 centimeters and 6 centimeters to 13 centimeters. I would have to trim off some paper. → If you make the height of the sides 4 centimeters, it works perfectly; 19 + (2 × 4) = 27 and 13 + (2 × 4) = 21.

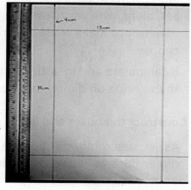

T: By making the height of the box 4 centimeters, the measurements do work out perfectly.   Watch as I model the four steps to make Box 1.   (Consider posting the steps.)

Step 1   Measure and mark two points 4 centimeters in from the edge on each side.

Step 2   Connect those marked points to draw the lines of the 19 cm × 13 cm base. (Shown on the previous page.)

Step 3   Cut out the small rectangles in each corner.

Step 4   Fold up the sides and tape the corners together.

Part 2: Determine the dimensions of Box 2 and the lid.

Distribute the Problem Set, rulers, and the other pieces of cardstock.

T: You'll decide on the exact dimensions of Box 2 and the lid for Box 1. What will you use to guide your decisions?

S: First, I'll think about the materials that have to go inside. → I'll think about making Box 2 fit inside of Box 1. → Box 2 can't be taller than Box 1 if the lid is going to fit. → The lid has to be just a tiny bit longer than Box 1 so it fits nicely.

T: To complete the project, you each will receive three 27 centimeter by 21 centimeter pieces of cardstock, one to make Box 1, one to make its lid, and one more to make Box 2. After you fold the edges of the cardstock to make the box or lid, will the inner dimensions still be 27 by 23 centimeters?

S: No, they'll be smaller than that.

T: Take a moment to talk with your partner about how the different sizes of your summer materials will influence the dimensions of Box 2.

S: We have Problem Sets, which are pretty big, and fluency cards and vocabulary cards that are smaller. → We might want the vocabulary cards to go in Box 2. → Problem Sets can still go at the bottom of the bigger box, and smaller things can go in the smaller box.

MP.1

T: Use a ruler to measure your summer practice materials and decide how you'll store them. Will they be rolled, folded, or flat? Then, decide on reasonable whole number dimensions for Box 2.

NOTES ON MULTIPLE MEANS OF ENGAGEMENT:

T: In order to make the lid fit snugly, you'll need to make it only slightly larger than the box. Record the dimensions of each box and the lid on your Problem Set, along with your reasoning about why those dimensions make sense. Work with a partner if you choose.

Some students will benefit from loosely folding the boxes into shape to find dimensions. It may be helpful to have scratch paper at the ready for visual and kinesthetic learners who prefer to manipulate in this way as they work. Also consider having more than enough paper on hand for the inevitable do-overs.

S: (Manipulate and measure summer practice materials, then decide on dimensions and record.)

Part 3: Construct the boxes and lid.

T: As you assemble your boxes and lid, if you find that you need to make adjustments to the dimensions as you work, record your updated thinking in the space remaining on your Problem Set, or on a separate sheet of paper.

S: (Draw dimensions and assemble boxes and lids, making adjustments to each if needed.)

COMMON CORE™

Lesson 33:   Design and construct boxes to house materials for summer use.
Date: 1/31/14

6.F.76

Have students decorate and personalize their boxes with designs that show what concepts they have learned in math this year. They will have some time to complete their designs and place their summer practice materials inside the boxes during G5–M6–Lesson 34.

Sample Folded Box 1 and Lid

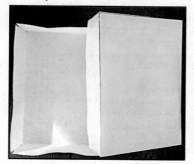

Sample Box 2 Inside of Box 1

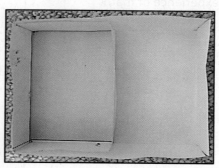

Student Debrief (10 minutes)

Lesson Objective: Design and construct boxes to house materials for summer use.

The Student Debrief is intended to invite reflection and active processing of the total lesson experience.

Invite students to review their solutions for the Problem Set. They should check work by comparing answers with a partner before going over answers as a class. Look for misconceptions or misunderstandings that can be addressed in the Debrief. Guide students in a conversation to debrief the Problem Set and process the lesson. You may choose to use any combination of the questions below to lead the discussion.

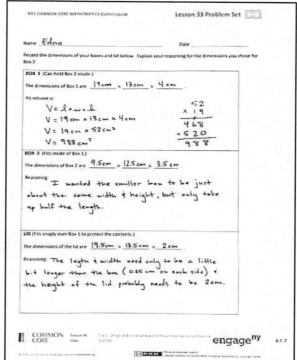

- What were the most important factors to consider as you decided on the dimensions of your boxes? Why did those things matter so much?

- To design these boxes we considered the materials that they would store. What specifically did we take into account? Volume, area, length, width, height? When would it be appropriate to consider other properties?

- What boxes do you see that have been designed for a specific purpose? What are some of the choices that were made to best serve that purpose?

- What was your biggest challenge in designing your boxes? Explain.

Reflection (3 minutes)

In G5–M6–Topic F, to close their elementary experience, the Exit Ticket is set aside and replaced by a brief opportunity to reflect on the mathematics done that day as it relates to their broader experience of math.

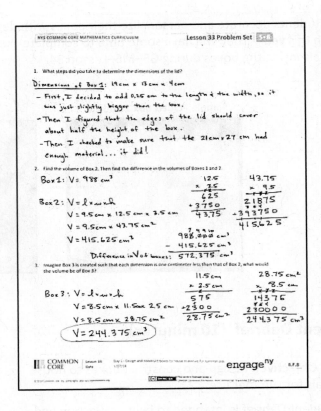

A

Divide.

Correct _____

1	$1 \div 1 =$		23	$5 \div 0.1 =$	
2	$1 \div 0.1 =$		24	$0.5 \div 0.1 =$	
3	$2 \div 0.1 =$		25	$0.05 \div 0.1 =$	
4	$7 \div 0.1 =$		26	$0.08 \div 0.1 =$	
5	$1 \div 0.1 =$		27	$4 \div 0.01 =$	
6	$10 \div 0.1 =$		28	$40 \div 0.01 =$	
7	$20 \div 0.1 =$		29	$47 \div 0.01 =$	
8	$60 \div 0.1 =$		30	$59 \div 0.01 =$	
9	$1 \div 1 =$		31	$3 \div 0.1 =$	
10	$1 \div 0.1 =$		32	$30 \div 0.1 =$	
11	$10 \div 0.1 =$		33	$32 \div 0.1 =$	
12	$100 \div 0.1 =$		34	$32.5 \div 0.1 =$	
13	$200 \div 0.1 =$		35	$25 \div 5 =$	
14	$800 \div 0.1 =$		36	$2.5 \div 0.5 =$	
15	$1 \div 0.1 =$		37	$2.5 \div 0.05 =$	
16	$1 \div 0.01 =$		38	$3.6 \div 0.04 =$	
17	$2 \div 0.01 =$		39	$32 \div 0.08 =$	
18	$9 \div 0.01 =$		40	$56 \div 0.7 =$	
19	$5 \div 0.01 =$		41	$77 \div 1.1 =$	
20	$50 \div 0.01 =$		42	$4.8 \div 0.12 =$	
21	$60 \div 0.01 =$		43	$4.84 \div 0.4 =$	
22	$20 \div 0.01 =$		44	$9.63 \div 0.03 =$	

COMMON CORE

Lesson 33: Design and construct boxes to house materials for summer use.
Date: 1/31/14

6.F.79

B

Improvement _____   # Correct _____

Divide.

#	Problem		#	Problem	
1	10 ÷ 1 =		23	4 ÷ 0.1 =	
2	1 ÷ 0.1 =		24	0.4 ÷ 0.1 =	
3	2 ÷ 0.1 =		25	0.04 ÷ 0.1 =	
4	8 ÷ 0.1 =		26	0.07 ÷ 0.1 =	
5	1 ÷ 0.1 =		27	5 ÷ 0.01 =	
6	10 ÷ 0.1 =		28	50 ÷ 0.01 =	
7	20 ÷ 0.1 =		29	53 ÷ 0.01 =	
8	70 ÷ 0.1 =		30	68 ÷ 0.01 =	
9	1 ÷ 1 =		31	2 ÷ 0.1 =	
10	1 ÷ 0.1 =		32	20 ÷ 0.1 =	
11	10 ÷ 0.1 =		33	23 ÷ 0.1 =	
12	100 ÷ 0.1 =		34	23.6 ÷ 0.1 =	
13	200 ÷ 0.1 =		35	15 ÷ 5 =	
14	900 ÷ 0.1 =		36	1.5 ÷ 0.5 =	
15	1 ÷ 0.1 =		37	1.5 ÷ 0.05 =	
16	1 ÷ 0.01 =		38	3.2 ÷ 0.04 =	
17	2 ÷ 0.01 =		39	28 ÷ 0.07 =	
18	7 ÷ 0.01 =		40	42 ÷ 0.6 =	
19	4 ÷ 0.01 =		41	88 ÷ 1.1 =	
20	40 ÷ 0.01 =		42	3.6 ÷ 0.12 =	
21	50 ÷ 0.01 =		43	3.63 ÷ 0.3 =	
22	80 ÷ 0.01 =		44	8.44 ÷ 0.04 =	

Lesson 33:   Design and construct boxes to house materials for summer use.
Date: 1/31/14

6.F.8

Name _____   Date _____

Record the dimensions of your boxes and lid below. Explain your reasoning for the dimensions you chose for Box 2.

BOX 1 (Can hold Box 2 inside.)

The dimensions of Box 1 are _____ × _____ × _____ .

Its volume is _____ .

BOX 2 (Fits inside of Box 1.)

The dimensions of Box 2 are _____ × _____ × _____ .

Reasoning:

LID (Fits snugly over Box 1 to protect the contents.)

The dimensions of the lid are _____ × _____ × _____ .

Reasoning:

1. What steps did you take to determine the dimensions of the lid?

2. Find the volume of Box 2. Then, find the difference in the volumes of Boxes 1 and 2.

3. Imagine Box 3 is created such that each dimension is 1 cm less than that of Box 2, what would the volume of Box 3 be?

 Lesson 33:   Design and construct boxes to house materials for summer use.
Date: 1/31/14

6.F.8

Name _____   Date _____

Today you made a box for a special purpose. It shows one way that math is used all the time to create containers. When might there be other opportunities for you to use the math you have learned in elementary school?

Name _____   Date _____

1. Find various rectangular boxes at your home. Use a ruler to measure the dimensions of each box to the nearest centimeter. Then, calculate the volume of each box. The first one has been done for you.

Item	Length	Width	Height	Volume
Juice Box	11 cm	2 cm	5 cm	

2. The dimensions of a small juice box are 11 cm by 4 cm by 7 cm. The super-size juice box has the same height of 11 cm, but double the volume. Give two sets of the possible dimensions of the super-size juice box and the volume.

Lesson 34

Objective: Design and construct boxes to house materials for summer use.

Suggested Lesson Structure

■ Fluency Practice   (12 minutes)
■ Application Problem   (5 minutes)
■ Concept Development   (33 minutes)
■ Student Debrief   (10 minutes)
   Total Time   **(60 minutes)**

Fluency Practice (12 minutes)

- Multiply **5.NBT.5**   (4 minutes)
- Divide by Two-Digit Numbers **5.NBT.6**   (4 minutes)
- Find the Volume **5.MD.5**   (4 minutes)

Multiply (4 minutes)

Materials: (S) Personal white boards

Note: This drill reviews year-long fluency standards.

  T: Solve 97 × 64 using the standard algorithm.

  S: (Write 97 × 64 = 6,208 using the standard algorithm.)

Continue the process for 897 × 64, 89 × 67, 789 × 67, and 698 × 86.

Divide by Two-Digit Numbers (4 minutes)

Materials: (S) Personal white boards

Note: This fluency activity reviews content from G5–Modules 2 and 4.

  T: (Write $\frac{163}{12}$.) Write the quotient as a mixed number.

  S: (Write $\frac{163}{12} = 13\frac{7}{12}$.)

Repeat the process from G5–M2–Lesson 21 for the following possible sequence: $\frac{278}{51}$ and $\frac{741}{23}$.

NOTES ON MULTIPLE MEANS OF EXPRESSION:

Rather than dictate a solution strategy for the calculation, allow students to choose to use a mental strategy or the algorithm. Students might solve $\frac{163}{12}$ by adding another 12 to 12 twelves, and finding 7 more is needed to get to 163. Likewise there are 5 fifty-ones in 255 with 23 more needed to get to 278.

Lesson 34:	Design and construct boxes to house materials for summer use.
Date:	1/31/14

6.F.85

Find the Volume (4 minutes)

Materials: (S) Personal white boards

Note: This fluency activity reviews G5–Module 5 content.

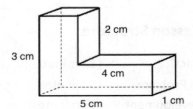

- T: Say the formula for finding the volume of a rectangular prism.
- S: Length times width times height.
- T: (Project composite figure.) Sketch the composite figure.
- S: (Sketch.)
- T: Draw a line that breaks the figure into 2 rectangular prisms.
- S: (Draw line..)
- T: Find the volume of the composite figure by adding the volumes of each rectangular prism.
- S: (Write 3 cm × 1 cm × 1 cm = 3 cubic cm. 4 cm × 1 cm × 1 cm = 4 cubic cm. 3 cubic cm + 4 cubic cm = 7 cubic cm.)

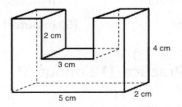

Continue the process for the other composite figure.

Application Problem (5 minutes)

Steven is a _____ who had \$280. He spent $\frac{1}{4}$ of his money on a _____ and $\frac{5}{6}$ of the remainder on a _____. How much money did he spend altogether?

Note: As this is the last day of lessons, you might bring some humor into the word problem by having students determine Steven's identity and the items purchased using a science fiction, futuristic, or fantastical setting.

Concept Development (33 minutes)

Materials: (S) Rulers, Problem Set (same page printed on 2 sides), G5–M6–Lesson 33 Problem Set

Begin by giving students time to assemble the notes and tools they created in G5–M6–Topic F lessons in their boxes. You might also want to give time for finishing designs or personalizing touches started in G5–M6–Lesson 33. Remind students that these are boxes of resources they can use to practice Grade 5 skills over the summer. In this lesson, their boxes will be evaluated to see how well they house the materials and meet the criteria below.

- ▪   Boxes must store all summer materials.
- ▪   Box 1's base must measure 19 cm by 13 cm.
- ▪   Box 2 must fit inside Box 1 when Box 1 is closed.
- ▪   The lid for Box 1 must fit snugly to protect the contents.

T: (Divide the class into groups of four students.) Your job today is to evaluate your group members' boxes to assess how well their materials fit inside.

T: Each student will review two other group members' boxes. Take a moment to decide with your group who will review which boxes.

S: (Divide the review work.)

Distribute the Problem Set.

T: Use a ruler to measure the dimensions of your friend's boxes and lid, and then calculate the volume of the boxes. You'll record that information on the Problem Set, and then assess the suitability of the boxes for the job of storing summer materials. What things will you look for to decide whether the box is suitable?

S: We can see how organized the materials are in the boxes. → If the materials stick out or get squished inside, then Box 2 may not have been thought out well. → We could check to see if the lids are tight enough to stay on and keep everything safe inside.

T: In the final column, you're asked to make suggestions for improvement of each box or lid. Be as specific as possible. For example, rather than saying, "The lid should be smaller," you might make a comment like, "The width of the lid should be 3 tenths centimeter smaller so that it fits more snugly."

S: (Evaluate one another's work.)

T: Debrief your evaluation with the creator of the boxes and lid. Work together to compare your measurements with the ones they recorded on their G5–M6–Lesson 33 Problem Set. Then, discuss the points you made about suitability and improvements. If your suggestions are easily implemented, go ahead and make adjustments together.

S: (Debrief evaluations together.)

> **NOTES ON MULTIPLE MEANS OF ENGAGEMENT:**
>
> Students may react differently to having their work critiqued. Therefore, it is important to discuss with students what types of comments or critiques are appropriate for their evaluation. Students might benefit from working as a class to develop a list of specific characteristics which should be commented upon.

Mixed Review Fluency Activities

If time permits after students evaluate their two boxes, invite them to play the games from G5–M6–Lesson 28 again in groups using the materials inside their boxes.

Student Debrief (10 minutes)

Lesson Objective: Design and construct boxes to house materials for summer use.

The Student Debrief is intended to invite reflection and active processing of the total lesson experience. Invite students to review their solutions for the Problem Set. They should check work by comparing answers with a partner before going over answers as a class. Look for misconceptions or misunderstandings that can be addressed in the Debrief. Guide students in a conversation to debrief the Problem Set and process the lesson.

COMMON CORE	Lesson 34: Date:	Design and construct boxes to house materials for summer use. 1/31/14

6.F.87

- (Have students share their boxes.) What designs did you choose to put on your box? Why?

- What was your favorite math topic in Grade 5?

- What models or manipulatives helped you with new concepts?

- What was your biggest accomplishment in math this year?

- What are some ways you can keep your math skills sharp during the summer?

Reflection (3 minutes)

In G5–M6–Topic F, to close their elementary experience, the Exit Ticket is set aside and replaced by a brief opportunity to reflect on the mathematics done that day as it relates to their broader experience of math.

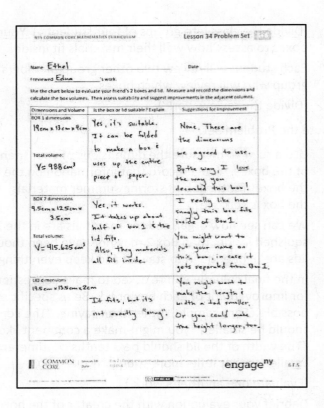

Name _____   Date _____

I reviewed _____'s work.

Use the chart below to evaluate your friend's two boxes and lid. Measure and record the dimensions and calculate the box volumes. Then, assess suitability and suggest improvements in the adjacent columns.

Dimensions and Volume	Is the box or lid suitable? Explain.	Suggestions for Improvement
BOX 1 dimensions: Total volume:		
BOX 2 dimensions: Total volume:		
LID dimensions: 		

Name _____   Date _____

What are you most looking forward to learning about in Grade 6 or in math in your future?